Law and Policy for China's Market Socialism

This edited volume presents fresh empirical research on the emerging outcomes of China's law reforms. The chapters examine China's 'going out' policy by addressing the ways in which the underpinning legal reforms enable China to pursue its core interests and broad international responsibilities as a rising power. The contributors consider China's civil and commercial law reforms against the economic backdrop of an outflow of Chinese capital into strategic assets outside her own borders. This movement of capital has become an intriguing phenomenon for both ongoing economic reform and its largely unheralded underpinning law reforms. The contributors ask probing questions about doing business with China and highlight the astonishing escalation of China's outbound foreign direct investment (OFDI).

Law and Policy for China's Market Socialism includes contributions from leading China-law scholars and specialist practitioners from the People's Republic of China, Hong Kong, the United States, the United Kingdom and other countries who all extend the examination of powerful influences on China's law reforms into new areas. Given the forecast for the growth of China's domestic market, those wishing to gain a better understanding and seeking success in the world's most dynamic marketplace will benefit greatly from reading this book.

This book is essential reading for anyone interested in Chinese economics and business, Chinese law, Chinese politics and commercial law.

John Garrick is a solicitor of the Supreme Court of New South Wales and former judge's associate of the Supreme Court. He is a Senior Research Fellow at MGSM and convenor of the Business Law and Corporations Law programmes at Macquarie University, Australia.

Routledge Contemporary China Series

1 **Nationalism, Democracy and National Integration in China**
   Leong Liew and Wang Shaoguang

2 **Hong Kong's Tortuous Democratization**
   A comparative analysis
   Ming Sing

3 **China's Business Reforms**
   Institutional challenges in a globalised economy
   Edited by Russell Smyth, On Kit Tam, Malcolm Warner and Cherrie Zhu

4 **Challenges for China's Development**
   An enterprise perspective
   Edited by David H. Brown and Alasdair MacBean

5 **New Crime in China**
   Public order and human rights
   Ron Keith and Zhiqiu Lin

6 **Non-Governmental Organizations in Contemporary China**
   Paving the way to civil society?
   Qiusha Ma

7 **Globalization and the Chinese City**
   Fulong Wu

8 **The Politics of China's Accession to the World Trade Organization**
   The dragon goes global
   Hui Feng

9 **Narrating China**
   Jia Pingwa and his fictional world
   Yiyan Wang

10 **Sex, Science and Morality in China**
   Joanne McMillan

11 **Politics in China since 1949**
   Legitimizing authoritarian rule
   Robert Weatherley

12 **International Human Resource Management in Chinese Multinationals**
   Jie Shen and Vincent Edwards

13 **Unemployment in China**
   Economy, human resources and labour markets
   Edited by Grace Lee and Malcolm Warner

14 **China and Africa**
   Engagement and compromise
   Ian Taylor

15 **Gender and Education in China**
Gender discourses and women's schooling in the early twentieth century
Paul J. Bailey

16 **SARS**
Reception and interpretation in three Chinese cities
Edited by Deborah Davis and Helen Siu

17 **Human Security and the Chinese State**
Historical transformations and the modern quest for sovereignty
Robert E. Bedeski

18 **Gender and Work in Urban China**
Women workers of the unlucky generation
Liu Jieyu

19 **China's State Enterprise Reform**
From Marx to the market
John Hassard, Jackie Sheehan, Meixiang Zhou, Jane Terpstra-Tong and Jonathan Morris

20 **Cultural Heritage Management in China**
Preserving the cities of the Pearl River Delta
Edited by Hilary du Cros and Yok-shiu F. Lee

21 **Paying for Progress**
Public finance, human welfare and inequality in China
Edited by Vivienne Shue and Christine Wong

22 **China's Foreign Trade Policy**
The new constituencies
Edited by Ka Zeng

23 **Hong Kong, China**
Learning to belong to a nation
Gordon Mathews, Tai-lok Lui and Eric Kit-wai Ma

24 **China Turns to Multilateralism**
Foreign policy and regional security
Edited by Guoguang Wu and Helen Lansdowne

25 **Tourism and Tibetan Culture in Transition**
A place called Shangrila
Åshild Kolås

26 **China's Emerging Cities**
The making of new urbanism
Edited by Fulong Wu

27 **China–US Relations Transformed**
Perceptions and strategic interactions
Edited by Suisheng Zhao

28 **The Chinese Party-State in the 21st Century**
Adaptation and the reinvention of legitimacy
Edited by André Laliberté and Marc Lanteigne

29 **Political Change in Macao**
Sonny Shiu-Hing Lo

30 **China's Energy Geopolitics**
The Shanghai Cooperation Organization and Central Asia
Thrassy N. Marketos

31 **Regime Legitimacy in Contemporary China**
Institutional change and stability
Edited by Thomas Heberer and Gunter Schubert

32 **U.S.–China Relations**
China policy on Capitol Hill
Tao Xie

33 **Chinese Kinship**
Contemporary anthropological perspectives
Edited by Susanne Brandtstädter and Gonçalo D. Santos

34 **Politics and Government in Hong Kong**
Crisis under Chinese sovereignty
Edited by Ming Sing

35 **Rethinking Chinese Popular Culture**
Cannibalizations of the canon
Edited by Carlos Rojas and Eileen Cheng-yin Chow

36 **Institutional Balancing in the Asia Pacific**
Economic interdependence and China's rise
Kai He

37 **Rent Seeking in China**
Edited by Tak-Wing Ngo and Yongping Wu

38 **China, Xinjiang and Central Asia**
History, transition and crossborder interaction into the 21st century
Edited by Colin Mackerras and Michael Clarke

39 **Intellectual Property Rights in China**
Politics of piracy, trade and protection
Gordon Cheung

40 **Developing China**
Land, politics and social conditions
George C.S. Lin

41 **State and Society Responses to Social Welfare Needs in China**
Serving the people
Edited by Jonathan Schwartz and Shawn Shieh

42 **Gay and Lesbian Subculture in Urban China**
Loretta Wing Wah Ho

43 **The Politics of Heritage Tourism in China**
A view from Lijiang
Xiaobo Su and Peggy Teo

44 **Suicide and Justice**
A Chinese perspective
Wu Fei

45 **Management Training and Development in China**
Educating managers in a globalized economy
Edited by Malcolm Warner and Keith Goodall

46 **Patron–Client Politics and Elections in Hong Kong**
Bruce Kam-kwan Kwong

47 **Chinese Family Business and the Equal Inheritance System**
Unravelling the myth
Victor Zheng

48 **Reconciling State, Market and Civil Society in China**
The long march towards prosperity
Paolo Urio

49 **Innovation in China**
The Chinese software industry
Shang-Ling Jui

50 **Mobility, Migration and the Chinese Scientific Research System**
Koen Jonkers

51 **Chinese Film Stars**
Edited by Mary Farquhar and Yingjin Zhang

52 **Chinese Male Homosexualities**
Memba, Tongzhi and Golden Boy
Travis S.K. Kong

53 **Industrialisation and Rural Livelihoods in China**
Agricultural processing in Sichuan
Susanne Lingohr-Wolf

54 **Law, Policy and Practice on China's Periphery**
Selective adaptation and institutional capacity
Pitman B. Potter

55 **China–Africa Development Relations**
Edited by Christopher M. Dent

56 **Neoliberalism and Culture in China and Hong Kong**
The countdown of time
Hai Ren

57 **China's Higher Education Reform and Internationalisation**
Edited by Janette Ryan

58 **Law, Wealth and Power in China**
Commercial law reforms in context
Edited by John Garrick

59 **Religion in Contemporary China**
Revitalization and innovation
Edited by Adam Yuet Chau

60 **Consumer-Citizens of China**
The role of foreign brands in the imagined future china
Kelly Tian and Lily Dong

61 **The Chinese Communist Party and China's Capitalist Revolution**
The political impact of the market
Lance L. P. Gore

62 **China's Homeless Generation**
Voices from the veterans of the Chinese civil war, 1940s–1990s
Joshua Fan

63 **In Search of China's Development Model**
Beyond the Beijing consensus
Edited by S. Philip Hsu, Suisheng Zhao and Yu-Shan Wu

64 **Xinjiang and China's Rise in Central Asia, 1949–2009**
A history
Michael E. Clarke

65 **Trade Unions in China**
The challenge of labour unrest
Tim Pringle

66 **China's Changing Workplace**
Dynamism, diversity and disparity
Edited by Peter Sheldon, Sunghoon Kim, Yiqiong Li and Malcolm Warner

67 **Leisure and Power in Urban China**
Everyday life in a medium-sized Chinese city
Unn Målfrid H. Rolandsen

68 **China, Oil and Global Politics**
Philip Andrews-Speed and Roland Dannreuther

69 **Education Reform in China**
Edited by Janette Ryan

70 **Social Policy and Migration in China**
Lida Fan

71 **China's One Child Policy and Multiple Caregiving**
Raising little suns in Xiamen
Esther C. L. Goh

72 **Politics and Markets in Rural China**
Edited by Björn Alpermann

73 **China's New Underclass**
Paid domestic labour
Xinying Hu

74 **Poverty and Development in China**
Alternative approaches to poverty assessment
Lu Caizhen

75 **International Governance and Regimes**
A Chinese perspective
Peter Kien-Hong Yu

76 **HIV/AIDS in China**
The economic and social determinants
Dylan Sutherland and Jennifer Y. J. Hsu

77 **Looking for Work in Post-Socialist China**
Governance, active job seekers and the new Chinese labour market
Feng Xu

78 **Sino-Latin American Relations**
Edited by K.C. Fung and Alicia Garcia-Herrero

79 **Mao's China and the Sino-Soviet Split**
Ideological dilemma
Mingjiang Li

80 **Law and Policy for China's Market Socialism**
Edited by John Garrick

Law and Policy for China's Market Socialism

Edited by
John Garrick

LONDON AND NEW YORK

First published 2012
by Routledge
2 Park Square, Milton Park, Abingdon, Oxfordshire OX14 4RN

Simultaneously published in the USA and Canada
by Routledge
711 Third Avenue, New York, NY 10017

First issued in paperback 2014

Routledge is an imprint of the Taylor & Francis Group, an informa business

© 2012 editorial selection and matter, John Garrick; individual chapters, the contributors.

The right of John Garrick to be identified as editor of this work has been asserted by him in accordance with the Copyright, Designs and Patents Act 1988.

All rights reserved. No part of this book may be reprinted or reproduced or utilised in any form or by any electronic, mechanical, or other means, now known or hereafter invented, including photocopying and recording, or in any information storage or retrieval system, without permission in writing from the publishers.

Trademark notice: Product or corporate names may be trademarks or registered trademarks, and are used only for identification and explanation without intent to infringe.

British Library Cataloguing in Publication Data
A catalogue record for this book is available from the British Library

Library of Congress Cataloging in Publication Data
Law and policy for China's market socialism / edited by John Garrick.
    p. cm. – (Routledge contemporary China series)
    Includes bibliographical references and index.
    1. Commercial law–China. 2. China–Commercial policy. 3. China–Economic policy. 4. Investments, Foreign–Law and legislation–China. 5. Foreign trade regulation–China. 6. Law reform–China. 7. Socialism–China. I. Garrick, John.
    KNQ920.L35 2012
    330.951–dc23
             2011038415

ISBN 978-0-415-69285-4 (hbk)
ISBN 978-1-138-85738-4 (pbk)
ISBN 978-0-203-12436-9 (ebk)

Typeset in Baskerville
by Taylor & Francis Books

Contents

List of illustrations — xi
List of contributors — xii
Preface — xvii
Acknowledgements — xviii
List of abbreviations — xix

Introduction: law and policy for China's market socialism — 1
JOHN GARRICK

PART I
China's evolving investment, company and business law environment — 19

1 China's outward direct investment in context: from 'open door' to 'going out' — 21
   JIANFU CHEN

2 Company law reform in China — 39
   XIANCHU ZHANG

3 China's enterprise bankruptcy law: implementation of the corporate reorganization provisions — 55
   ROMAN TOMASIC AND ZINIAN ZHANG

4 Chinese contract law after the UN Convention on Contracts for the International Sale of Goods — 70
   YAN CHANG BENNETT

PART II
Critical issues for China's law and policy reforms — 85

5 Understanding Chinese real estate: the property boom in perspective — 87
   RICHARD HU

6 The political economy of China's environmental law reforms   101
   FENG LIN, ANDREW CHAN AND WILSON CHEUNG

7 Implementing China's labor law reforms: interests and obligations at the firm level   118
   WILLIAM J. HURST, JONATHAN KINKEL AND ALEXANDRA SOWASH

8 Chinese outward direct investment: case studies of SOEs going global   131
   YINGJIE GUO, SHUMEI HOU, GRAEME SMITH AND SELENE MARTINEZ-PACHECO

9 China's taxation law reforms in the context of 'market socialism'   144
   JOHN GARRICK

PART III
Courts, alternative dispute resolution and anti-corruption measures in China   165

10 Economic and social rights: the role of courts in China   167
    RANDALL PEERENBOOM

11 Alternative dispute resolution in China   185
    FAN YU

12 Organized crime in China: the Chongqing crackdown (重庆打黑行动)   202
    NORMAN P. HO

13 Conclusion: law and policy for 'opening up' [kaifang] and 'going out' [zou chu qu]   215
    JOHN GARRICK

Bibliography   227
Index   253

Illustrations

Figures

1.1	China's GDP since 1990	24
1.2	China's foreign exchange reserves since 1990	24
1.3	China's ODI since 1990	24
9.1	China's landmark tax law reforms 1980–2010	154

Tables

4.1	Issues based on CISG Articles	80
4.2	Number of CISG decisions	82
7.1	Conceptual framework presenting the effects of four types of labor law reforms on three categories of firms conducting business in China	121

Contributors

Alexandra Sowash is a PhD scholar in the Government Department at the University of Texas, Austin. After receiving her BA in Chinese at UT-Austin in 2006, she studied intellectual property law in China on a Fulbright grant and interned at the US Patent and Trademark Office and a major foreign law firm, both in Beijing, before beginning graduate school.

Andrew Chan is Associate Professor in the Department of Management at the City University of Hong Kong. He is widely published in *Organization Studies, Journal of Organizational Change Management, International Journal of Human Resource Management* and *Asia Pacific Business Review* and is the author of several books including the acclaimed *Critically Constituting Organization* (2000) and a contributor to *Blackwell Encyclopedia of Sociology* (2007) and the *International Encyclopedia of Organization Studies* (2008).

Feng Lin, LLB (Fudan), LLM (Wellington), PhD (Peking), Barrister (Middle Temple, England, Wales and Hong Kong) is currently Director of the Centre for Chinese and Comparative Law and Associate Professor of Law at the City University of Hong Kong. His primary research interests are public law (constitutional law, administrative law), environmental law, comparative labour law and intellectual property law. He is widely published on topics including Chinese constitutional law, administrative law procedures and remedies in China and strategic moves in China's environmental protection laws. He is an expert member of the Technical Committee of the HKQAA.

Graeme Smith is a postdoctoral fellow and member of the advisory board of the China Research Centre, University of Technology, Sydney. He is also a visiting fellow in the State, Society and Governance in Melanesia programme at the Australian National University. His current AusAID-funded research examines Chinese investment in the Pacific region. He has explored the demand for organic produce in Chinese urban centres, the political economy of service delivery in rural China, and the redistribution of land among Chinese farmers. His PhD was in environmental chemistry and he was the first Australian to win the Gordon White Prize.

Jianfu Chen is Professor of Chinese Law and Legal Globalisation, School of Law, La Trobe University, Melbourne, Australia, and a '1000-Plan Scholar' (awarded under the National Thousand Talents Plan, China) with the University of International Business and Economics, Beijing, China. Specializing in international and comparative law, international business and trade law, human rights law, globalisation and law, and Chinese law, he has published (authored, co-authored and co-edited) 15 books and over 70 book chapters and journal articles. His main publications include *From Administrative Authorisation to Private Law: a Comparative Perspective of the Developing Civil Law in the PRC* (1995), *Balancing Act: Law, Policy and Politics in Globalisation and Global Trade* (co-editor, Sydney: Federation Press, 2004); *Rights Protection in the Age of Global Anti-Terrorism* (co-editor, Sydney: Federation Press, 2007); *Chinese Law: Context & Transformation* (Leiden/Boston: Martinus Nijhoff Publishers, 2008); and *International Law in East Asia* (co-editor, London: Ashgate Publishers, 2011). He is also General-Editor of the CCH International loose-leaf service *China Business Law Guide*.

John Garrick, LLB (Hon 1, UTS), M.Soc Stud (Sydney), PhD (UTS), is a solicitor of the Supreme Court of New South Wales and former judicial officer of the Supreme Court. Until 2006 he was in private legal practice with the major Sydney firm Ebsworth & Ebsworth, lawyers specializing in commercial law. He is Senior Research Fellow at MGSM and convenor of the Business Law and Corporations Law programmes at Macquarie University's City Campus (Sydney). He is the author and co-editor of a wide range of scholarly publications including *Law, Wealth and Power in China: Commercial Law Reforms in Context* (2011) and several well-known Routledge books on power relations, and has worked extensively in both legal practice and academia in Hong Kong, the Middle East, North America and Australia.

Jonathan Kinkel is a PhD scholar in the Government Department at the University of Texas, Austin, where he currently focuses on the political economy of China's legal development. He previously earned a JD from Wisconsin Law School and served three years as an Assistant Attorney General at the Wisconsin Department of Justice.

Norman P. Ho is an editor on the *New York University Journal of International Law and Politics* and a research assistant at the US–Asia Law Institute. He previously received his AB and AM degrees from Harvard University, studying pre-modern Chinese history. He was from 2007 to 2008 a Harvard–Yenching Institute Exchange Fellow in the Department of History at Peking University, working also as an intern in the ABA Rule of Law Initiative's Beijing office. Selected publications in English and Chinese include: 'Law, literature, and gender in Tang China: an exploration of Bai Juyi's (772–846) selected *Panwen* on women', in the *Tsinghua China Law Review*, and '*Ying jiang gudai chuantong falv shiwei zhengui ziyuan – Meiguo de Zhongguo falv yanjiu*' ['The Chinese legal tradition should be viewed as a resource for modern Chinese legal reform – suggestions for American scholarship on Chinese law'] in *Zhongguo shehui kexue bao* [*China Social Sciences Today*].

Randall Peerenboom is a Law Professor at La Trobe University and an associate fellow of the Oxford University Centre for Socio-Legal Studies. He was a professor at UCLA Law School from 1998 to 2007 and Director of the Oxford Foundation for Law, Justice and Society Rule of Law in China programme. He has been a consultant to the Asian Development, Ford Foundation, EU–China, UNDP and other international organizations on legal reforms and rule of law in China and Asia, and is the Co-Editor in Chief of *The Hague Journal of Rule of Law*. He is also a CIETAC arbitrator, and frequently serves as expert witness on PRC legal issues. His recent sole-authored and edited books include *Judicial Independence in China* (2010); *Regulation in Asia* (2009); *China Modernizes: Threat to the West or Model for the Rest?* (2007); *Human Rights in Asia* (2006); *Asian Discourses of Rule of Law* (2004); and *China's Long March toward Rule of Law* (2002).

Richard Hu is Assistant Professor of Urban Planning at the University of Canberra. Dr Hu's prior experience includes being an urban researcher at the University of Sydney and an urban professional in China (in Shanghai and Beijing), America and Australia. He received his professional and academic training in urban planning and development at the University of Sydney and UC Berkeley with research interests being global cities, CBD transformations, urban competitiveness and city governance. Richard is a columnist of urban studies in China for *Urban Planning International* and *Beijing Planning Review* and has published widely on Chinese urbanization, urban transformation and urban problems.

Roman Tomasic is Chair in Company Law at Durham University in the United Kingdom. Having previously worked in Australian law schools including as Head of the School of Law, University of Canberra, and Dean of the Faculty of Business and Law, Victoria University, Melbourne, he was founding editor of the *Australian Journal of Corporate Law* and has undertaken research into comparative corporate and commercial law including (with Neil Andrews and Jane Fu) the corporate governance practices of China's top 100 listed companies. Recently, with co-author Xinting Jia, he addressed *Corporate Governance and Resource Security in China* (2010) and has edited *Insolvency Law in East Asia* (2006) and *Company Law in East Asia* (1999). For many years he has served as a law reform consultant to the German government agency (GTZ) in support of the PRC National People's Congress – Finance and Economic Committee; this included work on developing China's new PRC Enterprise Bankruptcy Law.

Selene Martinez-Pacheco is a PhD scholar at the China Research Centre, University of Technology, Sydney, with research on China's foreign policy challenges in Latin America, particularly those that emerge from Chinese oil investments in that region.

Shumei Hou is a Postdoctoral Research Fellow at the Griffith Asia Institute, Griffith University, Australia. Her doctorate is from the University of Technology, Sydney. She was formerly Associate Professor and Head, Department of Administrative Law, Henan University of Political Science and Law, and remains a certified Chinese lawyer and in-house legal consultant to international companies doing business in China. Her publications concentrate on Chinese law in the areas of foreign investment, public administration, intellectual property, medical negligence, technical patents and the application of Chinese law on commercial and state secrets.

William J. Hurst is currently Assistant Professor of Political Science at the University of Toronto and was previously Assistant Professor of Government at the University of Texas at Austin (2007–11) and Postdoctoral Fellow in Modern Chinese Studies at the Faculty of Oriental Studies, University of Oxford, UK (2005–7). Among his numerous publications are authorship of *The Chinese Worker after Socialism* (2009) and co-editorship of *Laid-Off Workers in a Workers' State: Unemployment with Chinese Characteristics* (2009). His ongoing research explores the institutional politics of the Chinese and Indonesian legal systems in comparative context.

Wilson Cheung is an adviser to the Ministry of Environmental Protection in China on pollution liability insurance issues and General Manager of Shenzhen CIG-AMTD Insurance Brokers. He has legal and insurance qualifications from the UK, Canada and the US (FCII, FCIP, CPCU, and ARM); Grad Dip. Law, Nottingham (Trent University) and LLM (City University of Hong Kong). With over 28 years of insurance and risk management consultancy in mainland China, Hong Kong and Canada, he was Head of Business Development for leading global insurance broker Marsh, with responsibility for covering business development in the Pearl River Delta region, and ran his own broking firm specializing in project insurance for Chinese infrastructure projects including Daya Bay Nuclear Power Plant and other power and toll road projects. His research specialty is insurance for nuclear power plants and environmental insurances more generally.

Xianchu Zhang (张宪初) is a Professor of Law and Associate Dean of the Faculty of Law, University of Hong Kong, specializing in commercial law, Chinese law and comparative law. He has published on a wide variety of topics related to Chinese law. His LLB was taken at the China University of Political Science and Law and his MCL and JD were taken at the Indiana University School of Law, Bloomington, USA. He currently serves as the Co-Director of the Hong Kong University–Peking University Legal Research Centre and is an arbitrator of the China International Economic and Trade Arbitration Commission (CIETAC) and a trustee of the Legal Education Trust Fund of Hong Kong.

Yan Chang Bennett is a lawyer and the Assistant Director for the Princeton–Harvard China and the World programme, Woodrow Wilson School for International and Public Affairs, Princeton University. Before coming to Princeton University, Ms Bennett was a Foreign Service Officer with the US Department of State and served overseas in China and Bosnia-Herzegovina. As a diplomat serving in China, she had the opportunity to report on US corporate labour practices and intellectual property issues. She has received awards for superior performance from the State Department, including a personal commendation from the Secretary of State. Ms Bennett has a BA in Political Science, an MA in International Affairs from George Washington University and a JD from Syracuse University College of Law, and has practised in the areas of business and international law.

Yingjie Guo is Associate Professor in Chinese Studies at the Faculty of Arts and Sciences, University of Technology, Sydney. Educated at Shanghai International Studies University and the University of Tasmania, his research is related to nationalism in contemporary China, the domestic political impact of China's WTO membership, discourses of equality and the politics of class analysis.

Yu Fan is Professor of Law at the Law School of Renmin University of China (Beijing) and currently Vice President of the Comparative Law Research Association of China Law Society. Her LLM (Master of Law) is from Renmin University of China and her PhD in Law from Nagoya University, Japan; she has also been a visiting scholar of the University of Wisconsin (Madison). Extensively published in China with her landmark texts *The Theory and Practice of Dispute Resolution* (2007) and *Governing Principles of the Chinese Judicial System* (2004), she is actively involved in current legislative developments, judicial interpretation, judicial system and legal education reform in China.

Zinian Zhang worked as a lawyer from 1999 to 2009 in China, advising clients on banking, construction and contracting. From 2006, he was a senior partner in Zhejiang Brighteous Law Firm, a leading firm in Zhejiang Province, and is currently a part-time lecturer in insolvency law in the Law School of Durham University, UK, where he is a PhD candidate, supervised by Professor Roman Tomasic. He completed a master's degree in law (LLM) at Durham University in 2009 having previously been granted a judicial master's degree (JM) in 2008 by Zhejiang University Law School, China. His PhD research covers the corporate reorganization regime in China, making comparisons with the UK and USA.

Preface

Perceptions of the continued legitimacy of the Communist Party of China (CPC) now rest heavily on the successful implementation of its economic strategies. The success of its economic strategies is, to an extent, co-dependent on whether associated legal and policy settings can provide a stable foundation for development. China's economic and law reforms thus go hand in hand. The connections are vitally important as the much heralded Chinese economic 'miracle' may be unsustainable in the longer term, characterized by several contradictions in both theory and practice between relatively liberal rhetoric on the one hand and conservative, state-centric policies on the other hand. The volume contributes to the legal and policy areas examined from the theoretical standpoints of Chinese law reform, comparative law, policy, economics, political-economy and practice. Illustrations are drawn from the fields of commerce and investment, taxation, the environment and civil and administrative reforms including the courts, alternative dispute resolution and anti-corruption measures.

Law ought to be distinguished from mere decree. But is it? Contributors debate a range of questions including the directions of Chinese socialism under a new leadership. What outcomes are emerging for this vast one-party state from its evolving, 'hybrid' form of rule of law? What do the critical boundaries between economic and legal reform *signify* about China's role as a global power and how do the changes affect ordinary citizens at local levels? China is now 'going out'. New assumptions underlie China's ability to exercise political power on a global scale and new empirical research is presented as China asserts her superpower status. Set against this power backdrop, will contracting with PRC state-owned entities take on new dimensions? What policy directions will China set for 'going out' following the 18th party congress? Are there emerging signs that power will be exercised in new, strategic ways? What are the implications for cross-border commercial dispute resolution and enforcement? What might both foreign and domestic investors expect of China's regulatory, court and mediation processes in the foreseeable future? What instruments are available to help through international treaties and institutions and in what circumstances are these effective?

This volume probes such questions, contributing to several fields including the promotion of the rule of law and good governance, the political economy of law reform, Chinese commercial and business law, Asian legal studies and the environment, and comparative law more generally.

John Garrick
10 September 2011

Acknowledgements

In addition to the contributors themselves, this volume received helpful suggestions, ideas and generously shared knowledge from each of the following: Christine Chung, David S.G. Goodman, Jennifer Genion, Jiao Zhang, Judith Gibson, Laurelle Wishart, Luke Nottage, Minglu Chen, Qianfan Zhang, Rachel E. Stern, Scott Kennedy, Vivienne Shue and Xiaowei Zang. The editor sincerely thanks each of them.

Abbreviations

ACFTU	All-China Federation of Trade Unions
ADR	Alternative dispute resolution
AGOA	Africa Growth and Opportunity Act
CBRC	Chinese Bank Regulatory Commission
CCCPLC	Chinese Communist Central Political and Legal Committee
CCOIC	China Chamber of International Commerce
CCPIT	China Council for the Promotion of International Trade
CDM	Clean Development Mechanism
CEDR	Commission for Economic Development and Reform
CESRC	Committee for Economic, Social and Cultural Rights
CIC	China Investment Corporation
CIETAC	China International Economic and Trade Arbitration Commission
CISG	Contracts for the International Sale of Goods
CPC	Communist Party of China
CPPL	Clean Production Promotion Law
CPR	Civil and political rights
CSR	Corporate social responsibility
CSRC	China Securities Regulatory Commission
DMEQ	Queensland's Department of Mine and Energy
EIA	Environmental impact assessment
ENFI	Engineering and Non-Ferrous Institute
EPD	Environmental Protection Department
EPL	Environmental Protection Law
ESR	Economic and social rights
EU	European Union
EuP	Energy-using Product Directive
ETS	Emissions trading scheme
FDI	Foreign direct investment
FECL	Foreign-Related Economic Contract Law
FNTMMSP	National Federation of Miners, Metalworkers and Steelworkers of Peru
GDP	Gross domestic product
GFC	Global financial crisis

GHG	Greenhouse gas
ICCPR	International Covenant on Civil and Political Rights
ICESCR	International Covenant on Economic, Social and Cultural Rights
JSC	Joint stock company
LCL	Labour Contract Law
LLC	Limited liability company
M&As	Mergers and acquisitions
MCC	China Metallurgical Corporation
MOA	Memorandum of Agreement
MoE	Ministry of Environment
MOFCOM	Ministry of Commerce
MOFTEC	Ministry for Foreign Trade and Economic Cooperation
NAFTA	North American Free Trade Agreement
NPC	National People's Congress
NPPCC	National People's Political Consultative Committee
ODI	Outward direct investment
OFDI	Outbound foreign direct investment
PBOC	People's Bank of China
PLI	Pollution liability insurance
PRC	People's Republic of China
REACH	Registration, Evaluation and Authorization of Chemicals Directive
RoHS	Restriction of Hazardous Substances Directive
SAFE	Administration of Foreign Exchange
SASAC	State-owned Assets Supervision and Administration Commission
SAT	State Administration of Taxation
SEPA	State Environmental Protection Agency
SOE	State-owned enterprises
SPC	Supreme People's Court
TNC	Transnational corporation
TVE	Township and village enterprise
UCL	Uniform Contract Law
UNFCCC	United Nations Framework Convention on Climate Change
VAT	Value Added Tax
WEEE	Waste Electrical Electronic Equipment Directive
WTO	World Trade Organization

Introduction
Law and policy for China's market socialism
John Garrick

The political economy of China's law reforms

Since its foundation in 1949 the People's Republic has developed its legal system under the guidance of the Communist Party of China (CPC) and laws have evolved through different eras of CPC leadership. Never has the law in China been an expression of popular will. It has been shaped by very different understandings of the relationship between state and society compared to Western societies. Indeed, the struggle between 'the socialist road and the capitalist road' was enshrined in the 1974 Constitution.[1] Under the leadership of Deng Xiaoping, however, China's relationship with the law set a new course. By the end of the 1970s a fundamental change in direction had occurred to support the policies of 'opening up' and a 'socialist market economy'.

The pragmatic approach to the law, characteristic of Deng's era, evolved further under Jiang Zemin and then Hu Jintao, with a 'rule of law' narrative gaining unprecedented significance. In part this was due to China's new economic directions. But this discourse also performed a legitimizing function for the CPC's continuing power and the Chinese legal system remains a work in progress (Gillespie and Chen 2010). Jianfu Chen (2011: 109) asserts that China has in fact laid the *foundations* for the rule of law. Yet these 'foundations' are often borrowed, hybrid laws some of which are imported from foreign cultures. Some suggest this 'hybridity' means that China has yet to establish a 'coherent view' of the role of law in the governance of China.[2] Guo (2011: 53) argues instead that 'hybridity needs to be taken seriously instead of being treated as something transient'; others promote more optimistic political interpretations.[3]

The evolution of China's legal system is clearly connected to its economic reform model. For the past 30 years this model has relied heavily on global trade and investment, much of it export-oriented foreign direct investment (FDI), together contributing a high proportion of gross domestic product (GDP). Recently, however, China has announced an intriguing shift in emphasis with her vast US foreign reserves treasure (at least $2.4 trillion) to be used to secure exclusive access to raw material and other essential strategic assets. This was closely followed by China's announcement of the establishment of the National Energy Commission headed by Premier Wen Jiabao with a Vice Premier as deputy head.

This strategic move escalates China's plans to secure energy resources and raw materials globally and is a contemporary expression of China's 'going out' policy, of utilizing its vast 'treasure-chest' built upon years of domestic savings and trade surpluses to ramp-up investments *outside* of China.

China's outbound foreign direct investment (OFDI) has spectacularly expanded since 2004, reaching 'commercially and geo-economically significant levels that challenge international investment norms and affect international relations' (Rosen and Hanemann 2009: 1). The 'going out' strategy is, however, poorly understood and needs to be seen in context. There is a range of questions to be explored. What will this strategy encompass? How is China's OFDI to be interpreted? Will it be sustainable? What are the implications for making laws that support China's market economy (and promotion of rule of law more generally)? What sort of great power is China shaping up to become? How secure are China's foreign holdings given that its investments in some key assets may be of questionable value (including investments in dollars and US Treasury bonds) and limited liquidity to finance global consumption?[4] A significant decline in the value of the US dollar or Treasury bonds can hurt China. Alternatively, a rise in the value of the yuan could also hurt.[5]

At the same time, domestic consumption has been kept low. In the US, the contribution of direct consumption to GDP is around 71 per cent, while in China it is around 37 per cent. Given China's GDP is about $4–5 trillion versus $15 trillion for the US and average income in China is about 10–15 per cent of US earnings, the difficulty of using Chinese consumption to drive the global economy becomes apparent. But this is changing and the US credit rating is coming under extreme stress. Since Deng's reforms began Chinese savings have risen and exports have been a growth engine. Given that a significant proportion of exports is ultimately driven by US and European buyers, lower global growth and declining consumption can create problems for China. Foreseeing this, Premier Wen has indicated that 'Chinese growth was becoming increasingly unstable, uncoordinated and ultimately unsustainable'.[6] Driving up internal consumption, however, carries a number of deep-seated dilemmas. The relationship between internal consumption and currency valuation is co-implicated and some stark tensions exist between economic growth theories on the one hand and sustainable environment discourses on the other hand.

The artificially low ¥

Reserve currency issuance and regulation are points of international consternation. The OECD Economic Survey of China (OECD 2010) noted that China has a remarkably strong public finance position but that the 'real exchange rate will need to appreciate as is normal for a rapidly developing economy where rising incomes push up the price of non-tradable goods and services'.[7] China's economic problems, to a degree, mirror the earlier problems of Japan whose export-driven model successfully generated strong average growth of 10 per cent in the 1960s, 5 per cent in the 1970s and 4 per cent in the 1980s. Direct comparisons between the control of the yen and RMB are however spurious given significant differentiation of macro-economic factors. Yet there are some parallels that, on the surface, appear striking. Japan's export-driven growth through these years was underpinned by a number of factors including an artificially low exchange rate for the yen. In the 1990s a stronger yen triggered recession in Japan's export-dependent economy. Consequently, massive budget deficits were used in attempts to finance large public works to stimulate the economy. Only structural reforms in the late 1990s and early 2000s restored modest growth rates. China, unlike Japan, has a vast population mass and the deposit to loan ratio of China's national banks did not change that much in the global financial crisis (GFC) of 2009. As UBS International Bank Managing Director Jonathan Anderson (2011: 52) argues, this means that China's financial system has reasonable prospects for sustainable growth for some time to come.

Since the introduction of a large reform package in 1994 (the Tax Sharing System), China has rebuilt its revenue mechanism, and recent growth has brought annually double-digit increases in revenue that have filled government coffers, especially at the central government level. This strong fiscal position enabled the government to roll out the biggest fiscal stimulus programme in the world in 2009 to combat contagion from the global financial crisis. Indeed, the economic backdrop to broader reform is reasonably sound. During the 2009 calendar year alone, Chinese companies sold US$54 billion worth of goods and services and 45 per cent of global initial public offering (IPO) shares by value.[8] By the end of March 2011, China's foreign reserves increased by $197 billion to more than $3 trillion for the first time, a rise of 24 per cent from the previous year.[9] With the support of China's government, its companies are reaching beyond their borders to capture limited capital and, where possible, control allocation of natural resources. The central bank is also planning new investment funds to diversify the foreign reserves holdings. China's new rich also have new expectations and new understandings of contemporary China. An informed knowledge of China's objectives, drivers and restraints will become compulsory for political, business and social leaders globally, if this is not already the case.

Despite arguments that China's economic model may be unsustainable for reasons similar to the Japanese ascension and demise of the 1980s and 1990s, and because of property and equity market speculation bubbles (including debt levels carried by local government investment vehicles[10]) and significant debt carried by other government entities such as the Ministry of Railways, the current hype about China's so-called 'economic miracle' is not without some foundation. The success of China's economic reform has thus far occurred in conjunction with the significant evolution of the legal, regulatory and policy systems supporting it. The extent of reform success to date indicates China's dominant position on global well-being is a short to medium term certainty. The domestic Chinese consumer market will grow as China sets its sights on better educating its own citizens and developing its services sector including the education industry as an export earner.[11]

In 1978, when Deng Xiaoping urged his nation to adopt the 'open door' policy, China's GDP was estimated at ¥3,645.2 million. By 2008, GDP had increased to approximately ¥30.067 billion. At the end of 2009 China had the world's largest foreign exchange reserve at US$2.4 trillion and by 2010 China's share of global GDP had risen to 9.5 per cent (from 6.3 per cent in 2007).[12] The rise continues and China's economic, legal, political and social stability is now vital to the global community, and the key indicators of China's future directions are examined in depth in this collection of essays. In particular, China's 'going out' strategy and the internal legal developments that provide its foundations are examined with past and present indicators considered. Critical sub-themes include China's reform policies enabling ownership of private property, private entrepreneurship and large scale foreign investment in China's enterprises as well as the outward movement of Chinese capital into strategic assets in a range of countries. The contributors examine key effects of China's 'opening up' and 'going out' policies, offering specific examples of China's law reforms in the context of 'market socialism'.

The law, wealth and power nexus

A key for understanding the law, wealth and power nexus in China rests with the largely unheralded law reforms that are rapidly evolving to support a market economy and access to markets. Key reforms to company law, business, commercial, labour, the environment, tax and the courts encompass attempts to improve transparency, predictability and consistency. Following some major controversies in production liability a new *Tort Law* (2010) has also recently been adopted in China to tighten product liabilities.[13] Efforts have been made to improve 'level playing conditions' for companies, domestic and foreign investors, private entrepreneurs and so on in the so-called 'socialist market economy'. Trade and Intellectual Property (IP) laws have been introduced as China strives to become an innovator and 'not just an absorber of science and technology' (Stoianoff 2011: 188).[14] Indeed, technology transfer whereby companies doing big business in China are obliged to disclose the content of their technology is 'a big issue'.[15] WTO-compliant regulations also include institutional upgrading and policies related to the allocation of capital and these are now well documented.[16]

It is equally well documented that innovators cannot always connect well with each other without the current dominant ingredient of *CPC patronage*.[17] With few exceptions, Chinese firms and foreign investors alike have needed to 'focus on developing privileged relations with officials in the CPC hierarchy' (Garnaut 2010a: 5). Although business and social opportunities have certainly expanded since Deng's reforms began, the privileged power of strategic state-owned enterprises has actually grown since the GFC began, and arguably at the expense of the private sector. Furthermore, recent analyses indicate that the CPC will continue to have the final say on China's law reforms in the immediate to mid-term future (Lin 2011; Zhu 2010). The longer term is less foreseeable. Lin argues it is possible that we may see within our own lifetimes the evolution of both internal democratization of the party and movement towards China's broader political democratization (with 'Chinese characteristics'). Zhu (2010: 68) argues that in fact the Party's influence has diminished in many ways and its role has changed towards macro-management and policy setting 'with considerable de facto separation of party and state since the early 1990s'. Although some state organs may have assumed greater responsibilities and are acting more autonomously, indicators following the GFC are that China has actually tightened its control over political reform and democratization initiatives. As an illustration, Liu Xiaobo, a Beijing based pro-democracy and human rights activist, was sentenced on Christmas Day 2009 to 11 years' imprisonment by China's government for the so-called crime of 'enticing subversion of state power'. This was made despite sympathy, pressure and criticism from both home and abroad. Liu's sentence signifies a firm message from the CPC, one of denying political liberalization.[18] The brief detention in mid-2011 of dissident Ai Weiwei appears to have been part of the government's crackdown on the so-called Chinese 'Jasmine Revolution' which was a distant echo of the Arab Spring of 2011 (Cohen 2011: 17). Cohen (ibid.) further notes that China is preparing to revise its *Criminal Procedure Law* and that this review may provide 'additional impetus for the introduction of meaningful protections for future suspects'. Chinese authorities on the other hand are often sceptical of vitriolic Western interpretations of 'crackdowns on dissidents', citing difficulties in managing such a huge population and the concurrent need to take decisive steps to maintain social order. Although the current atmosphere may not be conducive to law reform, Party leaders are well aware of growing societal pressures against abuses of power and that practical law reforms are a way of defusing public hostility.

If there is a major cultural, political or strategic policy shift with China's next generation of leaders it is possible the 'new guard' may well have expectations that the fruits of successful economic and legal reforms ought to include political reform. Such expectations are not without foundation as an ideological platform has existed for some time for both internal party democratization and its expansion to the broader community (see Lin 2011). Progress on this front has, however, been quite limited. Premier Wen's repeated calls in the mass media for more political reform over the past few years and inaction of the CPC Politburo in this regard indicates Wen has not had sufficient support in the top Party-state leadership to bring about significant political reforms under President Hu Jintao.

It appears logical that as China's stature rises in the world order it will exert greater influence over international systems. Some China observers already suggest that China is being more assertive (perhaps even aggressive) in implementing its 'going out' policies; some even accuse it of seeking to undermine the current international infrastructure to reflect a 'balance' more favourable to itself. Others dispute such claims and the veracity of these arguments is methodically evaluated in the following chapters.

At the same time it must be remembered that Chinese courts handle more than eight million cases a year. As Fu and Peerenboom (2010: 133) put it, 'most cases are neither political nor politically sensitive'. China's sweeping legal reforms do however have strong connections to political science and political economy. The term 'judicial independence' can carry clear political connotations. In Common Law legal systems this term is normally associated with the doctrine of 'separation of powers' and is linked to democratic political systems. In China, where there is no separation of powers and the legal system is directly subject to CPC power, this legal term can have different connotations and interpretations. In some circumstances a judge may simply be required to fulfil a party-line.[19]

State advancing/private withdrawing (*guo jin, min tui*)

China's exercise of great wealth and power through her so-called 'command economy' has opened new research and development opportunities. This is especially so after China's economy seemed better positioned to withstand the impact of the 2009 GFC compared to some of the so-called 'free market' economies of the West (some of which have been accused of actually causing the GFC). In the period following the GFC the phenomenon sometimes called 'state encroaching and private withdrawing' has gathered some momentum in China. That is, the state-owned enterprises, previously perceived as a heavy burden to be liberalized and disposed of less than a decade ago, have been re-presented as 'champions' of China's economy. They have been very aggressive in investing in almost all important industries, with comparatively easy access to government-supported finance. During the immediate post-GFC period the private sector has somewhat receded against this strategic exercise of state power. This is reflected in bank lending patterns and government anti-inflation policies. For instance, required reserve ratios for major banks have risen from 15.5 per cent in December 2009 to a record 20.5 per cent, with Zhou Xiaochuan, governor of the People's Bank of China, warning (in April 2011) that 'there was no absolute limit to how high they could go' (Garnaut 2011c). A key has been that the big banks have responded by cutting off loans to private lenders while keeping credit channels open to state-owned enterprises. Some private sector borrowers have thus been forced to choose between bankruptcy and taking underground loans at up to ten times official benchmark rates (ibid.). The role of the state with respect to SOEs provides an example of the constantly changing nature of the state encroaching/private withdrawing relationship. SOEs are legal entities that are wholly or majority owned by the central, provincial or city governments. The CPC's reform strategy on these entities has evolved slowly, yet radically, over the past 30 years or so. There has been a reasonably consistent movement from communist planning to a socialist market economy and the government has been decisive in making landmark decisions such as opening the economy and closing major loss-making enterprises. China has also avoided some potentially calamitous mistakes such as creating cross-sectoral state holding companies or mass subsidization of the SOEs.

It is generally accepted that China's modern enterprise reforms began around the 1980s. From a completely planned system, authorities introduced some market elements, for instance SOEs were taken off budget, independent profit and loss accounting was introduced, a commercial banking system to finance enterprise needs (and liberalize prices) was created. These initiatives were not, at that stage, intended to reduce the role of the state sector *per se*. Rather they were to improve the performance of a fully state-owned economy. TVEs and collectives were allowed to compete in small-scale, labour-intensive manufacturing and services areas, but as part of a greater state economy.

The end of the 1980s then saw the initial major opening of China to domestic and external competition. Despite fierce ideological debate over the issue, the CPC for the first time gave up the idea that the economy would be fully state-owned (although there was collective ownership through neighbourhoods, production teams and so on in addition to state/public ownership even under Mao). Perhaps as a consequence of internal political divisions there was no consensus on the divestment or privatization of existing state enterprises. Nonetheless, the CPC opened up the field for new investment by both non-state and foreign-owned companies. It was no coincidence that this action led to 'the beginning of China's big wave of foreign direct investment inflows – and to the most significant domestic bubble in mainland history' (Anderson 2008: 22).

The economic costs of this bubble period became apparent as 'the government began to grapple with the idea of shutting down hopelessly unprofitable SOEs and divesting its assets in overheated, excess-capacity sectors' (ibid.). At the same time, planners were excited about consolidating the large-scale state economy into a limited number of *chaebol*-like 'national champion' holding companies with a cross-sectoral profile, similar to the experience of Japan and particularly Korea.[20] Zang Xiaowei (2008) notes this period also saw a spike in wealth inequality in China. A select few well-connected entrepreneurs became extraordinarily rich in a relatively brief period of time, spawning what Zang Xiaowei (ibid.) among others refers to as 'wealth hatred'.

Wealth hatred is a phenomenon the government still seeks to diminish. For instance, over the past decade, numerous programmes have been introduced including the rural fee reform, which abolished fees and taxes in the rural sector, the free rural compulsory education programme, which ensures rural children can attend basic education free of charge, and the rural cooperative medical scheme, which has enrolled much of the rural populace in a highly subsidized medical insurance programme. These all aim at 'reducing inequalities, promoting fairness and improving public services, as part of the shift to a service-oriented government and building social harmony' (Wong 2011).

Arguably, the most important trend of the post-bubble period was the historic wave of closures and layoffs of the late 1990s and early 2000s. These affected both the state enterprise sector and the non-state economy. Anderson (2011, 2008) argues that for the remaining SOEs, this period was of 'relative limbo' in terms of reform momentum. Anderson's point is that the Asian financial crisis ended the idea of large cross-sectoral state holding companies as being 'a good thing'. Authorities retreated from aggressive plans to recast and consolidate entire industries but instead progressed on an enterprise-by-enterprise basis. The key innovation associated with this shift was the discovery of 'foreign markets' after the landmark Hong Kong flotation of China Petroleum in 1999–2000. At that point the government realized that an overseas listing was an ideal way to restructure large state enterprises. In this way 'companies could get a significant overhaul, an inflow of external capital and oversight by a professional investor base – without giving up majority state control' (Anderson 2008: 22).

While authorities proceeded with the principle of 'enterprise privatization' there was no clear legal or administrative framework to support it. Consequently, China has not had the experience of mass privatization as occurred in the former Soviet countries of Eastern Europe. Rather, Chinese companies were bought out over time by local managers and/or outside investors. There has also been uncertainty associated with the ownership of state shares and local governments' ability to sell companies that had been state assets. Many of these companies are still formally listed as 'state enterprises' and were being consolidated to fewer than 100 by the end of 2010. At least that was the stated objective. Arguably, this concentrates state power in the fewer SOEs under its control as distinct from improving market competition through supply and demand forces.

Over the decade 2000–10, China has seen several crucial changes in the way state ownership is conceptualized. Anderson (2008: 23) notes three of them as follows:

1 The historic decision to open up the state banking system to outside ownership and privatization: from virtual stagnation around 2003, when large commercial banks were still 100 per cent state-owned, and also technically insolvent due to the extremely large accumulated stock of non-performing loans in the system. Chinese banks have now seen the largest cleanup and recapitalization program in mainland history, costing hundreds of billions of US dollars, followed by a rapid sell-off of state shares. To date, three of China's 'big four' state commercial banks have listed both at home and abroad, with nearly one-third of each bank now held in private hands, including more than 20 per cent foreign ownership.

(ibid.)

2 The opening of large SOE privatization through mergers and acquisitions. For the previous two decades the bulk of de facto privatization activity was aimed at small and medium-sized companies. There has been rapid change over the past few years with the rise of private equity investment now affecting some of China's larger companies and foreign capital now competing with domestic capital for transactions (Huang 2009). This trend remains in a relatively early developmental stage as much is learned on both sides (as evidenced by Chinalco's failed takeover attempt of Australian mineral giant Rio Tinto in 2009).

3 The adoption of a state enterprise dividend policy (see Anderson 2011: 49). Although this conceptualization may appear to economic and legal analysts from capitalist countries as a relatively minor step in that it applies only to a limited number of companies, it is not. It marks the first time the CPC has taken action to curb a structural bias favouring over-investment by state companies.

To the above three conceptualizations we might now add a fourth: of consolidated SOEs as 'strategic', providing a dominant platform for China to exploit a favourable economic position following the GFC of 2009 and subsequent world stock-market fluctuations of 2011–12. Supporting this interpretation is a report prepared for China's State Council (2010) finding that 81 per cent of 298 outbound investments between 2004–9 were by SOEs.[21] China's 'going out' policy rests significantly on the strategic success of its SOEs and an often expressed view in the West (and among some intellectuals in China) that China's political and wealthy elite corruptively collude to utilize SOEs to gain unfair commercial advantage is far too simplistic. At the same time the extensive state-led bias, reflected through for instance bank lending, favouring the 120,000 SOEs (and their subsidiaries) over the five million private companies (and 45 million informal private businesses) has resulted in a structural imbalance: while SOE revenues have been growing at 15–20 per cent a year, mean household incomes have been expanding at a rate of just 1–3 per cent over the past decade (cited in Lee 2011). As Lee (2011) points out, 'it is no wonder that domestic consumption is languishing at about 30% of GDP – the smallest percentage for any major economy in the world'. There are also intriguing conflicts of interest within and around SOEs such as between owner/regulator, the place of related party or connected transactions, and with regard to the discharge of political responsibilities.

Hybridity and the 'Chinese rule of law'

Debates about the trajectory of China's legal reforms are ongoing. Some argue that China has laid a 'foundation' for rule of law; others claim it is stagnating or even regressing on important measures (see Cohen 2011; Hurst 2011). Yu (2010), Peerenboom (2010b, 2011) and Hurst (ibid.) highlight various changes and challenges in the development of China's law reforms including new benefits and protections for particular social groups or economic practices; others focus on rights and provisions that are still absent or that may have been eroded. According to Hurst (2011: 72):

> Some scholars have even looked to the legal system to provide new means for Chinese citizens to challenge abuses of state authority, especially at the local level; others have emphasized legal reform's role in bolstering the power of the state and Party centre.

Hurst's point is that there is no overarching claim to 'truth' in this terrain. His call is for studies that look at several areas of Chinese law in a disaggregated way rather than in a monolithic, one-dimensional way, or through a single theory lens. This perspective is shared by contributors to this volume in that they draw on a range of theories from comparative law, business, economics, political economy and social science.

In China, neoliberal deregulation is essentially treated as a technical instrument for engineering economic reform. Non-state actors are not necessarily given more access to the regulatory space. This differs from the regulation/deregulation dynamic elsewhere in East Asia 'where numerous state, non-state and hybrid actors are influencing, adapting and localising global forces' (Gillespie 2009: 43). Key new rules and practices, how these are shaped, and pivotal international institutions are examined to maximize interpretive insights into recently decided landmark cases of the People's Courts, new environmental laws, tax law reforms, anti-corruption measures, judicial law reform and new initiatives promoting alternative dispute resolution. Critically, contributors to this volume examine key *emerging outcomes of reform*, reviewing how the philosophical justifications of reform are being played out in specific areas of practice.

This volume thus focuses on the issue of whether the legitimizing government narrative of law reform is backed up in practice, and searches for answers to some complex questions. How is the government's constant flow of rhetoric about the promotion of 'rule of law' reflected in actual practice? With China having borrowed and adapted many laws for internal use, what are the implications of this rapidly evolving 'hybrid' set of laws? Is a foundation for rule of law really being laid? Or are the reforms, when test cases are carefully examined, more cosmetic in nature or, even worse, new instruments for the organs of propaganda? Can a suite of laws borrowed from other jurisdictions be so readily transplanted to another culture so rich in its own traditions? Are there hidden 'transplantation' costs? What is the evidence that the law reforms can be sustainable under current one-party state power arrangements? What are the defining legal considerations when trading with a China that now flexes her wealth and power globally? What are the implications of China's 'superpower' status for managing and resolving cross-border legal disputes going forward? In order to examine these questions in detail, the theoretical framework of the volume is divided into three parts. Part I is based on the broad context of China's evolving investment, company and business law environment; Part II addresses some of China's most critical areas of law reform (property, the environment, labour, outward bound investment and tax), and Part III the role of courts with respect to economic and social rights, alternatives to litigation and anti-corruption measures. These various matters may appear disparate and unconnected. Indeed there are many other issues which have not been mentioned. However, all should be understood as having a synergistic relationship as progress and expanded cross-cultural understanding in one context can help in others.

Part I deals with China's outbound investment regime, company and business (including contract) law reforms which have opened up opportunities for both domestic and foreign investors. This Part examines China's outwards flows of capital, company law reform including what can happen in cases of corporate insolvency from several points of view – including the range of actors now seeking to influence regulation-making – and the politically sensitive areas of SOE reform, bankruptcy and corporate reorganization, and contracting with Chinese enterprises and legal mechanisms to resolve disputes related to the international sale of goods.

Part II examines several critical and interrelated aspects of China's law reform and policy agendas. The focus here turns to some of China's most controversial and contested reforms including the pivotal role to the market economy of new property laws, critical developments in environmental law, implementation issues for labour laws at firm level, experience of SOEs in foreign host-countries and taxation law reforms. These reforms have significant local and global implications whether they are viewed separately or collectively.

Part III then examines the role of China's courts with respect to economic and social rights, the current and emerging roles of alternative dispute resolution (ADR) and China's crackdown on corruption. At the heart of this Part is an implied question of great relevance to both foreign and domestic investors alike: 'Just how safe is it to do business with China?' What might foreign and domestic investors expect of the Chinese legal system if something goes wrong? What key issues surround judicial decision-making and reform? How influential does the CPC remain in determining court outcomes in 'sensitive' cases? What exactly constitutes a politically sensitive case? If contracts need to be enforced, what mechanisms will apply and what is to be expected in the future administration of Chinese justice? How are China's court reforms and judicial upgrading coping with the astonishing levels of legal change? How are the People's Courts responding to new community expectations for a fair, transparent legal system whereby rights are upheld on the legal merits (rather than the politics) of the case?

The authors examine these key questions, issues and dilemmas associated with making laws for China's market economy, commencing with Jianfu Chen's analysis in Chapter 1 of the policy shift from *opening up* to *going out* from the perspective of China's legal and regulatory reforms on cross-border investing. Chen sheds light on the global implications of China's outward bound investment strategy, noting that China is now clearly 'going global'. Xianchu Zhang in Chapter 2 then considers the development of company law in the PRC as an indicator of the legal environment *and* the competitiveness of the economy. With China still in transition from a planned to a market economy accompanied by rule of law, company law reforms are viewed as a reflection of the prevailing political ideology. Zhang refers to the pivotal role played by SOEs in the evolution of China's company laws and how this role has directly affected the economic integration of China into markets worldwide, with '*guo jin, min tui*' [the state advances, the private sector retreats] a common phrase over the last three years.

Roman Tomasic and Zinian Zhang explore China's implementation of the *Enterprise Bankruptcy Act* (2006), examining in Chapter 3 specific illustrations of corporate insolvency and company reorganization. Commencing with a brief overview of the new laws, they consider the winners and losers in the bankruptcy process, insolvency practitioners as potential new rule-influencers, and banks and creditors as rule-makers. Corporate liquidation in China is viewed against the backdrop of changes in the global financial order and they draw on recent case studies of major corporate bankruptcies with implications for future directions in Chinese corporate insolvency.

Private law and contract law issues concerning the international sale of goods foreground Yan Chang Bennett's analysis in Chapter 4 of the application of the United Nations Convention on the International Sale of Goods (1980; CISG) in China. Bennett assesses CISG contributions to Chinese jurisprudence with respect to Chinese contract law. Unlike other states with a long history of established contract law, China amended its contract law in 1999, more than a decade after its ratification of the CISG, to create the *Uniform Contract Law of the PRC* (UCL). Bennett argues that Chinese jurisprudence on contract law has been inspired by the CISG, and she assesses Chinese and US CISG case law to reveal the issues that are most often the subject of litigation and arbitration between these two giant trading partners.

This foregrounds Richard Hu's analysis in Chapter 5 of real estate property which has been one of *the* most contested issues during China's transformation towards a market economy and touches the very heart of China's socialist doctrine: the state/collective ownership of land. Hu notes that the evolution of real estate property law in contemporary China has been driven by the dual tropes of *market economy* and *urbanization* and that China's government has reformed laws to 'marketize' real estate property for investment, ownership and transaction. There are constantly new winners and losers. In this, Hu identifies *the* key drivers of, and impediments to, property law reform including the political paradoxes embedded within them such as state/collective ownership of land vs market transaction of land-use rights, and state ownership of land vs private ownership of property fixed on the land. Hu contends that these paradoxes contain the potential to eventually challenge China's socialist system of public ownership and the associated legitimacy of the CPC.

Chapter 6 overviews China's environmental law reforms from several perspectives: political economy, business development, foreign direct investment (FDI) and enforcement. Lin Feng, Andrew Chan and Wilson Cheung examine the connections between the philosophies and policies reflected in contemporary CPC slogans 'Harmonious Society', 'Putting People First' and the 'Scientific Perspective on Development' and environmental law reform. They assert that these slogans resonate with the Marxist paradigm of 'equitable societal development' as well as Chinese traditional values. President Hu's vision of striking a balance between economic growth and environmental protection may be foregrounding a logical route to sustainable development in China. Other motives are also noted: some policy corrections have been required following criticisms that modernization and 'open door' policies have been too economically driven at the expense of *loupeixin* (ordinary citizens). The authors also draw attention to significant moves in China's 12th Five-Year Plan (2011–15) including heavy penalties for polluters, carbon emissions trading, the introduction for selected high-risk industries of mandatory *Pollution Liability Insurance* (PLI) in 2015, and the implications of Premier Wen's 2010 announcement that 'the government shall close energy inefficient factories and restrain growth of high energy consumption industries to achieve the political objective of significant energy consumption reduction'.[22] The costs associated with doing business in China are about to rise. But the alternatives are bleak. Clean Development Mechanism (CDM) projects, energy-efficiency projects and related 'clean' technologies are thus being encouraged to make them more financially viable to investors.

William Hurst, Jonathan Kinkel and Alexandra Sowash in Chapter 7 present new research on the implementation of China's new labour laws highlighting key legal and policy reforms affecting China's business environment at firm level. In Chapter 8 Yingjie Guo leads a team of researchers who conducted recent case studies of Chinese SOEs' experience in several host nations including in Latin America, Papua New Guinea and Australia.

John Garrick's analysis in Chapter 9 of China's taxation law reforms is developed in the context of the recent push for greater recognition of the need for environmental sustainability and against the policy-making backdrop of the mid-1990s which saw market reforms pushed through in the face of opposition from powerful, entrenched interests. Since then the government has faced many difficult problems including downsizing SOEs, forcing the military to sell off its interests in commercial enterprises, abolishing allocation of foreign exchange and the dual-tier foreign exchange system, and most importantly regaining central control over the fiscal system through tax reforms. At the heart of tax law reform is the ongoing dilemma of how best to redistribute wealth in this vast socialist country while it is promoting a market economy with Chinese characteristics.

Randall Peerenboom's Chapter 10 overviews the role of the judiciary in enforcing economic and social rights (ESR) comparing the courts of several countries. He argues that Chinese courts are inhibited in implementing ESR by a variety of factors, including shortcomings in the regulatory framework, the lack of specific and robust individual remedies in many laws, institutional designs limiting the power of the judiciary within the Chinese constitutional structure, political limitations, ideological conflicts between New Left advocates of socialist justice and New Right proponents of neoliberalism and resource constraints.

Fan Yu's main purpose in Chapter 11 is analytical and descriptive, arguing that predictions about the demise of ADR in China were largely wrong. In the era of Hu Jintao, the role of mediation has been strengthened, becoming a vital element of China's movement towards a socialist market economy. She examines the combined effects of the Supreme People's Court's recent confirmation that the 'People's Mediation Agreement' is binding and the *People's Mediation Law* (2011), arguing that these are generating a special place in the reconstruction process for ADR. By considering the evolution of ADR from Mao's era through Deng's 'opening up' era to Hu's 'going out' era, this chapter highlights the intricate connections between political ideology, law reform and dispute resolution programmes in Chinese culture.

In Chapter 12 Norman Ho asserts that China has, over the past few decades, witnessed a gradual intensification of the power nexus between some corrupt government officials and organized crime groups. This intensification has been met with a 'crackdown' on corruption. This chapter, presented through a new case study of the Chongqing crackdown on organized crime, notes that activities of organized gangs have extended beyond prostitution and the drug trade, with gang elements infiltrating Chongqing's mainstream economy. Corrupt officials are known to have actively participated in criminal operations and many executions have been carried out in enforcing the government's crackdown, led by senior Party figure Bo Xilai. It appears that corruption probes such as this are too sensitive to be left to the ordinary Chinese judicial system. In this way, the Party system can decide not only who is punished but what evidence is passed onto the judicial system. Further, the propaganda organs may determine what evidence, if any, is revealed to the public and each stage of the legal process can be a matter of intense political negotiation. Ho explores the composition and operations of organized crime in China by historically situating the Chongqing example, noting that in heading the crackdown Bo has revived some Maoist slogans and strategies.

Critical issues for rule of law promotion

As one of China's most influential political commentators, Yang Hengjun, recently wrote about the 'rule of law':

> If you are serious about spreading the 'rule of law' in China I have a suggestion ... all legal elites and opinion leaders can join hundreds of thousands of netizens in demanding that Chongqing's fight against gangsters be introduced across the whole nation so that it can terminate unlawful rule of law by corrupt officials.
>
> (Cited in Garnaut 2010c)

Clearly, corruption is being targeted by the government, with the Premier stating in his 2010 report to the National People's Congress:[23]

> We will give high priority to fighting corruption and encouraging integrity. This has a direct bearing on the firmness of our grip on political power, ... We will promote transparency of administrative affairs, improve regulations for transparent governance and administrative review, create conditions for the people to criticize and oversee the government, let the news media fully play their oversight role, and exercise power openly.
>
> (Wen Jiabao 2010: 30–1)

Premier Wen further emphasized the government's plan to uphold the *rule of law* and further improve the legal system, 'particularly laws concerning the standardization and oversight of the exercise of power'. The importance the government places on law reform is highlighted along with the 'economic reforms and political restructuring' (2010: 27–8). China's reform agenda signals monumental changes not only for China's own internal legal, monetary and fiscal systems but for world markets, international relations and directions in international law more generally.

Critical issues covered include property laws, environmental laws, and the broader business and social implications of China's labour law reforms. Many international investors and companies are interested in having new products manufactured in China, to benefit from less expensive labour costs and tax advantages (compared to the West), but are fearful their product patents may be reproduced without permission and their intellectual copyright protections ignored, and they will be 'ripped off'. There are, of course, many precedents that justify such concerns.

Other concerns for both Western investors and domestic developers alike relate to China's unique and often contradictory constitutional entitlement to and legal claims on land (as well as the fixed properties on it). In China, urban land ownership belongs to the state, and the property on land is only entitled to land-use rights for a certain number of years depending on the type of land usage. This leaves some uncertainty and legal ambiguity as to when land-use rights may expire. Furthermore, foreign investors may face an additional hurdle in that China currently sets visible *and invisible* restrictions on FDI's access to real estate development, acquisition and transaction. Further, private land ownership in the countryside continues to be outlawed under the Chinese Constitution and this subject is at the centre of raging political, economic and social policy debates. Poor peasants do not have secure title to trade and mortgage their land efficiently and land is often the only asset they have. Yet officials still manage to find ways to procure it for developers at enormous mark-ups. As an illustration, in 2009 local governments received 22 per cent of their total income from land sales.[24] Property-related law is a critical issue for China's harmonious society policy.

China's labour law reforms are also intimately connected to such debates and a range of questions surround the government's determination to protect Chinese workers from being exploited in its new capitalist-style enterprise regime. At the same time it is sometimes argued that another major platform of capitalist exploitation is *the environment.* This issue is examined from the standpoint of China's strengthening of environmental laws and associated new cost implications for doing business in China. There are plans by the Chinese central government for mandatory insurance by 2015 on business developments that have an environmental impact and other tough measures are also proposed. There are global implications for the way China approaches environmental protection and climate change and these are addressed in the volume. Not only are the rules of the money-making game changing exponentially, so too are the grounds upon which the game is being played, literally and metaphorically. Cheap land and cheap labour to be ruthlessly exploited are beginning to diminish. So too will some of China's competitive advantage. Strategies to adjust to these new realities include 'going out' investments in developing nations such as Papua New Guinea and in Africa and Southeast Asia, and also commodities-rich countries including Australia and those of Latin America. Although the book has a law-policy focus, such macro-considerations frame its contextual backdrop.

Notes

1 Constitution of the People's Republic of China (1974) Article 8, Beijing: Foreign Languages Press. The Constitution was amended in 1982 to embody Deng's economic reforms and embed the notion of law in the government (see Article 5). At the same time the new Constitution reaffirmed socialism as China's guiding philosophy.
2 See for instance the arguments of Lubman (2006) and Peerenboom (2010b, 2011).
3 The State Council Information Office (2008) China's Efforts and Achievements in Promoting the Rule of Law, State Council White Paper at: www.china.org.cn/government/news/2008–02/28/content_11025486_12.htm.
4 For instance as China's US$2.4 trillion foreign currency reserves have a large proportion denominated in US dollars, it may be of more limited value in that they cannot be

liquidated or mobilized without massive losses because of their sheer size. Wen Jiabao recently stated that: 'if anything goes wrong with the US financial sector, we are anxious about the safety and security of Chinese capital', quoted in S. Das (2009: 22).
5 The People's Bank of China has ruled out any significant revaluation of the yuan exchange rate even though China suffered a loss of about $271.1 billion on its foreign exchange reserves accumulated between 2003 and 2010 because of the depreciation of the US dollar. Zhang Anyuan, head of the fiscal and financial policy research division of the NDRC's Institute of Economic Research, says China is likely to lose $578.6 billion if the US currency's exchange rate sinks to six yuan to the dollar (7 May 2011; see: http://english.sina.com/business/p/2011/0506/372155.html).
6 Cited in Satyajit Das (2010: 4). Also see Ye Xie (2010: 6).
7 OECD *Economics and Growth* website at: www.oecd.org/document/43/0,3343,en_2649_34571_44477419_1_1_1_37443,00.html.
8 This amount was raised by mainland China companies in IPOs; sources: http://english.people.com.cn/90001/90776/90882/6864500.html; http://english.people.com.cn/90001/90776/90883/6864519.html.
9 *China Daily* (7 May 2011) 'China loses $271b from debt holdings', at: http://english.sina.com/business/p/2011/0506/372155.html.
10 Oxford University Professor Christine Wong (3 August 2011) referred to the 'blurry' level of debt in local government investment vehicles in China as likely to be 'somewhere between ¥9–14 trillion', indicating there would be 'a day of reckoning on this level of debt', public lecture presented at the UTS China Research Centre.
11 Value-added services are now perceived as having a 'higher earnings margin than physical labour' (Chan 2011: 180). Hence the rapid development of some areas of the services sector, including the education industry in China and Hong Kong, as the interests of government and industry merge.
12 According to China's National Statistic Bureau, the 1978 GNP (then based on gross industrial and agricultural value of output) was ¥568,980 million. The GNP index was used from 1979 to 1991, see: www.stats.gov.cn/tjgb/ndtjgb/qgndtjgb/t20020331_15372.htm. The first use of the GDP index was 1992 and was ¥2,393,800 million. Earlier GDP figures are estimates. The official GDP for 2009 was ¥33,535,300 million, see: www.stats.gov.cn/tjgb/ndtjgb/qgndtjgb/t20090226_402540710.htm.
13 The Tort Law of the PRC was approved on 26 December 2009 (effective 1 July 2010). See the Chinese government's official web portal: http://english.gov.cn/2009-12/26/content_1497415.htm.
14 China's *National Intellectual Property Strategy* came into operation on 5 June 2008 resulting in some reductions in piracy rates and which recognizes enforcement shortcomings at this stage (see Stoianoff 2011 for detailed analysis).
15 Friedolin Strack, the director of the Asian Department of the Federation of German Industries, states:

> intellectual property rights are underpinned by WTO rules ... but in most cases [German] companies have no choice. The Chinese government is formally correct to underlie the 'voluntary' status of the transfer of technology from German companies to the Chinese authorities, state-owned companies or even private joint venture partners ... but [the reality is] if they want to enter the Chinese market they are often forced to disclose sensitive technology know-how.
> (see J. Dempsey at: www.nytimes.com/2011/06/25/business/global/25iht-wen25.html?_r=1&scp=1&sq=Wens%20visit%20shows%20concern%20over%20euro&st=cse)

16 Zhang (2011) argues that the current legal framework still suffers from the political ideology of the transitional period from the planned economy to a market economy in that it fails to provide a level playing field on the market. Even after 30-plus years of

state-driven market reform the government still shows signs of suspicion of non-state institutions.
17 See Donald C. Clarke (2007: 560); Link and Kurlantzick (2009: 13).
18 While in jail Liu Xiaobo was awarded the 2010 Nobel Peace Prize for 'unflinching and peaceful advocacy for reform'. The official Chinese line is disapproval of this award.
19 See for instance Fu and Peerenboom (2010: 95) on analytical frameworks for understanding and promoting judicial independence in China.
20 The main slogan of this period was '*zhua da fang xiao*' ('seize the large and let go of the small').
21 Cited in Garnaut (2010f). The report adds: 'half of [these] investments involved majority control of the target company, but Chinese companies have recently commenced to shift towards smaller and more "politically acceptable" [i.e. in the foreign country] stakes'. The report to the State Council further says: 'the government background of state-owned enterprises will be a problem that China's resource enterprises have to face while going out'.
22 温家宝:落实责任 确保实现'十一五'节能减排目标 中央政府门户网站 www.gov.cn2010年05月05日来源：国务院办公厅
23 See Xinhua (2011a).
24 UBS economist Wang Tao, cited in Garnaut (2010d: 9).

Part I
China's evolving investment, company and business law environment

1 China's outward direct investment in context

From 'open door' to 'going out'

*Jianfu Chen**

Introduction

There has been considerable debate in Europe, the US, Japan and other countries in recent years over the nature and implications of China's outward direct investment (ODI) around the world (Ferguson 2010; Rosen and Hanemann 2011: 64). These discussions resemble the ones relating to Japan's global investment in the 1970s and 1980s (ibid.; ITS Global 2009: 3; Rosen and Hanemann 2011: 14; Milhaupt 2008), although anxieties about Chinese investment seem to be even more intensive (Rosen and Hanemann 2009: 1). The debate has, however, suffered 'from too much speculation and too few facts' (Scissors 2010).

The current status of the debate is not surprising considering that, until quite recently, there has been a conspicuous lack of legal or policy studies about this important development in China's economy and its global strategies, despite the fact that China actually introduced ODI from the beginning of its 'open door' policies launched some 30 years ago, and that China has become the largest outward investor among developing countries since the 1990s (Wang 2002: 188). The less than transparent practice (especially regarding financial support, foreign exchange control, and sovereign wealth investment; Rosen and Hanemann 2009: 5–6) and the constantly evolving policy and legal framework governing outward investment have only intensified existing confusion.

On the other hand, it is not surprising that for a rather extensive period of time Chinese ODI has not formed a part of the core discussion in English writing on China's 'open door' policies and practices (Wang 2002; Buckley *et al.* 2007: 499).[1] In these years China's ODI, although steadily increasing, has been largely overshadowed by the very high level of inward FDI (Wang 2002: 187). Even when such studies emerged in the last ten years or so, they have been principally economic analyses, and occasionally analyses by political scientists; legal analysis hardly exists. While political and economic studies form a critical part of any thorough understanding of China's ODI, its trends, economic rationale, scale, and development, no such analysis is complete without a clear understanding of the policy and legal framework guiding and regulating Chinese ODI.

One of the most contentious issues regarding Chinese ODI, especially in relation to investment in the resource sector,[2] is the potential of direct state control over the Chinese companies making the investments (see Salidjanova 2011: 11; and Hilton 2011: 17).[3] This is not surprising given that the great majority of companies in resource-related areas are state-owned or controlled entities. While China has consistently rejected the claim that the government exercises any direct control over its state-owned or controlled companies, and has insisted that these companies operate on market principles, the reality is more complicated than an 'either/or' situation.

Chinese economic development is clearly 'guided' by an evolving policy framework, often reinforced by law and regulations after a period of trial implementation. This framework applies to both state-owned and private economic entities. Closer to the daily operation of these economic entities are issues relating to corporate governance and decision-making processes and mechanisms. Any satisfactory explanation of the Chinese transnational corporations' behaviour, present or future, requires a thorough understanding of these two aspects – the policy and legal framework, and corporate governance – both of which are evolving rapidly.

This chapter does not deal with corporate governance, as the issue itself would require a separate and comprehensive study, and as there is considerable research on the issue (albeit, few are specifically on Chinese transnational corporations) (e.g. Tomasic 2005; Leng 2009). Instead, the focus here is on general trends and motivations, the evolving policy and legal framework for China's ODI including developmental and strategic trends over the last 30 years or so.

China's ODI from a developmental perspective: the macro-economic context

After three decades of 'self-reliance' and 'self-sufficiency' under the influence of the conventional understanding of socialism, China was on the edge of economic collapse at the end of the so-called 'Cultural Revolution'. When China opened its doors for foreign business in 1978 there was neither the money nor the advanced technology that China could utilize for outward investment. Not surprisingly the principal objective then was to attract foreign capital, technology and know-how, management expertise, marketing experience and marketing networks. Nevertheless, the need for trade to generate foreign exchange and the corresponding need for overseas marketing networks necessarily led to some small outward investment. Indeed, as early as 1979 the State Council in its *Fifteen Measures on Economic Reform* had already explicitly stated that 'enterprises are *allowed* to establish factories overseas' (Ministry of Commerce 2011: 203) – a policy that has been described as the first initiative to incorporate 'going out' into the 'open door' policies (Zhou 2009). The first such investment was made in 1979 by a Beijing services company in a joint venture in Japan, with an investment of US$220,000 from China (Ministry of Commerce 2011: 3–4).

However, in the early years of economic reform, both trade and investment were strictly controlled by the government (Chen 2008: ch. 17). Thus only state-owned trading corporations and 'economic and technological cooperation enterprises' under direct state or provincial control were allowed to invest abroad (Buckley *et al.*

2007: 500). Further, foreign exchange, and especially its outflow, was under strict control by the government. Most importantly, China at that time simply did not have the necessary foreign exchange reserves to make any significant investments overseas.[4] Thus there was little to talk about in relation to ODI from China.

While in the 1980s China did not have any large trade surplus in any given year and, in fact, trade fluctuated, the consistent inflow of foreign investment nevertheless propelled a steady increase in foreign reserves. By 1990 China's foreign reserves had reached US$11.1 billion (State Administration of Foreign Exchange 2011). Nevertheless, foreign exchange was still under strict control and the first ever significant regulation concerning ODI was issued by the State Administration of Foreign Exchange (SAFE),[5] concerning more about the control of outflow of foreign exchange than about investment overseas.

If the 1979 State Council Measures only 'allowed' Chinese enterprises to establish factories overseas, the tone changed in the 1990s. In 1992 the Party Report to the 14th Party Congress explicitly stated that ODI and the transnational operation of enterprises should be 'actively expanded' (Jiang 1992: Part II). Soon thereafter a policy bank – the China Import and Export Bank – was established in 1994 to provide support for ODI as well as for trade (Ministry of Commerce 2011: 204).

'Going out' as a formal national policy strategy was proposed by the Communist Party of China (CPC) in 2000 (Ministry of Commerce 2011: 204),[6] and a national policy and legal framework for ODI began to appear in 2004, signifying the emergence of an active 'going global' strategy as part of the 'open door' policy (Zhao and de Pablos 2010: 149). As a result, China gradually changed from being a receiver of foreign direct investment to becoming an exporter of ODI (Zhao and de Pablos 2010: 149).

For all practical purposes ODI from China only became visible in the 1990s and significant after 2000. While the growth of ODI is determined by many factors, both domestic and international, two factors are obviously critical – the size of foreign exchange reserves and the size of the national economy, as indicated in Figures 1.1, 1.2 and 1.3. In this context, with foreign reserves of more than US$3 trillion,[7] and an economy poised to overtake the US as the world's largest economy in the foreseeable future,[8] we will certainly see much more ODI from China in the future, with strategic and other investments in developed and developing countries.

Some context is required in relation to Figure 1.3 on ODI. First, it should be noted that the total amount does not include ODI originating from Hong Kong, through which China also made considerable but unknown amounts of ODI to other countries,[9] nor portfolio investment, which is the main means of investment by Chinese sovereign wealth funds and the Chinese Central Bank (see Salidjanova 2011: 3).[10] Further, as Davies has pointed out, official ODI figures from China need to be read with caution. On the one hand such amounts could be over-estimated as a result of the 'round-tripping' practice and, on the other hand, underestimated as a result of private entities evading government exchange controls, investment through tax havens, and different definitions of ODI used in different countries (Davies 2010: 2).[11]

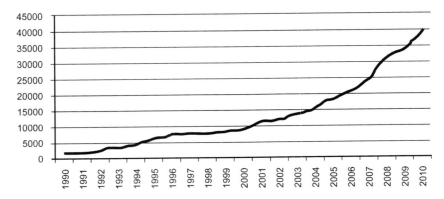

Figure 1.1 China's GDP since 1990
Note: Nominal GDP (RMB Millions).

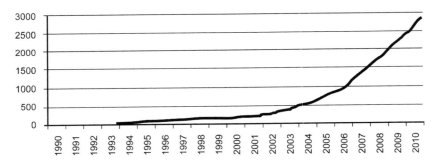

Figure 1.2 China's foreign exchange reserves since 1990
Note: Foreign Exchange Reserves (US$ billion).

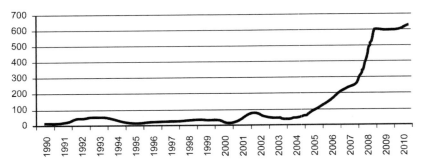

Figure 1.3 China's ODI since 1990
Note: ODI (US$ 100 million).

Second, while the speed of Chinese ODI growth is remarkable, and China has been the largest ODI originator among developing countries for many years, the total stock of ODI from China is in fact rather small in the global context. As at the end of 2010 the total cumulative amount of Chinese ODI stood at US $273.83 billion.[12] In comparative terms, as at the end of 2009, total Chinese ODI accounted for a mere 1.2 per cent of the global stock (Rosen and Hanemann 2011: 18), or about 6 per cent if ODI originating from Hong Kong and Macao is included (Salidjanova 2011: 1). By comparison, at the end of 2009 Japan's global ODI share was three times, and the US's 20 times, that of China. In this comparison it should also be noted that China has an 8 per cent share of global trade and a 9 per cent share of global GDP (Rosen and Hanemann 2011: 18).

Third, at the end of 2009, some 12,000 Chinese enterprises had made ODI abroad, establishing around 13,000 enterprises in 177 countries/regions. Among the enterprises investing overseas, 69.2 per cent were state-owned enterprises and only 1 per cent were private companies (Ministry of Commerce 2011: 11). The remaining distribution is as follows: limited liability companies: 22 per cent; companies limited by shares: 5.6 per cent; cooperative enterprises: 1 per cent; foreign investment enterprises: 0.5 per cent; collective enterprises: 0.3 per cent; enterprises established by Hong Kong, Macao and Taiwan investors: 0.1 per cent; and other unspecified enterprises: 0.3 per cent (Ministry of Commerce 2011: 11). Here we do not know the ownership structure of the limited liability companies or of companies limited by shares. It can, however, be assumed that many involve majority control by governments at central or local levels. Among the industries invested in by the Chinese enterprises, direct mining investment reached a total of $40.58 billion at the end of 2009 (Ministry of Commerce 2011: 72) accounting for about 20 per cent of the total non-financial ODI stock.[13]

Finally, while many headlines opposing Chinese ODI have appeared in major developed countries such as the US, the UK and Australia, the largest share of Chinese ODI was in Asia, accounting for 75.5 per cent of the total stock at the end of 2009. The remaining stock was distributed as follows: Latin America: 12.5 per cent; Africa: 3.8 per cent; Europe: 3.5 per cent; Oceania: 2.6 per cent; and North America: 2.1 per cent (Ministry of Commerce 2011: 7).

China's ODI strategy in context – the evolving policy and regulatory framework

If 'globalization' is not to mean 'Westernization', then ODI from China, and indeed from any developing country into developed countries, is to be expected. Thus, it is reasonable to say that ODI from China *per se* should not be controversial. Further, all governments play a role in regulating their domestic economic activities, whether in the name of protecting the 'national interest' or 'security' or otherwise. The real issue for our policy study is the extent of such regulation and its level of transparency.

While some economists have described the Chinese government as the 'Visible Hand' (Wang 2002: 192), strategically organizing Chinese transnational activities

(Wang 2002: 187), and some of its policies as 'interventionist' (Zafar 2007: 104), others disagree, arguing that Chinese firms do have their own interests to consider and do not always accept government directives or initiatives. As such they reject the view that China's ODI operations are largely driven by a dominant state (see for example Liou 2009). However, given the Chinese government roles as described, it seems obvious that Chinese governments at central and local levels play important strategic roles in guiding China's outward investment, as they do in managing inward foreign investment through various policy measures and regulations. What is also clear is that the role of government has not been constant or consistent; it has evolved in line with China's economic development and reform. Coupled with institutional and administrative changes, the general trend in regulation has been toward simplification, relaxation and liberalization (Buckley *et al.* 2007: 500), a process described as one of 'limiting–loosening–tightening–opening' (Zhao and de Pablo 2010: 149). This is not dissimilar to the development pattern in inward foreign investment in China.

As mentioned earlier, ODI by Chinese enterprises was *permitted* from the beginning of China's 'open door' policy, but that permission was only granted on a selected basis under certain very strict conditions (Buckley *et al.* 2007: 500), and typically strict control was effectively exercised through an administrative examination and approval system.

Initially, examination and approval was conducted on an *ad hoc* basis. The issuance of *The Circular Concerning the Approval Authorities and Principles for Opening Non-Trade Joint Ventures Overseas and in Hong Kong and Macao* (1984) and *The Implementing Provisions on the Administration and Approval Procedure for Opening Non-Trade Enterprises Overseas* (1985), both by the then Ministry for Foreign Trade and Economic Cooperation (MOFTEC), signified the beginning of a more institutionalized examination and approval system (Yu and Zhao 2007: 3). The policy then was about control, requiring all ODI, whatever the size or whoever wished to invest, to be approved by MOFTEC on behalf of the State Council (ibid.).

Control and restrictions were then easy to exercise as major reforms of China's foreign exchange system were yet to be introduced in 1994. Indeed, in the 1980s the most important policy on ODI was the *Measures on the Administration of Foreign Exchange for Overseas Investment*, issued by SAFE on 6 March 1989,[14] which reinforced the already strict control of foreign exchange. These Measures (and their Implementing Rules) not only exercised control over the outflow of foreign exchange, they also demanded repatriation of all profits derived from overseas investment. Clearly, the policy then was not designed to encourage ODI. The *Opinion of the State Planning Commission on Strengthening the Administration of Overseas Investment Projects* (1991) clearly stated this policy:

> At the present, our country does not have the conditions for large scale overseas investment. Overseas investment by enterprises should be conducted according to our nation's needs, focusing on utilising overseas technologies, resources and markets so as to overcome our domestic shortages, and on the basis of mutual benefit strengthening 'South–South' cooperation and thus

enhancing the development of our friendly cooperative relationship with the Third World.

(Item 1)[15]

The *Opinion*, having been endorsed by the State Council, was quickly implemented by the State Planning Commission through the *Provisions on Formulation, Examination and Approval of Project Proposals and Feasibility Reports on Overseas Direct Investment Projects* on 17 August 1991, by MOFTEC through its *(Trial) Provisions on the Examination, Approval and Administration of the Overseas Establishment of Non-Trade Enterprises* on 23 March 1992, and by SAFE which issued a number of strict measures on the use of foreign exchange for ODI. Under the State Planning Commission Provision, provincial authorities were given some limited approval powers.[16] But the same Provision subjected all ODI to examination and approval with the *(Trial) Provisions* of MOFTEC imposing four strict criteria for ODI. Approval could only be granted if an investment project served one of the following purposes:

- facilitating the export of equipment, materials and technologies and hence increasing earnings of foreign exchange;
- expanding overseas project contracts and labour cooperation;
- importing advanced technologies and managerial methods; or
- maintaining, over a relative long period, a stable supply of raw materials and products that China needed or was short of.

(Article 4)

Together, these Provisions effectively established some very strict and restrictive rules for Chinese ODI. Apparently a part of the justification for imposing such strict control was the fear of illegal capital flight and the loss of state assets through ODI (Liou 2009: 674; Wong and Chan 2003: 277).[17]

Deng Xiaoping's Southern Tour in 1992 effectively re-launched China's 'open door' policy. Thus it followed that the CPC for the first time officially called for active efforts to expand ODI and transnational operations as part of China's national economic development plan (Jiang 1992: Part II; Tan 1999: 18). Encouraged by this policy turn of the Party, Chinese firms became enthusiastic again. However, the above-cited *Opinion* of the State Planning Commission and the *(Trial) Provision* of MOFTEC continued to dominate policy-making. Further, although a new round of reform of foreign exchange control started in 1994 after the State Council issued its *Notice on Further Reforming the Foreign Exchange Administrative System* in December 1993, the *Regulations on the Foreign Exchange System of the People's Republic of China*, issued by the State Council on 29 January 1996, continued the strict control over the outflow of capital, as well as imposing an examination system over the sources of foreign exchange funds for ODI (Article 21; see also S. Li 2009: 2).

The strict control mechanisms established in the 1990s served China well. On the one hand it was able to control the outward flow of capital, such as during the Asian financial crisis in 1997, through its administrative approval procedures. On the other hand the government was able to actively and selectively encourage

ODI in specific industries (mostly in exports or resource-related areas) through export tax rebates, foreign exchange assistance and direct financial support (Ministry of Commerce 2011: 150–1). At the same time we also began to see some non-state-owned enterprises investing overseas, especially in Hong Kong in real estate and stock market speculation, apparently encouraged by both central and local governments (Chan 1995), despite the fact that private firms were not officially permitted to engage in ODI until 2003 (Buckley *et al.* 2008: 725).

It was also in the 1990s that we began to see some frequent but not always consistent overtures towards a 'going global' policy from state and Party leaders.[18] Sometimes explicit statements were made by these leaders. For instance, in a speech at a Party meeting in February 1998, Jiang Zemin specifically stated that

> While actively expanding our exports, we should take leadership to organise, step by step, and to support a group of strong state-owned enterprises to go out to other countries, principally to Africa, Central Asia, the Middle East, Central Europe, South America etc. to invest and to establish factories.
>
> (Yu and Zhao 2007: 6)

As a result of strict control over capital outflow and the sometimes contradictory overtures towards a 'going global' policy, the actual policy practice in the 1990s appeared to be *ad hoc*, confusing and contradictory, and practices lacked transparency. Not surprisingly, ODI from China remained flat in the 1990s.

The various overtures to ODI finally led to the official initiation of a 'going out' policy in 2000, as part of a national social and economic strategy by the CPC (CPC 2000: Item 12). In its Proposal for the Making of the 10th Five-Year National Economic and Social Development Plan, the Party called for financial and insurance support for transnational operations of enterprises, overseas processing trade and overseas contracting projects. It also called for speeding up the formulation and adoption of rules and regulations regarding the administration, supervision and coordination of ODI. The Party's 'going out' policy soon was officially translated into national policy and incorporated into the 10th Five-Year Plan adopted in 2001 (Section 17(4)), thus initiating China's official 'going out' strategy.[19] Importantly, while these are very general documents without much detail, the language used was no longer 'to permit' but had become 'to encourage'.

In response to the policy initiative, and in addition to the establishment of the China Import–Export Bank in 1994, the China Export Credit Insurance Company was swiftly established in 2001. An ODI data collection system was also established in 2002 (Ministry of Commerce 2011: 204). However, major policy and regulatory measures were not issued until 2004.[20]

The year 2004 represents a landmark in China's effort to reform and formalize its regulatory framework on ODI. First, the Ministry of Commerce, in conjunction with the Ministry of Foreign Affairs, issued the *Industry Catalogue of Individual Countries for Outward Investment*,[21] providing much needed information guidance for Chinese enterprises eager to make outward investments. This information assistance was further supplemented by the Ministry of Commerce through the establishment of a *Reporting System for Operational Barriers in Individual Countries* (November 2004). In July 2004, the State Council issued its important *Decision on the Reform of the Investment System*. Essentially, this Decision was to abolish the 'examination and approval' system, which had been the hallmark of China's administrative system for the control of investment since the 'open door' policy was introduced in 1978. In its place two new investment approval systems ('verification and approval', and 'filing-for-record') were to be established in accordance with the principle that 'whoever invests decides and whoever takes profit assumes risks' (Item I (2) of the State Council Decision). Under the 'filing-for-record' system, the 'old' 'examination and approval' system was effectively abolished. Under the 'verification and approval' system, the various administrative authorities would no longer examine project proposals, feasibility studies and reports on project commencement. Instead, the authorities would only examine project applications in relation to

- economic security,
- the appropriate use of natural resources,
- environmental protection,
- optimal industrial distribution,
- the protection of public interests, and
- the prevention of monopoly.

For this purpose, a *Catalogue of Investment Projects subject to Government Verification and Approval* was attached to the State Council *Decision on the Reform of the Investment System*, making the 'verification and approval' system reasonably transparent.

The State Council Decision was swiftly implemented by the Ministry of Commerce through the issuance of the *Provisions on Matters subject to Verification and Approval in relation to Overseas Investment to Establish Enterprises* (1 October 2004), and by the State Development and Reform Commission through its *Interim Measures on Matters subject to Verification and Approval in relation to Outward Investment Projects* (9 October 2004). Under the Ministry of Commerce Provisions, this Ministry further delegates its verification and approval powers to provincial authorities for commerce, but retains the powers over ODI of state-owned enterprises under direct control of the central government. Under the Interim Measures, the State Development and Reform Commission only exercises the verification and approval power in relation to ODI projects where the Chinese investment is over US$10 million for non-resource projects, and over US$30 million for resources-related projects. The State Council retains the final verification and approval power over investment of US$50 million or more for non-resource projects and US$200 million or more for resources-related projects. Additionally, the Provisions and the Interim Measures provide some transparent criteria for the exercise of the 'verification and approval' powers.

Clearly the 2004 reform indicated a transition from 'control' to 'encouragement and facilitation' through information assistance to enterprises' decision-making in outward investment, as well as a reasonably transparent regulatory framework for examination and approval of ODI. In this sense the 2004 State Council Decision effectively initiated a new era for the development of the Chinese ODI (Zhou 2006).

Not surprisingly, therefore, Chinese ODI only took off in a significant way from 2004 onward.

It is however wrong to assume that the 2004 reform was intended to abandon government control over ODI. Foreign exchange control and government financial support continued to be critical elements in regulating ODI activities, though both were moving towards further liberalization. In 2005 SAFE issued the *Circular on Expanding the Pilot Programme Concerning Overseas Investment*, under which the total allocated foreign exchange funds for ODI were increased from US$3.3 billion to US$5 billion, and local authorities' approval limit was also increased from US$3 million to US$10 million. Soon, however, the cap of the US$5 billion ODI funds was abolished by the *Circular on Revision of Certain Foreign Exchange Control Policies Relating to Overseas Investments*.[22] On the financial support front, the State Development and Reform Commission and the Import and Export Bank jointly issued the *Notice Concerning the Policy on Providing Credit and Loan Support for Overseas Projects Encouraged by the State* on 27 October 2004.[23] According to the Notice, each year the Import and Export Bank was to allocate specific funds to support ODI projects and a preferential interest rate would apply to loans for projects that met one of the following criteria:

- resource development projects that address a shortage of domestic resources;
- manufacturing or infrastructural projects that promote the export of domestic technology, products, equipment and labour;
- R&d projects that utilize international advanced technology, managerial experience and expertise; and
- M&a projects to enhance the international competitiveness and market development of Chinese firms (Items I and II of the Notice. For further discussion, see Yu and Hwang 2005).

Clearly China's financial support policy is formulated on the basis of strategic considerations, and is not just intended for profit-seeking.

Significantly, reforms of the administration and regulation of ODI continued after 2004, and once again the reform was led by the State Council. In October 2006 the State Council adopted its *Opinions on Encouraging and Regulating Enterprises involved in Outward Investment and Economic Cooperation*[24] which called for, *inter alia*, the strengthening of:

- policy guidance;
- regulation of market order;
- overall coordination;
- rational distribution;
- prevention of disorderly competition; and
- the protection of national interests ('State Council adopted *Opinions on Encouraging and Regulating Enterprises involved in Outward Investment and Economic Cooperation*').

Meanwhile, in September 2007, China established its sovereign wealth fund, the China Investment Corporation (CIC), with an injection of US$200 billion as its initial capital, thus making CIC the largest sovereign wealth fund in the world (Congress Research Service 2008). This clearly signified a more direct involvement by the government in ODI activities in accordance with its own strategic considerations, while liberalizing ODI administrative regimes for enterprises. It is in this context that a new round of decentralization and liberalization was promulgated.[25]

In 2009 two important sets of regulations were issued: the *Administrative Measures on Outward Investment* (issued by the Ministry of Commerce, 16 March 2009),[26] and the *Administrative Measures on Foreign Exchange Used by Domestic Enterprises for Outward Investment* (issued by the SAFE, 13 July 2009). These two sets of administrative measures completed the long process of rule-making to establish a formal and more transparent regulatory framework for ODI, although further supplementary or implementing measures and rules continued to be issued in 2010 and 2011.

The Ministry of Commerce's Administrative Measures, which are also applied to ODI to Hong Kong, Macao and Taiwan,[27] focus on further decentralizing the power of regulating ODI activities to provincial authorities, and simplifying the verification and approval procedures. Under the new Measures, ODI projects with Chinese investment of US$100 million or less would only need verification and approval from provincial authorities, unless such investment is made in a country which has no diplomatic relationship with China, or in a country that is specifically identified as needing central government approval, or for projects that involve multiple countries or projects to establish 'special purpose' firms (Article 6 and 7 of the Administrative Measures).[28] Once again, the feasibility of any project is a matter for the investing firms to determine. Further, the Ministry also undertakes to provide information assistance to enterprises, through the issuance of *Guides to ODI in Specific Countries* and *Catalogue of Industries for Outward Investment*, as well as providing information on ODI statistics, investment opportunities, investment barriers and risk warnings (Article 28 of the Administrative Measures).

The SAFE Administrative Measures were formulated in consolidation of the previous *ad hoc* policies and measures, but also provided further liberalization in the control of foreign exchange.[29] Thus these Measures greatly expand the sources of foreign exchange funds available for ODI, which now include all self-owned foreign exchange, foreign exchange loans, foreign exchange purchased with Renminbi, in-kind contributions, intangible property, profits obtained from previous ODI, and any other foreign exchange funds approved by the foreign exchange authorities (Article 4 of the Administrative Measures). Further, a registration and filing-for-record system, replacing the previous prior examination of foreign exchange fund sources, is established so that the process of actual transfer of the foreign exchange for ODI is greatly simplified (Article 6 of the Administrative Measures). The Administrative Measures also allow domestic institutions to provide guarantees for overseas commercial loans and financing for the purpose of ODI (Article 11 of the Administrative Measures). Continuing this liberalization trend, in January 2011 the People's Bank of China issued its *Administrative Measures on the Trial Implementation of Renminbi Settlement for Overseas Direct Investment* (issued by the

People's Bank of China on 6 January 2011). These Measures have for the first time allowed the direct use of Renminbi for ODI, albeit on a very limited trial basis.

With the 2009 reforms in place, it can be said that on paper at least the transformation of the examination and approval system from 'control' to 'guidance' has been completed.[30] If Chinese enterprises need no financial support from the government and have sufficient funds of their own in foreign exchange, they will be able to make their own ODI decisions. Those requiring government financial or exchange assistance would have to accept government guidance to only invest in the 'encouraged' areas or industries. This suggests that we will see much more ODI from China in the coming years as liberalization has only just been put in place and private enterprises have only come onto the scene since then.[31] Indeed, an official from the Ministry of Commerce has recently stated that ODI will grow by between 20 and 30 per cent in the next five years and will overtake inbound foreign investment within three years (see Ding and Bao 2011).[32] Other studies also confirm this growth trend (Salidjanova 2011).

The above review indicates that government policy on ODI has involved some major changes, and the Chinese government currently sees its role as a dual function: to provide information assistance and to guide ODI into strategic areas through the use of financial support and foreign exchange resources. In theory it is fairly clear that business decisions on ODI are now to be made by firms themselves, but one must keep in mind the crucial link between business decisions and government strategic considerations. The largest firms, especially those in the area of banking, resources and insurance, are principally state-owned enterprises. This means that despite the apparent policy liberalization, the Chinese government will still be able to direct ODI by state-owned firms through the exercise of 'ownership rights' in these firms,[33] direct financial support, favoured loans, allocation of foreign aid projects, etc. (Salidjanova 2011: 11). In terms of government strategic considerations, priority has always been access to resources and markets, and acquisition of technology, know-how and brands – summarized as the 'two resources and two markets' strategy.[34] Additionally, there are political and diplomatic goals to be achieved (Tull 2006; Zafar 2007; Salidjanova 2011: 4; Wang 2002: 194).

Between macro-economic control and micro-economic management

The Chinese government has a reasonably clear strategy of using ODI for specific goals. Chinese enterprises, on the other hand, have their own economic and financial objectives for their market operations. Even for directors and managers of state-owned enterprises, who are mostly appointed by government and form part of Chinese officialdom, career development depends more on achieving economic results than being simply compliant with government directives or obedient to their superiors. Put simply, Chinese firms, whether state-owned or private, must have their own motivations for ODI and often have their own objectives in making investment decisions.[35] As such, the realization of ODI is a product of the interplay between government policies and enterprise motivations.[36] Government control is only one element in the realization of Chinese ODI, with the exception of investment activities by sovereign wealth funds.[37]

Chinese firms share, to varying degrees, the government's strategic goals for energy security, acquisition of technology, brands and access to markets. The need for energy security, whether for price or availability reasons, requires little explanation in a country where economic growth has been maintained at or near 10 per cent for more than two decades.[38] The need for new markets is also understandable in a country where the rate of saving is high and economic growth is fast (see Wang 2002: 200).[39] With regard to advanced technology, the need for ODI arose directly from the failure of inbound foreign direct investment to attract sufficient technologies and market information (Zhao and de Pablo 2010: 149), despite the tax incentives and the establishment of high-tech parks to attract such investment (Wang 2002: 203–4.).[40] Not surprisingly, Chinese firms are often encouraged to invest in 'economies with significant levels of human and intellectual capital, and in particular in the industrialized countries' (Buckley *et al.* 2007: 505).

As with many other countries, there was also external pressure originating from regional and international groupings (Wang 2002: 189) to increase ODI, either to avoid being left out by the movement of economic regionalization or to bypass trade protection.[41] The risk of blockage was even greater when the United States imposed high tariffs on certain products originating from China before China joined the World Trade Organization (WTO). The Chinese government's response was to establish offshore firms in other countries such as Australia in order to infiltrate the American market. This strategy proved to be useful with Chinese textile, clothing and footwear products prior to China joining the WTO (Wang 2002: 202). There were similar considerations for Chinese investment in Africa. China sees Africa as a lucrative market for Chinese products as well as an export transition point to the American market through the Africa Growth and Opportunity Act (AGOA) (Zafar 2007: 121).

While much of the public attention has been fixed on large-scale resource-related or brand name related investment by Chinese firms, it should be pointed out that most of Chinese firms involved in ODI are small and medium-sized firms, making investments of under US$5 million (CCPIT 2010a, 2010b, 2011a, 2011b; Salidjanova 2011: 3). Their motivation is quite different from that of large enterprises. For these small-scale investing firms the principal motivation is achieving sales networks, market access and expansion, and sometimes even for the purpose of gaining foreign residence or social security benefits (Antkiewicz and Whalley 2007: 210), though some of them also have the aim of acquiring natural resources and raw materials as well as technologies and know-how (Cheng 2004: 52–4; CCPIT 2010a, 2010b, 2011a, 2011b).

Firms' objectives do not, however, always match government strategic goals. The political and diplomatic motivation in investing in some African countries is a good example (Buckley *et al.* 2008: 730). Several studies have suggested that Chinese investment, from the very beginning in the 1970s to the 1990s, was sometimes designed to fulfil geo-politic and diplomatic goals (Buckley *et al.* 2008: 722), such as the political rivalry with the United States and Taiwan (Zafar 2007: 106), and the outcome of such investments was in practice unproductive (Wang 2002:

204–5). Clearly such investments are not always in the best interests of Chinese firms, whether state-owned or private. However, the strict conditions for government financial support and exchange control have meant that the government is capable of directing investment into these areas by ensuring that firms nevertheless derive economic or other benefits from such ventures through government financial support, aid projects, or by applying political and administrative pressures.

Finally, government financial support, whether in direct financial aid, loans or foreign exchange assistance, continues to play an effective role in guiding and directing ODI from China.[42] With the simplification and liberalization of the ODI examination and approval regime, surveys have indicated that the principal barrier for Chinese firms in investing overseas, among other issues such as the lack of international networking expertise and personnel with sufficient ODI experience, is difficulty in financing (Cheng 2004: 54; CCPIT 2010a, 2010b, 2011a, 2011b).[43] This, coupled with the strict control over foreign exchange, has given the government much needed leverage in controlling ODI direction and development.[44]

Conclusion

As with other areas of China's 'open door' practice, Chinese ODI strategy has been transformed from a 'political device' to a more 'market-oriented exercise'.[45] Chinese policy and regulation of ODI have been gradually transformed from a strictly controlled trial-and-error practice to a regime which may be described as 'guidance'. Under this regime, the examination and approval framework has been both simplified and liberalized. But financial support and foreign exchange control remain firmly in government hands. While the government may promote its role as information provider and administrative supervisor, leaving feasibility decision-making to enterprises and much to the market, it certainly retains the capacity to strategically guide ODI through various financial means, although to varying extents. Further, with US$3 trillion in reserve, China by necessity must find a way to utilize the money, if only to reduce losses due to the appreciation of the yuan.[46]

Although it is difficult to measure the extent to which the government is involved in decision-making by large state-owned firms in resource-related ODI, it has been argued that such intervention is selective, operating more through providing financial and other supports rather than by vetoing such investment. Given the significant growth in ODI in the last few years (and in the foreseeable future), and the liberalization of the ODI examination and approval regime, the government's capacity to control and direct ODI is now more limited. As such ODI is bound to be shaped more by commercial than political considerations (Buckley *et al.* 2008: 724). What is now clear is that China, whether for national strategic reasons or enterprise business considerations, needs to and will 'go global'.

Notes

* I thank Enshen Li and Maya el Khoury for their research assistance.
1 Indeed major studies on Chinese ODI only emerged after some 'large-scale buyout attempts in the US became widely publicized' (Cheung and Qian 2009: 312).

2 For a summary of recent investment in gas and oil by Chinese companies, with the controversial practice of loan supports from Chinese state-owned banks (China Development Bank and China Export and Import Bank) to Chinese companies and hosting countries, see Evans and Downs (2006); Zweig and Bi (2005); Ma and Andrews-Speed (2006); Dittrick (2010); and Tudo (2011).
3 Another major controversial aspect is Chinese investment in countries like North Korea and a number of African countries. See Kim (2006) for analysis of Chinese investment in North Korea; for investment in Africa see Zafar (2007), Servant (2005), Tull (2006).
4 At the end of 1979, China's foreign reserves stood at US$840 million. See State Administration of Foreign Exchange (2011).
5 Measures on the Administration of Foreign Exchange for Overseas Investment, issued by the State Administration of Foreign Exchange, March 1989.
6 The strategy was contained in the Proposals of the Communist Party of China on the Making of the 10th Five-Year National Economic and Social Development Plan, October 2000.
7 China's foreign exchange reserve, being the largest in the world, exceeded US$3 trillion at the end of March 2011 and together with the continuing inflow of FDI and a large annual trade surplus, China is now the world's largest capital-surplus country (Salidjanova 2011: 1).
8 While some economists in the West now agree that China will overtake the US as the world's largest economy in the near future, there is no agreement as to when this will happen. The latest prediction from the International Monetary Fund projects this could happen by 2016 in terms of China's real economic output (see Colebatch 2011).
9 This aspect of Chinese ODI is particularly 'non-transparent' (Wong and Chan 2003: 277). Chinese statistics simply treat Hong Kong as an 'investment destination rather than a transitional point', as is often the case (Scissors 2010: 3).
10 According to Ministry of Commerce data (Ministry of Commerce 2011), as at the end of 2009 overseas assets owned by Chinese firms amounted to US$1 trillion – indicative of Chinese portfolio investment being large in volume (see also Fung *et al.* 2007).
11 'Round-tripping' is a practice whereby Chinese funds are injected into overseas entities and then returned to China to take advantage of financial incentives for foreign investment (see Davies 2010: 2; Wong and Chan 2003: 276–7; Salidjanova 2011: 1; Buckley *et al.* 2008: 733; Cai 1999: 857). Some economists believe that the data of the Ministry of Commerce have seriously underestimated the actual amount of ODI, at least in the early years (Zhan 1995: footnote 1). It should be noted, however, that most financial incentives for inward FDI have now been abolished in China and, as a result, the practice of 'round-tripping' will eventually disappear.
12 My calculation of US$273.83 billion is based on Chinese Ministry of Commerce (2011: 5), and other reported data from the Ministry of Commerce at: http://www.mofcom.gov.cn/static/column/tongjiziliao/dgzz.html/1?3046609383=755335131. Also NB. the sources of *Figure 1* compiled from 'GDP growth in China 1952-2009' are at: http://www.chinability.com/GDP.htm (last accessed 26 April 2011), and 'Annual Statistics Report' by National Bureau of Statistics of China. 'Year' refers to end of year. *Figure 2* is compiled from 'Scale of China's foreign exchange reserves, 1950-2010'. 'Year' refers to end of year. *Figure 3* is compiled from the Chinese Ministry of Commerce 2011: 5, and other reported data from the Chinese Ministry of Commerce (op. cit).
13 At the end of 2009, total non-financial ODI stock was US$199.76 billion (Ministry of Commerce 2011: 9). In the first three months of 2011, China had already made a total of US$8.51 billion, involving 974 ODI projects in 98 countries: http://www.mofcom.gov.cn/aarticle/tongjiziliao/dgzz/201104/20110407517370.html?479695335=19103707 (last accessed 11 May 2011). For Chinese non-trading ODI growth from 1979 to 1993, see Ding 2000: 123.
14 These Measures were further implemented by a set of Implementing Rules, issued by SAFE on 26 June 1990.
15 The *Opinion* was formulated by the State Planning Commission but issued by the State Council as *Guofa* (1991) No. 13, on 5 March 1991.

16 Under the Provisions, investment under US$1 million without the need for state financial support might be approved by provincial authorities. Investment between US$1 million and 30 million would need the approval of the State Planning Commission, and any investment over US$30 million would require the approval of the State Council.
17 For detailed studies on illegal capital flight (amounting to tens of billions a year) and informal privatization of public assets, see Ding (2000) and Gunter (1996).
18 See various statements quoted in Yu and Zhao (2007).
19 There are arguments about the precise timing of the official start of the 'going out' policy. For example, Kaartemo (2007: 9) identifies the commencement year of the policy as 2003, while K. Zhang (2005: 5) refers to the year as being 2000 and initiated by the then Premier Zhu Rongji.
20 Some specific interim measures had been issued in 2003 including the SAFE *Notice on Certain Issues Concerning the Simplification of Examination of Foreign Exchange Fund Sources for Overseas Investment* (19 March 2003), the SAFE *Circular on Issues Relating to Further Intensifying the Reform of Foreign Exchange Administration of Overseas Investment* (15 October 2003), and the *Circular on Issues Relating to Granting Financial Support to Key Overseas Projects Encouraged by the State* (jointly issued by the State Development and Reform Commission and the Import and Export Bank, 9 May 2003. The Circular was soon replaced in October 2004). The foreign exchange measures relaxed the examination of fund sources as well as delegating certain approval powers to local authorities, and the State Development and Reform Commission measures provided support for ODI projects encouraged by the state (see also discussions in Mao 2003; Yin *et al.* 2003).
21 This has been supplemented twice – in 2006 and 2007.
22 Issued by SAFE on 8 June 2006. On these specific liberalization measures, see Geng (2007) and Stender *et al.* (2006).
23 This Notice replaced the *Circular on Issues Relating to Granting Financing Support to Key Overseas Projects Encouraged by the State* issued in 2003.
24 The Opinion, although not formally published, has been widely discussed in Chinese media and in academic and policy studies.
25 The new measures have typically concentrated on strengthening the 'file-for-record' system and the abolition of certain administrative examination and approval processes/powers. Chinese texts of these policies can be found in China Overseas Investment Promotion Network at: www.coipn.cn (last accessed 25 May 2011).
26 The Measures also abolished the *Provisions on Matters subject to Verification and Approval in relation to Overseas Investment to Establish Enterprises* (1 October 2004), and the *Provisions on Matters subject to Verification and Approval in relation to Outward Investment to Establish Enterprises in Hong Kong and Macao Special Administrative Regions* (jointly issued by the Ministry of Commerce and the Hong Kong and Macao Office of the State Council, 2004).
27 Although Article 38 of the Measures specifically states that these Measures apply to investment to Hong Kong, Macao and Taiwan, the State Development and Reform Commission, the Ministry of Commerce and the Taiwan Office of the State Council jointly issued (on 9 November 2010) the *Administrative Measures on Outward Investment to Taiwan Region by Mainland Enterprises* specifying all outward investment to Taiwan would require verification and approval of the central government authorities; provincial authorities only having the power to undertake preliminary examination.
28 A 'special purpose' firm is defined by Article 37 as an overseas listed firm that is established to control and realize interests in a domestic firm.
29 The Measures abolish a series of measures and rules on foreign exchange control over ODI issued since 1990.
30 An issue not explored here but worthy of future research is whether this government-controlled transformation is a reason for China's ODI development not following traditional internationalization patterns, such as the 'Uppsala model', Dunning's 'Eclectic

Paradigm' or the 'international product life-cycle theory', etc. (see Syed Tariq Anwar 2010: 422). For comparative studies on the Chinese ODI pattern, see Buckley *et al.* (2008).

31 In fact, in May 2010 the State Council issued its *Certain Opinions on Encouraging and Guiding the Healthy Development of Investment by the Private Sector*. These Opinions (Items 27 and 28) specifically encourage private enterprises to invest overseas and state that they will enjoy the same treatment as other enterprises in the area of financial support, insurance, foreign exchange control, customs and quality control. In a survey undertaken between December 2009 and March 2010 on *Current Conditions and Intention of Outbound Investment by Chinese Enterprise*, conducted by the China Council for the Promotion of International Trade in conjunction with the European Commission and UNCTAD, (involving 3,000 enterprises, 1,377 responding to questionnaires, 69 per cent being private enterprises), 56 per cent indicated their intention to increase or maintain their current level of ODI in the next 12 months, and 61 per cent indicated their intention to increase their ODI in the next two–six years. Also importantly, the government 'going global' policy and its related incentives were seen as the most decisive factors in their consideration of ODI (CCPIT 2010a, 2010b, 2011a, 2011b).

32 Rosen and Hanemann (2011: 16) estimate Chinese ODI could reach US$2 trillion by 2020.

33 Corporate governance and government influence in decision-making in state-owned enterprises warrant separate research attention; however, it is commonly recognized that senior SOE executives are appointed by governments at central and local levels, and if finance is required this is provided through state-owned banks (see Salidjanova 2011: 4 and 13).

34 That is to target both domestic and overseas markets and to seek resources (including capital, technologies and know-how) domestically and internationally (Wang 2002: 194).

35 As demonstrated by Chih-shian Liou (2009), even among the closely controlled oil oligopolists, government directives are sometimes circumvented to protect the companies' economic interests. Government capacity to directly control SOEs' ODI activities is also questioned by some Western economists (Salidjanova 2011: 12). See also: Schüller and Turner (2005: 10, Table 4).

36 Government and enterprise motivations or rationales for ODI form the core of existing studies on ODI from China. Instead of repeating these studies, this section provides a summary.

37 In 2007 the China Investment Corporation (CIC) was established as a sovereign wealth fund, but CIC is not the only investment vehicle directly controlled by the government. See Chapter 1 of the *Report to Congress of the US-China Economic and Security Review Commission* 2008: Section 2.

38 For instance, in relation to Chinese investment in Australia (Wang 2002: 201) notes that

> the high quality natural resources has been the most attractive factor: Australian iron ore has over 60 per cent iron content and it has been estimated that, if a similar grade and scale of iron ore deposit was developed in China, the total cost would be eight times the amount that China has invested in Australia ... Such huge cost gaps explain why China selected Australia as its source of resources ... From the central government's perspective, China has to find stable and cheap raw material sources to meet its rapid industrialization needs, especially in a fluctuating global market.

39 Thus there was a rise in 'offensive market-seeking motives' among both government and Chinese firms (Buckley *et al.* 2007: 503).

40 This is not a unique problem for China. It is generally agreed that

> [b]ecause developed countries have stringent restriction policies on the output of advanced technologies, ODI is an important way for developing countries to acquire the most advanced technologies ... [T]he technology gap was one of the driving forces of ODI for developing countries; developing countries should not

only rely on foreign investment to fill the technological gap, but should also actively increase ODI.

(Zhao and de Pablo 2010: 151)

41 Important blocs to China, for example, are the North American Free Trade Agreement (NAFTA) and the European Union (EU) (see Wang 2002: 202; Zhao and de Pablo 2010).
42 This happens mostly in investment in resources and it is difficult to determine the extent of such financial support or subsidies (see Evans and Downs 2006; Dittrick 2010).
43 Z. Li (2010: 4) points out that at the end of October 2009 loans (both in RMB and foreign exchange) to private enterprises and individuals accounted for 1.7 per cent of all financial loans in China.
44 This is especially true in 'resource and telecommunications areas' (Salidjanova 2011: 4).
45 Some have described the pre-1990 policy as 'purely political' (Cheung and Qian 2009: 315).
46 According to Chinese media reports, in the last eight years Chinese reserves have lost US$271.1 billion due to yuan appreciation alone (see Xinhua 2011c).

2 Company law reform in China

Xianchu Zhang

Introduction

The development of company law in the People's Republic of China (PRC) is viewed in this chapter from the perspective of how the overall company law regime provides a gauge for evaluating the corporate legal environment specifically and the competitiveness of the economy more generally.[1] The context is China's modernization of its own legal system coinciding with reform to company law worldwide; the global focus on company law being hastened by the 2009 global financial crisis (GFC). With China still in transition from a planned to a market economy accompanied by the rule of law, company laws are examined through the lens of how their development reflects prevailing political ideology and in turn how the reforms affect contemporary China's 'going out' policy. It is argued that the evolution of China's company laws has directly affected the economic integration of China into markets worldwide and thus how competitors may respond (Vining 2010).

Evolution of company law in the PRC

Although the introduction of company law into China may be traced as far back as the Qing Dynasty, the practice of the planned economy since 1949 by the communist government decimated for three decades the basic conditions of corporate operations. As a result, when economic reform was implemented in 1978, state-owned enterprises (SOEs), where all management, personnel appointments, finance and production were controlled by the government through its central plans, were the dominant business form, making almost 80 per cent of national industrial outputs (Jefferson and Singh 1999; Garnaut *et al.* 2005). Given the extent of their power and gross economic effects, reform of SOEs was inevitably taken as a commencement point to pave the way for developing company practice and legislation.

The SOE reform

The SOE reforms of 1978–93 went through two discernable stages: the first (1978–83) characterized by the primary theme of 'deregulation' was to enable

SOEs to operate with more business autonomy. The second (1984–93) focused on separating SOE business management rights from state ownership and control. *The State Enterprises Bankruptcy Law (on Trial)* and *Law of the Enterprises of the Whole People* were promulgated in 1986 and 1988 respectively, starting a new era of SOE regulation based on formal legislation. Soon after these laws were proclaimed, stock corporations with public issuing emerged under a central government pilot scheme in Shanghai and Guangzhou. Under these pilots Tsingdao Beer became the first company of mainland China to be listed on the Hong Kong stock exchange in June 1993 – even before the *Company Law* was adopted on 29 December 1993 (CL 1993). As a parallel development, a large number of foreign investment enterprises were established in the form of limited liability companies since the reform policy was implemented under the foreign investment enterprise laws including the *Sino-Foreign Equity Joint Venture Law*, *Sino-Foreign Contractual Joint Venture Law* and *Wholly Foreign Owned Enterprises Law*.[2]

In addition to the enactments and administrative policies outlined above, SOE reform has been guided by decisions of the Communist Party of China (CPC). The movement of incorporation was accelerated after the CPC adopted its 'Decision on Certain Issues Concerning Establishment of the Socialist Market Economy' on 14 November 1993. This called for the introduction of a modern enterprises system into China, characterized by well-defined ownership, clear accountability, separation of enterprise functions from political responsibilities and scientific management. This decision reoriented China to the so-called socialist market economy and was soon recognized as a national goal reflected in Article 7 of *Amendments to the 1982 Constitution* (29 March 1993).

The SOE reforms illustrate not only rapid progress in modernizing the economic system and legal institutions but also the continuation of the 'Chinese characteristics' in developing the socialist market economy. The characteristics include a 'top-down' approach to governance commencing with the leadership of the Party-state (Chao 2005: 91). In contrast to the former Soviet Union and other Eastern European countries where entire political regimes were overturned, the purpose of introducing a modern enterprises system to China was to preserve socialism by taking advantage of capitalist institutions. The Decision of the CPC Central Committee on 'Major Issues Concerning the Reform and Development of State Owned Enterprises' of 22 September 1999 explicitly declared one of the objectives of the SOE reform was to make the state economy play a more leading role in the national economy. The CPC General Secretary Hu Jintao's report to the 17th National Congress of the Party (15 October 2007) stated that 'deepening the SOE reform and the introduction of the modern enterprises system were intended to rationalize the structure of the public economy to increase the vitality, control and influence of the public sector in national development'. The State-owned Assets Supervision and Administration Commission (SASAC) has also been established with the intention that instead of CPC powerbrokers directly appointing SOE directors, SASAC would supposedly present objectivity and transparency. SASAC's much touted role in the system is itself, of course, subject to CPC oversight.

Tensions have long existed between the favoured political ideology of state control and public ownership, and market reformists' demands for increased business autonomy, property rights and private sector protection for a level playing field (see Lan 2000: 13; Chao 2005: 91).

CL 1993

CL 1993 was the first Company Law legislation passed in PRC history. It was promulgated only after ten years of drafting and debate. In fact the promulgation was celebrated as a milestone of market development and a catalyst for further SOE reform. CL 1993 introduced two company types into China: (i) the limited liability company (LLC), and (ii) the joint stock company (JSC). These are basically equivalent to 'private' and 'public' companies in many other jurisdictions. CL 1993 set out the organic corporate structure whereby shareholders' meetings were defined as the corporation's power body. The board of directors and the supervisory board were to operate side by side, as the 'executive organ' and the 'watchdog' respectively. Furthermore, it streamlined establishment requirements, capital registration and operational scope (Zhang 2003).

CL 1993 suffered from inherent deficiencies in the early years of market development. For example, the law subjected corporate practices to rigid administrative regulation with strict *ultra vires* rules,[3] and statutory capital requirements.[4] Some rules further reflected the prevailing political ideology including special provisions to 'preserve state assets',[5] the mandate for corporations to enhance 'socialist spiritual civilization',[6] and the statutory privilege granted exclusively to SOEs to form 'one-man companies'[7] and issue corporate bonds.[8] Moreover, the Law was defective in many aspects in that it failed to stipulate any rules governing 'majority' and 'minority' shareholder relations. This soon became problematic due to lack of clear provisions in place over shareholders and shareholder remedies. Although the Law required directors to carry out their duties 'in good faith', the crucial concept of *fiduciary duties* was missed out from the legislation. In a sense, such omission might be intended to accommodate the potential conflict facing the management between business efficiency and political objectives. To a large extent most listed companies are controlled or influenced by the government with a majority equity ownership directly or indirectly. In this environment despite the supervisory board being institutionalized in the law, the short and general provisions rendered it a toothless tiger in practice.[9]

CL 1993 was, in due course, criticized and its defects were soon amplified on the securities market.[10] Rampant abuses and violations required legislative amendments, judicial interpretations and new government regulations. Before the 2005 reform improvement of the company law regime was thus progressed through criminalization of false capital contributions and fraudulent company registration,[11] civil action against false statements of listed companies,[12] and introduction of an independent director system.[13] This piecemeal approach to reform could not, however, effectively improve the corporate legal regime and its operating business environment. The deficiencies were particularly exposed after China joined the World Trade Organization (WTO). Against this background of rising domestic and international pressure, the new *Company Law of China* together with the *Securities Law* were promulgated on 27 October 2005, effective 1 January 2006 (CL 2006) (see Zhang Xianchu 2011).

Company Law 2006

CL 2006 overhauled the old legislation and introduced new philosophies and institutions. In line with the worldwide trend for company law reform, the Law includes the rule to promote corporate social responsibility (CSR)[14] and places an emphasis on labour participation and protection.[15] The comprehensive amendments also attended to the need for efficiency in corporate operations. For instance, Article 38 allows an LLC to decide a matter without a shareholders' meeting if the agreement is approved in writing with unanimous consent. Furthermore, Article 72 sets out a statutory limitation of 30 days for shareholders to exercise their pre-emptive rights; the notice period of a JSC annual general meeting is shortened from 30 days to 20 days;[16] the length of public notice for capital reduction is reduced from 90 days to 45 days;[17] and the minimum statutory capital for LLC and JSC is reduced from RMB100,000 and RMB10 million to RMB30,000 and RMB5 million respectively.[18]

The progress of market reform and corporate practice since 1993 are well reflected in CL 2006 with the relaxation of the *ultra vires* doctrine;[19] abolition of some state privileges for state-owned companies; recognition of more operational autonomy by permitting companies to more freely appoint their own legal representatives[20] and decide on their own guarantee arrangements.[21] In addition, the ceiling on corporate investment was deleted.[22] The shift in regulatory philosophy to a more market-friendly approach is further evidenced with replacements to a number of mandatory provisions with default rules enabling companies to make decisions by following their own company articles, and compulsory approval from the state authority for establishment of any JSC is no longer required.[23]

Reforms to the capital contribution rules also demonstrate the government's new pro-business attitude. In order to restrict commercial risk in business transactions, CL 1993 had set a high statutory minimum capital threshold and required all the registered capital to be paid in full before a company could be established. Under the Law limited capital contribution in intangible form was capped no more than 20 per cent of all the company's capital. This limitation was to a large extent due to concerns about the possible diminution of capital value.[24] CL 2006, however, significantly reduces the amount of statutory capital and allows shareholders to make their capital contributions in instalments for up to five years – as long as the minimum contribution requirement was met. Capital contribution in intangible forms (such as intellectual property rights) may now account for up to 70 per cent of all company capital.[25] At the same time, some measures are maintained to ensure capital contribution is made as promised. Articles 31 and 94 make shareholders in both LLC and JSC jointly liable if a member fails to contribute his capital, or if the value of his 'in kind' contribution is below the value stipulated in the articles of association. Article 35 further sets out the general principle that shareholders of LLC shall receive a dividend in accordance with actual paid-in capital, unless a unanimous agreement of shareholders stipulates otherwise.

New institutions introduced

In addition to the reform measures outlined above, CL 2006 introduced a number of new institutions from foreign countries, with common law jurisdictions in particular. The most notable transplantations include the doctrine of *lifting the corporate veil*,[26] the statutory decision-making power of shareholders and directors without conflict of interest in connected transactions with affiliates,[27] one-man company,[28] cumulated voting power in management elections,[29] fiduciary duties of directors, supervisors and senior officers (with regard to loyalty and due diligence),[30] and a statutory derivative action enabling shareholders to initiate lawsuits on behalf of the company to stop management wrongdoing.[31]

Significant achievements of CL 2006 were thus improvements to corporate governance. Specifically, with respect to new legal rights and remedies that have been created for shareholders' protection there is now the right to claim damages arising from abusive or oppressive conduct by controlling shareholders in connected transactions.[32] This is a major shift as minority shareholders are now entitled to better participation and a stronger voice in company proceedings to safeguard the best interests of the company as a whole against abuse and violation. Protections include the right to annul a resolution of the management board or the general meeting for a violation of the law (or articles of the company) within 60 days of its adoption;[33] the right to inspect company records or even account books;[34] the right of minority shareholders in CCL to request the company to buy back their shares at a reasonable price if they are in dissent from the majority on certain important matters;[35] the right of 3 per cent shareholders to forward a motion to the shareholders' meeting of JSC;[36] the right of JSC shareholders to approve, by a two-thirds majority, transfer of important assets or guarantee provisions involving more than 30 per cent of the company's total assets;[37] the right to sue management for wrongdoing,[38] and the right of 10 per cent shareholders to petition to dissolve the company.[39]

Corporate accountability

Accompanying better legal protection for shareholders are enhanced accountability requirements. First, CL 2006 expands the regulatory spectrum to bind directors, supervisors, senior officers, controlling shareholders, *de facto* controllers and affiliate relations to the legal regime.[40] Second, the conduct of shareholders' meetings, the board of directors and the supervisory board has been rationalized to improve working relations. Under CL 2006 the powers of both the shareholders' meeting and the supervisory board have been enhanced. In addition to the shareholders' rights discussed above, Article 170 entitles the shareholders' meeting to choose the company's accounting firm (if the articles of the company so stipulates);[41] in JSC such power may extend to approval of all important transactions involving the company's material assets.[42]

The 2006 reform has attempted to address weaknesses in the 1993 design of the supervisory board. Under the 2006 law, in addition to the routine functions of inspection, the supervisory board now has the power to propose dismissal of directors and senior officers, convene the shareholders' meeting with its own motions, sit in meetings of the board of directors (with the right to make inquiries and proposals), investigate abnormal situations and appoint outside accounting professionals and take legal action against directors and senior officers for wrongdoing.[43] In other words, the watchdog has been given some teeth!

The corollary to the power expansion of the supervisory board is that CL 2006 subjects boards of directors to tighter accountability. Improvements to corporate law and governance have imposed more stringent duties and responsibilities on directors and senior officers, making them more accountable for liabilities in situations not covered by CL 1993. Specific examples include, *inter alia*, appropriating company funds, providing finance in violation of the law or the articles, usurping corporate opportunity, taking secret commissions from company transactions, disclosing company secrets without authorization, or receiving bribes.[44]

Even more restrictive rules apply to JSCs in line with common law jurisdictions for public companies. Article 116 prohibits a JSC from providing any loan to its own directors either directly or indirectly through a subsidiary; Article 117 mandates directors must report their remuneration to the shareholders on a regular basis; Article 125 bans a director from voting on any connected transactions in order to avoid conflicts of interest, and Article 113 holds that all the directors are collectively responsible for damage caused by their resolutions that violate the law, regulations, articles of the company and also a shareholders' resolution. A director may only be exempted if his objection to the resolution is raised and recorded in the minutes of that meeting. This exemption may, of course, have implications for individual directors for their future liability (or non-liability) with regard to a particular resolution.

Having highlighted specific progress made by amendments to the *Company Law* in 2006, it should be noted that the relative immaturity of the Chinese market and the short time-span of modern corporate practice have constrained further development of the legal regime. As a result, defects remain. There is considerable room for further improvement to corporate governance in China.

Problems unsolved

To adopt a special resolution in a company's general meeting, CL 2006 insists on a two-thirds majority (see Arts 44, 104 and 122). This compares with the requirement in most Western jurisdictions of a 75 per cent majority. The Centre of Corporate Governance Study of World Economy and Politics Institute and the Social Science Academy of China (2010) found that in 77 of the top 100 listed companies the shareholdings of the first five largest shareholders (most being state-owned or controlled companies) amount to more than 50 per cent. In 82 of the 100 top listed companies, it is the state company that is the first and largest shareholder. Such holding concentration makes the low passing threshold a design favouring this powerful majority in significant ways. A result is that any abusive or oppressive conduct of the powerful majority over minority shareholders is too easily hidden or obscured. Such corporate dominance has become a serious problem in practice and will continue to challenge the development of sound corporate governance in China (Tomasic and Andrews 2007: 88)

CL 2006 treats the general meeting similarly to CL 1993 in that neither stipulates any quorum requirement. This omission has repeatedly invited the scenario in listed companies whereby the person representing the majority shareholders is the only participant at the shareholders' meeting and makes all key decisions. The net effect is that power over important decisions can be concentrated in a single shareholder giving rise to the gross potential for the abuse of power.[45] Some limits to corporate power have been inserted into CL 2006 with a JSC now required under Article 117 to disclose management remuneration to shareholders on a regular basis. To get around this stipulation, however, this matter is treated as an internal one and only subjects directors' pay to the general meeting for approval.[46] Executive remuneration is then left to the directors themselves.[47] Compared to developed countries across Europe and the United States where management remuneration has been increasingly subjected to legislation and regulatory schemes, the approach taken by CL 2006 seems weak and outdated (Feinerman 2007: 609).

The new Law, while attempting to enhance corporate governance by granting more powers to the relevant parties, has created a complex legal apparatus which includes the 'two-tiered' management model borrowed from Germany and the 'independent director system' borrowed from the US.[48] At the same time Chinese institutions, such as the grass-roots organizations of the CPC, trade unions, the supervisory board (standing side by side with the board of directors) as distinct from the two boards used in the German unitary system, have been maintained. China's model with its borrowed legal concepts grafted onto its own top-heavy characteristics has created not only responsibilities and powers on both boards, but arguably unnecessary layers of complexity. For instance, without clear, rational divisions of duty, both the supervisory board *and* the independent board of directors may enjoy some supervisory and checking powers, which may in turn lead to functional overlaps, inefficient management and even internal power struggles.[49]

Consistent with socialist principles, Article 18 of CL 2006 guarantees employee participation in the supervisory board,[50] permits employees to be appointed to the board of directors,[51] and mandates that companies practise 'democratic management' through workers' assemblies and other forums. In this regard, further attention should be drawn to Article 5 of the Provisions on Enterprise Trade Union Work adopted by the All China Federation of Trade Unions on 11 December 2006, which explicitly stipulated that enterprise trade unions should be led by the CPC organization as well as the trade union at the upper level.

CL 2006, in attempting to correct past wrongs, may have lost some balance. Directors' duties, liabilities and penalties have all been significantly increased without providing any statutory protections and defences such as a 'business judgement' rule characteristic of many common law jurisdictions. As such the imbalance is not in line with international practice,[52] rendering the current market and legal environment in China less favourable for developing professional and risk management skills and director level than it ought to be.

The adoption of CL 2006 has led to a new round of promulgation of administrative regulations in order to put the law into effect and further improve China's overall company law regime. They include the Regulation on Administration of Company Registration of the State Council of 2005, Measures to Administrate Capital Contribution in Form of Equity Holdings of the State Administration of Industrial and Commerce of 2009, Rules Governing Shareholders' Meeting of Listed Companies of 2006, Measures to Administrate Information Disclosure of Listed Companies of 2007 and the Basic Norms of Internal Risk Control of Enterprises of 2008 known as 'the Chinese version of the Sarbanes–Oxley Act'.[53]

Judicial activism

The judiciary in China has played an active role dealing with problems of corporate law practice and filling legal gaps in the rapid legal and social transition. As such, the development of company law has been fuelled by judicial activism since the economic reform. Even before the adoption of CL 1993 certain rules similar to the 'lifting the corporate veil' doctrine had been developed by the Supreme People's Court (SPC) and applied to judicial proceedings (Zhang 1996: 129). Before the 2005 company reform, the Court took the initiative to relax the strict *ultra vires* rule of CL 1993. In its Interpretation on Certain Issues Concerning Application of Contract Law of PRC (Part I) 1 December 1999, the SPC was of the opinion (Article 10 of the Interpretation) that a contract should not automatically be made void if it was concluded *ultra vires*, as long as no state prohibition was violated.

As more stakeholder entitlements are recognized, CL 2006 has built up a broad arena for intervention and adjudication for the People's Court. The reform therefore not only modernized the company law regime, but promoted capacity building of the People's Courts, particularly in the application of mechanisms transplanted from foreign jurisdictions such as lifting the corporate veil, the statutory derivative action and rights of inspection to the conditions of China. Moreover, since CL 2006 the SPC, in addition to many concrete rules scattered throughout various judicial interpretations, has promulgated three sets of provisions specifically dealing with application of the law in judicial proceedings. In the Provisions on Certain Issues Concerning the Application of Company Law of PRC (Part I) (28 April 2006), the SPC authorized (Article 2) the People's Courts to apply CL 2006 retrospectively 'by reference', if the earlier law at that time (when the dispute arose) did not have clear rules.

In the SPC Provisions (Part II) promulgated 12 May 2008, more detailed and comprehensive rules are set out dealing with company dissolution and liquidation including dissolution for serious mismanagement, inability to convene a shareholders' meeting or to adopt any valid resolution at the general meeting for more than two years, deadlock inside the company, or other difficulties leading to material loss of shareholders (Article 1 of the Provisions (Part II).

To further prevent abusive behaviour, Article 18 of the SPC Provisions (Part II) stipulates that shareholders of LLC and directors and controlling shareholders of JSC shall be liable to creditors if they fail to form the liquidation group in the statutory period and causing damage to creditors. Moreover, Article 19 holds them liable even after dissolution of the company if corporate assets are disposed in bad faith or the cancellation of the business was made with deceitful means.

Part III Provisions were promulgated by the SPC on 27 January 2011 focusing on promoters' liability, capital contribution and share transfer. Certain points are worth noting in the Provisions as they reflect a more pragmatic approach of the SPC in guiding judicial practice. For example, in addition to the means of capital contribution specified in the Company Law, Article 11 permits equity interests in other companies to be used as a lawful means of capital contribution; Article 16 stipulates that the People's Court may not entertain any claims against a shareholder for devaluation of his non-cash capital contribution due to the market fluctuation, unless parties agree otherwise. Under Provisions, the legal status of dormant shareholders is recognized. According to Articles 25 and 26, the People's Court may uphold the validity of the contract between the dormant and the nominal shareholders in dealing with their disputes and the nominal shareholder may be liable for damages if he disposes of the shares concerned in breach of the agreement with the dormant shareholder.

The judicial activism of the SPC appears to have encouraged local courts to make input to company law development. As a result, a number of provisions have been adopted according to the needs of local practice and adjudication, although such local judicial rule-making cannot be readily found in any law! Since the adoption of CL 2006 at least the High People's Courts of Beijing, Shanghai, Shangdong, Shanxi, Guangdong and Hunan have all issued *local rules* applicable to local company dispute hearings. This 'enthusiasm' may promote the development of company law by pooling local-level wisdom and effort. As China is such a large and diverse country with a centralized system, however, the trend of local rule-making has much potential to generate conflicts of law in practice. This is the case following Article 12 of the Guiding Opinions on Certain Issues Concerning Trials of Company Disputes (Beijing High People's Court) 21 April 2008 which states that the voting procedure in LLC as stipulated by its articles of association cannot be changed unless there is unanimous agreement of the shareholders. This provision appears inconsistent with CL 2006 (Arts 43 and 44) which merely provides for a 'two-thirds majority' with default permission. Another example is Article 50 of the Opinions on Certain Issues Concerning Hearings of Company Disputes (On trial basis) issued by the High People's Court of Shandong on 26 December 2006 which provides that a purchaser may revoke share transfers on the ground of fraud if defective capital contribution is not disclosed. Such an approach appears heavy-handed in that linking fraud to defective capital contribution may not be reasonable in all circumstances.

The contribution of case law to corporation law development

As a country with strong civil law tradition China does not follow the common law doctrine of precedent. Nevertheless, case law has, in addition to rule-making at different levels of the judiciary, increasingly been used as a means of promoting company law development. In the Second Five-Year Reform Plan of the Supreme People's Court (2004–8) dated 26 October 2005, establishment and improvement of a case guidance system to streamline judicial practice were officially set out as important tasks of judicial reform. Since then numerous company law cases have been published with a nationwide impact. In October 2008 the First Intermediate People's Court dismissed Ding Liye's action against the China Securities Regulatory Commission (CSRC) for wrongful imposition of a penalty. The plaintiff, a director of a listed company, was found liable for the material omission of his company's annual report for two years and fined for RMB30,000. He challenged the CSRC's decision, arguing his appointment was merely 'nominal' by the controlling shareholder and thus without substantive power. On certain occasions he simply entrusted his voting power to the chairman of the board. The People's Court upheld the CSRC's decision on the ground that the plaintiff failed to carry out his due diligence duty as a director. Moreover, the court shifted the burden of proof in this case by asking the plaintiff to prove he performed his director's duty as required by law. The case attracted wide media attention and provides valuable guidance for assessing directors' duties in practice (*Fazhi Ribao*: 2008).

In dealing with its many new and varied challenges, the Supreme People's Court has cautioned lower courts to ensure they strike a sensitive balance between market freedom and government regulation, internal remedies and judicial intervention, minority protection and the majority rule, honouring internal authorization and the necessary protections to outsiders, shareholders' interests and management powers, and breaking deadlocks in companies and respecting corporate efficiency.[54] Inherent in the caution is an intricate set of dilemmas. Each has no easy answer and therefore judicial activism will continue to make its indispensable contribution to institutional innovation to China's company law regime.

The reasonably foreseeable challenges and difficulties ahead

The politics of Chinese company law

A thorough examination of the current company law regime in China would reflect on both the impressive progress made thus far and also the challenges and uncertainties that can be anticipated in its future development. First, it must be acknowledged that CL 2006 is still deeply inscribed by the socialist political ideology. In some senses, and ironically, this is even more enhanced than it had been in CL 1993. In addition to the provision of CL 1993 to permit activities of grass-roots organizations of the CPC, Article 19 of CL 2006 further stipulates that 'the company concerned shall provide the necessary conditions for the Communist Party's activities'. This raises several fundamental issues with regard to the exercise of power and influence in corporations including the deployment of company resources. In a highly competitive world, a number of questions and conundrums arise. Should the cost of CPC political activities be paid for by the company and should such political spending be viewed as 'for best interest of investors and creditors'? In practice, what are 'necessary conditions' that the company must provide for CPC activity? What would happen if a company refused to provide resources to the CPC on the grounds that it is unnecessary in that particular company's circumstances? What circumstances would justify exemption (if any)? Could a company litigate a dispute in the courtroom against the CPC and would a People's Court be required to accept the case?

In virtually every working unit in China, a CPC hierarchy runs parallel to the administrative one. According to a recent report, the CPC has established its working branches in 95 per cent of 190,000 larger private enterprises (Xinhua 2010c). Their main function, in addition to management and decision-making roles, is to carry out *political and patriotic education* so as to make workers 'integrate their communal spirit' (Garnaut 2010h).

The Communist Party remains as comfortably in control as it was in 1978 China even though it has taken huge strides in marketization since then. Despite judicial enthusiasm and rapidly improved competence in practice, the People's Courts are still influenced by the political ideology and policies of the Party-state. As a result, even after 30 years of reform, judicial independence may only be recognized and realized to a limited extent. Howson (2010: 134) found that although progress had been made with regard to judicial independence in company law practice in Shanghai, in a large number of cases: 'the courts actually worked against the law in the service of state policy aims', particularly in cases involving the Party-state backed companies. When high profile cases of public companies reached the court, the Party-state policy [cadres] often prevented them from accepting the cases or invoked *social stability* as taking priority over fairness in decision-making (see Howson 2010; and Hung 2005). At the same time, some leading Chinese scholars are taking a different approach to these issues, arguing that judicial function and independence of the People's Court should be judged by the concrete conditions that apply in China and that there are no other institutions or political forces like the CPC capable of overseeing China's drive to modernization and overcoming the complex social conflicts in the transition (Zhu 2010: 52–69).

Regulation and market access

At the same time, although some provisions of government approval were deleted from the CL 1993, the Party-state at both the central and local level still routinely insert their control and influences on the market (*China Daily* 2008). According to the World Bank's *Doing Business in China Report* (2008: 7), as compared with the global best practice the number of days needed and the procedures to open a business made China rank 79th and 140th places respectively, which render market entry in China a lengthy and cumbersome process.

CL 2006 has, to an extent, reoriented corporation law from a *regulatory* to a more *enabling* philosophy. In some respects, however, the traditional cautious mentality has prevented the legal regime from making more breakthroughs. Taking capital contribution as an example, despite the reforms, the 'autonomy' of a company to decide its own capital amount and structure is still not fully recognized. Both the statutory minimum capital and the registered capital have still been maintained. Moreover, capital contributions, particularly those of an 'in kind' nature, have to go through the appraisal, verification and certification process with the institutions designated by the government.[55] Such administrative vigilance against frivolous or fraudulent incorporation is even more manifest in the introduction of the one-man company into China. The measures include that one natural person may establish only one one-man company; the statutory minimum capital was raised to RMB100,000 and must be fully paid before incorporation. Further, the account of a one-man company must be audited by a professional firm, and the sole member shall be liable (jointly with his company) if he fails to carry out the burden of proof on him to show the separation of his own assets from those of the company.[56] This cumbersome and over-regulated approach has in effect offset the merits of having one-man companies. It is also in stark contrast to the EU rules, which now encourage the merits of 'thinking small first' in relation to the one-man company as a market device.

The dual track incorporation system

Another task unfinished in the company reform is the failure of CL 2006 to unify the current dual track incorporation system with different rules applicable to general companies and foreign joint ventures. Article 218 maintains this system by providing that both LLC and JSC with foreign interests shall be governed by Company Law; however, if the foreign investment enterprises laws provide otherwise, such provisions shall prevail. For instance, under the equity and contractual joint ventures laws an LLC does not need to have shareholders' meetings and instead the board of directors will be the highest power organ. Also, decisions on certain important matters will not be made by voting, but through consultation under the principle of equality and mutual benefit.[57]

Lack of a unified and uniform framework and parallel development of both regimes have made China's company law regime (and incorporation) increasingly complicated. On the company law side, regulations have been adopted to deal with JSC with foreign interest, foreign holding companies and foreign regional headquarters in China.[58] On the joint venture side, rules have been promulgated to streamline foreign venture capital joint ventures, dissolution, liquidation and dispute resolution of Sino-foreign joint ventures.[59] According to Neumann (2006: 30–1) there are as many as 13 different classifications of foreign investment enterprises in the form of LLC and 10 of JSC due to different governing laws, capital structures and sources of investment. As a result, the Implementing Opinions on Certain Issues Concerning Application of Laws in Approval and Registration of Foreign Investment Companies was issued on 24 April 2006 by several state authorities jointly to streamline the practice. Whether it has been successful warrants further specific research.

Seeking a level playing field

Beyond the differences and conflicts of rules at a technical level, the long divergence has raised further concerns about 'level playing field' conditions at an institutional level. Despite claims about its 'market economy', China has been struggling to implement its WTO commitments as to market non-discrimination (see Xianchu Zhang 2011). An example is the recent reform of the legal regime of foreign mergers and acquisitions (M&As) by the Ministry of Commerce after the promulgation of the Antimonopoly Law of the PRC. As a positive sign, the amendment has merged the special regulation governing foreign M&As into the newly established uniform antimonopoly regime. However, a separate set of rules is maintained in addition to antitrust clearance that subjects foreign M&As to the scrutiny of 'public interest', 'social and economic order' and 'loss of state assets' tests'.[60]

In a further sign of tightening foreign M&A rules, the State Council issued a special notice with detailed rules on 3 February 2011 to establish a 'scrutiny regime' to safeguard state security. The notice sets out the examination scope, contents and working procedures. For implementation purposes a special joint meeting involving the relevant ministries is to be set up reporting directly to the State Council.

The gap between the legislation and practice

A recent study on the top 100 listed companies in China has clearly demonstrated the resistance to the company law reform in practice.[61] The study reveals the impact of CL 2006 on improving corporate governance has been very limited. In certain aspects, such as function of the supervisory board, information disclosure, control of majority shareholders' abusive conduct and management remuneration, the situation has even become worse (ibid.). Indeed, there is always a gap between legislation and practical reality. The task is made more daunting in China as the transitional socialist market economy challenges not only the political will of the Party-state and institutional capabilities to enforce the law, but also the development of professionalism and a transparent and accountable business culture. The imposition of penalties by the CSRC against 738 directors of listed companies alone in 2004–8 for various violations illustrates the depth of the challenge (ibid.).

In this context, the development of company law in China faces several dilemmas: It can be argued that a more liberal, facilitating approach is needed to enable Chinese companies to compete in international markets, with better efficiency and to catch up on trends in company law reform. Yet the problems and constraints in the transitional period are not easy to quickly overcome, such as insiders' control (and abuse), lax enforcement of laws, limited transparency, defective market infrastructure, heavy-handed government involvement, the resistance emanating from political ideology, and mitigate against company law being further liberalized (see Zhong Zhang 2007).

Conclusion

In the course of China's economic reforms and increasing integration into international markets, the company law regime has developed rapidly. It has become more sophisticated with profound political implications for rule of law promotion. The implementation of CL 2006 has accelerated comprehensive company law reforms and significantly closed gaps between China and international best practice. This is reflected in developments in corporate governance, corporate social responsibility and business enabling approaches in legislation. At the same time China has transplanted a range of legal doctrines from developed countries, particularly common law jurisdictions. The reforms remain incomplete. As this chapter has outlined, there are imbalances that promote stringency in directors' duties and liabilities, yet statutory protections and defences remain undeveloped. In practice this lack may add a complication to the unclear business and political relationship in China whereby directors and other senior officers may have to seek protection from the political side in dealing with risks. Thus, despite significant endeavours of both legislature and judiciary, processes of modernization have faced the interrelated challenges of political ideology, infrastructure and cultural constraints. Taken together these influences indicate the foreseeable future of company law development in China is likely to continue on a path of 'selective adaptation' (Potter 2003: 119). This pathway would allow for compliance with international norms whilst remaining contextualized to local Chinese conditions.

Notes

1 The World Bank (2010) in its *Doing Business Report* uses 'freedom of business operation' and 'creditor protections' as main indicators for analysing economic outcomes and for identifying the effectiveness of reforms in 183 economies under the fundamental premise that economic activity requires good rules.
2 These three laws were adopted in 1979, 1988 and 1986 respectively, with amendments in 2001 and 2000.
3 See Art. 11 of CL 1993.
4 *Id.*, Arts 23–27, 78 and 80.
5 *Id.*, Arts 4 and 81.
6 *Id.*, Art. 14.
7 *Id.*, Arts 64–72.
8 *Id.*, Art. 159.
9 *Id.*, Arts 124–8.
10 See Fang (1995: 149–269); Nicholas C. Howson (1997: 127–73); Zhang (1998: 248–60); and Zhu (2004: 248–67).
11 Arts 158–61 of the *Criminal Law* 1997.

12 *Provisions of the Supreme People's Court on Hearing of Civil Claims for False Statement on the Securities Market*, 26 December 2002.
13 *Guiding Opinions of China Securities Regulatory Commission to Establish an Independent Director System in Listed Companies*, 16 August 2001.
14 Art. 5 of CL 2005.
15 *Id.*, Arts 17 and 18. These provisions are upgraded to the chapter of the general principles from the low-rank subordinate stipulations.
16 Compare Art. 103 of CL 2005 with Art. 105 of CL 1993.
17 Compare Art. 178 of CL 2005 with Art. 186 of CL 1993.
18 Compare Arts 26 and 81 of CL 2005 with Arts 23 and 78 of CL 1993.
19 The compulsory rule of CL 1993 that a company should carry out its operations within its registered business scope has been deleted (compare Art. 12 of CL 2005 with Art. 11 of CL 1993).
20 Art. 13 of CL 2005 allows a company to appoint its legal representative among the chairman of the board of directors, executive directors or managers, whereas Arts 45 and 113 of CL 1993 only allowed the chairman of the board of directors to serve the corporate legal representative.
21 *Id.*, Art. 16 empowers the board of directors *or* the shareholders' meeting to decide on provision of guarantees.
22 According to Art. 12 of CL 1993, a company's accumulated investment in another company should not exceed 50 per cent of its own net assets (compare Art. 15 of CL 2005 with Art. 12 of CL 1993).
23 Art. 77 of CL 1993 has been deleted.
24 Arts 23–5, 78, and 80 of CL 1993.
25 Arts 26–7, 81, and 83 of CL 2005.
26 *Id.*, Art. 20.
27 *Id.*, Arts 16 and 125.
28 *Id.*, Arts 58–64.
29 *Id.*, Art. 106.
30 *Id.*, Art. 148.
31 *Id.*, Arts 150 and 152.
32 *Id.*, Arts 20–1.
33 *Id.*, Art. 22.
34 *Id.*, Arts 34 and 98.
35 *Id.*, Art. 75.
36 *Id.*, Art. 103.
37 *Id.*, Art. 122.
38 *Id.*, Art. 153.
39 *Id.*, Art. 183.
40 In addition to the rules discussed above, Art. 217 provides the relevant definitions.
41 *Id.*, Art. 170.
42 *Id.*, Art. 105.
43 *Id.*, Arts 54, 55 and 119.
44 *Id.*, Arts 148 and 149.
45 See the report on the general meeting of ST Shengda on 27 January 2010, at http://finance.ifeng.com/stock/ssgs/20100128/1769751.shtml; the general meeting of ST Qiong-Huaqiao on 26 April 2004, at www.5i8866.com/bbs/id_100402594362@questioninfo.shtml; and the general meeting of Yimei B on 11 September 2000, at www.sdtv.com/compere/zy/lwsb/sb64.htm.
46 Arts 38 (2) and 100 of CL 2005.
47 *Id.*, Arts 47 (9) and 109.
48 Art. 123 of CL 2005 reads that listed companies shall have independent directors and the detailed rules shall be stipulated by the State Council. However, the central government has not as yet promulgated any rules in this regard.

49 Overview of Governance of State-owned Listed Companies in China, OECD Document (DRC/ERI-OECD) for Policy Dialogue on Corporate Governance in China (19 May 2005) at: www.OECD.org/dataoecd/14/6/34974067.pdf.; also see Donald C. Clarke (2006: 125–228); and Jiangyu Wang (2007: 47–55).
50 Arts 52 and 118 of CL 2005.
51 *Id.*, Arts 45 and 109.
52 For example, Australia has adopted 'the business judgement rule' from the US, see s. 180 (2) and (3) of the *Corporations Act of Australia 2001*; Hong Kong has also allowed companies to purchase insurance for directors, see s. 73 of the *Companies (Amendment) Ordinance 2003*.
53 The Basic Norms of Internal Risk Control of Enterprises were adopted jointly by five state ministries (Finance, the China Securities Regulatory Commission, the Audit Commission, the China Banking Regulatory Commission and China Insurance Regulatory Commission) in 2008 and will become effective on 1 January 2011. This is considered 'the Chinese version of the Sarbanes–Oxley Act' applied to all listed companies, while other companies are encouraged to follow the Norms (see Wang and Zhang (2008)).
54 Speech of Xi Xiaoming, Vice President of the Supreme People's Court, 30 May 2007, National Conference on Civil and Commercial Trials of the Supreme People's Court, at: http://vip.chinalawinfo.com/newlaw2002/slc/slc.asp?db=chl&gid=110729.
55 Arts 27, 29, 83 and 84 of CL 2005 – see K.L. Alex Lau (2007: 248–52).
56 *Id.*, Arts 59–64.
57 Art. 6 of the *Sino-Foreign Equity Joint Venture Law* as amended in 2001, and Art. 12 of the *Sino-Foreign Contractual Joint Venture Law* as amended in 2000. For more detailed discussions see Vivienne Bath (2009); and Hui Huang (2009: 189–218).
58 The regulations promulgated by the Ministry of Commerce in this regard include the *Interim Provisions on Certain Questions Concerning Establishment of Foreign Investment Companies Limited by Shares* dated 10 January 1995, the *Provisions on Investment Companies Established with Foreign Investment* dated 17 November 2004 and the *Supplementary Provisions on Foreign Investment Companies* dated 26 May 2006.
59 The enactments include the *Interim Provisions Concerning Establishment of Foreign Venture Capital Investment Enterprises* jointly promulgated by the Ministry of Commerce, the State Administration of Industry and Commerce and the Ministry of Science and Technology on 28 August 2001, the *Guiding Opinions on Dissolution and Liquidation of Foreign Investment Enterprises* of the Ministry of Commerce on 5 May 2008, and the *Provisions on Certain Issues Concerning Trials of Foreign Investment Enterprises Disputes* of the Supreme People's Court dated 5 August 2010.
60 Art. 3 of the *Provisions on Mergers and Acquisitions of Domestic Enterprises by Foreign Investors*, promulgated 23 July 2009 by the Ministry of Commerce.
61 The Centre of Corporate Governance Study of World Economy and Politics Institute, China Social Science Academy and others (2010), *2009 Nian Zhongguo Shangshi Gongsi 100 Qiang Gongsi Zhili Pingjia* (Assessment of corporate governance of top 100 listed companies in China).

3 China's enterprise bankruptcy law

Implementation of the corporate reorganization provisions

Roman Tomasic and Zinian Zhang

Introduction

Understanding the *Enterprise Bankruptcy Law (2006)* is enhanced with awareness of pre-existing legal provisions. Two decades earlier, the *Enterprise Bankruptcy Law (For Trial Implementation) 1986* (EBL 1986), had been enacted, but with a very narrow remit. This cautious approach subsequently dominated the way bankruptcy laws were implemented in China. Apart from some provincial rules, prior to the enactment of the EBL 1986 there had not been a broad-ranging bankruptcy law since the 1949 founding of the PRC;[1] during this period it was left to the government's planned economy rather than 'market socialism' to determine the fate of SOEs.

The drafting process for the *Enterprise Bankruptcy Law 2006* took almost two decades before the new more comprehensive law was enacted to replace the 1986 EBL (see Shi 2007; Booth 2008; Tomasic and Wang 2006). The EBL 1986 had been amended in 1994 to better align legal provisions with the newly established socialist market economy (Booth 2008). In updating the EBL 1986, China showed a willingness to embrace international bankruptcy norms (Tomasic 1998) to improve its economy, notwithstanding the fear of massive unemployment associated with the likely rigorous enforcement of bankruptcy law upon under-performing and often insolvent SOEs (Halliday and Carruthers 2009).

At the same time, to take advantage of foreign 'best practice' in bankruptcy law, China's law reformers examined bankruptcy regimes in Australia, Britain, France, Germany and the United States to help fashion their own new law. This process was also used to gain time while the internal political battle was fought between law reformers responding to the rise of the market economy and more ideologically driven hard-liners who saw bankruptcy law as a foreign set of values that were in conflict with traditional socialist ideas (Tomasic and Little 1997: 48–56).

During the decade or so before the enactment of the *Enterprise Bankruptcy Law 2006* (EBL 2006), Chinese law reformers participated in many international bankruptcy law reform meetings, including the annual meetings of a regional forum for the discussion of insolvency law reform in Asia set up by the OECD in collaboration with the Asian Development Bank, Japan and Australia (the Forum for Asian Insolvency Reform).[2]

On its face, the EBL 2006 is rescue friendly; even during its drafting the bill was named China's Enterprise Bankruptcy and Reorganization Law (Wu 2004). It is noteworthy that the EBL 2006 locates 'reorganization' in Chapter 8, ahead of Chapter 9 (dealing with Composition) and Chapter 10 (dealing with Liquidation). By adopting the new corporate reorganization regime, China's legislators were convinced that the new law could preserve the going concern value of enterprises and maximize the recovery to creditors whilst seeking to protect the interests of a wider group including employees, suppliers, revenue authorities, customers and local communities (Wang 1995).

As is well known, the law in the books does not always translate into the law in action; this reality is strikingly demonstrated by the way that corporate reorganization is handled by the legal system in China. According to data collected in 2010 by Zinian Zhang,[3] about 105 in-court reorganization cases were heard between June 2007 and November 2010.[4] It should however be noted that the vast majority of reorganized companies in China are economic giants; Zhang's data shows that 32 out of 99 reorganized companies were listed on the Shanghai or Shenzhen Stock Exchanges and that the average unsecured debt per company amounted to ¥1,511,295,550 (equivalent to US$225,517,003 in value in November 2010).[5] Regarding the legislative aims of maximizing creditor recovery, this is likely to be partly achieved as the amount recovered for general creditors through the reorganization of companies has increased to 21.33 per cent when compared with the less than 10 per cent recovery in liquidation cases prior to the EBL 2006 (see Booth and Zhang 2001).[6]

However, during the first four years of its implementation,[7] some problems emerged as a result of legislative vagueness of the 2006 Law and the effects of China's changing social context. Among these, the most salient problem involved the assessment of companies to be seen as eligible for reorganization. Most practitioners, especially judges,[8] struggled with the concept of eligibility for reorganization, misunderstanding this aspect of the legislation. Meanwhile, in stark contrast to more democratic countries, social stability is seen as a huge political and social concern in China. This concern about social unrest has led to pressure to reshape some core insolvency law principles (Kan and Lam 1999).

This chapter examines corporate rescue in China in two substantial parts: first, the selection of rescue candidates, and second, the balancing of social stability considerations and basic reorganization norms in corporate reorganizations, followed by a brief conclusion.

Eligibility for company reorganization in China

In terms of corporate reorganization, we first need to ask which type of company is most likely to be rescued. Some viable companies may be improperly liquidated if it is too difficult for them to gain entry to the reorganization process; equally, the timely liquidation of failed companies may be impeded if it is too easy for them to gain entry to reorganization proceedings. This calls into question the appropriateness of China's corporate rescue threshold.

The statutory threshold for corporate reorganization

Under Article 2 of the EBL 2006, the debtor company must be liquidated if it cannot pay its due debts *and* if its debts exceed the whole of its assets. This effectively means that the debtor will be bankrupt. Paragraph 2 of Article 2, however, provides that a bankrupt debtor may still be reorganized. Therefore, all insolvent companies could in theory be subject to corporate reorganization. In 2009, the Supreme People's Court released its latest judicial interpretation of the EBL 2006 in which it was stated that a debtor could be reorganized on the grounds that its business was important to national economic strategies and where it could possibly survive.[9]

In terms of conformity with national economic strategies, this may not be difficult to achieve as China's National Development and Reform Commission published a detailed list stating that certain industries may be 'encouraged, constrained or even abolished'.[10] However, it is more difficult to establish whether the company can survive into the future as this requirement is uncertain. Professor Weiguo Wang suggested that this 'future survival' concept was borrowed from Australia (Wang 1999: 15). Indeed, section 435A of the Australian *Corporations Act* (2001) sets out the goals of the Australian rescue procedures whereby rescue procedures should seek to maximize 'the chances of the company, or as much as possible of its business, continuing in existence'.

The Australian Law Reform Commission report which recommended company reorganization reforms, held that the 'legislation may be used not only by a company which is presently unable to pay its debts but also by a company which is facing that prospect' (Harmer 1988: 33).[11]

One reason for the success of the apparent Australian corporate rescue reforms is that, in contrast to China, Australia has long had a skilled cadre of insolvency practitioners who may make independent and expert assessments of survival prospects of corporate rescue candidates (Anderson 2010). China is still building a comparable group of insolvency practitioners (see S. Li 2009). Professor Li Shuguang reported in July 2009 that there were about 9,000 registered bankruptcy administrators in China (S. Li 2009; Parry 2010). However, only a very small fraction of these Chinese bankruptcy administrators have had any experience in company reorganization matters.

In other words, without fully considering the differences in legal infrastructure between Australia and China, Chinese practitioners and judges have complained that they have had considerable difficulty in assessing which companies are likely to be suitable candidates for reorganization (Wang and Liu 2009). This is in part due to the statutory oversimplification of the 2006 EBL (Fan *et al.* 2011: 8). Various foreign experts have thus argued that China should nurture a pool of qualified and skilled insolvency practitioners when giving advice to Chinese legislators during the drafting of the new bankruptcy law (Tomasic 1998: 211). The ease of entry into corporate reorganization need not be a bad thing, as the aim of Australian corporate rescue law has been to rehabilitate as many distressed companies as possible (Anderson 2001: 112). Therefore, it is not surprising to see that the number of reorganizations in Australia was nearly equal to the number of liquidations, such as in the year 1996–7.[12]

However, the low statutory threshold for corporate reorganization under the EBL 2006 does not mean that such a rescue vehicle is practically accessible in China. As Zhang's data indicates, there were merely 105 reorganizations in the three and a half years after the EBL 2006 came into effect in June 2007. Put differently, there were only 30 in-court corporate rescue cases each year, despite the fact that there were 2,631 corporate bankruptcies in China on average annually from 2007 to 2010 (Siyuan Think Tank 2010). As a result, the actual threshold for corporate reorganization, in contrast to the broad legislative wording, is probably still too high. But discussion of the difficulties of launching a court-centred corporate rescue falls outside the concerns of this chapter.

Financial distress and economic distress

Before selecting an appropriate candidate for rescue, the first step is to ascertain the nature of the company's distress. Scholars have widely agreed that an insolvent company may suffer two broad types of difficulty: financial distress or economic distress (Baird 1998: 580). Financial distress arises where the company cannot pay its due debts because of distress resulting from its cash flow management. This might be caused by excessive leverage even though its actual business may still be viable. In contrast, economic distress may arise where the company's business operations cannot generate enough income to cover its costs.

Companies in financial distress are the ideal candidate for reorganization as they can be rehabilitated by means of debt reduction, debt postponement or other such methods. By contrast, with an economically distressed company, quick liquidation is likely to be in the best interests of both its creditors and other parties. Bearing in mind the academic recognition of selective rescue objectives, China's approach to the possibility of a company's survival should go a step further so as to more clearly identify the type of difficulties faced by companies. It is the financially distressed company rather than the economically distressed one that should be the more appropriate candidate for corporate rescue.[13]

Useful sources in assessing a company's viability

In practice, prior to the formal acceptance by China's courts of a corporate reorganization filing, a court is likely to convene a hearing in order to assess the possibility that the company will survive. This meeting will be attended by the debtor, substantial creditors such as banks, and the government body in charge of the debtor, whose attitude is critical to the possibility of its rescue.[14] At this stage, the administrator has not been appointed (Art. 17, EBL 2006), and so cannot be consulted by the committee. Ironically, given the small number of bankruptcy cases in China, even if an insolvency practitioner is available, he or she usually does not have the knowledge to be able to offer any support in identifying the nature of the company's distress as there are few cases for them to learn from.

Because of the lack of sufficient information about the company's business, it is unlikely that creditors and the government bodies involved in dealing with such cases 'will be able to form an accurate judgement of the nature of the company's distress' (Kahl 2002: 136). Such a meeting may test the related parties' attitudes towards the prospective rescue solution; the key problem as to whether the company's business deserves to be kept afloat might not, however, be explored in any depth. In the absence of expert practitioners to assess the prospects for a successful rescue of the company,[15] the viewpoint of the debtor may provide the most influential information in appraising the future viability of its business. But it should be noted that it is commonly believed in China that company insolvency is mainly caused by fraud or incompetence on the part of the company's managers (Rapisardi and Zhao 2010). So, as a compromise in tackling this dilemma, a pragmatic balance may need to be struck by interested parties.[16]

In these circumstances it might be a rational approach for judges to solicit the views of the company's chief accountant, who is usually the officer best placed to ascertain whether the company's business is viable. Possessing first-hand accounting documents and information, the chief accountant is more likely to make an informed appraisal of whether the company's business operations could generate profits after meeting their costs. In these circumstances, a practical solution that emerges relies on the technical judgement of the chief accountant as to the viability of the business and this is then submitted to the court when the debtor applies to be reorganized.

The government's role in the assessment

Consideration of corporate reorganization by a court is unlikely to arise in China unless such a filing is supported by the local government. Zhang's data suggests that local government support or intervention is evident in 73 per cent of reorganizations.[17] As a result, local governments' attitudes seem to play a significant role in helping companies to become eligible for rescue. It is also noteworthy that over 50 per cent of reorganized Chinese companies are state-owned, state controlled or formerly state-owned. In other words, their government background is likely to be a key factor in ensuring their future business survival.[18] In these circumstances, political considerations appear to take precedence over business judgements in the selection of rescue cases. Indeed, different countries invariably apply their own legal rules and standards for entry into corporate reorganization.

International comparison

Globally, at least three different rescue eligibility assessment systems can be identified. The narrowest criteria for entry are in the UK which holds that 'helping hands should only be extended to purely financially distressed companies, whereas economically troubled ones should be immediately liquidated' (Frisby 2004: 248). The intermediate model is in the USA, where most scholars favour narrowly interpreted eligibility of rescue candidates (proceduralists), while practitioners including judges (traditionalists) tend to save as many companies as possible, relying on 'social policy considerations' (Baird 1998: 580). A wide approach to admission into corporate rescue procedures is found in Australia where, as noted above, the number of corporate reorganizations is greater than the number of liquidations, and where the intention of the Australian legislature (to set a low threshold for corporate rescue) has been fully exploited by both practitioners and other related parties (Anderson 2001: 108).[19]

China has in some respects, at the legislative level, substantially followed the Australian approach in adopting eligible rescue objects or purposes. But, at present, a serious concern in China is the court's attitude as this has yet to be fully aligned with the broad intentions of the legislature. The courts are well aware, however, that not all companies entering the rescue process should be reorganized as some may use the rescue procedure to liquidate or sell the business as a going concern.[20] Furthermore, the eligibility test to become a candidate for rescue might also depend on different philosophies towards the nature of a company. In the purely economic sense, a company is simply deemed to be a business entity whose survival should be subject to market forces. The fate of the company would thus depend less upon the intervention of the legislature than upon a kind of corporate Darwinism. This is expressed in the UK in this way: 'not all lame ducks can, or should be rescued' (Frisby 2004: 248). Frisby's viewpoint is echoed by proceduralists in the USA and is influenced by market economic models.

In contrast to this market-based view of a company, scholars adhering to a traditionalist perspective are more willing to deal with a company not only as an economic organization but also as a political, moral and social entity. Consequently, a company's rescue in this view should be seen in a wider social context with the belief that saving a company may preserve the interests of a wider range of related parties whose interests might be seriously impaired by a particular company failure (Baird and Rasmussen 2002). Moreover, from the traditionalist perspective, corporate reorganization aims to establish space for interested parties to bargain for a solution (Baird and Rasmussen 2002).

Why a low threshold is desirable in China

So, which of these positions is appropriate and should be adopted in China? On the basis of China's recent law reforms more generally (see Garrick 2011), pragmatism is likely to characterize bankruptcy law reform on the basis of theoretical issues and practical features in the environment. In spite of academically defined differences between economic distress and financial distress, untangling these models is quite problematic. As Baird (1998: 581) aptly states:

> [T]o be sure, many firms face financial distress because they are in economic distress. The restaurant cannot pay its creditors because no one wants to eat there. There can also be a feedback loop between the two, such that financial distress causes economic distress. For example, a restaurant that is insufficiently capitalized may, in order to pay its bills, cut corners on food and service. As a result, patrons eat elsewhere and the restaurant encounters economic distress, which in turn aggravates its problem of financial distress.

Indeed, there are blurred boundaries between economic and financial distress. One may refer to the practice of corporate rescue in Japan where Eisenberg and Tagashira (1994: 155) noted that '[E]ven firms troubled enough to file for bankruptcy often have a going-concern value worth preserving ... some companies deemed to be economically distressed are still recovered through rescue efforts.' Rescue success may also depend on the confidence of interested parties who may marshal the company's assets more efficiently and effectively than its former management. While the company's difficulties may ultimately arise from underperforming business operations, these can still be altered, updated or reformed.

China's experience with corporate reorganizations demonstrates that a company's viability can be radically improved where its business strategy is strengthened after restructuring; others without a successful business transformation (model) are still mired in distress (Xuqiang He 2011). By way of contrast, in the USA in February 2009, automobile manufacturer Chrysler was not economically viable, lacking 'a developed product pipeline or the international reach to compete in an increasingly globalized auto market' (White House 2011). As a result of this US government assessment, President Obama refused to assist the failing auto giant despite the prospect of significant social dislocation as a consequence. However, one month later, the White House reversed its decision when another automobile giant, Fiat, was willing to establish a partnership with Chrysler. This meant the business plan of the distressed American company would be refreshed. One year later, after its corporate rehabilitation, Chrysler had largely returned to profitability with the fiscal support of the US federal government (ibid.). In this regard, the Chrysler case illustrates the view that economically failed business operations can be renewed under a robust restructuring plan. Opponents of this view might cite the US government debt crisis (July–August 2011) as evidence that market forces should determine the fate of distressed companies rather than government intervention. Indeed, strict distinctions between economic distress and financial distress models may be quite spurious.

In China's context, it may be appropriate to weaken any artificial differentiation between these two types of distress. In ascertaining the debt model appropriate to the particular debtor seeking reorganization, it should be acknowledged that the initial aim of corporate rescue is to recover companies in financial trouble and that court intervention is unnecessary where agreement has been reached by the impaired parties. However, where there is a dispute regarding the viability of the business, the court may look at the type of business distress, especially when a 'cram down' procedure is applied (Article 87, para. 2 of the EBL 2006).

The social environment in China makes a 'low threshold' approach necessary

Taking the unemployment rate in China into account, both the legislature and the courts have supported more corporate rescues. World Bank statistics (2011) show China's unemployment rate has been around 4 per cent in recent years. But these figures are unreliable as they are readily manipulated by China's government

(Giles *et al.* 2005: 150). Giles *et al.* found that the 'actual unemployment rate' in urban areas in China was 14 per cent in 2002 in contrast to the official statistic of 4 per cent (2005: 168).

Even the academically derived figure only reflects unemployment in China's *urban* areas, whilst the huge numbers in the rural countryside have been largely ignored although Xinhua reported that 'every year 150 million migrant workers leave their rural homes to look for jobs in cities' (Xinhua 2010b). At the end of 2009, there were 120 million migrant workers who lost their jobs because of the global economic crisis affecting China's manufacturing industries (Ifeng TV News 2009). Given this scale of unemployment, giving a second chance to distressed companies is seen by many as essential in China.

Besides the unemployment problem, China's social insurance system is still at a primitive stage of development. Government departments have been unable to offer adequate social security benefits to employees facing redundancy (Leung 2003: 81–4). As a consequence, even deeper social problems may be triggered if more companies were allowed to dissolve or be liquidated.

In summary, it makes good sense for China to have a lower threshold for entry to its rescue proceedings than the US or UK, for example. But what remains imperative is for local courts to fully appreciate the intentions of the national legislature rather than their own local concerns alone. This may include allowing the courts to hear more reorganization petitions. In China, however, courts are very wary of the social unrest which may be caused by in-court bankruptcy cases and therefore may wish to distance themselves from ruling on bankruptcies. Concerns for social stability definitely affect corporate reorganization practice in China and this is examined in the following section.

The impact of social stability on corporate reorganization in China

Social stability concerns have several effects on corporate reorganization. It took the legislature 12 years to finalize the bankruptcy law amendment (*Asia Times* 2006) due to fears of massive social unrest from liquidating underperforming SOEs (Halliday and Carruthers 2009: 249). Even after the EBL 2006 was implemented, the courts still see social stability concerns as a priority over some basic norms embedded in the legislation.

Social stability concerns delayed the process of the EBL 1986's reform

By postponing the reform of China's bankruptcy laws until 2006, China's rulers seemed to have been responding to pressures caused by perceived negative effects of SOE reform. For instance, the contribution of SOEs to urban employment has steadily declined from 66.4 per cent (in 1994) to 34 per cent (in 2006) (OECD 2009). Not all of the displaced workers found new employment. As a result of this decline, the number of mass incidents comprising riots, strikes, demonstrations and protests soared from 8,700 in 1993 to 740,000 in 2004; the primary concern leading to these protests seems to have been 'employee redundancy' (Halliday and Carruthers 2009: 287–8).

It was foreseeable that this unstable situation would be exacerbated if the bankruptcy laws were to be stringently enforced, as virtually all China's medium and small SOEs were, technically, insolvent at that time (Halliday 2007). Anecdotally, the national government was able to promulgate the EBL 2006 partly because the pressure from SOE workforce layoffs had been immensely alleviated by large-scale SOE reform coming towards its end by 2006. Before this there had been considerable tension between those concerned about the position of workers and those who advocated a more effective bankruptcy law in China.

Advocacy for reform deepened after 2000. For example, in 2003 one NPC representative, Professor Wang Liming, appealed to the 10th National People's Congress to introduce a new bankruptcy law as this was seen as essential to a market economy (*China Daily* 2003). By April 2006 a major OECD-organized international conference was held in Beijing to discuss bankruptcy reform; the local convenor was the powerful PRC State Council's Development Research Centre.[21]

At the policy level, the fear of social unrest caused by workforce retrenchments as a result of bankruptcy has been progressively mitigated in China. Protests in relation to bankruptcy had mainly occurred amongst SOE employees (Chen 1999: 60), while the level of private sector employment in China has grown steadily (Garnaut and Song 2004). Anger of the employees in redundancy appears to be twofold. First, there has been a sense of unfair treatment compared with employees in the seemingly profitable SOEs who had stable jobs (even though profitability of their enterprise was not the result of their employees' commitment or performance but rather government policy).

Second, the collapse of SOEs was often caused by a company's incompetence (or even fraud) amongst directors and other senior managers (Rapisardi and Zhao 2010: 59). These actors have been rarely held legally or politically accountable (Lewis and Litai 2003). Without investigation into manager misconduct, there is a public perception that ordinary workers, rather than the managers, will bear the cost of the latter's misbehaviour (see Cai 2002). Large-scale job losses can certainly trigger social unrest and subject the vulnerable to injustice (Halliday and Carruthers 2009: 288).

However, over the last two decades the SOE situation in China has begun to change. After shutdowns and privatizations, *inter alia*, China has substantially tackled the losses incurred by its SOEs, with their contribution to overall industrial production having fallen from about 73 per cent in 1978 to approximately 30 per cent in 2004 (OECD 2009). For the most part, China's huge project of reforming its SOEs had come to an end by 2010.[22]

In the wake of the closure or disposal of most loss-making SOEs, the remaining government-controlled SOEs are now more economically viable and even more aggressive as the majority now dominate or control various markets in China and thereby gain monopoly profits (Gao 2010). Indeed, as Chen points out in Chapter 1 of this volume, some of these SOEs are now leading China's corporate 'going out' strategy.

On the one hand it could *now* be argued that it is obsolete for policy makers to worry about the social unrest caused by the bankruptcy of SOEs. Pure job loss in China is no longer directly associated with widespread social unrest. On the other hand, there are studies that show protests have been caused by other factors such as unpaid wages, poor conditions and exploitation of migrant workers. There has indeed been anger towards the government because of perceived collusion between some government officials and some employers resulting in the encroachment of workers' rights (Keidel 2005).

Fear of social instability thus remains a barrier to the full implementation of the EBL 2006, and this can have a profound impact on how the basic principles of corporate reorganization are interpreted, even if reorganization is to take place.

Employment relocation plan prior to the reorganization filing

Under Article 8 of the EBL 2006, when a corporate reorganization petition is filed a comprehensive employee redeployment plan must then be submitted to the court. This is to prevent perceived unrest and, in effect, forestalls protests that might otherwise be launched by unpaid workers. Further, the debtor needs to obtain the support of local government which has authority to mobilize the police if required to maintain order. Not all companies can routinely obtain access to government support in China. Over half of reorganized companies do, however, have a government background as they are state-owned, state-controlled or formerly state-owned.[23]

As far as the policy of protecting employees is concerned, this might be legislative rhetoric as, in practice, it is common for the debtor to terminate all previous labour contracts to give more latitude to new investors. For example, in the reorganization of Yangdong Engine Manufacture Ltd in Jiangsu Province, all previous employees were sacked and re-employment was up to the reorganized company.[24] In principle, this approach is not consistent with either the legislative spirit or the letter of the law.

Small-creditor-first approach rather than creditor equality

In addition to the fear that employees may cause social unrest by public protest caused by an enterprise bankruptcy, corporate reorganization cases can also involve a large number of potentially disgruntled small creditors. For example, in the reorganization of Zhonggu Sugar Ltd in Guangdong Province, there were nearly 300,000 small farmer creditors who supplied sugar cane to the company (Feng and Li 2010). Upon the company entering reorganization, the farmers pressured the local government by assembling before its building, knowing this would raise social instability fears. The farmers had known that under the *pari passu* bankruptcy law principle, they would not be able to recoup all of their losses in reorganization (Feng and Li 2010). The *pari passu* principle is at the heart of bankruptcy norms (Tomasic 1998: 214) and this principle is also recognized in Chinese legislation with Art. 113 (EBL 2006) providing that: 'Where the bankrupt property is not sufficient to satisfy the demands for repayment that are arranged in the same group, it shall be distributed on a pro rata basis.'

Similarly, in the reorganization of Xiaxing Electronic Ltd, a Shanghai Stock Exchange listed company based in Fujian Province, there were nearly 4,000 unsecured creditors (Jia 2010). In China's social context this was unusual. The number of creditors is an issue in that it may provoke government fears that large numbers of unsatisfied creditors may initiate social 'trouble'.

Under pressure from local governments, the courts have been forced to adjust this principle by repaying the farmer creditors in full. This occurred in Zhonggu Sugar Ltd's reorganization; similarly, in the Xiaxing Electronics case, full repayments were made to small creditors with claims of less than RMB10,000. Other general creditors who were *entitled* to equal treatment in the Zhonggu Sugar case were only paid 28.3 per cent of their claims (Feng and Li 2010: 3) and in Xiaxing Electronics they were paid 21.77 per cent of their claims.[25]

The *pari passu* principle has been adjusted in 14 (27 per cent) out of 52 reorganizations where the relevant information is publicly available.[26] Clearly, the scales of justice in such cases have favoured small creditors, achieving social peace; however, whether it is fair to other general creditors who bear the cost of maintaining this social stability is another matter. Apart from pressure from local governments which fund them, the courts in China are also held politically responsible for ensuring social stability (Wang 2001: 3). That courts appear to favour small creditors in politically sensitive cases is hardly surprising given their responsibility for ensuring social stability. The EBL 2006 also requires that any reorganization plan be approved by over half the creditors by number and by over two-thirds of creditors by the value of their claims (Article 84).

It may seem pragmatic for the *pari passu* principle to be adjusted with the support of a creditors' meeting. In Western insolvency law, for instance, the *pari passu* principle is regarded as sacrosanct and not available to the parties to contract out of.[27] Where such a deviation from this principle is not agreed to by parties involved in the creditors' meeting, Chinese courts can and do occasionally intrude by applying a 'cram-down' (with a cram-down procedure enforced in five out of 14 reorganizations).[28] These five reorganizations took place in north China where the economy is not as well developed, and, correspondingly, the judicial infrastructure might be less sophisticated than that found in the southern parts of China (see Howson 2010 and Balme 2010).

It can be argued that creditors are most concerned by the lack of transparency in reorganizations, rather than by adjustments in the application of equality principles. Wang (2001: 3) notes that prior to the EBL 2006, creditors usually could not get sufficient information in relation to the debtor's 'assets, claims, pre-bankruptcy transactions, assets valuation and disposition'. Therefore opaqueness in the substantive information of the debtor may lead to creditors being even more suspicious. This situation has not greatly improved since the EBL 2006, as shown in the reorganization of the company Haiji Lujian Ltd in Mongolia. There, the general creditors were told of the reorganization plan merely two hours in advance of the vote at a creditors' meeting. Even more critically, the creditors' request for copies of the company's financial reports, assets valuation reports and detailed reports of the debts was directly rejected by the court (A. Zhang 2009). In this sense, it appears to be the court, or the local government acting behind closed doors, rather than creditors, who are endangering social stability. Without adequate transparency, the confidence of creditors cannot be established. As a result, this can give rise to social tensions which might otherwise be pre-empted or removed.

The 'absolute priority' principle gives way to shareholders

Another large group of stakeholders in any reorganization are *shareholders*. Because of their significant numbers they are also given special treatment in corporate reorganization. Under the absolute priority norm (Ayer 1989), junior creditors will receive nothing until senior creditors are paid in full. This doctrine has been derived from Chapter 11 of the US Bankruptcy Code that gives priority to senior over junior creditors. In China, the rule has been codified in Article 113 of the EBL 2006. The rule requires that claims by creditors will have absolute priority over claims by shareholders. In Commonwealth jurisdictions, such as the UK and Australia, this rule has been codified and reflects a long-established practice associated with the UK decision in *Houndesworth v. City of Glasgow Bank* ((1880) 5 Appeals Cases 317).

Normally, a company may have fewer than 50 shareholders (Article 24 of Company Law 2006). In such smaller companies it would be easy for the government or the court to limit any form of protest initiated by this small number of shareholders. By contrast, where a public company listed on the Shanghai or Shenzhen Stock Exchanges is involved, the court has to give more weight to shareholders who may be much more numerous. For instance, in Xiaxing Electronics Ltd's reorganization in Fujian Province, there were about 50,000 public shareholders.[29] Indeed, it is not uncommon for a listed company to have over 20,000 public shareholders.

To remove the threat of possible social unrest in connection with mass meetings of shareholders in listed company reorganizations, the Supreme People's Court, via one of its senior judges, Mr Song Xiaoming, expressed its clear opinion that a certain number of shares should be retained for the small and medium shareholders for purposes of maintaining social stability and for maintaining public confidence in the stock market in China (Song 2006).

Not surprisingly, in 11 (48 per cent) out of the 23 listed company reorganizations, the shares held by members of the general public retained their value, and such public shareholder shares in the remaining listed companies were reduced in value by just 22.17 per cent. This amounted, however, to a sharp reduction in the rights of creditors.[30] For example, in the reorganization of Dixian Textile Ltd, a listed company in Hebei Province, the general creditors were repaid 2 per cent of the amount due to them, while all pre-existing shares, including those of the controlling shareholders and those of the public shareholders, remained unaffected.[31]

In the case of company reorganizations involving non-listed companies, due to the small number of shareholders in such companies the absolute priority principle tends to be rigorously enforced. This is because it is common for the old shares in a reorganized company to be simply cancelled or given to new investors for free. Out of 21 non-listed company reorganizations examined by Zhang, the original shareholders were deprived of their shares in 17 cases (81 per cent of the reorganizations). Therefore, the decision to deviate from the absolute priority rule in China seems to depend upon whether there are large numbers of shareholders who can raise social stability concerns during a reorganization and hence trump established bankruptcy law principles.

Conclusion

Generally, the corporate rescue mechanism has theoretically been available in China since the enactment of the EBL 2006. But, in contrast to the relatively broad-minded approach taken by China's bankruptcy law-makers, China's bankruptcy judges appear to be extremely cautious in accepting corporate reorganization petitions.

Although the use of bankruptcy and company reorganization under the EBL has increased since the enactment of the law, it would be desirable for the Supreme People's Court to give lower court judges specific guidelines[32] in relation to the entry test for corporate rescue; in practice, partly due to a misunderstanding of rescue eligibility, judges have refused to hear the vast majority of corporate reorganization petitions. As a result, if the present situation continues, China's court-based company reorganization procedures face being stifled.

Meanwhile, the biggest barrier to in-court corporate reorganization is the fear of social unrest in China; however, given the significant changes that have occurred in China's major enterprises over the last two decades, it seems unnecessary for the legislature and the courts to worry about this issue as much as they may once have done, as this fear has undermined a commitment to the consistent application of legal principles.

Notes

1 For further insights into the history of China's bankruptcy legislation see Chen (1999) and Li (2001).
2 In addition, the German government played a critical role in channelling China's internal debates on bankruptcy law through the joint project involving the German aid agency GTZ and the Finance and Economic Committee of the PRC National People's Congress (Tomasic 2007: 2–7). Eventually, China's State Council took over management of the reform process that quickly led to the passage of the new Enterprise Bankruptcy Law on 27 August 2006 (and this Law took effect on 1 June 2007).
3 There are no comprehensive official statistics in relation to reorganizations in China. Some reorganization data reported by government bodies may be deliberately manipulated. It has been argued by Professor Charles Booth (2008: 279) that even insolvency data from China's Supreme People's Court is not reliable.
4 From unpublished data collected by Zinian Zhang in 2010.

5 The average unsecured debt is calculated from 46 reorganized companies in China from June 2007 until November 2010.
6 This figure is drawn from 46 company reorganizations; publicly available information from June 2007 to November 2010 – collected by Zinian Zhang in 2010.
7 This chapter is focused on the corporate reorganizations conducted from June 2007 to November 2010 in China.
8 Judges have complained that the legislative requirement of reorganization entry is too vague (see generally Wang and Liu 2009).
9 The Supreme People's Court Interpretation on Corporate Bankruptcies in Enhancing the Socialist Market Economy, Article 3, 12 June 2009, at: http://rmfyb.chinacourt.org/public/detail.php?id=129395.
10 The National Strategy of Promoting Certain Industries, Products and Technologies was issued by China's National Development and Reform Commission in 2000: www.ndrc.gov.cn/zcfb/zcfbl/zcfbl2003pro/t20050708_28193.htm.
11 Australian Law Reform Commission, *Report No. 45: General Inquiry into Insolvency* Chapter 3 paragraph 8: www.alrc.gov.au/report-45 (accessed on 1 June 2011). This reorganization scheme was eventually implemented in Australia in 1993 in Part 5.3A of the Corporations Law in the form of the new deed of company arrangement procedure. Some in Australia have however argued that this threshold may need to be raised to prevent the abuse of corporate rescue procedures (Robinson 1996: 433). Nevertheless, in 2004 the Australian reorganization procedure was successfully reviewed by an Australian Parliamentary committee of inquiry (PJC 2004: Chapter 5).
12 According to Anderson (2001: 108), in the financial year 1996–7, there were 1,937 Voluntary Administration appointments made and there were 2,035 liquidator appointments in Australia.
13 Zinian Zhang examined China's corporate reorganization literature and found that there is little if any discussion seeking to distinguish different business distress models.
14 The Intermediate Court of Hangzhou, China, 'The principles of in-court corporate reorganization' (5 January 2010, Hangzhou, China) at: http://wenku.baidu.com/view/75dc5835f111f18583d05a62.html; accessed on 1 June 2010 (in Chinese). Such court behaviour is also described by Lu (2010); see also Zhang and Tan (2010).
15 In the UK, it is the appointed administrator who makes a professional judgement on whether the company's business is economically viable and deserving to be rescued (see further Frisby 2004).
16 There was a long-term legislative and practical struggle in the USA's bankruptcy legal history as to whether to 'leave the old management in the driving seat during the company's rehabilitation' (Warren and Westbrook 2009: 387–90).
17 In 70 Chinese reorganizations whose relevant information is publicly available, local governments initiated the establishment of 40 liquidation committees which then were appointed by the courts as the administrators in charge of the whole reorganization process. Apart from liquidation committees, local governments formed special working teams to intervene in 18 other reorganization cases. Thus, governments were directly involved in 73 per cent of reorganizations. This data archive was collected by Zinian Zhang in 2010.
18 In 79 Chinese reorganizations, there are 42 companies that are state-owned, state controlled or previously state-owned. Therefore 54 per cent of reorganized companies have a government background (data collected by Zinian Zhang in 2010).
19 The 2004 report of the Parliamentary Joint Parliamentary Committee on Corporations and Financial Services found that the Australian reorganization procedures under Part 5.3A of the Corporations Act were 'the most commonly used form of external administration in Australia' (PJC 2004: 7–3), finding that around 40 per cent of all external administration cases in Australia in 2003 were handled in this way. Unlike the position in China and the United States, this Part 5.3A reorganization procedure is a non-court-based procedure which places the company in the hands of an external

administrator. The Australian voluntary administration procedures in Part 5.3A of the Corporations Act 2001 were first introduced in 1993–4 and proved popular, reducing the number of insolvency cases handled by the courts.
20 In the USA, Chapter 11 is frequently used by the debtor to sell the business by virtue of its unique procedural protection, and the general discussion can be seen in Baird and Rasmussen (2002: 248).
21 Some of the Chinese speakers at this conference included: Mr Chen Xioahong and others from the Development Research Centre of China's State Council; Mr Zhu Shaoping, a leading figure on the Finance and Economics Committee of the National People's Congress; Mr Song Xiaoming, Chief Justice of the No. 2 Civil Court of the PRC Supreme People's Court; and Professor Wang Weiguo, a member of the drafting committee of the Enterprise Bankruptcy Law (see OECD 2006). Responsibility for the preparation of the final draft of the EBL was moved to the Legislation Committee of the State Council and strong political support for the enactment of the law came from the leadership of the Standing Committee of the National People's Congress, leading to the compromise that produced the successful passage of the EBL 2006.
22 Also see the Chinese Communist Party (1999); and Brandt and Rawski (2008).
23 In Zinian Zhang's 2010 collected data, 43 reorganized debtors out of the total of 79 cases studied were state-owned, state-controlled or formerly state-owned.
24 Yangdong Engine Manufacture Ltd, 'The proclamation of soliciting the strategic investor to recapitalize Yangdong' (July 2009) at: http://hs.hongdou.gxnews.com.cn/viewthread-4407688.html.
25 The administrator of Xiaxing Electronic Ltd, 'The reorganization plan of Xiaxing Electronic Ltd' (November 2009).
26 This finding is based on Zinian Zhang's unpublished data archive.
27 The *pari passu* principle cannot be compromised by mutual agreements in the UK as a recent case confirms that this principle is public policy which cannot be easily altered by contracts among parties. *Belmont Park Investments PTY Limited v. BNY Corporate Trustee Services Limited and Lehman Brothers Special Financing Inc.* [2011] 38 UKSC 2.
28 This is based on Zinian Zhang's unpublished data.
29 'The reorganization plan of Xiaxing Electronics Ltd is passed in the first creditor and shareholder meeting', *Quick News of the Southeast* (Fuzhou, China, 19 November 2009) at: www.dnkb.com.cn/archive/info/20091119/212026545.html.
30 Zinian Zhang's collected data.
31 The administrator of Dixian Textile Ltd, 'The reorganization plan of Dixian Textile Ltd' (15 December 2008, Chende, Hebei Province, China), and this public notice can be found at: www.cninfo.com.cn.
32 The Supreme People's Court 2009 judicial interpretation on bankruptcy generally urges courts to accept bankruptcy petitions but does not offer any specific approach.

4 Chinese contract law after the UN Convention on Contracts for the International Sale of Goods

Yan Chang Bennett

Introduction

This chapter focuses on the interpretation and application of the United Nations Convention on Contracts for the International Sale of Goods (CISG) in China and assesses CISG contributions to Chinese jurisprudence specifically with respect to Chinese contract law. It is argued that Chinese jurisprudence on contract law has been significantly influenced by the CISG. To assess CISG's impact on Chinese contract law, the chapter is divided into four parts commencing with an overview of the CISG. The second section compares and contrasts the CISG and China's Uniform Contract Law (UCL). The third section gives a brief analysis of both Chinese and US case law on the CISG, assessing the issues most litigated. The final section analyses where CISG has made its greatest impact on Chinese jurisprudence.

It was on 1 January 1988 that the CISG first took effect in 11 countries, including China and the United States. The purpose of the CISG is to provide a unified body of law governing agreements between parties involving the international sale of goods and to pre-empt domestic law of member nations with regard to certain contract elements. The CISG was conceived to provide 'neutral law' in that the CISG, as the governing law in such contracts between parties of differing nations, would offer neither party any particular 'home advantage', such that sales contracts would be interpreted and applied neutrally. The theory is that adoption of the CISG as governing law would also add a level of predictability for such international trade agreements on goods.

Today, the CISG has 74 member states. With the globalization of business, the volume of world trade of goods has rapidly increased since 1988 with only a significant dip in 2008–9 due to the financial crisis. In 2008, export trade of the top ten trade nations comprised more than 50 per cent of the total (WTO 2009: 12). In China's case, its export market totalled 8.9 per cent of the total market. Of the CISG's member states, six are China's top ten trading partners.[1] Undoubtedly, the CISG has importance to both China and world trade.

China makes a unique case study in that the CISG was adopted before China revised and consolidated its several domestic contract law codes to form the Uniform Contract Law of China (UCL). China amended its domestic law in 1999 to create the UCL, more than a decade after its ratification of the CISG.

Overview of the CISG

The United Nations Convention on Contracts for the International Sale of Goods is a unified body of law for contracts on the sale of goods between nations that have ratified the Convention (CISG 1980). Promulgated in 1980 by the United Nations, the CISG is a self-executing treaty entered into force on 1 January 1988. The sphere of CISG's application encompasses 'contracts of sale of goods between parties whose places of business are in different States when the States are Contracting States or when the rules of private international law lead to the application of the law of a Contracting State' (CISG 1980: Article 1). Where it applies, it pre-empts domestic contract law; one of the primary purposes of the CISG was to create 'neutral law' by pre-empting the domestic contract law of both Contracting States so that both parties would be on the same legal footing (Flechtner 2008: 5). Additionally, Article 7 of the CISG provides that interpretation of the Convention requires regard to be given to the CISG's 'international character and to the need to promote uniformity in its application and the observance of good faith in international trade'. Ambiguities in the CISG are to be settled 'in conformity with the general principles on which it is based or, in the absence of such principles, in conformity with the law applicable by virtue of the rules of private international law' (CISG 1980). Thus, the CISG was drafted with the intent to create truly international law without being influenced by the domestic legal traditions of Contracting States.

The CISG provides a body of law governing contract formation, obligations of the buyer and seller, remedies for breach, passing of risk and assessing damages for breach. The CISG applies to contracts formed after the CISG entered into force and to the rights and obligations of the seller and buyer to a sale of goods. The CISG does not apply to sale of goods bought for 'personal, family or household use', auction or on execution or otherwise by authority of law. Nor does the CISG apply to the sale of investment securities, negotiable instruments or money, or to sea-going vessels or aircraft (CISG 1980: Article 2). The CISG also does not apply to mixed contracts of goods and services that are preponderantly service-based (CISG 1980: Article 3). The CISG does not apply to contract validity, which must be resolved under domestic law. The CISG also does not apply to the effect the contract has on the property in the goods sold, or upon tort liability of the seller for death or personal injury caused by the goods (CISG 1980: Articles 4 and 5). The CISG does not have statute of fraud or parol evidence provisions as many domestic commercial codes do.[2]

Pursuant to the CISG, 'declarations made under this Convention at the time of signature are subject to confirmation upon ratification, acceptance or approval' (CISG 1980). The CISG permits Contracting States to make declarations to the CISG and allows Contracting States to opt out of certain provisions. An Article 95 declaration would prevent the indirect invocation of the CISG through Article 1(1)(b), which determines choice of law 'when the rules of private international law lead to the application of the law of a Contracting State'. An Article 96 declaration allows a Contracting State to opt out of Article 11, which states that contracts 'need not be concluded in or evidenced by writing and is not subject to any other requirement as to form. It may be proved by any means, including witnesses'. Such a declaration would thus institute writing and form requirements.

Adoption of CISG by China

China was one of the 11 original Contracting States to ratify the CISG. China has entered two declarations. China entered an Article 95 declaration to not be bound by Article 1(1)(b), thereby disallowing the invocation and application of the CISG through domestic choice-of-law rules. The Article 95 declaration would also prevent the application of the CISG on a non-Contracting State. China made a second declaration on the general subject of Article 96 that China 'does not consider itself bound by ... Article 11 as well as the provision of the Convention relating to the content of Article 11'.

The status of Hong Kong and Macao should be noted. Hong Kong, as it was then a British protectorate, was not subject to the CISG because the United Kingdom was not and is not a signatory of the CISG. In 1997, China made Hong Kong a 'Special Administrative Region' that enjoys a relatively high degree of legal and financial autonomy from Beijing. Pursuant to Article 93(1) of the CISG, if a Contracting State has territorial units to which different systems of law are applicable, the Contracting State, 'at the time of ... accession, declare that this Convention is to extend to all its territorial units or only to one or more of them' thereby requiring a Contracting State to make a declaration whether such territorial units are subject to the CISG. China has so far been silent as to whether CISG applies to Hong Kong. The Chinese government deposited with the Secretary General of the United Nations a written declaration announcing the conventions that would apply to Hong Kong upon its transfer. The CISG was not included among the 127 listed treaties, indicating that the Chinese government did not intend to extend the CISG to Hong Kong (Letter of Notification dated 27 June 1997). Furthermore, the Hong Kong Justice Department has taken the position that 'no new conventions apply to Hong Kong as a result of the handover' (Institute of International Commercial Law 2010b). For the same reasons, Macao is most likely also not subject to the CISG as Portugal was not a signatory of the CISG and the CISG was not named as one of the treaties that applied to Macao (Letter of Notification 1999). The status of Hong Kong will be addressed in more detail in the fourth section of this chapter.

CISG in practice

While the CISG was heralded by the United Nations as a transformative body of law that would alter the landscape of international trade agreements on goods, use of the CISG has been uneven. In part, practitioners in international trade are still slowly developing familiarity with its application, even 20 years after its inception (Schwenzer and Hachem 2009: 463). Second, practitioners from certain countries prefer to adhere to the domestic law with which they are familiar. In the United States particularly, practitioners often choose to opt out of the CISG by making an Article 6 reservation due to their unfamiliarity with and general suspicion of the CISG (Philippopoulos 2008: 358). This is due to a lack of precedential decisions on the CISG and certain trepidation in how courts will interpret the CISG in litigation given American judges' unfamiliarity with its provisions.[3] Parties from European nations, on the other hand, tend to require the application of the CISG for a variety of reasons, including that the CISG parallels their own domestic law or that the CISG is more easily understood than law from another nation (Philippopoulos 2008: 364).

In China, some practitioners are uncertain whether the CISG is legally advantageous to Chinese parties to trade agreements on goods. Some indicate that the choice of CISG must be made on a case-by-case basis. Others indicate that foreign parties would be more likely to select the CISG as choice of law and/or choice of forum because of their unwillingness to select Chinese law (Koehler and Yujun 2008: 56). Use of the CISG seems most prevalent in the context of alternative dispute resolution and arbitration (see Fan Yu in Chapter 11).

CISG in context with China's domestic provisions

The CISG has been used in part as a model code for China's domestic contract law. When the CISG's Diplomatic Convention was first convened in 1980, there was no Chinese domestic legislation on contract law, primarily because China's economy was state-planned and China had just begun its economic opening up in 1978. At the time that China ratified the CISG in 1986, China's domestic contract law comprised of the Economic Contract Law, the Foreign-Related Economic Contract Law (FECL), the General Principles of Civil Law and the Technology Contract Law (Xiao and Long 2008: 62). On 15 March 1999, China enacted the UCL (as preparation for admission to the WTO), repealing and replacing the aforementioned civil contract codes. Given the antecedent, the UCL features many similar, if not identical, provisions to the CISG, which will be discussed below.

Contract formation

Under the UCL, it became possible for 'natural persons' to be parties to a contract with foreign individuals, enterprises, or other economic organizations, unlike the FECL which disallowed such contracts. This places the UCL in accord with the CISG.

The formation of contracts is addressed in Chapter Two of the UCL. Under the UCL and consistent with the CISG, a contract is concluded by the exchange of an offer and an acceptance (UCL 1999: Art. 13). The offer must be sufficiently specific and definite and that, if accepted, the offeror will be bound thereby (UCL 1999: Art. 14). The CISG differs only in that it expressly states that an offer is 'sufficiently definite if it indicates the goods and, expressly or implicitly, fixes or makes provision for determining the quantity and the price' (CISG 1980: Art. 14). The UCL states once the offer has been accepted, the terms of the contract 'shall be prescribed by the parties and generally include the names and domicile of the parties, subject matter, quantity, quality, price or remuneration, time, place and method of performance, liabilities for breach of contract, and method of dispute resolution' (UCL 1999: Art. 12). This seems to indicate that most of the aforementioned terms are not necessarily required in the offer, but necessary to having an enforceable contract.

Under the UCL the definition of acceptance is conceptually the same as under the CISG, as are the other provisions governing acceptance.[4] Acceptance of an offer under article 18(1) of the CISG requires that 'a statement made by or other conduct of the offeree indicating assent to an offer is an acceptance. Silence or inactivity does not in itself amount to acceptance'. Acceptance becomes effective when assent reaches the offeror. Acceptance fails if it does not reach the offeror within the designated time, or within a 'reasonable time'; an oral offer must be accepted immediately unless circumstances require otherwise.

Article 17 of the UCL is identical to the CISG regarding withdrawal of an offer, which may be made before or at the same time as the offer. Revocation under the UCL is also identical to the CISG in that an offer may be revoked before notice of acceptance has been dispatched. Article 19 of the UCL is also identical to the CISG's Article 19 provision governing irrevocable offers, which may not be revoked if it expressly indicates it is irrevocable or if the offeree has reason to regard the offer as irrevocable and has undertaken preparation for performance.

Both the UCL and CISG state that a reply to an offer that contains material differences to the offer is considered a rejection and constitutes a counter-offer (UCL: Article 30 and CISG: Article 19(1)). Both the UCL and CISG contain the same definition of 'material change', stating that change in the subject matter, quantity, quality, price, time, place and method of performance, liabilities for breach of contract or method of dispute resolution constitute material changes.

Article 19(2) of the CISG states that a reply to an offer which purports to be an acceptance but contains additional or different terms that do not materially alter the offer, constitutes an acceptance. However, the offeror may make timely objections to the non-material modifications contained in the acceptance. The UCL also follows the CISG regarding acceptance containing non-material changes.

Article 10 of the UCL states that a 'contract may be made in a writing, in an oral conversation, as well as in any other form' but that if relevant law or administrative regulation so requires, a contract shall be in writing if the parties have agreed. This is in accord with the CISG, which does not require a written or form requirement. However, China declared an Article 96 reservation to this CISG Article, thereby requiring parties to evidence contracts in writing and to adhere to form requirements, which contradicts its own domestic provision on a writing requirement in Article 10 of the UCL, a contradiction that will be addressed in the conclusion.

Contract validity

The CISG does not speak to contract validity and expressly states in Article Four that the CISG is 'not concerned with the validity of the contract or of any of its provisions or of any usage or the effect which the contract may have on the property in the goods sold'. Thus, the domestic law of the Contracting Parties determines contract validity. This may become quite complicated if only the CISG has been selected as governing law without mention of which domestic law should be used to determine contract validity or issues on which CISG is silent.

Chapter Three of the UCL speaks to contract validity. In general, Chinese contract validity follows Western common law concepts, but with 'Chinese characteristics'. For instance, in Article 52, Invalidating Circumstances, a contract is invalid if such contract would harm the interests of the state or if the parties 'colluded in bad faith, thereby harming the interests of the state, the collective, or any third party'. Article Seven of the UCL, Legality, states that 'In concluding or performing a contract, the parties shall abide by the relevant laws and administrative regulations, as well as observe social ethics, and may not disrupt social and economic order or harm the public interests', which indicates such contracts would be illegal or void. Some scholars have interpreted this provision to be analogous to the Western concept of a contract being void as against public policy, but also caution that the terms 'public policy', 'social ethics' and 'public interests' are ambiguous and are yet to be clearly defined (Pattison and Herron 2003: 470).

Contract performance

The CISG addresses performance of contracts in Article 71, which states that a party may suspend the performance of his obligations if it becomes apparent that the other party will not perform a substantial part of his obligations as a result of 'a serious deficiency in his ability to perform or in his creditworthiness; or his conduct in preparing to perform or in performing the contract'. If so, a seller who has already dispatched the goods is not obligated to hand over the goods to the buyer even though the buyer holds a document to obtain them. A party suspending performance must immediately give notice to the other party, but must continue with performance if the other party provides adequate assurance of his performance.

Chapter Four, Article 60 of the UCL governing the performance of contracts, requires parties to a contract to 'fully perform their respective obligations in accordance with the contract', in addition to abiding by 'the principle of good faith, and perform obligations such as notification, assistance, and confidentiality in light of the nature and purpose of the contract and in accordance with the relevant usage'. The UCL also speaks to performance by third parties, consecutive or simultaneous performance, or when performance may be suspended or terminated. In contracts where performance by the parties has not been ordered, the parties must perform simultaneously (UCL: Article 66), which has no CISG analogue. In suspension of performance, a party may suspend performance if the other party's business has seriously deteriorated, the other party has engaged in transfer of assets or withdrawal of funds for the purpose of evading debts, lost business creditworthiness, or in any other situation where the other party has lost its ability to perform (UCL: Article 67).

Breach of contract

Article 25 of the CISG defines a fundamental breach of contract as one that results

> in such detriment to the other party as substantially to deprive him of what he is entitled to expect under the contract, unless the party in breach did not foresee and a reasonable person of the same kind in the same circumstances would not have foreseen such a result.

The UCL does not define 'breach', but implies that in circumstances where consecutive performance is required, suspension of performance would be considered a breach (UCL: Article 67).

Obligations of the seller

Under the CISG and UCL, the obligations of the seller are the same. The seller is required to provide delivery of the goods and handing over of documents as required by contract (CISG: Article 30). The seller, if not bound to deliver the goods at a particular place, is obliged to deliver the goods to the first carrier and, generally, to place the goods at the buyer's disposal at the place where the seller has his place of business or where it was manufactured or produced (CISG: Article 31).

Under Articles 35–44 of the CISG, the seller's obligations regarding conformity of the goods and third-party claims are outlined. Article 35 states that the seller must 'deliver goods which are the quantity, quality, and description required by the contract and which are contained or packaged in the manner required by the contract'. Article 35 also provides warranties regarding the goods' fitness for an ordinary purpose, fitness for any express or implied purpose as expressed by the seller, possession of the qualities which the seller had held out to the buyer in a sample or model and warranty of adequate packaging. Article 41 provides the seller must have proper title to the goods, which must be 'free from any right or claim of a third party, unless the buyer agreed to take the goods subject to that right or claim'.

The UCL differs in that it speaks to 'quality specifications' of the goods, requiring the seller to 'deliver the subject matter in compliance with the prescribed quality requirements. Where the seller gave quality specifications for the subject matter, the subject matter delivered shall comply with the quality requirements set forth therein.' The UCL does not speak to a warranty of fitness for a particular purpose or for purposes for which the goods are known specifically. Article 62(i) of the UCL provides that if the quality requirements are not clearly prescribed, 'performance shall be in accordance with the state standard or industry standard; absent any state or industry standard, performance shall be in accordance with the customary standard or any particular standard consistent with the purpose of the contract'.

The UCL also differs with respect to implied warranties. Article 62 of the UCL states that in situations where the quality of goods had been inadequately described, a gap-filling measure may be taken and the seller shall provide goods 'in accordance with the state standard or industry standard; absent any state or industry standard, performance shall be in accordance with the customary standard or any particular standard consistent with the purpose of the contract'.

Obligations of the buyer

Under the CISG, the buyer is required to pay the price and take delivery of the goods as required by the contract. The CISG also dictates method and place of payment (CISG: Article 57). While the UCL does not have a specific section on the obligations of the buyer, it requires the buyer to pay for the goods (Article 159) in the prescribed place and time (Articles 160 and 161). The UCL makes an express provision regarding an excess of goods delivered; the buyer may accept or reject the excess. If accepted, the buyer shall pay the contract price; if rejected, the buyer must give timely notification (UCL: Article 162).

Passing of risk / risk of loss

Chapter Four of the CISG states risk of loss passes to the buyer when the goods are handed over to the first carrier for transmission in accordance with the contract, commonly known as 'risk passing at ship's rail'. If the seller is bound to hand the goods over to a carrier at a particular place, the risk transfers at the designated place. Risk at this point does not pass to the buyer unless the goods are clearly identified to the contract. Unlike the CISG, UCL Article 142 states that 'the risk of damage to or loss of the subject matter is borne by the seller *prior to delivery* and by the buyer *after delivery*, except as otherwise provided by law or agreed by the parties' (emphasis added).

Remedies

The CISG articulates in Articles 45–52 remedies for breach of contract by the seller and in Articles 61–65 remedies for breach of contract by the buyer. For breach of contract by the seller, remedies include entitlement to direct damages, specific performance, substitute goods for nonconforming goods, contract avoidance and entitlement to consequential damages. For breach of contract by the buyer, sellers are entitled to a remedy – if the buyer fails to perform any of his obligations under the contract or the CISG. Such remedies include requiring the buyer to take delivery and pay the price, to give additional time for performance, to avoid the contract and entitlement to damages.

The UCL was written to address a more market-oriented economy and redress of breached contracts. Previously, contract law in China demanded specific performance in all contracts as part of a command economy. As with the CISG, the UCL provides non-breaching parties may seek specific performance, except where performance is impossible, if the subject matter does not lend itself to enforcement by specific performance, if the cost of performance would be excessive, or if the obligee's time requirements for performance are unreasonable (UCL: Article 110). The non-breaching party is entitled to damages under Article 112. Under Article 111, the non-breaching party may require the breaching party to repair, replace, re-manufacture the nonconforming goods, accept returned goods, or reductions in price or remuneration.

Damages

Under the CISG, the non-breaching party is entitled to direct damages and consequential damages suffered from the loss. However, such damages may not exceed the loss which the breaching party foresaw or ought to have foreseen at the time of the contract as a possible consequence of the breach (CISG: Article 74). The CISG is silent on liquidated damages. Although the UCL section on damages is patterned after the CISG (Articles 112, 113), it does add a liquidated damages provision (Article 114) whereby the non-breaching party is entitled to liquidated damages if this is provided for in the contract.

Other provisions of law affecting CISG application and contract interpretation

With regard to the CISG within China's legal framework, Chapter Eight, Article 142 of the PRC General Principles of Civil Law states 'the application of law in civil relations with foreigners shall be determined by the provisions in this chapter' and holds that:

> If any international treaty concluded or acceded to by the PRC contains provisions differing from those in the civil laws of the PRC, the provisions of the international treaty shall apply, unless the provisions are ones on which the PRC has announced reservations. International practice may be applied to matters for which neither the law of the PRC nor any international treaty concluded or acceded to by the PRC has any provisions.

Article 150 of the General Principles of the Civil Law of the PRC states: 'the application of foreign laws or international practice in accordance with the provisions of this chapter shall not violate the public interest of the PRC'. In theory, if a CISG provision were in violation of the public interest of China, it would be void and unenforceable by law.

Article 145 of the General Principles of the Civil Law of the PRC state that parties to a contract involving 'foreign interests may choose the law applicable to settlement of their contractual disputes, except as otherwise stipulated by law'. Thus, China's civil code allows freedom of contract in making an express choice of law provision. In the event the contract is silent as to choice of law, Article 145 states 'the law of the country to which the contract is most closely connected' shall apply, thus legislating a theory of proximate connection to determine applicable law to govern the contract. Article 126 of the UCL also states that parties to a 'foreign-related contract' may select the applicable law, and if the parties are silent, then the contract will be 'governed by the law of the country with the closest connection thereto'.

To see how this pans out in practice, the following section overviews Chinese court and arbitration decisions and briefly examines US case law to contrast the differences in legal analysis and issues litigated.

Interpretation and application of the CISG within China's legal framework: case law and arbitration decisions

Although China is a civil law nation where judge-made rules of interpretation are not precedential, such rulings are nevertheless instructive as to how Chinese courts and arbitration panels interpret the CISG. Chinese arbitration decisions are determined by the China International Economic and Trade Arbitration Commission (CIETAC) and conducted in accordance with the Commission's arbitration rules. Such decisions are binding upon the parties and are not, by law, precedential. Awards are made based on the facts in accordance with relevant law and international practices.[5] By way of contrast, the United States, as a common law country, follows the principle of *stare decisis* with case law being precedential and binding on future decisions of relevant courts (Garrick 2011: xix).

A total of 125 Chinese and American legal opinions and arbitration decisions involving parties of US and Chinese origin were reviewed. Of those, 96 were CIETAC arbitration decisions, with 14 Chinese and 15 US legal decisions. First, a few general observations. In Chinese arbitration decisions, one clearly sees an evolution of arbitration tribunals' understanding and application of CISG within the domestic law framework. Several early decisions stated that the governing law was Chinese with no reference to the CISG, even if the parties were differing Contracting States and otherwise met the requirements for application of the CISG. During the 1980s and 1990s, several courts and tribunals stated the CISG is applicable 'together with Chinese domestic law' (CIETAC Arbitration Proceeding 1991). Technically, this is not a correct statement of law since CISG is Chinese law as it is an international treaty adopted by China. As explained earlier, Chinese law may be applied as a 'gap filler' where the CISG is silent or where the CISG has no jurisdiction. Recent arbitration decisions generally state the CISG applies without mention of Chinese law or that 'Chinese law shall apply to issues not governed by the CISG' (CIETAC Arbitration Proceeding 2006). Other tribunals have applied the principle of CISG Article 7 whereby 'international practice shall be applied to the case when neither the law of PRC nor the Convention has any provisions' (CIETAC Arbitration Proceeding 2003). Such decisions show the sophistication and experience tribunals have with disputes involving the CISG, although at times some confusion has clearly existed about the status of CISG within China (see Table 4.1).

In both the US and China decisions, the primary issues consisted of the buyer's obligations to pay and take delivery (Article 53), conformity of the goods in accordance with the agreement (Article 35) and obligations of the seller to deliver

Table 4.1 Issues based on CISG Articles

CISG Article	Cases
25	2
29	1
30	24
32	1
33	1
34	2
35	29
36	1
50	1
53	47
54	1
79	1
86	1

the goods and transfer the documents relating to them (Article 30). On the whole, CISG litigation in both countries is generally simple contract breaches. Litigation or arbitration of these three areas of contract breach should be relatively straightforward and arbitration tribunals, in particular, should be able to adjudicate without great difficulty.

In many of the Article 53 cases, it was the failure of the buyer to pay for goods delivered. In a number of the Article 35 cases, the goods were damaged during transit, making them nonconforming to the contract. In such cases, the tribunal or court acknowledged CISG Article 67 that risk of loss passes to the buyer when the goods are handed to the first carrier for transmission and correctly determined that the seller was not liable for such damage (CIETAC Arbitration Proceeding 1999). In several Article 35 cases, the parties had negotiated passage of risk to the time of delivery rather than time of shipment or had made concurrent agreements as to damages to goods during delivery (CIETAC Arbitration Proceeding 1995).

Chinese arbitration tribunals

The review of the 96 CIETAC decisions from 1988 to 1999 found that, in general, the arbitration tribunals had a sophisticated understanding of CISG within China's domestic framework. For instance, they often applied the principle of decoupage to adjudicate issues that involve the CISG and other areas of law such as law on letters of credit (CIETAC Arbitration Proceeding 1997c) and agency (CIETAC Arbitration Proceeding 2011). Furthermore, Chinese arbitration decisions reveal the tribunals' understanding of CISG Articles 74 on damages and 78 on interest. Of the 81 decisions reviewed, 90 per cent of the claimants received some compensation. Arbitration tribunals consistently applied Article 74 in determining damages, and 61 per cent of the awards included compensation in the form of interest calculated from the date of breach to the decision date and pegged to

LIBOR or bank rates. US courts, however, seem unable to properly interpret Article 78 on interest, as shown below.

Chinese case law

In the Chinese legal decisions examined, the courts give little analysis on choice of law, so it is somewhat unpredictable whether and how the CISG will be applied. Chinese courts sometimes exhibit a lack of understanding as to when the CISG applies. For example, in *Carl Hill v. Cixi City Old Furniture Trading Company* ((2001) Cijingchuzi No. 560), the court held that, in accordance with the closest connection principle, Chinese law governed, but if 'international treaties concluded or acceded to by China contain provisions differing from those in the civil laws of China, the international treaties should apply'. Yet the court followed the UCL in upholding the validity of an oral contract despite the CISG Article 96 declaration of a formality requirement. In determining damages, the court cited the General Principles of Civil Law and the UCL while citing only CISG Article 32(2) on 'shipping requirements'. The selective use of laws may illustrate that some parochialism exists.

Several opinions and arbitration tribunal decisions have stated the CISG applies only when it differs from domestic provisions (*Carl Hill v. Cixi City Old Furniture* (2001) Cijingchuzi No. 560; *Shanghai Weijie Electronic Devices Ltd. v. Superpower Supply Inc* (2000) Hu Yi Zhong Jing Chu Zi Di No. 727t; *Shanghai Wangruixiang Fashion Co. Ltd. v. U.S. Trend Co. Ltd., Shanghai Silk (Group) Co. Ltd.* (2003)). Other decisions excluded the application of the CISG with little or no reasoning when it is clear that the CISG should apply (*XM International Inc. v. Jiangsu Metals & Minerals Import & Export (Group) Corp* (2000) Su Jing Zhong Zi Di No. 380; *Y.L.F. (USA) Inc. v. Jiangsu Overseas Group Haitong International Trade Co. Ltd.* (2006); *Shanghai Yanko Engine Co. Ltd. v. Shanghai Materials & Equipment Group Import & Export Co. Ltd.* (2004)). In *Global Nutri Co. v. Sichuan Xinguang Industrial Import & Export Co. Ltd* (2005), the court applied Chinese domestic law on the ground that the parties had chosen Chinese law in the contract. Although China's Article 95 declaration would prohibit the application of the CISG, it is unclear from the opinion whether this was the reason for CISG's exclusion.

Twelve arbitration tribunals adjudicated cases between Chinese and Hong Kong parties. All but one stated that the CISG has been agreed upon as the governing law or had been impliedly accepted since both parties used the CISG in argumentation during arbitration proceedings (CIETAC Arbitration Proceedings 1997b). Three cases involved Chinese and Macao parties. In each case, the arbitration tribunal wrongly stated that because Portugal is a Contracting State of the CISG, then it applies to Macao. Portugal is not a signatory and China did not include the CISG as one of the treaties to apply to Macao. Thus, even though it appears that China does not want the CISG to apply to Hong Kong or Macao, Chinese arbitration panels will, nevertheless, apply the CISG.

Table 4.2 shows the number of decisions, in both China and the US, and arbitration tribunals where the CISG applied. On the whole, China correctly applies

Table 4.2 Number of CISG decisions

Governing law	Total
CISG	77
Concurrent CISG and Chinese law	15
CISG is not deemed governing law, but clearly relevant	9

the CISG with some minor exceptions. Chinese courts and arbitration tribunals have stated that the CISG and Chinese law are concurrent, but in interpretation, applied the CISG without reference to Chinese law. US courts are not as consistent, most likely due to general unfamiliarity with the CISG in the US.

US legal decisions

In the United States, cases dealing with the CISG most often involve procedural matters without addressing the merits. In the few opinions on the merits, it is clear that US domestic courts are not familiar with the CISG and sometimes fail to consider obvious issues. Given the volume of litigation in the United States and the relatively little experience some US courts have in applying the CISG, this is not unexpected.

In *Guang Dong Light Headgear Factory Co. Ltd. v. ACI International Inc.* ((2007) 2007 521 F.Supp.2d 1153), the court correctly interpreted that contract validity is outside the jurisdiction of the CISG, validity being a matter of domestic law, but was in actuality addressing the issue of contract formation, an issue within the jurisdiction of the CISG.

In *Beijing Metals & Minerals v. American Business Center Inc.* ((1993) 993 F 2d 1178), the court stated 'we need not resolve this choice of law issue [between Texas law and the CISG], because our discussion is limited to application of the parol evidence rule'. The parol evidence rule prevents a party to a written contract from providing evidence that contradicts or adds to the terms of the final contract. Because of China's Article 96 declaration of contract formality, the CISG was in fact relevant and the court should have addressed the choice of law in this case. No appeal was filed, but this would have been grounds for appeal if resolution of choice of law proved substantive.

Several US cases involved plaintiffs seeking enforcement of Chinese arbitral decisions against US defendants. Whether the plaintiff was entitled to interest, the courts were divided. In *Guang Dong Light Headgear Factory Co, Ltd. v. ACI Intern. Inc.* ((2008) 2008 WL 1924948), the court determined under article 78 of the CISG, the non-breaching party is entitled to interest and that failing to award prejudgment interest would impede the purpose of the CISG, which favours arbitration as a means to resolve disputes by promoting the enforcement of arbitral agreements in international commerce. In direct contradiction, the court in *Zhejiang Shaoxing Yongli Printing and Dyeing Co. Ltd v. Microflock Textile Group* ((2008) 2008 WL 2098062) simply stated the CISG is silent on the issue of interest and the plaintiff was not entitled under the substantive domestic law. This is wholly untrue as Article 78 of the CISG addresses interest issues.

Three cases dealt with the issue of whether the CISG applied to contracts between US and Hong Kong parties. In *CNA International Inc. v. Guangdong Kelon Electronical Holdings et al.* ((2008) No. 05 C 5734 (N.D.Ill.)), the court held Hong Kong is a Contracting State of the CISG because under Article 93(4), 'if a Contracting State makes no declaration under paragraph (1) of this article, the Convention is to extend to all territorial units of that State'. The court reasoned China, at the time of Hong Kong's takeover, had the opportunity to declare that the CISG should not extend to Hong Kong when it resumed sovereignty over it, but did not. The court also held that a 'state must affirmatively opt-out of the CISG on behalf of one or more of its territories in order to avoid this provision'.

Innotex Precision Limited v. Horei, Inc., et al. ((2009) 679 F.Supp.2d 1356) came to the opposite conclusion that the CISG is inapplicable to Hong Kong because China did not formally declare the CISG applies to Hong Kong. Furthermore, the Chinese government deposited with the Secretary General of the United Nations a written declaration announcing the conventions that should apply to Hong Kong upon its transfer. The CISG was not included among the 127 listed treaties, indicating that the Chinese government did not intend to extend the CISG to Hong Kong. (*Innotex Precision Ltd*, pp. 1358–9).

In *Electrocraft Arkansas Inc. v. Super Electric Motors Ltd.* (2009) 70 UCC Rep. Serv.2d 716, p. 5), the court initially followed the *CNA International* holding that Hong Kong is a contracting state but noted in a subsequent motion for summary judgment that the court had been made aware of *Innotex Precision* and that it was a real possibility that the CISG is not in fact the governing law in this action.

In *Guang Dong Light Headgear Factory Co, Ltd. v. ACI International Inc.* ((2007) 521 F.Supp.2d 1153), the court analysed whether a joint venture agreement between the parties had been terminated in accordance with the CISG. The court, in applying the CISG to an agreement that did not involve the international sale of goods, erred.

In a procedural matter whether to execute a writ of attachment on respondent's domestic property for a contract dispute to be arbitrated in China, the court had to determine whether the plaintiff had a valid claim and probability of success in order to issue the writ. The court analysed the validity of the claim using the California Commercial Code rather than the CISG to determine whether the defendant had provided nonconforming goods (*China National Metal Products Import Export Company v. Apex Digital Inc.* (2001) 141 F.Supp.2d 1013). As the CISG would be the governing law in the upcoming arbitration tribunal, this court incorrectly applied the California code to a nonconforming goods analysis, grounds for appeal if proved substantive.

Conclusion: CISG's impact on Chinese jurisprudence

China has made phenomenal headway in transitioning from a command economy towards a market economy. Since 1978, China has made exceptional steps to enter the global competitive market by both first codifying contract law and then creating uniform contract law with the expectation that foreign companies doing business in China might seek to litigate their concerns in Chinese courts and arbitration tribunals. The CISG, as shown in the second section of this chapter, has made a great impact on China's UCL which, in no small part, brings China's contract law into conformity with international standards.

Chinese courts and arbitration tribunals have also shown growing sophistication in applying the CISG, given that Chinese courts have been in operation for only several decades. CIETAC arbitration decisions, particularly, show China's increasing ability in the application of law to specific cases and in determining damages and interest. That said, the application of CISG is still uneven across Chinese courts and arbitration tribunals. In addition, there may also be a 'fear factor' for some litigants apprehensive of taking on a Chinese enterprise in arbitration (including fear of losing future business even if their case is successful). Finally, the contradiction between the Article 95 declaration of contract formality requirements with the UCL must be resolved, most likely by doing away with the Article 95 declaration.

But generally, the review of Chinese decisions over time shows that the unevenness is levelling out. As time goes on, Chinese jurisprudence on the CISG is likely to influence decisions in other countries and create new international standards of interpretation and application. It follows that comprehension of and familiarity with the CISG and UCL will become *a must* for international lawyers who practice in China and for judges in all jurisdictions in which the CISG applies. On the evidence at hand, China's involvement with the CISG may well foreground broader engagement with and influence over a range of international legal architecture.

Notes

1 As of 2009, China's top trading partners are: the US, Japan, Hong Kong, South Korea, Taiwan, Germany, Australia, Malaysia, Singapore and India. Hong Kong, Taiwan, Malaysia and India are not contracting states. The 2009 statistics are provided by the US–China Business Council at: www.uschina.org/statistics/tradetable.html.
2 Article 6 of the CISG does however permit parties of Contracting States to 'exclude the application of the Convention or … derogate from or vary the effect of any of its provisions'.
3 For a review of practitioner opinions and preferences regarding the CISG, refer to Koehler and Yujun (2008).
4 Articles 21–4 of the UCL govern acceptance and follow the conceptual principles of the CISG. It is noteworthy that both the CISG and UCL require acceptance of an oral offer to be immediate unless otherwise agreed by the parties or dictated by circumstances. There is no similar analogue in the Uniform Commercial Code of the United States.
5 US arbitration decisions are difficult to follow in that they are administered separately by each state and, in addition, there are several national bodies such as the American Arbitration Association which are not required to be publicly available.

Part II
Critical issues for China's law and policy reforms

5 Understanding Chinese real estate

The property boom in perspective

Richard Hu

Introduction

Real estate property has been one of the most contested issues of China's transformation from a planned economy to a market economy. It touches the very heart of China's socialist doctrine: the state/collective ownership of land. This chapter analyses the evolution of land and real estate property laws in contemporary China. Outcomes and implications for both foreign and local investors are examined against the backdrop of the privatization of real estate property fixed on land. This has occurred during China's unprecedented process of urbanization along with the much heralded economic reforms. Driven by the dual tropes of 'market economy' and 'urbanization', China's government has made laws to 'marketize' real estate property for investment, ownership and transaction. These reforms have very different implications for the various social groupings. As Peerenboom (2011: 285) notes there are constantly new 'winners *and* losers' in revisions of the law.

The drivers of and impediments to property law reform are identified including inherent policy paradoxes: state/collective ownership of land vs market transaction of land use rights, and state ownership of land vs private ownership of real estate property fixed on the land.

The chapter argues that these paradoxes spring from the hybrid nature of China's market economic reforms and the socialist system of public ownership. Left unaddressed, such underlying paradoxes may challenge the legitimacy of the continuing rule of the CPC. For the moment, China has buoyant expectations of growth in its developing market economy. Yet these unresolved paradoxes may hint at an element of pessimism with China's further reforms to laws on land and real estate property likely to be consistent with 'socialism with Chinese characteristics'.

Law reforms on land and real estate property

China's land and real estate markets have been developing concurrently since China's 'reform and opening up' (*gai ge kai fang*) in 1978. Strictly speaking, China does not have a 'land market' in that constitutionally land ownership is vested in the state in urban areas and collectives in rural areas. When people talk about China's land market, they are actually referring to the 'land use right' market.

China's land market and real estate market reforms are interlinked given that real estate property is fixed on land. However, these two concurrent (and bound) reforms have been proceeding along different tracks over the past three decades. For the land market, the overarching reform theme has been *from* non-transferable land use right *to* transferable land use right. For the real estate property market, the theme has been *from* public provision and ownership *to* privatization.

The importance of land in China's contemporary political and economic context cannot be overstated. Public ownership of land is one of the fundamental principles of the CPC. Historically, land reform was marked by the confiscation of private land for redistribution in rural areas. This appealed to peasants, playing a pivotal role in the CPC's victory over the Chinese Nationalists (*guo ming dang*) in the civil war before 1949. Based on the ideology of all land being common property, large-scale nationalization was carried out after the establishment of the PRC. The *PRC Land Reform Law* was announced in June 1950 with a focus on land confiscation and redistribution, mainly in rural areas. In the same year, the *Regulation on Urban and Urban Fringe Land Reform* stipulated that urban land was to become state land, managed by city governments. This nationalized urban land system was in force from the early 1950s until the mid-1980s. During the period between the 1950s and 1980s, China's urban land system was characterized by three features summarized by Li (1999) as follows:

- *The administrative allocation of land*: Land was allocated for purposes determined by the administrative authorities. Land users such as the state authorities, army, schools or state enterprises could lodge land use applications to the relevant levels of governments. Land was then granted when the land use application was approved.
- *Land use without charge and compensation*: When land was granted through the administrative allocation, no charge or compensation was made for land use. The period of land use was not specified either. Theoretically the users could occupy the land for an unlimited time unless future state construction was going to take place on the same site.
- *No transfer right*: Land users had no right to transfer the land through selling, leasing, mortgaging, donating or exchanging. Constitutionally land could not be transferred in any form. Land had to be returned back to the relevant levels of government agents if land users did not need any particular piece of land, though this seldom occurred.

China's current land system is a result of a series of land law reforms, commencing in the early 1980s, that moved from administrative allocation of land use rights to an hierarchical system of primary and secondary land use *markets* (Ho and Lin 2003). A further significant breakthrough in property law reform came in 1988 with the amendment to Article 10 of the *Constitution* adding that: 'the right to use land may be transferred in accordance with the provisions of law'. This effectively separated 'ownership' and 'use rights' pertaining to urban land in order to establish a *land use right market* for private purposes (Hsing 2006). Thus a 'dual track' land use system is in practice in China determined by the purposes of the land.[1] Allocation (*hua bo*) is used to grant land use rights to state or non-profit users; conveyance (*chu rang*) is used to transfer land use rights to commercial users for fixed terms (40 years for commercial land, 50 years for industrial land and 70 years for residential land). Major land reforms have thus been centred on defining and granting land use rights through the second track of 'conveyance' and this carries significant implications for investors explored below.

Land use right markets in China

The two tiers of land use right markets in China are the (i) allocation, and (ii) conveyance of land use rights from the state. Together, these form the 'primary market' (*yi ji shi chang*) of land use rights. Land use rights through allocation are obtained by paying an 'allocation price' consisting of three major parts: the expropriation fee of land (*zheng di fei*); stipulated land fees (*tu di gui fei*); and allocation fee (*hua bo fei*).

Land use rights through conveyance are obtained by paying a 'conveyance price' consisting of three major parts too. The first two parts are identical to those in the allocation price. The third differentiating part is a conveyance fee (*chu rang jin*), which is the largest and most important portion of price paid to obtain land use rights through conveyance. The conveyance fee is supposed to be the market price of land use rights and can be determined by negotiation (*xie yi*), tender (*zhao biao*) or auction (*pai mai*). To curb corruption in determining the conveyance fee through negotiation between the government and the land users, the State Council promulgated in 2002 the *Regulation of Granting State-Owned Land Use Rights by Tender, Auction and Quotation* (the No. 11 Decree). This sought to end obtaining land use rights through negotiating the conveyance fee. An outcome has been that land use right holders who obtained land use rights through paying the conveyance fee in the primary market can transact or circulate (*liu zhuan*) their land use rights through transfer (*zhuan rang*), rent (*chu zu*) or collateral (*di ya*). This has the effect of forming a secondary market of land use rights. Circulating land use rights in the secondary market adds significant value to the land use rights. But land use rights obtained through allocation in the primary market cannot be circulated in the secondary market. As to whether the original intention of curbing corruption was fulfilled is a very moot point.

Land market reforms

Land market reforms had an immediate impact on the formation and evolution of China's real estate market. The real estate market has also developed along two tracks, but with differences to the land market. One track has been developing in parallel with the land market evolution as described above. The commercialization of land use rights was the first step to build a real estate market. The land use rights for real estate development can be obtained in both the primary land market and the secondary land market. Real estate developers can be public (state enterprises) or private (private investors from home or overseas).

The other track has been the process of privatization and marketization of *housing*. This track represented a transition from an administrative system to a market system under a 'top-down reform package' (Lee 2000; Zhang 2000). There was no housing market in China before the early 1980s. Housing was provided by the state as social welfare through the work units (*dan wei*) for which individuals worked. The ownership of housing belonged to the state and could not be circulated or transacted. Public provision of housing proved to be a major barrier to alleviating financial burdens on the state or state enterprises and enhancing residents' living conditions. The solution was dual: on the one hand, public-owned housing was privatized; on the other hand, real estate development through multiple modes of investment was allowed and encouraged. This extensive housing privatization was then supported by a system of urban housing property rights and growing availability of mortgage finance (Stephens 2010).

A dividing line in the evolution of China's real estate market came in 1998 with the State Council's Notice on *Further Deepening Urban Housing Reform and Accelerating Housing Construction*. This formally ceased all public provision of housing as a form of welfare from work units (including both government departments and state enterprises). The Notice marked a complete transition to market-based housing (Ye *et al.* 2006). From this point, the market became the only source for purchasing housing. This provided an overwhelming impetus to the real estate market in China, sustaining a property boom for over two decades. Generally, this property boom mainly refers to housing development, but in leading cities such as Beijing, Shanghai, Shenzhen, Guangzhou and so on, it also includes commercial property development such as office, hotel and retail. The commercial property boom has, to an extent, reflected China's macro economic growth and need for expanded infrastructure and facilities for economic development.

Property law reform: drivers and impediments

China's land and real estate property law reforms were initially facilitated by economic drivers. Further reforms have been shaped by political considerations including China's local government investment model which involves appropriating land from peasants and urban households and transferring it into government investment vehicles. The land is then used as collateral for debt, or portions of land are sold to fund ongoing constructions costs. This model is in part dependent on constantly rising land prices and use of coercive force to hold down compensation payment for the dispossessed. Garnaut (2011d: 5) describes this as a 'battle for land … where China's economic and political crises intersect'.[2] In addition to Beijing's influential monetary and fiscal policies, there is in fact a range of reform drivers that contribute to this battleground.

Drivers of reform

Foreign investment

A main economic driver involves an interwoven process of non-state investment and urbanization. Non-state investment refers to both foreign investment and domestic private investment. An important aim of the 'opening up and reform' policy in the early 1980s was to attract foreign investment (as well as so-called 'advanced technology and management experience') to grow the Chinese economy – initially in the coastal cities. Foreign investment in China in the 1980s mainly came from Hong Kong, Taiwan and Singapore, which had traditional links with mainland China. From then, inbound investment came from other East Asian countries like Japan, South Korea and other Southeast Asian countries, and then from North American and European countries. Foreign investment in China has not come without its problems, however, the first arising from the land use rights and real estate property rights. Early distinctions were made between enterprises that were completely foreign investment, and joint ventures between foreign investors with Chinese partners. A common practice in the early stages of reform was for Chinese local governments to provide land use rights as a contribution and to 'share in the joint ventures with foreign investment' (Wu *et al.* 2007). This nexus was problematic and the need to urgently clarify and define the land use rights (as well as the real estate property on the land) in relation to foreign investment became apparent to the central government in the early 1980s. The reforms had significant implications not only for foreign investors but also for domestic private investment.

Domestic private investment

Domestic private investment in China constituted the other important part of China's non-state investment. In the 1980s, domestic private investment did not impose a strong push on law reforms on land and real estate property in China because it had not yet evolved into a power force in the political-economic sphere in terms of scale or influence. Private investment was mostly made in the form of individual household business (*ge ti hu*) largely of vendor retailing or small-scale manufacturing workshops. In the 1990s, especially after Deng Xiaoping's Southern Tour Talk in 1992,[3] private investment grew massively along with foreign investment. Two factors well justified the rapid growth of private investment in the 1990s. First, after Deng's pro-market doctrine of building a Socialist market system with Chinese characteristics, favourable and encouraging investment policies were carried out by all levels of government. Second, some individual household businesses which commenced and accumulated in the 1980s were able to improve their strength and scale at an accelerating speed in the 1990s. Coupled with those who could access power in the transition from a planned economy system to a market economy system to grasp their 'first bucket of gold' (*di yi tong jin*), the domestic private investors were able to invest in enterprises with scales which involved land use rights and real estate property, such as factories, farming and real estate development projects. Thus domestic private investment joined the force requesting law reforms on land and real estate property.

Urbanization

The other significant driver of China's law reforms on land and real estate property has, of course, been its massive urbanization process. China's urbanization rate was 45 per cent in 2008, growing from 20 per cent in 1980, while the central government's target was set to be 60 per cent in 2020 (Hu 2008). The magnitude and speed of China's urbanization were unprecedented and unparalleled in its ambition of urbanism (Campanella 2008). China's urbanization is a concurrent dual process of urban population growth and urban construction growth. Urban population growth has been largely a result of rural population moving into cities for employment, education and residence under the context of macro economy boom. Urban construction growth has been more than a process of providing accommodation for the burgeoning urban population. It was first of all to provide spaces for production and business activities in factories, offices and commercial facilities of hotels, exhibition and conference centres, etc., in addition to the infrastructures which support the urban systems. It then involved the massive urban housing construction to provide shelters for people who work and live in cities. For local governments, one important fiscal source has been from leasing land for urban housing development to fund the expanding public services since the 1980s (Tang *et al.* 2010). This is a factor of urban growth driven by local governments.

The massive and rapid process of urbanization has imposed imperatives for property law reforms to land use and real estate properties in two senses. The first relates specifically to urban housing, which was previously provided by the state as in-kind welfare *for workers*. Now it is privatized and commoditized. Private ownership and transferability of real estate properties required that relevant law reforms must be made. The second relates to the *private corporate subjects* that invested in urban properties for business purposes – including foreign or domestic investment. As corporate assets, real estate property – including the land invested in, occupied and used – needed to be legally clarified and defined. For individuals and/or corporate subjects in China's urbanization process, it has thus been essential for the government to reform land and real estate property laws to cater for the new economic settings and 'actors' such as state regulators, hybrid state/private developers and wealthy private entrepreneurs.

Impediments to further reform

Political factors

There are a few deeply rooted impediments restricting further law reforms on land and real estate properties which are mostly political factors in China. The first impediment is the practice of the rule of party (the CPC) despite the rhetoric of the rule of law. People, including cadres and ordinary citizens in China, tend to attribute Chinese contemporary problems to the so-called 'systematic problem', which is essentially about the centralized governing system by one party. After attempts to begin liberalizing the political system in the late 1980s, culminating in the Tiananmen Square 'Incident'[4] in the spring of 1989, the CPC has tightened its political control throughout the 1990s. Some scholars assert this tightening has included enhanced economic control in recent years as evidenced by the strengthened, strategic position of state-owned enterprises in the Chinese economy (see Garrick's Introduction to this volume).

Making law for building a market economy is a paramount goal of the government. But it is not the only goal as the CPC seeks to justify and sustain its rule. Thus, on the one hand Chinese politics is an obvious driver of reform; on the other hand it can also be an impediment by restricting further law reforms on land and real estate property in some arbitrary ways. Achieving transparency and accountability under an impartial rule of law system may be a future goal of China's market economy system. At the moment, however, there remain some deficiencies in the rule of law system as applied to China's land and real estate property market. For example, a series of incidents has occurred in recent years whereby some property owners have committed *self-burning* to protect their properties from being arbitrarily demolished by local governments or government-backed developers. Popular media has dubbed this as 'blood demolition', with claims that such conflict between 'the haves' and 'have-nots' in China are reaching crisis point due to the lack of a clearly defined, effectively implemented legal system (Rui 2010; *Sydney Morning Herald* 2010).

Lingering ambiguity

The second category of impediment is 'ambiguity' in the interpretation and implementation of the rule of law in China. Ambiguity is related to the first impediment described above. There are some philosophical tensions for the CPC in that some socialist doctrines are now at an ideological crossroad between a forward vision and historically based legitimacy. Every generation of CPC leadership has generated its own governing 'concepts' and 'theories', such as Mao Zedong Thought, the Deng Xiaoping Theory, the Three Represents Theory and the Scientific Outlook on Development.[5] Such variations in the party's ideology have affected the rule of law development with Jiang Zeming in 2000, then as CPC Secretary General and China's National President, expanding the rule of law (*yi fa zhi guo*) to incorporate the 'rule of virtue' (*yi de zhi guo*) – so as to 'run the country by combining the rule of law with the rule of virtue' (Xinhua 2003). This statement was highly praised in the mainstream Chinese media or propaganda mechanism. However, intellectuals have privately challenged the 'real' implications of this call for 'rule of virtue' through blogs and conversation circles arguing the 'rule of virtue' is problematic because of its vague definition and arbitrary criteria. The core issue for the dissidents is 'whose virtue' – that is, who defines, judges and implements 'the virtue' to rule the country. An intrinsic presumption is that the CPC will turn to 'rule by the virtue of the CPC', which is essentially a euphemism for 'rule of party' (*dang zhi*), perhaps even leaving scope for a reversion to the 'rule of man' (*ren zhi*) (as in Mao Zedong's era). Indeed, the present generation of CPC leadership came into power in 2002 with some contradictions as to the meaning for China of 'rule of law'. Here, this uncertainty affects both the pace and clarity of land and real estate property law reform and this 'space' has played into some hands more than others, as the following section explains.

The power–wealth coalition

The third category of impediments relate to the so-called power–wealth coalition which has been developing in conjunction with China's economic growth over the past three decades (Hu 2011; Garrick 2011). Vested interest groups in the power–wealth coalition have grown out of a number of sources. China's popular media has frequently referred to corruption and 'illegal power rent' as elements of China's transition from a planned economy to a market economy. Deng legitimized this as 'groping for stones while China crosses the river' of market reform. Together, a centralized power structure and liberalized market have enhanced the possibility (and profitability) of transactions between power and wealth. The formation of such a power–wealth coalition has been accelerating during the last decade since both parties had consolidated their primitive accumulation of power or wealth. Although both allusive and elusive, the power–wealth coalition has become a feature of contemporary China and for some time regarded as a significant barrier to further reform of China's political, economic and legal structures (see Peerenboom 2011; Li Ling 2010: 196).

The power–wealth coalition is exclusive, protecting its elitist interests while its legitimacy is highly problematic and yet often relatively unchallenged. The nexus of wealth and power can be hidden. Members of the coalition may have high-level connections with access to both finance and decision-makers. Examples are now coming to public attention, and even China's media notes that some of the current CPC leaders are the offspring of the older generation of leaders.[6] This group includes Xi Jingping, the current National Vice President (and someone often touted as a potential successor to Hu Jintao as the CPC Secretary General and China's National President), Bo Xilai, the Party Secretary of the Chongqing Municipality, Wang Qishan, the Vice Premier, and Li Xiaopeng, the Vice Governor of the Shanxi Province, to name a few. They are referred to in China as *tai zi dang* (prince party or 'princelings') and are appointed to top political positions where they can guard their vested interests and those of their favoured connections. Under such political conditions it may not be so easy for China to deepen its law reforms on land and real estate property if the reforms risk impairing the interests of the most powerful and well connected.

Restrictions on foreign investment in real estate property

Foreign investors can obtain land use rights to establish foreign enterprises in China through either an allocation from the government, or a transfer in the land market. The common practice is that foreign investors pay certain allocation fees and a land use fee to the government, or cooperate with Chinese partners who own the land use rights. However, policies on foreign investment in real estate property have been very restrictive since 2006.

The 2006 reform package was developed as policy to tighten both management and finance in the real estate market. Both domestic and foreign investors were targeted. Intended to cool down a heated economy (as well as the real estate market) the restrictive tone lingers today with Premier Wen Jiabao (2010) reaffirming the government 'will rein in speculative housing purchases'. Aiming specifically at foreign investment, however, six ministerial departments including the Ministries of Construction, Commerce and the State Commission of Development and Reform co-issued the 'Opinion on Regulating the Entry and Management of Foreign Investment in Real Estate Market' (No. 171 Decree) in July 2006. The core theme of this Opinion was to apply an 'authorized system' and 'national treatment' to foreign investment in real estate market, and apply strict approval and registration (with true names) of real estate purchases by foreign bodies or individuals. Decree 171 sets restrictive policies on the ownership, capital structure and financing of real estate property by foreign investors in China, stipulating that foreign investors cannot invest in the Chinese real estate market by directly owning the property. First, they must register their businesses in China (or transact through a China-based investment agent). This blocks foreign investors from directly investing in Chinese real estate property in the form of equity investment. Second, only after having transferred all registered capital in the designated accounts and having obtained the state land use right certificate are foreign real estate developers eligible for bank loans. For a total foreign investment of more than US$3 million in the real estate market, the amount of registered capital for the development company should not be less than 50 per cent of the total investment.

The Opinion was followed by a series of other related policies and regulations restricting foreign investment in the real estate market. For instance, in July 2007 further restrictions to foreign investment in the real estate market were announced by the State Bureau of Foreign Exchange Management with the 'Notice on the List of the First Group of Foreign Invested Real Estate Projects Approved and Recorded in the Ministry of Commerce' (No. 130 Decree). An important issue for foreign investors was whether or not they were listed in this Notice, as it stipulates 'any foreign invested real estate company approved and recorded by the Ministry of Commerce or its delegated bodies *may not be registered to borrow foreign loan*'. This regulation means that new foreign-invested real estate companies can no longer access overseas loans to invest in the Chinese real estate market.

The Law refers to 'foreign real estate investment' as forms of Sino-foreign joint investment, Sino-foreign cooperation and foreign independent investment, and can, if approved, include investment in residential units, apartments and houses, as well as commercial properties such as hotels, resorts, offices, conference and exhibition centres, retail and theme parks. Foreign investment can include *development* of land sites. Compared to other (non-land or real estate) businesses in China, the registration requirements for foreign capital investment in real estate development are high. Foreign real estate companies cannot borrow from overseas, but they are allowed to borrow RMB within China. Foreign real estate enterprises need to be registered in the form of a 'project company' for any one specific real estate development project. To register a real estate project company, the foreign investor thus needs to have already obtained the land use right, ownership right of the real estate property on the land (or the land/property transaction agreement), signed by the foreign investor, the government land department and land developer/real estate property owner (and if loans are required these must be procured in China). Registration for foreigners has thus become significantly tougher since the 2006–7 reforms.

The registration process

Apart from foreign real estate investors, Chinese policies also restrict foreign *end users* with regard to purchasing real estate property, whether a foreign enterprise or an individual. It is stipulated in the No. 130 Decree that two types of foreign entities and individuals can purchase commodity housing for self use or living according to 'actual need': (1) the branches or representative agencies of overseas bodies can purchase a commodity office where they are registered; and (2) foreign individuals who have been working or living in China for more than one year can purchase one commodity unit per person. The registration and approval procedure is very strict. In order to purchase housing for non-self use or living purposes, the transaction must be made through a locally registered investment company. If a foreign company wants to transfer the profit from selling its housing in China to its home country, approval from the Chinese government must be obtained.

Foreign investment in the Chinese real estate market is thus very restricted when compared to the inverse situation of Chinese property investment in Western countries. A point of difference is that great profits have accrued in China's overheated property markets over the past 30 years and the government's recent policy initiatives have sought to protect Chinese national interests. As to whether this represents a retreat from market forms is debatable, but clearly there is an argument that it is. Foreign real estate developers have mostly come from areas with traditional ties to China such as Hong Kong, Singapore, Taiwan and Malaysia. Some are not 'authentic' foreign investors in that the developers might have originally come from China (later becoming overseas residents), and then returning to invest in their country of origin – as 'foreigners'. Alternatively, foreign funds may have originally been transferred from China to an overseas destination then reinvested in China as 'foreign' funds. Despite the restrictions mentioned above, many of these 'foreign' real estate investors had been 'localized' before the 2006–7 policies were promulgated. For investors from North America or Europe without traditional links with China, however, the Chinese real estate market is now very difficult to access. With foreign investment in real estate property accounting for only 3.8 per cent of the total real estate investment in China in 2004 (Shu 2008) and with tightened policies since that date, it can be stated that for foreign investors, the Chinese real estate market is not 'reformed and opened up'.

The policy paradoxes

For foreign investment, the restrictions on investing in Chinese real estate can be interpreted as policies that seek to address cyclical economic overheating rather than a stable legal or political mechanism designed to serve narrow local interests. The restrictive policies are linked to how the Chinese economy proceeds. If China's economy turns stagnant, for instance, these restrictive policies are very likely to be adjusted to stimulate market growth. What is more concerning for anyone wishing to invest in Chinese real estate property, foreign or domestic, are the paradoxes currently embedded in Chinese land and real estate property law outlined as follows.

The state/collective ownership of land

One paradox is the state/collective ownership of land and the transferability of land use rights in *the market*. As stated earlier, China does not have a land market but rather a land use right market. This is so as only land use rights within certain years can be transacted in the market, depending on the categories of land use. Current land occupiers do not actually *own* the lands, but rather the land use rights. Land occupiers rent the lands by paying land allocation fees and land use fees. The land use rights can be transferred in the primary land market involving transactions between the government and the land users and the secondary land market which, in turn, involves transactions between different land users. No matter how the land use right is transacted and who owns the land use right, land ownership remains with the state. The separation of land ownership and land use right is a fundamental legal problem in the Chinese land system. This problem is acknowledged by the government, but it has not yet been confronted. Since China's land reforms were commenced three decades ago, none of the land use right contracts have yet to expire. The day of reckoning on this point has not yet arrived. When it does, the questions of how to terminate or renew the land use right when terms expire will be sharpened and the answers are not yet legally defined. Confusion as to how to address the real estate property fixed on the land when the land use terms expire is related to the second policy paradox.

State ownership of land and private ownership of real estate property fixed on the land

The second paradox in the Chinese land system is the relationship between the state ownership of land and the private ownership of real estate property fixed on the land. A central theme of the Chinese housing reform over the past three decades has been 'privatization' and how far it should go. Most housing provision today is privatized and belongs in private ownership and can be transacted in the market. However, as I have pointed out above, housing owners do not actually 'own' the land where the property is fixed. They rent the land use right for a certain number of years. Again, the separation of ownership of the land and ownership of the real estate property on the land is legally problematic. For example, the land use right for residential land use is 70 years, but for a residential unit which is transacted in the 20th year, the new owner will only have a land use right for 50 years. Despite owning the residential unit they will argue they have been 'short-changed' by 20 years. The 2007 Property Law echoes the long-standing principle in the Chinese Constitution that land belongs to the state or collectives (Wong and Arkel 2007). It stipulates that the land use right for residential will automatically renew when the 70 year land use right term expires. But it leaves open the issue of land premiums for renewals (Howlett and Hong 2007). How, and in what circumstances, land use rights may be renewed remains uncertain.

The selective desire for foreign investment

The above paradoxes directly impact on foreign investment coming into China and create an additional paradox. China has welcomed foreign investment since the opening up policy began. But investment in Chinese real estate is a special case. It is less welcome in this case irrespective of propaganda to the contrary. Here it is necessary to differentiate foreign investments that originate in areas with traditional links to China such as Hong Kong, Taiwan and Singapore from investments that do not. It is the latter category of foreign investors who face restrictive barriers to Chinese land and property, and the paradox is this: China welcomes foreign investment, but not *this type* of investment. Yet business investment is, of course, often interconnected with land and real estate property. The net outcome of such a discriminatory policy is that although there is some foreign (non-Chinese) commercial investment in Chinese real estate property (including in the form of real estate investment trusts) they are set up as short-term investments that aim at profits going overseas. The discriminatory policy in this way backfires as longer-term, more stable investment is lost. Indeed, this category of foreigner has very good reasons for being cautious of holding and owning real estate property in China as either long-term lessees or end users.

Conclusion

The Chinese government faces a range of powerful influences upon it to effectively address the policy paradoxes outlined in this chapter. Some of the influences come from within the Party itself and centre on the changing, hybrid nature of CPC ideology (and the tensions accompanying hybridism). Some critical issues relate to the thousands of local government investment platforms that have gone into significant debt to appropriate land and fund property development; at the same time some individuals have become enormously wealthy from such developments in China. Some of these new rich are themselves princelings. Herein lies another dilemma for China: how best to promote good governance and a transparent rule of law with respect to the privatization of land and ownership transferability in the land market. The feasibility of privatizing Chinese land has been the subject of ongoing discussion among law-makers and academics, but its practical application has not been as straightforward as some may have hoped. A source of difficulty has been that privatization of land represents a fundamental contradiction for the CPC's ideological foundations. Land is pivotal to the public ownership system. Land privatization would signify the collapse of one of the CPC's ideological platforms upon which the current central government is based. The existence of this dilemma does not, however, exclude the possibility of land privatization in China. Like housing privatization and the constitutional recognition of private property ownership, these too were unimaginable just 30 years ago. Land privatization may be possible in the longer term. This perspective is supported by two arguments. First, all stakeholders in the Chinese political-economic sphere are aware of this problem and are seeking constructive solutions, with the principles of land privatization in focus. Second, the CPC has shown flexibility in adjusting its ideological doctrines. The market reforms are testimony to this and the CPC's continued legitimacy is now inextricably linked to its reform programme. Building a 'socialist market economy' could certainly include privatization of land with Chinese characteristics.

China has already made significant property law reforms in just three decades centred on the:

- privatization of housing and real estate property ownership, and
- transferability of real estate property and land use rights in the market.

Together these themes represent a giant step in liberalizing the Chinese land and real estate markets. From a starting position of a planned economy with Stalinist governance, China's law reforms on land and real estate property have been a catalyst for rapid economic growth, urban and social transformation. These law reforms are far from complete. As argued, fundamental paradoxes exist, but as the reforms proceed the core contradictions of privatization of land vs the public ownership system may yet be addressed. Privatization of land is likely to be required by an increasingly liberalized market economy. A return to a more Stalinist form of governance is almost unthinkable now. Nonetheless, privatization will not be an easy task for future Chinese land-law reformers. But there are strong grounds for optimism and such reform may well suit the purposes of the princelings.

Notes

1 The 'dual track' land system is also called 'plan' track and 'market' track. The 'plan' track is a legacy of the land system in practice from the 1950s to the 1980s. The 'market' track resulted from the marketization of land use rights for market purposes.
2 By the end of 2010 the People's Bank of China estimated these county- and municipal district-owned companies had accumulated debt of up to 14.4 trillion yuan (or 30 per cent of China's outstanding loans, i.e. 35 per cent of China's GDP) (cited in Garnaut 2011d).
3 Deng Xiaoping was dissatisfied with the stagnant economic growth in 1989–92 under the governance of the conservative central leaders after the Tiananmen Incident in 1989. Deng had a series of pro-reform talks on a tour in southern China provinces, which is collectively called the Southern Tour Talk, and triggered a new round of economic reform and growth in China.
4 The Tiananmen Square Incident refers to the pro-democracy movement in Beijing in the spring of 1989. It was triggered by the university students' protests in the streets

calling for government actions to address corruption and democratization, but resulted in the killing of some students by the army when the CPC felt its statehood was threatened.

5 Deng Xiaoping first proposed the concepts of 'generation of CPC leaders' that Mao Zedong headed the first generation, Deng Xiaoping headed the second generation, and Jiang Zeming headed the third generation. Following this logic of classifying leaders by generations, the current generation of CPC is the fourth, led by Hu Jintao. Each generation of CPC leaders came up with respective governing concepts or theories, as summarized by the propaganda mechanism, which are interrelated as well as distinctive (see Chan 2011).

6 The nepotism that the offspring of the ex-generation of CPC leaders came into power as top leaders is an impressive phenomenon in the current generation of CPC leaders since 2002. There are two explanations for this phenomenon. One is that they are in the right age group of 50s and 60s to become top leaders. It was realized by the vested interest groups that they should have representatives to safeguard their interests, mostly economic interests gained in the 1980s and 1990s, in the political sphere so as to establish a firm power–wealth coalition. See Garnaut (2010i).

6 The political economy of China's environmental law reforms

Feng Lin, Andrew Chan and Wilson Cheung

Introduction

This chapter overviews China's environmental law reforms in terms of how they connect to political economy generally and to Chinese communist ideology in particular. That they are connected there is no doubt. In fact, environmental law appears to be one area in which the nation and its leadership may be prepared to synchronize with international standards and set futuristic sustainability goals – for very good reasons. The alternatives may be rather bleak.

China's environmental law reforms seek to mitigate pollution and there will be cost implications for investment. Compliance implications for businesses and manufacturers, as well as the options of outsourcing and setting up subsidiary companies, are examined in light of the Chinese government's five-year plans, the current plan being for 2011–15. The chapter closes with a brief analysis of future and international implications. Before this, however, we examine the dominant discourses about environmental law as, until very recently, the environment has played 'second fiddle' to the master discourse of economic reform. But this is changing. It has now become alarmingly apparent that the dominance of economic discourse over the environment is dangerously unsustainable. This is not lost on China's leadership.

Discourses of environmental law

There are different discourses of the 'environment' including scientific, economic, political, aesthetic, moral and legal discourses, to cite the most obvious.[1] These different conceptions of the environment have led to the development of different discourses of environmental law. This section will discuss the two most dominant and interrelated environmental law discourses at the present time in China.

Discourse 1: Balancing economic growth with environmental protection

Kuhn (2010) observed that Chinese leaders tend to strive to characterize their time in power with a slogan that can be remembered as a milestone achievement – after (and possibly even during) their own lifetime. He cites Mao Zedong's 'Getting

China to stand-up', Deng Xiaoping's 'Opening China's Door', and Jiang Zemin's 'Modernizing China' as examples that were predominantly economically based. Hu Jintao currently espouses philosophies and policies summed up in the slogans: 'Harmonious Society', 'Putting People First' and the 'Scientific Perspective on Development'. The principles of these slogans chime with the Marxist paradigm of 'equitable societal development' as well as traditional Chinese values. President Hu's slogans represent an attempt to balance economic growth *and* environmental protection as a logical way to sustainable development in China. But there is another motive in that modernization and the open-door policies appear to have been too economically driven at the expense of ordinary citizens. Some policy changes have been required.

The Chinese discourse of 'scientific perspective on development' is intended to help stakeholders and actors focus on what the government considers important issues for environmental protection, overcoming pollution problems and achieving sustainable development. This discourse has been central to environmental policy as reflected in the 11th Five-Year Plan (2006–10). This powerful and legitimizing discourse retains its status in the 12th Five-Year Plan (2011–15) as we shall see below. As most members of the current Chinese politburo have engineering backgrounds it is hardly surprising they are keen to establish measurable targets for holding stakeholders accountable and to track compliance and implementation.

At the same time quantifiable targets are made transparent to other industrialized countries and international agencies. Suitably publicized and visible gestures seem to highlight the nation's determination for China to be a world leader on environmental protection in the future. This discourse is not cosmetic or merely propaganda. Since the Copenhagen climate change conference of 2009, for instance, China has committed to lower its carbon dioxide emissions per unit of GDP by 40 per cent to 45 per cent by 2015 compared to the 2005 level (Susskind 2010: 16). Some may argue, however, that such promises are cheap and that enforcing them will be the true test of their merit as the targets are voluntary.

In balancing economic growth and environmental protection there are some challenging dilemmas ahead. As China seeks to promote internal consumption, to help move away from relying on its export strengths, there are immediate environmental consequences. The manufacture and use of motor vehicles is but one example. With 22 per cent of the world's population, the promotion of car use will have a range of negative environmental consequences. At present the 'balancing' discourse seems to conveniently slip over the surface of such potentially irreconcilable issues.

Discourse 2: Moving from fossil fuel dependency to sustainable new technology

As China relies so heavily on industrial production growth as a driving force of the economy it may also be argued that her environmental goals are more challenging than some other countries. Here it is coal usage that is a significant problem. Coal burning is a main cause of global CO_2 emissions and is still the main fuel for China's electricity. To offset this, China has agreed in the 2009 Copenhagen Accord to 'increase the share of non-fossil fuels in primary energy consumption to around 15 per cent by 2020 compared to 2005 levels and to increase forest coverage by 40 million hectares and forest stock volume [also by 2020]' (Susskind 2010: 16). Again the targets are voluntary. But the emerging power discourse is clear: modern state-of-the-art energy efficiency and pollution control technologies and equipment are being strongly encouraged. Perhaps this 'encouragement' will help promote the next wave of FDI and indeed influence China's outward bound investment strategy.

Recent rapid industrial growth in China was built significantly on the exploitation of cheap labour resources from rural areas.[2] Although perceived to be necessary in controlling China's vast population the Household Registration System has been criticized in recent times for contributing to the exploitation of some rural and migrant workers with benefits far less than those of city workers (see Kay-Wah Chan 2011). The high rate of growth of industrial factories also brought environmental problems emanating from industrial waste and other pollutants. For instance, there is a serious problem with water pollution. More than 70 per cent of rivers and lakes in China are now heavily polluted (Ansfield and Bradsher 2010). There are also limited long-term plans for garbage disposal in many of China's industrial cities. Indeed, water pollution and solid waste disposal are issues that are now directly impacting on the rural environment as well the urban. As a result the emerging power discourse is about sustainable development *and* social stability. The Chinese government knows that it faces discontent and it is determined to crush this in its promotion of the 'harmonious society'. But ordinary Chinese citizens are not easily duped and both sewage water processing plants and solid waste disposal facilities are being encouraged, with new technology projects now touting for domestic and foreign direct investment.

These powerful and emerging environmental discourses underpin some of the national legislative initiatives currently being promulgated in China to curb 'dirty' industries and polluters. The following overview is of course not exhaustive as this would require much more space than is available here. We highlight key illustrations of China's environmental laws and policy directions to analyse where these may lead and what is foreseeable in the interim period until new 'clean' technologies become more accessible and affordable.

China's environmental protection framework

China's environmental legal framework does not take a unified approach in legislative form such as in New Zealand where its *Natural Resources Act* has consolidated all environmental legislation. Rather, it is an integration of different kinds of special statutes and regulations at local and national levels, as well as some treaty obligations at international level. Articles 9, 10, 22 and 26 of the Chinese Constitution (1982) are the sources of Chinese environmental legislation, of which Article 26 is especially important, stating that: 'the state must protect and improve the living environment and the ecological environment and prevents and controls pollution and other public hazards. The state organizes and encourages aforestation and the protection of forests.'[3]

The first specific environmental law in China, the *Environmental Protection Law* (EPL), was adopted in 1979 as a trial and subsequently passed in 1989. The EPL elaborates principles rather than detailed rules on pollution prevention and control – including the 'polluter pays' principle. This law dictates the direction of national environmental policy. Since it was adopted there have been nine laws on environmental protection,[4] 15 laws on protection of natural resources,[5] 50 State Council administrative regulations, and more than 600 environmental rules or regulations under the supervision of different ministries and local governments.[6] Laws and regulations related to FDI also touch on environmental issues including the *Law on Foreign Capital Enterprises, Law on Chinese–Foreign Contractual Joint Ventures, Foreign Economy Contract Law, Foreign Trade Law, Interim Provisions for the Guidance of Foreign Businessmen in their Orientation of Investment* and a guiding list of Industries for Investment by Foreign Businessmen. There are also many local regulations concerning the coordination of environmental protection and utilization of foreign capital.[7]

In addition to domestic environmental legislation, China has also entered into more than 50 international legal agreements for environmental protection and around 26 bilateral environmental protection agreements.[8] China has actively participated in several UN Conferences on Environment and Development at Rio, Johannesburg and Copenhagen. Apart from endorsing the Rio Declaration, China was one of the first countries to sign the two Framework Conventions on Climate Change and Bio-diversity. China has also signed and ratified the Kyoto Protocol (2005)[9] for the implementation of the Framework Convention on Climate Change. At the contentious Copenhagen Summit, China also contributed to the conclusion of the Copenhagen Accord (2009).[10]

As such, China's environmental law framework is multi-dimensional, covering the local to the global. Indeed, landmark shifts are occurring in China characterized by a move away from local administrative regulation to comprehensive national legislation, participation in international agreements, adoption of trade practices (including modern process management methods), environmental policies (including 'corporate social responsibility' initiatives) and other hybrid legal-economic administrative measures such as a carbon tax and mandatory green insurance for some industries. We next turn our attention to these initiatives with a view to interpreting what they may mean when taken collectively.

Landmark environmental protection legislation and policy reform

International agreements

China's ratification of the Kyoto Protocol was a landmark decision of the Chinese government. Under this agreement, Parties in Annex I (developed countries) agreed to adopt measures to reduce greenhouse gas (GHG) emission by an average of 5 per cent below 1990 levels in the period 2008–12.[11] As China is a signatory with 'developing' status it is not obliged to compulsorily reduce its GHG emissions before 2012. In fact, it has been commonly expressed in popular media that China is the country which has benefited most from the Kyoto Protocol.[12] However, as mentioned earlier, China agreed to the 2009 Copenhagen Accord, committing to 'lower its CO_2 emissions by 40–45 per cent by 2020 compared to 2005 levels'. In so doing, China shows a willingness to engage with the global community on matters of environmental significance and indeed take a leadership role. At the same time Copenhagen has many critics who describe it as 'a fiasco, a disaster and a debacle' (Susskind 2010: 18) on the grounds that the dire consequences of global warming and environmental degradation demanded a stronger, binding international protocol to adequately follow up the groundwork of over a decade ago in Kyoto. That China (and India) agreed to the Copenhagen Accord is, however, encouraging and significant because the Copenhagen Accord has implicitly incorporated the principle of polluter-pays (see Lin and Buhi 2009). Though China is still a developing country, it is the second largest economy in the world and still rapidly evolving under 'market socialism'. Without the participation of the largest developing countries such as China and India, it would be fair to say that any effort to reduce the total amount of GHG emissions in the world would be fruitless. It is therefore imperative that developed and developing countries now work together rather than pointing accusatory fingers at each other.

Trade practice and process management

China has also made significant changes to her international trade practices. For instance, previously there had been a legislative trend to focus environmental responsibility for polluting factories onto 'finished goods producers'. These finished goods producers can be final assembling factories *or* distributors along the supply chain. This approach contrasted with that of the European Union (EU) which puts responsibility directly onto 'producers' to identify all environment-related data *along* the supply chain. Under the 'Energy-using Product Directive' (EuP) of the EU, companies have to report total energy used during a product's lifecycle, including the energy used during manufacturing and transportation. China has moved in this direction with the *Clean Production Promotion Law* (CPPL, enacted in 2002). This law has introduced the concept of producer responsibility and life-cycle approach for both resource use and waste management.[13] Other examples of new laws include the *Prevention of Environmental Pollution by Solid Wastes* (enacted in 1995, amended in 2004 and effective from 1 April 2005) and the *Law on Recycling Economy and Methods on Management of Urban Garbage* (enacted in 2008 and effective from 1 January 2009).

These reforms illustrate that traditional thinking about the control of sources of pollution has given way to a more proactive approach characterized by participation in international forums, endorsement of international agreements on environmental issues and adoption of certain European trade practices. To give effect to this proactive approach, a range of policy initiatives has been enacted and we highlight pivotal initiatives as follows.

Environmental policies

The State Council adopted in 2005 the 'Decision on Strengthening Environmental Protection by Implementing Scientific Development' (the Decision). This places 'environmental protection' more strategically, maintaining it as a basic state policy. With regard to the guiding principles, the Decision states that environmental problems should be resolved in the 'development process', a fundamental change from the traditional approach of 'pollution first, cleaning later, and destroying while cleaning'. The Decision made it clear that China will follow the principles of harmonious/sustainable development and rule of law in environmental protection. One specific mechanism to achieve harmonious/sustainable development is the use of total quantity control of pollutants in addition to an emission permit system. The Decision also emphasizes a reliance on science and technology, not only to develop new mechanisms to resolve environmental problems, but to develop a resource-saving and environment-friendly society.[14] The Decision further states the necessity to promote cleaner production (including related examination and verification), prevent pollution, and control the whole process of production (process management), renewable energy and circular (sustainable) economy.

The implementation of the Decision policies has been facilitated by the introduction of the 'corporate social responsibility' discourse backed up by incentives, environmental issues disclosure requirements, and a public supervision system. In December 2007, the SASAC issued 'Guidelines on Fulfilling Social Responsibilities for State-Owned Enterprises' (the Guidelines).[15] The purpose of issuing the Guidelines was to achieve 'comprehensively harmonious and sustainable development among enterprises, society and environment'. One specific corporate social responsibility in the Guidelines is for SOEs to be 'role models' in saving resources and environmental protection through reducing pollution, saving energy, adopting recycling measures, increasing investment in environmental protection, clean production and so on. Such responsibilities are in line with the discourse of balancing the growth of enterprises with social benefit and environmental protection.[16]

The government followed in July 2006 with the 'Restriction of Hazardous Substances Directive' (RoHS). This imposed restrictions on the use of certain hazardous substances in electrical and electronic equipment – for all electrical products entering into the EU market. The 'Registration, Evaluation and Authorization of Chemicals Directive' (REACH) was also put into effect whereby manufacturers are required to manage the risks from chemicals by providing *safety information* on the chemicals used to downstream users (again, in the EU).[17] The US has similar requirements to the EU.

Taken together this set of policy initiatives have clearly been driven by international demands that China, as the biggest manufacturing partner of Western countries, needs to cope with more stringent laws related to the *full life-cycle* of products in manufacturing, distribution and, where possible, recycling and waste management.

'Green credit policy', green securities, and licences

Green credit policy is a new policy introduced jointly by the State Environmental Protection Agency (SEPA), (the name has been changed to the Ministry of Environment, MoE), the Chinese Bank Regulatory Commission (CBRC) and the People's Bank of China (PBOC) since July 2007.[18] The purpose of this policy is to limit the expansion of high energy consumption projects and promote energy saving and emissions reduction projects. Under the new policy, all commercial banks need to review the environmental performance of borrowing companies as part of the credit risk management and lending criteria. Relevant environmental protection bureaux are required to provide the banks with information on compliance with environmental laws by the borrowing companies. Up to 2010, more than 40,000 pieces of such information have been provided to banks.[19] This new policy has linked banks with environmental protection bureaux and enabled banks to play an important role in achieving sustainable development.

The 'Green Securities' policy has also been introduced since February 2008 whereby environmental audits have become a prerequisite for IPO or refinancing for heavily polluting industries. A securities requirement is for disclosure of environmental risk information for all listed companies.

Furthermore, in October 2007 SEPA agreed with the Ministry of Commerce (MOFCOM) that export quotas and licences should not be granted to enterprises that violate environmental law.[20] This includes violating China's rules on carbon emissions.

It is clear from the above discussion that a series of new policies have been introduced in recent years by SEPA/MoE, together with other governmental organs at the central level. These policies aim to implement a comprehensive approach to environmental pollution prevention and control. Indeed, 'environmental performance' has become an essential criterion for any approval by governmental departments. Further, financial mechanisms and market means have also been introduced to supplement enforcement by the MoE.

CO_2 emissions and carbon taxes

To cope with the challenges of controlling the total quantity of polluting emissions, SEPA, starting from 2001, began to experiment with an emissions trading system (ETS) in various provinces and municipalities. Since 2007, the ETS has been expanded throughout mainland China and more local legislation has been enacted and various trading markets established in Beijing, Zhejiang, Wuhan and Shanghai for the trading of sulphur dioxide (SO_2) emission permits.[21]

The idea for trading carbon emission permits came from the Clean Development Mechanism (CDM) introduced by the Kyoto Protocol and trading has mainly been conducted between Chinese enterprises and purchasers from developed countries.[22] The Chinese government, with the assistance of the UNDP, established the first trading market for CO_2 in Beijing in 2008. Three similar markets have subsequently been established in Tianjin, Shanghai and Shenzhen and more provinces intend to establish such markets. But as yet there hasn't been much trading at all. The Beijing trading market had only one trading around the time of the first anniversary of its establishment.[23]

At a policy level, the Commission for Economic Development and Reform (CEDR) proposed in 2009 that China should further explore carbon emission trading. After China's Copenhagen commitments, the issue of establishing a carbon trading market was formally brought onto the agenda of the central government. This was because China faces the pressure of reducing its carbon emissions in order to fulfil its commitments. By 2010, a bill was introduced during the annual meeting of the National People's Congress (NPC) and the National People's Political Consultative Committee (NPPCC) to establish China's own carbon trading market.[24] It has also been proposed that China should establish its own carbon trading system for internal trading to promote carbon emission reduction within China, especially to encourage exchanges between CDM of east coast factories with environmental projects in the west. Premier Wen Jiabao has further declared that China will not only establish a chain of industries characterized by low carbon emissions, but also cultivate a 'consumption mode' based on low carbon emissions.[25]

The 12th Five-Year Plan makes it clear that China will reduce the intensity of its carbon emissions and promote low carbon technology[26] and, more specifically, will make substantial reductions in resource-consumption and carbon emission intensity compulsory targets so as to effectively control GHG emissions and gradually establish a carbon emissions trading market.[27] It is therefore clear at policy level that China is committed to reducing carbon emissions.

On the other hand, it should also be noted that China's commitment is to the reduction of *the intensity of carbon emission* per GDP, not to the reduction of total quantity of carbon emission. That position has been consistent. Since the most fundamental element of a successful ETS is the overall emission cap, a comparative study of the US emission trading system and the EU system has proven that without a firm emission cap the ETS is hardly likely to succeed (Lin and Buhi 2009: 150–3). Caution about the future of carbon emission trading in China is therefore justified.

The introduction of an environmental protection tax (carbon tax) and comprehensive reform of resources tax is another key policy initiative identified in the Proposal for the 12th Five-Year Plan. Essentially, a carbon tax is a tax based on the consumption of carbon through an internal allocation system. Another approach, however, could be to replace certain types of resource taxes with a carbon tax, thus shifting the focus of tax levying from the 'upstream' exploiting of fossil fuel resources to basing the levy on the carbon content used at any point along the supply chain. Whatever mechanisms are used, the government appears to view a carbon tax as an important source of taxation and a direct investment in environmental protection projects. This in part may be required to fund structural changes to the industrial sectors.[28] Industrial restructuring is expected to be aggressively pursued by the government following Wen Jiabao's recent announcement that energy-inefficient factories will be closed and the growth of high energy consumption industries restrained 'to achieve the political objective of energy consumption reduction'.[29]

Pollution liability insurance

Pollution liability insurance (PLI) is another market-related policy to resolve environmental issues. The idea is that insurance companies can effectively pool individual risks, fairly allocate premium costs to potential polluters, and have the financial capacity to pay for any potentially huge clean-up cost after an environmental disaster. In a recent circular from the China Insurance Regulatory Commission (CIRC), the Chinese government recognized the importance of PLI in environmental risk management to cope with the ever increasing pressure of controlling pollution in the fast growing economy. The MoE now intends to encourage third-party risk prevention and regulate consultants to direct the development of PLI on a risk management approach rather than a liability insurance product that is based on an actuarial compensation mechanism. There are two groups of authorized third-party environmental consultants. The first focuses on environmental risk management and risk identification and advice; the second focuses on quantifying environmental losses and damages. How far the reports of environmental supervisory authorities will go remains a moot point.

In December 2007, the SEPA (now MoE) and the CIRC jointly issued the *Guidelines on the Development of Pollution Liability Insurance*.[30] This states that PLI will be promoted in pilot cities and provinces including Hunan, Hubei and Jiangsu and at the major cities of Ningbo, Shenyang, Shanghai, Chongqing, Shenzhen and Kunming. This is to promote the market mechanism in conjunction with the government compensating victims in environmental pollution cases.[31] By the end of 2010, nine provinces had established PLI on a trial basis; however, the development of PLI in all pilot cities is low because of some negative responses from the relevant enterprises (ibid.). Nonetheless, officials from the MoE disclosed at a conference at the end of 2010 in Beijing that PLI is likely to be expanded throughout China during the 12th Five-Year Plan period and the relevant national legislation has already been drafted.[32] Of interest is that one of the trial cities, Wuxi (Jiangsu Province), adopted its own local legislation on PLI.[33] This provided the legal basis for the local Environmental Protection Department (EPD) to promote and enforce PLI. The objective is to embed a pollution liability system and promote it nationwide by 2015. But the benefits of environmental risk management through an insurance mechanism remain to be evaluated.

FDI options and preferences

China's environmental legal and policy frameworks directly impact on FDI and the Chinese government has divided foreign investment projects into four categories: 'Encouraged', 'Permitted', 'Restricted' and 'Prohibited'. Environmental friendliness is one of the criteria used to classify FDI projects.

The 'Encouraged' category includes new technology or new equipment projects that can make best use of resources and, in particular, renewable resources for the prevention and control of pollutants. China usually exempts customs duty and Value Added Tax (VAT) on most of the imported machinery or equipment (see Garrick's Chapter 9 in this volume) and this category is consistent with the discourse of *moving from fossil fuel dependency to sustainable new technology*.

China restricts foreign investment in relation to the exploration and mining of rare and precious mineral resources (and other projects which may prejudice the environment or cause pollution). Importing solid waste capable of use as raw material is also restricted. Besides, China demands that technology introduced from abroad must be advanced technology favourable to environmental protection. The State prohibits projects that may cause environmental pollution or damage natural resources or the health of the people. China prohibits foreign businessmen from employing technology and equipment that may seriously pollute the environment. Furthermore it is prohibited for solid waste coming from outside Chinese territory to be dumped, piled or disposed of in Chinese territory; importing solid waste incapable of use as raw material is also banned and violation of these rules carries criminal liability.

Projects of foreign investment except the above three categories are permitted. At the same time, such projects are required to conform to the regulations that they shall cause no (or little) pollution (Qin 2009).[34] Question marks remain, however, about the regulatory authorities' power and abilities to enforce the requirements of each category and concerns remain about corrupt connections between local government officials and big business (see Ho's Chapter 12 in this volume). It is thus worth a brief excursion into how the government enforces environmental law in China before we return to consider the landmark legislation that will take China into the future.

Supervision and enforcement measures and their effect

There is a range of administrative supervision and enforcement measures available through various environmental legislation. This section will first outline key ones and evaluate their effectiveness before discussing the enforcement of environmental law in China. A case study is provided.

The supervision and enforcement measures

The first important measure is environmental impact assessment (EIA), which has been available for a long time in China and was standardized by the enactment of a national law on EIA in 2002.[35] Both domestic and foreign investors must submit an Environment Impact Statement with full documentation explaining environment protection in the preliminary design of the construction project. Upon completion of the project, the developer must also submit a report on inspecting and accepting the completed environmental protection facilities.

The second is called 'Three-Simultaneity', meaning that the pollution prevention and control facilities of an enterprise must be designed, built and put into operation simultaneously with the principal part of any projects of an enterprise.[36] Only after satisfactory inspection can an enterprise start its production.

The first two measures focus on the environmental requirements at the *pre-operation* stage of an enterprise. Their objective is to prevent environmental problems at the source. The MoE and its local bureaux have strengthened enforcement of these two measures and the MoE has conducted a national inspection of the enforcement of the EIA Law for two consecutive years – 2009 and 2010. Furthermore, all information concerning application for approval of EIA reports at national level are available on the website of the MoE.[37] In January 2011, the MoE decided to defer the approval of one EIA report from Sichuan and refused to approve another EIA report from Xinjiang Uighur Autonomous Region, indicating the EIA is being taken seriously. However, every now and then news is reported of enterprises operating without complying with the EIA and the Three-Simultaneity requirement.

The third measure is the establishment of various environmental standards. Up to 1996, China had established 347 national environmental standards and 28 industrial sector environmental standards that must all be adhered to and are categorized in this way: (a) ambient environmental quality standards; (b) pollutant discharge standards; (c) monitoring methodology standards, environmental specimen-taking standards; and (d) basic scientific standards.

The fourth measure is the 'Discharge Permit' requirement.[38] Enterprises discharging pollutant(s) must, within a set time, hold the pollutant discharge declaration and registration forms approved by the local department of environment pollution administration and apply for a Discharge Permit. Enterprises with 'Temporary Discharge Permits' are required to reduce their discharge quantity within the set time. An enterprise cannot discharge pollutants without a discharge permit without incurring a penalty.[39]

The fifth measure is the requirement to pay a 'pollutant discharge fee' (ibid.). Various pieces of Chinese environmental legislation have incorporated the 'polluter-pays principle', and empowered environmental protection bureaux to levy pollutant discharge fees on enterprises (with domestic and/or foreign investment) which discharge pollutant(s). However, the payment of such fees does not exempt such enterprises from having to control pollution or compensate for damages caused, or from fulfilling other responsibilities as prescribed by the law.

The third, fourth and fifth measures target the *operation* of an enterprise. If an enterprise can meet all three requirements, environmental problems at the operational stage of an enterprise should be under control. If, however, an enterprise fails to meet any of these three measures, a sixth measure is needed to identify the problem: 'on-site inspection'. The environmental protection bureaux are empowered to make on-site inspections of enterprises which must report all relevant facts and provide all necessary information. The MoE and environmental protection bureaux at local level have the power to conduct annual inspections. In practice, however, through the shortage of appropriately trained staff, local environmental protection bureaux tend to conduct on-site inspections on a selective basis, or upon a report coming from a third party.

The strategy also includes 'emergency measures'. Any enterprise whose activities have resulted in any accident or other emergency must promptly take emergency measures to: (a) control and contain the pollution hazards; (b) make the situation known to inhabitants who are likely to be endangered by such hazards; (c) report the case to the competent Department of Environmental Protection administration concerned, and (d) accept their investigation and decision. Once an environmental disaster happens, the pollution is often beyond the control of any one enterprise.

This tough enforcement regime described above does not distinguish between different categories of enterprises. Where enforcement becomes intriguing is where powerful, strategic SOEs are involved. Some SOEs have been heavy polluters and to an extent this has been tolerated during China's modernization period and opening up policy. Some concessions are required, for example, for China's coal-fired power stations and iron and aluminium smelters. Heavy industry has been built on fossil fuels. Nuclear waste and disposal of other toxic wastes also remain problematic issues.[40]

Although there are comprehensive pollution prevention laws and administrative measures (identified below), their execution has met with questionable success. Before 2000 there was a lack of discretionary and monitoring power in the hands of local environmental officers at local government level. Arguably there has been improvement since then. At the same time the interests of local economic growth often conflict with environmental protection goals. Environmental protection has not been a top priority for many local officials.[41]

A case study of enforcement

With regard to the enforcement of environmental law, every unit within the MoE has a role to play. For example, the EIA Department will enforce the EIA Law at a national level, the Pollution Prevention and Control Department will enforce various kinds of pollution (air, water, solid waste and noise) prevention and control laws, and so on. There is also a special Department of Monitoring and Supervision. That Department has a particularly important role to play in monitoring national and cross-regional environmental problems or environmental pollution disputes that are deemed 'significant'. It is responsible for organizing nationwide inspection of the enforcement of *all* national environmental laws, and is in charge of administering penalties imposed by the MoE.

In July 2010, the MoE announced the first batch of environmental cases which make clear that it will properly investigate (polluters) and final results will be reached.[42] The MoE announcement said it had conducted on-site inspections of 461 pulp and paper mills located in 53 cities of 14 provinces and autonomous regions and found that 21 per cent of those enterprises had violated certain kinds of environmental legislation. Five cities were particularly problematic and more than 50 per cent of enterprises in four out of the five cities violated certain kinds of environmental legislation (ibid.). In the fifth city, though, there are less than 50 per cent of its relevant enterprises violating environmental legislation; four enterprises there either stopped the operation of their pollution prevention and control facilities or discharged polluted water without any processing.

The MoE decided not to approve any EIA reports for similar new plants or renovation of existing plants in those five cities. In the other cities inspected, the MoE found that nine enterprises were in serious violation of environmental legislation. They had either stopped the operation of pollution prevention and control facilities without permission, or did not normally run their own pollution prevention and control facilities, in violation of the EIA/Three-Simultaneity requirement, or discharged waste water in excess of discharge standards. The MoE has set out in detail its findings of violation of the relevant environmental legislation and specific decisions on what those enterprises need to do in order to address their environmental problems, as well as penalties imposed on them. Furthermore, the MoE has requested the relevant local environmental protection bureaux at provincial/autonomous regional and municipal levels to follow up these cases to make sure that they are compliant with the relevant environmental legislation (ibid.).

This reporting is of the first and most recent national law enforcement action taken by the MoE on such a scale and method. The MoE brief is clearly to take enforcement of environmental law seriously – especially with regard to the heavy polluting pulp and paper mills. Once those enterprises have been on the MoE 'blacklist' they become negative examples. The MoE is then charged with ensuring that those enterprises become compliant with the relevant environmental legislation within a specific period of time. Otherwise they can be closed down, potentially prohibited from resuming operations (ibid.).

This national enforcement action has, at the same time, revealed several serious defects relating to enforcement of environmental law in China. First, failure to comply with environmental law seems to be quite normal as 21 per cent of 461 enterprises inspected had violated certain environmental laws to varying degrees (ibid.). That may not surprise those familiar with China; there is still a long way to go before environmental law can be satisfactorily enforced. As far as enterprises are concerned, the balance between economic development and environmental protection still favours the former. Second, out of the 14 enterprises named in the Announcement by the MoE, only three have been ordered to stop production. The remaining 11 have been allowed to continue production with a time limit set for resolving their environmental problems. This indicates a degree of discretion may be exercised by the MoE as in these cases it has not vigorously enforced relevant environmental laws to the extent that it could have.[43] Further research into the triggers of the use (or otherwise) of this discretion may be helpful.

Conclusion

Several conclusions can be drawn about China's environmental law reforms at different levels. At the national legislative level China has since 1989 progressively enacted a broad suite of environmental laws governing pollution prevention and control. This national framework is characterized by a range of new legislation promoting local incentives and disincentives to control sources of pollution and encourage the development of new 'cleaner' technologies. China has also engaged internationally through various international agreements, protocols and accords.

Through her intricate environmental protection framework China has set herself challenging and quantifiable goals to 2020. These autonomous domestic mitigation actions are essentially voluntary in nature and thus enforcement is a key issue that will shape both market-based and government actions that emerge.

At another level of analysis, it is clear that there are several intersecting power discourses relating to the environment. We have identified two central discourses in this chapter which serve the government by legitimizing actions taken in the name of 'environmental protection'. We note, however, that in several instances there are virtually irreconcilable differences between the requirements of economic growth on the one hand, and environmental protection on the other hand. The balance appears still tipped in favour of economic growth. At the same time there are overt attempts by the government to increase consumerism in China to reduce dependency on its export-led economic model and this creates unprecedented burdens on China's environment. One of these burdens is the question of where toxic waste is to go in the future, and this will surely become increasingly contested.

The range of initiatives we have highlighted clearly provides some hope. There is hope in the form of new policies to promote technologies that will decrease dependencies on fossil fuels; there is hope that the citizenry is becoming better educated and more informed about environmental issues; and there is hope that a greater, more sustainable balance can be struck between economic growth and environmental needs. While some lawyers and business leaders not entirely helpfully describe the aspirational statements coming from China through international accords such as Copenhagen as being 'soft', in due course they might become hard law or legally binding obligations. Looking back over the past 60 years there can be no doubt that China today is taking environmental protection more seriously than ever before. Hopefully it is not too late.

Notes

1 'A discourse establishes meanings, confirms relations between actors and other entities, sets the boundaries for what is legitimate knowledge, and generates what is accepted as common sense' (Dryzek 2007: 46).
2 See for instance Hurst (2009); and Gallagher (2005, 2009).
3 This is based on the broad concept of environmental law which includes both preservation of natural and human resources as well as prevention and control of pollution. Historically, China has had a narrow understanding of environmental law and paragraph 3 of Article 11 of the 1978 Constitution provided for the first time that 'the state protects environment and natural resources, prevents and controls pollution and other public hazards'.
4 They include, *inter alia*, the *Marine Environment Protection Law of the PRC* (1999) at: www.fdi.gov.cn/pub/FDI_EN/Laws/law_en_info.jsp?docid=50970; *Law of the PRC on Prevention of Environmental Pollution Caused by Solid Waste* at: www.fdi.gov.cn/pub/FDI_EN/Laws/law_en_info.jsp?docid=50961; *Law of the PRC on Desert Prevention and Transformation* at: www.fdi.gov.cn/pub/FDI_EN/Laws/law_en_info.jsp?docid=50964; *Law of the PRC on Water and Soil Conservation* at: www.fdi.gov.cn/pub/FDI_EN/Laws/law_en_info.jsp?docid=50915; *Law of the PRC on the Prevention and Control of Environmental Noise Pollution* at: www.fdi.gov.cn/pub/FDI_EN/Laws/law_en_info.jsp?docid=50986; *Law of the PRC on the Prevention and Control of Atmospheric Pollution* at: www.fdi.gov.cn/pub/FDI_EN/Laws/law_en_info.jsp?docid=50974.

5 For instance, the *Forest Law of the PRC* at: www.fdi.gov.cn/pub/FDI_EN/Laws/law_en_info.jsp?docid=50875; *Land Administration Law of the PRC* at: www.fdi.gov.cn/pub/FDI_EN/Laws/law_en_info.jsp?docid=52290.
6 Some of the more prominent laws include, for instance: the *Marine Environmental Protection Law, Law on Prevention and Control of Solid Waste Pollution to the Environment, Interim Provisions Governing the Environment in Economy Open to Outside Region, Interim Provisions Governing the Environmental Protection Related to Imported Wastes and Supplementary Provisions*.
7 For instance: the Regulation of Shanghai Municipality for Environmental Protection, Regulation of Sichuan Province on Encouraged Foreign Investment Provisions of Xiamen Special Economic Zone on Introduction of Technology, Regulation of Ningbo Economic and Technological Development Zone, and so on.
8 For details refer to the MoE website at: http://gjs.mep.gov.cn/gjhjhz/.
9 China's ratification of the Kyoto Protocol has a range of legal and environmental implications, one being that as a 'developing nation' it can take advantage of Article 12 of the Protocol which permits developed nations to set up 'clean development projects' in developing countries and gain certified emissions reduction units towards emissions targets. One of the advantages for China is the gaining of new technology for renewable energy projects and pollution-reducing technology (Blazey and Govind 2008: 447).
10 For detailed discussion of the negotiation at Copenhagen and the bilateral diplomacy between China and the US, see Lin and Buhi (2009).
11 United Nations Framework Convention on Climate Change (UNFCCC) (2007) at: unfccc.int/Kyotoprotocol/background.
12 For instance, it has been reported that China has obtained 73 per cent of carbon credit under the Kyoto Protocol; see: www.rmloho.com/user7/51370/index.html (accessed 8 February 2011).
13 See Xinhua (2006). Also see *Clean Production Promotion Law* at: www.fdi.gov.cn/pub/FDI_EN/Laws/law_en_info.jsp?docid=50880 See *Law of the PRC on Prevention of Environmental Pollution Caused by Solid Waste*, at: www.fdi.gov.cn/pub/FDI_EN/Laws/law_en_info.jsp?docid=50961. See: *Circular Economy Promotion Law of the PRC* at: www.fdi.gov.cn/pub/FDI_EN/Laws/law_en_info.jsp?docid=97504; also see *Law on Recycling Economy and Methods on Management of Urban Garbage*.
14 See Xinhua (2006). Also see www.gov.cn/zwgk/2005-12/13/content_125680.htm. (NB: This is a Chinese government website that publishes all the State Council's decisions and orders; it does not, however, provide English versions.)
15 The purpose of these guidelines is stated in the first paragraph: 'to earnestly fulfill corporate social responsibilities (CSR), so as to realize coordinated and sustainable development of enterprises, society and environment in all respects': www.sasac.gov.cn/n2963340/n2964712/4891623.html.
16 Section 11 of the SASAC Guidelines is specific about SOE responsibilities and leadership in energy saving and emission reduction:

> the enterprises have to upgrade their technology and equipment, and engage in the recycling economy, so as to develop energy-conserving products and improve resource utilization efficiency. What is more, they should invest more in environmental protection, rationalize production procedures, try to decrease polluting emissions with the targets of lower energy consumption and less pollution but higher production efficiency and output.
> (www.sasac.gov.cn/n2963340/n2964712/4891623.html)

17 All hazardous substances identified as persistent, bio-accumulative or toxic have to be registered before sale in the EU. Another important EU Directive is the 'Waste Electrical Electronic Equipment Directive' (WEEE) whereby all producers who may be importers or manufacturers shall provide mandatory collection, dismantling and disposal measures for their products sold in the EU. The manufacturers or importers are required to either deposit the required funding, based on their trade volume, or arrange an

appropriate financial guarantee from banks or insurance companies for their commitment to recycle the electrical and electronic wastes of their used products.

18 The Opinions on Prevention of Credit Risks through Implementation of Environmental Protection Policies and Laws was jointly issued on 30 July 2007, see: 《关于落实环境保护政策法规防范信贷风险的意见》: http://websearch.mep.gov.cn/info/gw/huanfa/200707/t20070718_106850.htm (NB. This is the public website of Ministry of Environmental Protection of PRC but no English version is attached).

19 See: 四万条执法处罚信息纳入银行征信系统. www.legaldaily.com.cn/index_article/content/2010-12/10/content_2391569.htm?node=5955. (The Ministry of Environmental Protection of the PRC published the first 'Green Securities' report comprising some 40,000 pieces of information on penalties for banks, and initially released in legaldaily.com.cn on 10 December 2010.)

20 MOFCOM has also revised the 'Catalogue for Guiding Foreign Direct Investment' to include 'environmental related business' as an encouraged category.

21 For detailed discussion, see Lin and Buhi (2009: 142–8).

22 The proposal was raised by Zhang Hongli from Deutsche Bank in NPPCC 2010, and reported in Chinese at: www.ce.cn/xwzx/gnsz/zg/201003/12/t20100312_21110007.shtml. Also, see 'China innovation assists in building low-carbon society'; this article mentioned that a proposal on promoting China's low-carbon economy development submitted by Jiusan Society to CPPCC had been ranked as the first issue to be solved, at: www.caihuanet.com/english/ACN/201003/t20100326_1621984.shtml.

23 For details see CDM 方兴未艾 国内碳排放交易尚需政策推动 (CDM is developing and domestic carbon emission trading still needs policy promotion), at: http://www.cma.gov.cn/qhbb/newsbobao/201001/t20100119_57213.html.

24 中共中央关于制定国民经济和社会发展第十二个五年规划的建议（2010年10月18日中国共产党第十七届中央委员会第五次全体会议通过 This is the Proposal for the 12th Five-Year Plan adopted by the Central Committee of the CPC and recommended to the NPC for its endorsement in the NPC meeting held in March 2011. It is available at: http://news.xinhuanet.com/politics/2010-10/27/c_12708501.htm.

25 See Wen Jiabao (温家宝：将建设一个以低碳排放为特征的产业体系). For the full text of the Report of Government Work by Wen Jiabao, see: www.chinadaily.com.cn/china/2010npc/2010-03/15/content_9593380_8.htm.

26 中共中央关于制定国民经济和社会发展第十二个五年规划的建议（2010年10月18日中国共产党第十七届中央委员会第五次全体会议通过), at p. 5. Main targets of the CPC proposal on 12th Five-Year Plan include: 'China to make the reduction of energy consumption intensity and carbon dioxide emission "binding goals" in the 2011–15 period' at: http://news.xinhuanet.com/english2010/china/2010-10/27/c_13578315.htm.

27 Ibid. at pp. 16–17.

28 Indeed, China plans to target outdated, highly polluting industries with an electricity price surcharge as part of its push to dramatically slow the growth of the country's greenhouse emissions over 2011–15. The vice chairman of national development and reform in China, Xie Zhenhua, recently stated that 'outdated' companies were identified in eight energy-intensive industries including iron and steel, cement, aluminium and iron alloy for a special 20 cents per kilowatt hour surcharge on their electricity payments and another category of 'limited' enterprises would face a 5 cent per kilowatt hour surcharge (Taylor 2011).

29 温家宝:落实责任 确保实现"十一五"节能减排目标 中央政府门户网站 www.gov.cn 2010 年05月05日 来源：国务院办公厅 Wen Jiabao: 'Exhaust all means to meet emission reduction goal in 11th five-year plan' on 5 May 2010: www.gov.cn/ldhd/2010-05/05/content_1599918.htm (English version is unavailable, but see: http://news.xinhuanet.com/english2010/china/2010-09/14/c_13494507.htm, 'The nation has taken many steps to reduce carbon emissions, including scrapping preferential electricity rates for some high energy-consuming businesses, discouraging exports of energy-intensive products by removing export tax rebates on 406 products and shutting down of energy-intensive enterprises.'

30 See *the Guidelines on Environmental Pollution Liability Insurance* December 2007《關於環境污染責任保險工作的指導意見》. This is on the Ministry of Environmental Protection of the PRC's public website: www.zhb.gov.cn/gkml/zj/wj/200910/t20091022_172498.htm (NB: However, no English version is available).
31 中國將全力推進環境污染責任保險 已在9省試點. See: www.chinanews.com/ny/2010/11-15/2657297.shtml (Chinese).
32 See: 十二五期間環境污染責任保險制度將強制推行, www.lerong.com/Article/hydt/post-157eb9a4159f71a627fb.html.
33 See: 无锡在江苏率先推出环境污染责任险, from www.gmw.cn 2011-02-16 11:19:45 来源：光明网综合, resited from: http://tech.gmw.cn/2011-02/16/content_1618379.htm.
34 秦天宝, Chinese Environmental Law and its Impact on Foreign Investment, 文件提供：http://vip.chinalawinfo.com 北大法宝
35 The Law of the PRC on Environmental Impact Assessment, enacted 29 October 2002 and in effect from 1 September 2003.
36 The Law of the PRC on Environmental Impact Assessment.
37 See: www.mep.gov.cn/gkml/hbb/bgth/201101/t20110130_200382.htm; and www.mep.gov.cn/gkml/hbb/bgth/201101/t20110130_200387.htm (accessed 16 February 2011).
38 This is imposed where the limits on quantity and concentration of pollutant discharge are exceeded. The limits are defined clearly and both taxes and/or subsidies are available as either incentives or disincentives to enterprises.
39 See for instance the *Reply of the State Council on the Plan for Controlling the Nationwide Total Discharge Volume of Major Pollutants in the 11th Five-Year Plan Period* at: www.fdi.gov.cn/pub/FDI_EN/Laws/law_en_info.jsp?docid=73521; the *Circular of NDRC, MOF, MOFCOM, MLR, GAC, SAT, SEPA on Related Measures to Control the Exportation of Parts of High Energy-consuming Products, High-polluted Products and Resource Products* at: www.fdi.gov.cn/pub/FDI_EN/Laws/law_en_info.jsp?docid=52463, and *'Polluters should face higher discharge fees'* at: www.chinadaily.com.cn/bizchina/2007-8/06/content_6013457.htm.
40 For example, at the time of writing Asia has 112 nuclear reactors, with 37 more under construction, a further 84 planned and 80 under consideration. China has 20 more nuclear reactors under construction and eight more approved for completion by 2020 to meet rising demand for 'clean' energy. In this context it is salutary to consider the lessons from the nuclear disaster at Japan's Fukushima reactors in 2011. There, the weakness of the Fukushima No. 1 plant's seawater cooling system to earthquake and tsunami damage had been pointed out by opposition members of the Diet since 2006, but the private operator (Tokyo Electric) did not adequately respond. Notwithstanding reservations about the technology, the location and proximity to an earthquake-prone region, it was the 'cosiness and collusion between operators and regulators that was the immediate risk' (McDonald 2011: 16). Japan is far from unique in relation to this risk.
41 [Editor's note] Stern (2011: 294–312) traced the Pingnan civil environmental lawsuit from dispute to decision and found that getting a day in court is more often a 'hard-won privilege than a basic entitlement' (p. 296). By far the most frequently cited explanation for most litigant difficulties was that

> the local government shelters large polluters who prop up the local economy ... as one Environmental Protection Bureau (EPB) employee put it, 'if there wasn't a factory, there wouldn't be a [local] government' ... By 2003, tax revenues from the Rongping chemical plant comprised more than 25 per cent of the county's 20 million yuan (US$2.9 million) annual budget.
>
> (Stern 2011: 298)

42 See 环境保护部公布 2010 年首批挂牌督办案件 坚决查处环境违法行为 遏制污染反弹势头 www.mep.gov.cn/gkml/hbb/qt/201007/t20100706_191733.htm.
43 Please also refer to the above website (n. 42) but note there is no English version attached.

7 Implementing China's labour law reforms
Interests and obligations at the firm level

William J. Hurst, Jonathan Kinkel and Alexandra Sowash

Introduction

Many scholars have focused on the politics of labour in China's changing political economy (e.g. Hurst 2009a; Lee 2007; Gallagher 2005). Many others have examined changes to the labour law and the process of legal reform more broadly (e.g. Chan 2011; Chen and Funke 2009). Few have explicitly sought to link these two topics, however. We suggest that the state's application of labour regulations and – even more importantly – how firms respond to new labour rights provisions vary systematically across different types of firms, depending on the type of workforces they employ and their political economic position, rather than simply on their ownership structure.[1]

The past three decades have witnessed a sea change in the politics of China's labour relations. Workers are no longer assigned to lifetime employment in a work unit (*danwei* 单位) as they were in Mao's China; instead, any prospect of employment stability for workers is sourced in written contracts. The Labour Law (1994) and the Labour Contract Law (most recently revised and expanded in 2008) have been the two most substantial legislative elements of this shift to date.

Why should the CPC pursue labour reform with such resolve and alacrity? After all, foreign investors have flocked to China because of its status as 'the world's shop floor' – an outsourcing destination for low-skill, labour-intensive manufacturing (Chen and Funke 2009). Indeed, foreign investors had been encouraged to 'take advantage of the low wages of Chinese workers (particularly rural–urban migrants who toiled in the 'sweatshops" of southeastern China's Special Economic Zones) as well as the absence of strikes and other disruptive labor actions' (Hurst *et al.* 2009: 5). Given this starting point, it seems counterintuitive that China's top-down command structure would implement labour legislation that could significantly raise wages and costs, limit firms' labour flexibility, and generally make China a less favourable destination for production-related foreign direct investment (FDI).

China is, however, striving mightily to move up the product cycle and forward along the path to becoming an advanced industrial economy. Thus, along with others (Chen and Funke 2009; Chan 2011), we view the introduction of new labour laws as a signal that the state is beginning to de-emphasize low-end manufacturing ('low-skilled, low-cost, low-margin manufacturing') in favour of high-end production. Chen and Funke (2009: 570) sum up the point nicely:

> The underlying motivation for the new Labour Contract Law may therefore be that China no longer wants to be the home of low-skilled, low-cost, low-margin manufacturing. The government is backing the drive with a two-pronged approach: [encouraging companies to innovate and discouraging low-end manufacturers from operating in the country] ... The Chinese government policies now favour high-tech economic zones, research and development centres and companies that promise higher salaries and more skills.

Against this backdrop, we ask how China's recent labour law reforms affect foreign firms that must engage the changing legal-political structure of labour relations. We thus seek to move away from analysis of the state's underlying strategy for implementing labour reforms to examine how this strategy practically affects business practices and worker and state responses at the level of *the firm*. From this perspective, we address several critical and yet often unasked questions: which types of firms and which business practices are affected (and in what ways) by formal legal changes? When directly affected, do firms prefer to react and adapt to these legal developments? Or do they seek to block, ignore, or circumvent them? How successful (or otherwise) is each kind of strategy?

We argue, in a vein similar to Peerenboom's (2002: 475–92) explanation of different ownership categories of firms being more or less accepting of greater rule of law, that firms' reactions depend primarily on two variables: the skill-level of the firm's workers and the type of labour law reform implemented. Additionally, because foreign investment is both important and analytically distinct, we have narrowed our primary focus to the effect of labour law reforms on foreign firms, with a secondary focus on large Chinese firms. We also believe this focus will make our findings more directly useful to Western analysts and practitioners. This approach eschews the common framework for assessing the impact of legislation of Chinese firms, which generally assumes that the practical effect of legal reforms depends on ownership type. Hopefully, by structuring the analysis in this way, we will avoid some common classification problems. For example, it is difficult to assess law's impact on firms of different ownership type owing to the oscillation between state- and private-based capital investment; additionally, classifying firms based on geography or locality might become more skewed as investment within China continues to be increasingly mobile.

We will thus primarily focus on foreign firms who outsource different types of production operations to China, and how they must avoid or adapt to the new labour relations legal structure if they hope to remain competitive. Our focus on such 'export processing' firms essentially recognizes that export processing, or the labour outsourcing of the component processing stage of production, has played a major role in China's phenomenal economic development.[2] This chapter aims to illuminate how labour law reforms impact upon different firm types in China, thereby extending Kay-Wah Chan's (2011) consideration of the problems the labour law reforms were intended to address.

Conceptual framework: Different firm types, different reactions to reform

Labour law reforms, though nearly always intended to advance economic reform and improve operating efficiency (Hurst 2011: 73–6), affect different firms differently, depending on: (1) the skill level of the firm's workforce, and (2) the type of the labour law reform at issue. This framework reflects the reality that China's foreign-invested firms, which can vary wildly in terms of the level of technical skill required to produce consumer export goods, represent just one segment of the global production chain. Firms making everything from dolls to desktops operate supply chains that span multiple countries. Such multinational firms often produce components, process components and manage operations all in different locations; for many of them China is an attractive, low-cost alternative location where intermediate components are processed into finished products, then exported for sale in developed consumer markets.

Using this framework, we can then hypothesize that firms that have historically engaged in the type of low-skilled, low-cost, low-margin manufacturing that China's government would like to move past in the course of economic development will be the probable losers from, and most outspoken critics of, labour reform. Such firms have historically benefited from ambiguities in China's labour contract system, frequently failing to make wage payments, failing to enter contracts with their workers, and often opposing the state's emphasis on protecting the earning and consumption power of the country's workforce. Further, countering rising wages for China's workers is a 'sister issue' related to opposing the liberalization of the renminbi's (RMB, 人民币) foreign exchange trading and China's attempts to build a stronger consumer economy. In high intensity, low-technical-skill industries like textiles, the RMB's rising value has sparked acute opposition from industry groups, which argue that a dearer yuan would seriously damage textile companies' profit margins. Giving veracity to this assertion, China National Textile and Apparel Council Vice-President Gao Yong has stated, 'If the yuan actually appreciates 5 per cent against the US dollar, over half of China's textile companies will go bankrupt' (*People's Daily* 2010a).

The labour law reforms also represent, however, a set of incentives for companies to innovate (Chen and Funke 2009). Thus, foreign firms focused on research and development, and requiring more technical and scientific skilled workers at higher salaries, will most likely welcome most labour law reforms. High-skill workforce firms are already willing to create and honour labour contracts and pay slightly increased wages in return for better guarantees against unionization. They also benefit from the development of formal dispute resolution processes, which further limit the potential for work stoppages and labour activism. Finally, such firms stand to benefit from the state's emphasis on intellectual property rights protection reflected in articles of the Labour Contract Law that codify restrictive covenants and the protection of sensitive information and business secrets (Labour Contract Law, Articles 23–24). There is also a third category of firm, between low-skill and high-skill labour sectors of the economy: the 'transitional' firm. These firms' optimal responses to labour law reforms remain ambiguous. We summarize these dynamics in Table 7.1, which presents three different types of primarily foreign firms that have different reactions to the labour law reforms: (1) low-skill, labour-intensive, component processing firms; (2) 'transitional' firms caught between skill levels and production stages; and (3) higher-skill, high-tech component processing and basic service firms. Of course, we do not presume that these categories are necessarily mutually exclusive and collectively exhaustive. That is, there are certainly firms that fall in between our types or function as amalgams of multiple types. Also, there could be additional categories we have not yet observed or analysed.

Table 7.1 lists (across the top) the broad categories of labour law reforms that impact upon our typology of firms, viz: (a) an increasing emphasis on minimum wages, contract use, limited work hours and decent working conditions (Brown 2010: 36–42; 2008 Labour Law, Chapters 3–6; Labour Contract Law, Chapter 2); (b) the increasing role of labour unionization in China (Brown 2010: 44–58; Labour Law, Chapters 3, 11; Labour Contract Law, Chapter 5); (c) the increasing formalization, legalization and adversarialism of labour disputes (Brown 2010: 163–6, 168–98; Law of the PRC on Labour Dispute Mediation, Chapter 10; Labour Contract Law, Chapter 7); (d) and finally, the increasing burden of social welfare benefits that private enterprises increasingly assume (Brown 2010: 135–44; Labour Law, Chapter 9). In each cell, we provide a general assessment of how each firm type views each type of labour law reforms: highly unfavourably, unfavourably, neutrally, favourably, or highly favourably.

Table 7.1 Conceptual framework presenting the effects of four types of labour law reforms on three categories of firms conducting business in China

Type of firm	Management view of state's emphasis on wages, working conditions, and hours	Management view of increasing unionization (including collective bargaining and the potential for work stoppage)	Management view of increasing formalization and adversarialism of labour dispute resolution	Management view of private firms' increasingly heavy social welfare burden
Low skill, labour intensive component-processing firms [e.g. Walmart]	Highly unfavourable	Highly unfavourable	Generally unfavourable	Unfavourable
'Transitional' firms [e.g. Honda]	Neutral/variable?	Unfavourable	Favourable	Unfavourable
Higher-skill, high-tech component-processing and/or basic-service firms [e.g. Huawei]	Favourable	Unfavourable	Highly favourable	Neutral

The low-skill labour force firm

Foreign firms that employ a low-skill workforce tend to view the formal legal regulation of wages, working conditions, hours, as well as attending phenomena such as increasing unionization, highly unfavourably. Essentially, these firms benefited greatly from the extremely liberal environment and labour flexibility of China's early reform economy, and thus oppose labour reforms that might alter that environment in important ways. Additionally, such firms tend to require workers to assume individual responsibility for social welfare expenses, and are thus likely to oppose extension of employer contributions to or responsibility for social protection programs.

Low-skill firms might view the increasing legalization of labour disputes favourably because they could expect a reduction in informal protests against management. Preliminary data from the Ministry of Labour and Social Security suggest, however, that firms' resource advantages have not translated into success in court when labour disputes are adjudicated. Indeed, employees were successful in more than 80 per cent of cases adjudicated between 1996 and 2003, winning outright more than half of all cases. During this period, the total number of cases also rose by 470 per cent to more than 200,000 per year (Cooney 2007: 679).

With these patterns in mind, low-skill workforce firms generally take an unfavourable view of each of the four categories of labour law reform presented in Table 7.1. Thus, their strategy can be characterized as 'exit', in that they seek to play outside the system (rather than actively resisting or abiding by the new rules) by circumventing constraints and looking for ways to avoid complying with the law (Hirschman 1970: 4, 21). The one thing that might hold such firms back is the improvement in social stability provided by reforms, which in turn may help improve their bottom lines.

High-skill labour force firm

At the other end of the spectrum, foreign firms employing a highly skilled labour force usually take a favourable view of the increasing emphasis on wage constraints, labour contracts and civilized working conditions. They are frequently in compliance with many of these provisions already, as these are minimum requirements for attracting and retaining highly skilled workers. While they likely value flexibility in order to recruit new talent, such firms rarely view the basic requirements of the Labour Contract Law as particularly cumbersome (Labour Contract Law, Chapter 2).

High-skill firms like the increased legalization of dispute resolution because it offers them a legal means for resolving any contentious issues, while also codifying an important intellectual property right – that of protecting business secrets through the formal acknowledgement of restrictive covenants in the Labour Contract Law. Even high-skill firms might bristle at increasing unionization and difficulties in potentially having to provide more social services. They might not mind providing more social benefits, however, if they are already using such perks to recruit and retain employees. Thus, in the case of the high-skill firm, the firm's response to the labour law reforms will likely resemble, in Tsai's (2007: 145–9) terms, either a 'grudgingly acceptant' or 'loyally acceptant' response to the labour law reforms.

Transitional firms

What we call transitional firms find themselves in between stages of component production or basic service provision (i.e. between secondary and tertiary economies). These firms thus vary drastically in their compliance with the working conditions, wage and hourly requirements under the labour laws. Whether they choose 'exit' or 'loyal acceptance' depends on the extent they would have to reshape their policies in order to comply. Those firms that already largely comply with the new law's requirements stand to gain a competitive advantage from the labour law reforms. Transitional firms with long time horizons might likely tend to favour the increased legalization of dispute resolution. Should class action challenges to firms' activities become more robust over time, however, these companies might well change their views (see note in the *Harvard Law Review*, Anonymous 1998). In the short term, however, the labour laws provide aggrieved workers with a forum to voice complaints that would otherwise have gone unlodged, harming the interests of transitional firms.

Like most other firms, transitional companies view the increasing unionization of the labour force and social welfare burdens as cumbersome. This pressure is especially acute as they attempt to reconfigure their own business models in line with China's future development trajectory. Thus, transitional firms with short time horizons tend to opt for exit, while those with longer-term views are more often grudgingly – or even loyally – acceptant of the new labour reforms.

Our case studies illustrate how these issues in labour law and workplace relations play out in firms of each type. We examine Walmart, a low-skilled firm, where management did its best to resist granting workers new labour law protections. We then look at Honda, a transitional firm in which the situation was much less clear-cut. Finally, we turn to Huawei, a high-skilled company whose workers and managers have already established relations based on protections and obligations far exceeding those guaranteed even in most recent new labour contract law. By scrutinizing how the law is applied on the ground, we can get a better sense of the political and social implications of legal reforms.

Case studies

Walmart

With over 180 retail outlets in 101 cities (Walmart China 2010), Walmart has a noticeable retail presence in China. Walmart also contracts with over 20,000 different Chinese suppliers to manufacture its merchandise (ibid.). While much of this is exported from China to other markets around the world, 95 per cent of the merchandise that Walmart sells in its Chinese stores is manufactured in China (ibid.). Through these retail outlets and domestic suppliers, Walmart China directly employs over 50,000 Chinese workers (ibid.).

It appears that low-skill retail and manufacturing employers, including Walmart, have been extremely resistant to unionization and implementation of other provisions of the Labour Contract Law (LCL). Indeed, once unionization attempts began at Walmart facilities in China, a political and legal confrontation ensued. By examining what unfolded, we can gain insight into how foreign firms of a certain type manoeuvre to block or co-opt the growing power of Chinese unions.

In objections to early drafts of the LCL by the American Chambers of Commerce in China, Walmart is cited as one of the American companies that might be driven from China if the costs of implementing the LCL were too high. In the run-up to the passage of the LCL, Walmart resisted efforts by the All-China Federation of Trade Unions (ACFTU) to establish trade union branches in their local retail outlets. Despite the requirement that workers initiate the establishment of a local union by making a formal request with their employer and obtaining the approval of a higher-level union (ACFTU 2006; Trade Union Law, Article 11), the unionization of the first 17 Walmart retail outlets appears to have been covertly initiated by the ACFTU. In July and August 2006, the ACFTU approached workers from 17 different retail outlets outside of business hours to propose unionization and subsequently facilitated the election of trade union committees and trade union chairmen (Chan 2008).

When Walmart learned of these unions, it refused to recognize them. At one point, the corporation even issued a statement opining that trade unions 'are a divisive force that can threaten the company's competitiveness' (Wei 2010). After realizing that cooperation was a better tactic than recalcitrance, however, Walmart changed its stance and signed a memorandum with the ACFTU that supported the open establishment of trade unions at its remaining retail outlets in China. While certain unions have been co-opted by Walmart management, often with the help of local Party branches and district ACFTU offices (Wei 2010), some union branches remain independent. By examining two Walmart trade unions, one acquiescent and the other fiercely independent, we show how one foreign company has come into conflict with Chinese unions and workers over the implementation of key aspects of labour reform.

Soon after the first round of unionization, complaints against the trade union organized in Shenzhen (Guangdong Province) at the Jiali Centre (Walmart Store #3424) began to arise. On 14 December 2006, about four months after the original trade union was established, a Party branch (*dang zhibu* 党支部) was established within the Walmart store. The establishment of this Party branch reflected the government's stated goal of 'setting up trade union branches to facilitate the setting up of Party branches' (Wei 2008). With the Party branch's approval, management appropriated the functions of the trade union. In addition to union members not being able to select the candidates for union committee and chairman positions, union officials allegedly served at the pleasure of general management, sparking vituperative internet chatter and other grumbling (Baidu Bulletin Board 2007). Such subordination and cooptation of the Shenzhen union inhibited its ability to negotiate enforceable collective contracts.

While the trade union at Walmart's Bayi Square outlet in Nanchang (Jiangxi Province) also faced opposition from management, its leadership did not back down as easily. Given that the Chairman of this labour union, Gao Haitao, took pains to learn about the labour law and passed the Chinese bar exam (Wei 2008), the relatively uncompromising stance of this union branch is not surprising. On 5 September 2008, Gao engaged Walmart management in collective contract negotiations. When Walmart offered a collective contract with unfavourable terms, Gao reminded the company that the contract's content legally needed to reflect workers' interests and that workers should be treated as equals in the negotiation process (Wei 2008).

Although Gao made specific revision recommendations, Walmart ignored them and declared that its originally proposed contract had been approved by the ACFTU. When the Department of Collective Contracts at the ACFTU was contacted by the media for comment, they indicated that they could only encourage workers and companies to sign collective contracts, not advise them on the content of collective contracts, making it appear unlikely that Walmart received approval of its collective contract from the ACFTU. After Walmart announced this supposed support from the ACFTU for its collective contract, it bypassed Gao and obtained approval of the collective contract from 'employee representatives'. Other labour union branches around the country subsequently ratified this collective contract. Gao compared this process to concluding a treaty with the enemy once it has reached the city's walls (Wei 2008).

Walmart was lauded as a foreign company at the forefront of promoting labour rights, after concluding numerous collective contracts at different branches around China in late 2008. Even if all contract terms were to be honoured, hefty fees are often subtracted from workers' pay by some local governments when compensation exceeds the minimum wage. As a firm that employs low-skilled workers, Walmart has consistently opposed and frequently appeared to circumvent the LCL.

Honda

Having established its first joint venture in 1982, Honda was part of the first wave of foreign manufacturers of goods in China for export. While Honda has since expanded to supply the domestic market, its labour policies and provisions have not evolved in step with China's political and legal development. Indeed, the company has struggled to adapt to the gradual disappearance of low-cost production and continuing labour law reform. The strikes at Honda plants in southern China in May and June 2010 are indicative of these difficulties.

Beyond demands for higher wages, the Honda strikes were notable for their advocacy of at least relatively more independent trade unions and the democratic election of union leaders (Barboza 2010). The strikes were otherwise unremarkable, as such actions occur routinely in protests against poor working conditions or non-payment of wages. With at least the tacit acceptance of top leaders, labour activists have managed to improve working conditions and have grown increasingly emboldened by these successes (Solinger 2010; Lloyd 2010; Chang et al. 2010).

As a 'transitional' firm in our framework, Honda is not uniform in its approach to labour issues. Though Honda has been less resistant than Walmart to unionization efforts, the ACFTU has been less supportive of workers' rights and interests, even clashing physically with demonstrating workers during one recent strike at a Honda subsidiary (Lubman 2010). By comparing the handling of worker demands at a transmissions factory in Foshan (Guangdong Province) and an auto parts plant in Zhongshan (also in Guangdong), we show how higher-skilled workers were more successful at pressing their claims than their lower-skilled counterparts.

The strike among high-skilled workers at the Foshan transmissions factory was the first in a series that occurred between late May and early June 2010. The disruption it caused effectively shut down Honda's assembly operations in China and contributed to the setback of a little less than 20,000 vehicles in China's supply chain (Soble 2010). The lower-skilled workers also struck at the Zhongshan parts plant, but the company viewed these employees as essentially expendable and replaced them during the strike without compromising production. The high skill level of the transmission factory workers, however, made them hard to replace, forcing Honda to accommodate at least some of their demands. The different responses of the company to these strikes show how transitional firms can be willing to conform to new labour regulations in their relations with high-skilled employees; simultaneously they can seek to evade or resist labour protections when dealing with lower-skilled workers.

Huawei

Established in 1988 as a private company, Huawei quickly became the second-largest global supplier of mobile telecommunications equipment. While Huawei remains a private company owned by its founder and employees (Huawei 2010), it has become one of the most globalized of China's major firms, with much of its business originating abroad. Huawei has thus established 100 overseas branch offices and 17 R& d centres throughout the world. While its ownership structure might suggest labour-friendly policies, Huawei exploited loopholes to evade key contract provisions of the soon-to-be-implemented LCL in 2007.

As specified by the LCL, open-ended contracts differ from fixed-term or task-specific ones in their lack of expiration dates. Open-ended contracts are generally seen as more favourable to workers because they can be terminated only for certain causes. After 10 consecutive years of employment, the third renewal of a fixed-term labour contract, or the failure to sign a labour contract within a year of the start of work, an employee has the right, under the 2008 LCL, to demand an open-ended contract (Labour Contract Law, Article 14). The ambiguity of the calculation of this 10-year period of consecutive employment in the LCL gave Huawei and other companies an opportunity to deny long-term employees open-ended contracts by transferring them to subsidiary companies or different branches. The Implementing Regulations for the LCL that were adopted 18 September 2008 closed this loophole and Huawei was forced to reverse its actions.

Employers perceived the new regulations on open-ended contracts as akin to an 'Iron Rice Bowl', a guarantee of lifetime employment common in the Chinese state sector until the 1990s (S. Zhang 2008; Hang *et al.* 2008: 1–3). In fact, in marked contrast to the Iron Rice Bowl system, an employer can terminate an open-ended contract with an employee for 14 different reasons under the LCL. While severance pay or pledges to re-hire employees under certain circumstances are required by the new law, an employer can terminate staff for reasons such as changing economic conditions, advancing technology that makes the workers' services redundant, incompetence, or re-structuring due to bankruptcy. Fixed-term and task specific contracts can be terminated for these reasons, in addition to others, giving employers additional latitude and flexibility.

Starting in September of 2007, Huawei arranged for 7,000 of the workers with eight or more years of service at its Shenzhen headquarters to resign voluntarily. Most of these were re-hired under new fixed-term contracts soon afterwards. These new contracts did not specify new positions, duties or wages. But the new contracts crucially omitted any acknowledgement of the employees' years of service or seniority in the company. By the time the LCL went into effect on 1 January 2008, 10,000 workers, including the CEO and vice-president of the company, had to *xian cizhi zai jinggang* (resign first, then compete for a place) (Jiang and Li 2007).

Workers received monetary compensation based on their salary and length of service in exchange for resigning and re-applying. If an employee had worked for the company for eight years and received a monthly salary of RMB5,000 and an annual bonus of RMB60,000, his monetary compensation totalled RMB90,000 – a severance package far more generous than that required by the LCL. All together, the initial 7,000 employees that resigned received RMB1 billion (ibid.). Still, not all workers were satisfied.

Lower-paid employees, who had received less generous packages, and workers who realized the disadvantages of fixed-term contracts, were the most vocal opponents of Huawei's resign and re-apply policies. In early November 2007, soon after Huawei began arranging workers' resignations, Shenzhen's Municipal Labour and Social Security Bureau expressed concern, stating that this situation needed more study and attention (Jiang and Li 2007).

The LCL Implementing Regulations tied up many loose ends in the law exposed by practices like Huawei's. Specifically, the regulations stressed that workers' seniority needed to be counted from the date the employee began work for the employer, whether or not this was prior to 1 January 2008, and explicitly disallowed resetting the seniority clock through involuntary resignation or transfer of an employee. These Implementing Regulations, the scrutiny of the Shenzhen Municipal Labour and Social Security Bureau, and general public outcry, forced Huawei to end its 'voluntary' resignation programme.

Despite Huawei's attempts to circumvent the LCL, its treatment of its workers has been better than the treatment we have touched on at other companies, such as Walmart and Honda. As a technology company with high-skilled workers, this treatment fits well with the rubric that we laid out in the initial section. In addition to offering workers compensation packages that were more generous than those required by law, the management of the company showed solidarity with the workers by also resigning. Although Huawei was harshly criticized by local media outlets and relevant government bureaus, it was criticized for its alleged attempt to circumvent a law, not necessarily for its poor treatment of workers. In fact, Huawei's actions protected many workers' interests and appeared to be acting in strategic anticipation of the new law.

Capitalizing on its superior legal resources and information, Huawei management manoeuvred to bring itself into compliance with the LCL such that the firm's labour flexibility would be legalized moving forward. Though Huawei might not have liked all of the law's specific provisions, it was willing to think quickly and act legally. Also, as the company intended to re-hire the majority of the workers on three-year fixed-term contracts before the level of criticism and Implementing Regulations required them to honour the open-ended contract stipulations, many of the workers would not have suffered and, in fact, would have received compensation packages that were close equivalents to their annual salary.

Implications for firms' interactions with the state and China's development model

Several general hypotheses can be drawn from our ideas about firms and their attitudes toward implementation of different provisions of labour laws and regulations. First, low-skilled labour force firms should have closer ties to local governments (which seek to promote local economic development) and more tenuous relations with the central state (which seeks universal adherence to its regulations and laws); we would expect the inverse to be true for high-skilled labour force firms because in applying the law (or stricter internal standards) they conform to and endorse central policy, but, by employing a narrower segment of the workforce and doing much of their business abroad, they fail to support key local development priorities while showing up local violators or labour and environmental protections. Second, transitional firms' status is untenable in the medium to long term; they are likely either to exit the market arena of export producers in China or to upgrade to higher value-added production necessitating their evolution into high-skilled labour force companies. Third and most interestingly, the segmentation outlined above potentially undermines the sustainability of China's development model (Hurst 2009b), at least in the short run. While the first two claims are relatively straightforward and testable against observed behaviour by companies and government agencies, our third hypothesis requires a bit more explanation.

China currently follows what could be called an 'East Asian Model, plus two' development policy (Hurst 2009b: 16), focused on an explicit rejection of democratization or political liberalization and a heavy reliance on FDI in addition to the more general principles of export-led industrialization as described by the World Bank (World Bank 1993: 13–23). Maximizing participation by all three categories of foreign firms is thus critical. If FDI were to decline substantially, this could jeopardize China's continued economic growth and development. Retaining firms employing low-skilled workers is critical for providing employment opportunities and exploiting China's comparative advantage in labour-intensive industries. Fostering the development of high-skilled workforce enterprises is crucial for encouraging innovation and the development of higher value-added sectors. While allowing each type of firm to implement labour regulations differently may be conducive to short-run maintenance of China's development model, in the long run high-skilled firms will be hurt by the lack of more universal standards and transparent practices, while low-skilled companies may see their labour costs increase to the point where it will be difficult for them to keep pace with rivals in Southeast Asia or further afield.

Aside from these general points about political economy, segmentation in the application of labour law also threatens the popular legitimacy of the state and Party among both the most advanced leaders of the new economy and the most vulnerable (and numerous) sections of the population. High-skilled firms that see the government as unable to keep pace with industry standards in its labour regulations will be less and less likely to have faith in the CPC's overall competence and legitimacy, while workers in low-skilled firms that see their employers' practices falling further and further behind legal benchmarks will likely feel even greater resentment. All of this presents China's leaders with a dilemma: allow differentiated application of labour law and risk threats to the development model and popular legitimacy, or demand more universal adoption and enforcement of standards and risk either making no progress at all or causing insurmountable short-term disruptions. How this issue is dealt with over the next decade is likely to be a key in shaping the trajectory of China's political, economic and legal development.

Conclusion

Our case studies have revealed how high-skilled workforce firms appear to have embraced key provisions of the labour law, while low-skilled workforce firms have resisted. What we have called 'transitional' firms, meanwhile, were found to be in a more complicated position. Huawei management championed recent reforms, while Walmart looked to circumvent the law's requirements. Honda remained ambivalent and reacted equivocally.

Future research might usefully test empirically just how widely applicable our findings are across the Chinese economy. If they are proved to be so at the broader level, facile assumptions that firms of different ownership types (e.g. state-owned versus foreign-invested firms) exhibit systematic differences in the implementation of labour protections, or that new legal provisions are applied in similar ways by all employers, would be called into serious question.

Additional research on enforcement by state agencies would also be useful in that more knowledge of when and how the relevant bureaus or ministries are likely to use the tools at their disposal would be most valuable. For instance, which tools may be used to cajole or compel which recalcitrant employers to follow what specific requirements of the law? At what point will the competent authorities decide an employer is being 'recalcitrant'? What precisely will they do to enforce new labour regulations and what steps might the so-called recalcitrant employers take to avoid enforcement or perhaps minimize obligations? Clarification of such points would advance our knowledge of both Chinese labour politics and the effectiveness of the law reforms. Understanding that the skill level of a firm's workforce plays a significant, perhaps decisive, role in shaping its reaction to new legal protections for its workers is, however, an essential step in the analytical process.

As Chinese firms struggle to keep pace with the requirements of labour law reforms, the facts on the ground in its most cutting-edge firms indicate the government runs a risk of driving down the profitability of its most ubiquitous exporters. At the same time, however, the government is seeking to engineer a major industrial shift towards higher-skilled workplaces. This balance is clearly quite delicate and whether the Chinese leadership is getting this balance right by allowing regulations to be implemented in the segmented fashion we have outlined is a moot point. What is clear, however, is that continued and at times wrenching change appears almost certain in the short–medium term. Its effects both globally and locally are likely to be profound.

Notes

1 Kinkel completed much of the research and writing for the segment on our conceptual framework, with Sowash making similar contributions to the case studies.
2 We use Feenstra and Hanson's (2003) description to specify what we mean by export processing. During export processing, a firm in China imports intermediate inputs, processes the inputs, and then exports the finished goods. The allocation of ownership and control in processing exports of China 'tends to be shared between foreign and local parties, with foreign firms likely to have (at least partial) ownership in the Chinese plant, but the Chinese parties having control over input–purchase decisions' (Feenstra and Hanson 2003: 5, 31).

8 Chinese outward direct investment
Case studies of SOEs going global

Yingjie Guo, Shumei Hou, Graeme Smith and Selene Martinez-Pacheco

Introduction

China's remarkable economic rise and increasing political presence in international forums have raised concerns about its impact on the international community including the security of neighbouring and competing states. Recurrent questions in academic literature and mass media in the English-speaking world tend to revolve around what kind of global power the PRC will become as its comprehensive power grows. Will it be a responsible power as it says it will? Or are there emerging threats? Will it seek to maintain, reform or transform the international status quo? Despite the PRC's status as a global economic superpower alongside the US and the EU these questions have been explored predominantly from international relations, trade and security perspectives rather than through the lens of China's outward direct investment (ODI) (Buckley *et al.* 2010: 81).[1]

Although scholarly attention to Chinese ODI has recently increased, it has focused primarily on the motivations of PRC investors, and trends in the country's aggregate annual ODI flow, particularly its geographical and sectoral distribution and modes of entry (see Chen in Chapter 1 of this volume; Z. Li 2010; Buckley *et al.* 2010). This chapter, by way of contrast, turns to questions about China's international behaviour as a global power with reference to Chinese investor motivations, the behaviour of Chinese firms in host countries, and the lessons learnt from SOEs 'going out'.

This approach to Chinese ODI analysis assumes that China is not monolithic nor a homogeneous actor, as is often made out by mass media and in international relations and international security studies. Nonetheless, it has features as a global power that are discernable in the government's international behaviour, as international relations and security literature demonstrates, and in the engagement of China's SOEs with host countries. The latter includes the international socialization of SOEs themselves in ODI operations. Here, 'engagement' refers to the ways PRC firms and the PRC state cope with business practices in host countries. The term 'international socialization' refers to 'the process that is directed toward a state's internalization of the constitutive beliefs and practices institutionalized in its international environment' (Schimmelfennig 2000: 111). This chapter adopts this definition but also includes Chinese firms' own internalization of some of the beliefs, practices and established norms of the host country's domestic environment.

This analysis therefore links the international engagement and international socialization of Chinese 'going out' firms, on the one hand, with how this engagement influences the relationships between SOEs, the PRC and development of related state policy on the other hand. It is argued that Chinese firms and the Chinese state will tend to comply with local practices when and where there is sufficient pressure to do so, and that firm-level socialization will be manifested in both their international engagement and in changes at home that include, *inter alia*, the transference of management and technological skills to China and modifications to China's policies and regulations. The argument is developed through three contrasting 'going out' case studies. Before findings of the case studies are presented, the policy context of the PRC's engagement with ODI is briefly examined in the following section.

State engagement in ODI

The analysis essentially holds that SOEs are state agents whose assets are owned or controlled by the PRC. This assumption is not always easy to establish without evidence that they obey state directives and advance state interests. It is often difficult to find out precisely who are the 'real owners' of China's SOEs. But they are registered as such and state 'involvement' in their operations is beyond dispute. There are times when government departments and officials in China clearly do intervene in investment decisions. There are also times when enterprise managers make decisions independently without first obtaining approval from supervising government departments (see Chen in Chapter 1 of this volume).

The PRC's involvement in ODI is most notable in its policy initiatives that support Chinese investors – particularly SOEs. Most of China's pioneering ODI firms were hastily set up to fulfil state objectives (Cai 1999: 856). Since then policy objectives have been a major driving force for Chinese ODI, prompting some analysts to assert that it is actually 'a product of governmental policy' (Z. Li 2010: 6). At its inception, ODI was tied to the state's political agenda, primarily intended to develop trade relations and enhance China's economic and political influence in the world (Cai 1999; Z. Li 2010: 7). For some years, supervising bodies at various levels of the Chinese government were not obviously concerned that these firms were mostly in debt (Cai 1999: 856). Only since the mid-1980s has the 'profit motive' become a major concern for SOEs engaged in ODI (Z. Li 2010: 8). Still, profit maximization remains inseparable from any political imperatives.

Chinese ODI soared from US$622 million in the year 2000 to US$3.7 billion in 2004 (*People's Daily* 2010c) and US$16 billion in 2006 (UNCTAD 2007: 44). By 2009, the PRC had become one of the top six investors in the world, after the US, France, Japan, Germany and Hong Kong (UNCTAD 2010), and the trajectory of its investments is on the rise. This dramatic increase is attributable to the state's 'go-global' (*zou chu qu*) strategy launched by President Jiang Zemin in 2000 and implemented in the government's 10th Five-Year Plan (2001–5). Both

President Hu Jintao and Premier Wen Jiaobao have subsequently reaffirmed the importance of this policy. In his report at the 17th National Congress of the CPC, Hu (2007) announced that 'adhering to the basic state policy, we will better integrate our "bringing in" and "going out" strategies'. Wen reiterated the strategy at the 2010 National People's Congress, stressing that the government was keen to accelerate its implementation by supporting competent companies in their overseas investments, mergers and acquisitions.

Given the state's paramount role in Chinese ODI, it is not surprising that Chinese SOEs feature prominently in the strategy.[2] The first Chinese ODI operators were all SOEs (Zhu 2001: 23) because only selected state-owned trading corporations were allowed to invest abroad (Buckley *et al.* 2010: 127). ODI was then directed by the government towards supporting the export function of state-owned manufacturers (Ye 1992; Zhan 1995; Liu and Li 2002). In the mid-1990s, 'going out' and 'bringing in' became the two central planks of China's 'open door' policy, and the Chinese government encouraged ODI as a means of integrating the country into the global economy, restructuring domestic industries, enhancing firm competitiveness and reforming domestic institutions. Restructuring and strengthening the SOEs became a major objective of China's opening-up policy under Premier Zhu Rongji. More recently, the Hu–Wen leadership has directed Chinese ODI more towards resource development with a view to establishing global supply chains with the capacity to sustain Chinese economic activity (Hu 2007). SOEs have unquestionable advantages over private equity investors by virtue of their access to sovereign funds and, in some instances, monopolistic power in key industries such as oil and mineral exploration and exploitation.

The SOEs' privileged access to capital at below-market rates comes most notably in the form of state-sponsored 'soft budget' constraints (Lardy 1998; Scott 2002; Warner *et al.* 2004). Acquisitions by Chinese firms have become a normal mode of entering a host economy – often as a result of such soft budget constraints (Warner *et al.* 2004). Additionally, SOE investors receive direct government support in the form of export tax rebates (see Garrick's Chapter 9 in this volume), foreign exchange assistance and other financial support (Wong and Chan 2003). They also have access to low-cost capital as China's inefficient banking systems can provide soft loans to SOEs either as policy or through inefficiency (Warner *et al.* 2004; Child and Rodrigues 2005; Antkiewicz and Whalley 2006). Coupled with these capital advantages is the absence of private shareholder governance whereby some reckless risk-taking can be prevented through general meetings. This absence makes it easier for Chinese SOEs under command capitalism to venture into ODI and leads to overbidding (see Ma and Andrews-Speed 2006).

The sizable venture capital the state provides to SOEs is exemplified by the State Council's provision of the China International Trust and Investment Corporation (CITIC). CITIC was instructed to explore opportunities overseas in priority resource sectors (Y. Zhang 2003). The State Council in effect gave the state-owned Sinochem Group an 'internal bank' by directing the transfer of the China Investment and Trust Corporation for Foreign Economic Corporation and Trade to the

Group (ibid.). Similarly, the Shougang Group was allowed to have its own bank, relieving it of its hard budget constraints (Steinfeld 1998). Lenovo's acquisition of IBM's personal computer business was underwritten by the Chinese government which, at the time, held a stake of 57 per cent in the company (*Business Week* 2004).

There are numerous reasons why SOEs are given a dominant role to play in Chinese ODI and substantial support to play that role. Above all, SOEs belong to the people, at least according to the Constitution, while the state acts as owner-representative on their behalf. In theory, the SOEs' function in China's socio-economic systems is to prevent market failures, stabilize the economy, serve as policy instruments, generate revenue for the state and provide employment. With such an important role it is hardly surprising the state wishes to maintain effective control of at least the principal SOEs through supervision, monitoring by CPC cadres, and political appointments. According to a recent survey by the Chinese Association of Enterprises (cited in Zhu and Hua 2011), the managers of 57.5 per cent of the sampled SOEs were appointed by the supervising departments, and 31.5 per cent were elected by the boards of directors, which often included CPC cadres and Party members and thus were subject to state influence.

However, the state often fails to effectively supervise the management of the SOEs owing to the high costs of monitoring under market socialism and some perceived advantages of allowing company bosses leeway to run their enterprises. Indeed, a range of reform measures since 1978 have granted SOE managers greater managerial discretion in decisions related to production, pricing, materials purchasing, employment, personnel control rights and revenue redistribution. The *Contract Responsibility System*, for instance, significantly increased SOE autonomy through a process whereby the government would not intervene in the daily operations of firms that fulfilled their contracts. Under this arrangement it is difficult for the state to completely compel enterprise managers to work towards the maximization of 'owner interest', and insufficient monitoring allows some ambitious managers to pursue private interests at the expense of enterprise profit and the state. State control over transnational operations of SOEs, too, has been gradually relaxed. Since China joined the World Trade Organization in 2001, ODI policies have been liberalized in a number of ways. Buckley *et al.* (2010: 130) point out, for instance, that indirect 'hands off' policies have been replacing direct 'hands on' management. Consequently, the managers of SOEs often make decisions without consulting or informing their supervising departments at home.

Those SOEs which are under effective state control may well be considered state agents. In this case, their behaviour is more likely to be consistent with state directives and objectives while their ODI experience is also more likely to have an impact on state policies. This cannot be said about SOEs which enjoy operational autonomy or frequently fail to consult or inform their supervisors at home. In this case, the SOEs' international engagement can be somewhat disconnected from the state's information-gathering and decision-making processes, or at least more disconnected than media interests sometimes portray it to be. At any rate, whether their behaviour in the host country is related to state objectives or the calculus of self-seeking managers, learning about and adaptation to local practices is essential for success. The following cases suggest that the challenges that Chinese SOEs have encountered are not so much attributable to a tendency to throw their weight around as to the reluctance or failure to quickly adapt to local practices.

Case 1: Meitan (an Australian-based mineral resources project)

The Meitan Company (pseudonym) is one of the top 500 industrial companies in China and a diversified group of 12 subsidiaries in China and overseas that focus on coal, aluminium smelting and electric energy generation. It is a 100 per cent state-owned large enterprise whose board of directors is appointed by the local government. Under a 2006 Chinese municipal foreign trade approval, the company responded to the Chinese policy of 'going global' and self-financed a subsidiary Australian company primarily focused on coal exploration and mining (in Queensland). The subsidiary's board includes the chairman, the executive general manager of Meitan (based in China) and the deputy general manager of Meitan's subsidiary (based in Australia). The deputy general manager in Australia reports daily by phone to the company's executive general manager in China. According to the group's business plan and internal material provided to the researchers, parent board members visit the Australian subsidiary once every year or two.

The company brought to Australia its own Chinese experience and knowledge of doing business, and its board had little or no Australian experience and knowledge. Successive managers in Australia had no prior knowledge of Australian conditions, business law or government policy and regulation. Their limited English posed some problems for the expeditious acquisition of the appropriate level of local business understanding as dependence on interpreters is less reliable. For example, there were often delays in management communication and approvals and it can be readily inferred the company did not adequately invest in personnel with local knowledge and expertise. Much was contingent upon the signing authority of the company's executive general manager in China. Sometimes this resulted in delayed salary payments in Australia. The finalization of plans at the subsidiary was also delayed. The deputy general manager in Australia reported to Meitan's executive general manager, who then reported to the company's chairman, who would in turn request the approval of Meitan's board of directors. The parent board of directors in China made Australian business decisions on the basis of their own successful business experience in China, assuming the Australian government would expedite their position in any legal disputes, as may occur in China. They also expected that the Australian government would provide them with policy and legal knowledge and that such provision would reduce the local costs of lawyers and consultants. Such expectations were flawed.

In short, the company's personnel in Australia lacked the right combination of knowledge of the local legal, regulatory environment and business culture. The notion of conducting appropriate due diligence to comply with Australian contract law and culture, for example, came as an inconvenient surprise. It could be characterized this way: that the company adopted a 'learn-as-you-go' strategy. As a result some decisions were made without an adequate research base including Australian labour laws, the *Immigration Act*, tax, company management policies and business culture. They also had difficulty in establishing related networks. The lack of in-house English and culture skills meant that Meitan's staff were reluctant to engage extensively with local financial, legal, resource and business management circles. The directors in China did not provide training funds for staff to develop their English, cultural or legal knowledge in Australia. This was not recognized as essential to the tasks at hand.

In keeping with the learn-as-you-go strategy, the company did not have a long-term, focused business plan in the host nation. It adopted an experimental 'crossing the river by groping the stones' approach to investing in Australia. Local capacity for making an effective and long-term business plan was restricted by parent company micro-management and was compromised by the above lack of training and local understanding. Rough, uninformed local adjustment resulted in delays and the idling of personnel resulting in a lost opportunity to apply for upgrading port capacity in Australia five years ago.[3] Management has also undergone significant personnel changes with senior staff placed only on one-year contracts.[4] This lack of continuity has clearly impeded company management learning. The deputy general manager, for example, was on a casual contract, and this key authority has been changed three times in the last four years.

Meitan's experience in Australia is reflected in multi-layered battles. In December 2005, the company's board of directors engaged a local Australian businessman to help expedite the submission of an exploration permit application to Queensland's Department of Mine and Energy (DMEQ). Without speculating on the reasons for doing this, the businessman placed his own company's name on the application form, falsely claiming it to be a subsidiary of Meitan. The DMEQ thereupon issued a permit under the name of the businessman's company, which then became the legal person who owned the exploration rights. Upon receipt of this permit, the businessman raised the money for exploration under this permit, thus circumventing Meitan's potential rights in relation to the property, even though it had underwritten the application costs. The company's problems thus started with its initial failure to engage appropriate lawyers or consultants with Australian business and regulation expertise.

After a protracted and costly legal battle, the Queensland Supreme Court ruled in favour of Meitan. Despite this battle, no immediate adjustments to Meitan's management and personnel training strategies were made. Only recently did Meitan's parent company begin to make adjustments by encouraging new recruits to undertake MBAs in US universities, engaging a local resources and business law firm, and joining a statewide mining association.

The legal battle delayed the company's schedule and long-term planning was further compromised through a failure to acquire timely geological information on the quality of the coal. For instance, after expending $20 million on coal exploration and feasibility studies, Meitan belatedly commissioned a survey which revealed the very high acid content in the coal, the vast distance of rail transport from the mining site, and complicated infrastructure processes in Australia. The company therefore encountered unnecessary upfront costs resulting from an initial failure to operate on the basis of a long-term business plan and essential investment in the selection and training of suitable personnel with appropriate levels of local knowledge and experience. Such criticisms, however, must be put in context as China's enterprises have only quite recently commenced 'going out' and there is no substitute for 'on the job' learning.

Case 2: The China Metallurgical Corporation (in Papua New Guinea)

This study examines Chinese aid projects in the Asia-Pacific region and argues that the main game is often securing resources rather than helping vulnerable island nations through disbursing aid. The main project examined is the Ramu nickel/cobalt mine, a $1.4 billion dollar investment in Madang province, Papua New Guinea (PNG), managed by the China Metallurgical Corporation (MCC). The discovery of vast tracts of copper deposits has rekindled interest in Bougainville's mineral wealth following the election of PNG's former ambassador to China, John Momis, as president of the Autonomous Bougainville Government.

Much of what has unfolded in Madang is specific to both the structure and corporate culture of MCC, factors peculiar to the local communities at the Kurumbukare mine site and the Basamuk refinery site, and weaknesses of the local government in Madang. The background of MCC and its Engineering and Non-Ferrous Institute (ENFI) contractors in infrastructure have included both strengths and weaknesses. For instance, this background has allowed much of the hardware, including a 134 km pipeline to carry the ore slurry, to be built ahead of schedule. But emphasis on meeting construction deadlines has led to significant disputes with local communities that have been left unresolved long after the responsible ENFI contractors have returned to China. As is common with mining projects in PNG, Ramu Nickel has found itself caught up in local landowner disputes, many of which arise irrespective of the nationality of the mining company (Ballard and Banks 2003). High levels of expectation in this project (the exploration lease having initially been issued five decades ago; Zimmer-Tamakoshi 1997), the haste of construction and the failure of PNG Land Titles Commission to undertake due diligence work have exacerbated disputes.

Notable in the Ramu project, however, is that the Chinese and PNG governments have viewed it as a 'state-to-state' matter, leaving any private equity interests, provincial and local governments sidelined. At first, this approach appeared to benefit MCC, delivering a 10-year tax-free period, a zero-rating on VAT during the construction phase,[5] and a framework agreement which passed much of the sovereign risk to PNG (interviews, November 2009).

It appears that the preference for dealing with the central state arose partly from MCC's originating out of the Chinese Ministry of Metallurgical Industry, and also from the developing nation's lax level of local governance. To automatically conclude that this was opportunistic by the Chinese authorities may be unfair, as reliance on the PNG government (under the then Prime Minister Somare) has disadvantaged MCC in several ways. The PNG central government has failed to deliver on many projects in the Memorandum of Agreement (MOA), and has shifted blame for changes to the Environment Act to MCC, even though elements within the government were agents of the change. By contrast, even critics admit that MCC has delivered on the social and development commitments in the MOA (interviews, November 2009 and October 2010).

There is a well-known history of international mining companies lobbying the PNG government to rewrite law. This is not new and has been powerfully illustrated in the case of the nearby Ok Tedi gold mine.[6] Notwithstanding such 'lessons of history', MCC management has been reluctant to engage with local government, civil society and landowner groups on environmental issues. This reluctance arguably contributed to court action which delayed construction for a year (interviews, October 2009, February 2010, October 2010). There has, however, been evidence of management learning from experience in the region with a new willingness to draw on mining experts from Australia and elsewhere. At the start of the project, the company had refused to hire 'outsiders'.

It appears the pressures on Ramu Nickel to reform its practices have been accentuated by court proceedings rather than through regulation by either central or local government agencies. For instance, on 26 July 2011, after delaying construction of a deep sea tailings outlet at the refinery site for more than a year, the national court lifted its injunction, instructing that the plaintiffs 'be consulted and kept informed by the defendant company, at least every three months, on tailings and waste disposal issues concerning the mine, and this order shall continue for the life of the mine unless and until amended or set aside by the court' (Cannings 2011).

Other issues highlighted in the case study were extensive use of Chinese labour, low wages paid to local staff, and communication problems between the two (Chinese and local) workforces. Joint ventures that allow for real input from local partners may be a way forward, but local governance issues need to be addressed and greater transparency as to what future Chinese investors can and cannot do will need to be in place.

Studies from Africa have also suggested the possibility for 'horizontal learning' of international norms within mining companies, depending on what sorts of international projects the companies are exposed to (Haglund 2009). In the case of MCC's exposure to international norms, until now they have been exposed to regulatory regimes that are often as lax (or worse) than PNG, limiting the scope for positive horizontal learning.[7] As Shen Heting, the CEO of MCC, explained,

> High-quality resources have already been taken by others, so at present, we can only go wherever there are still good resources. Which regions we invest in aren't for us to choose. As for risks, we can only rely on the support of the central government and our own efforts to avoid them. As long as it is a good resource, we will go for it.
>
> (Yan 2010)

Whether such a strategy will be sustainable remains a critical question.

Case 3: Shougang Hierro Peru (in Latin America)

Established in 1992, Shougang Hierro Peru (SHP) was China's first investment project in the region. The company, previously American owned, was expropriated by the Peruvian government and later sold to Shougang. The latter has encountered numerous problems in Peru, but the most difficult to resolve have occurred at the iron ore mine at Marcona. There have been troubled relations here between the new Chinese owners and the local trade unions.

SHP has owned the iron ore mine at Marcona since 1992. This Chinese SOE bought the mine from the locally state-owned Empresa Minera de Hierro del Peru (Hierro Peru). As mentioned earlier, investments and acquisitions in energy and raw materials overseas have been part of Chinese foreign policy in the twenty-first century under the 'going out' strategy. However, the buying of the Marcona mine in Latin America was one of the first overseas ventures by a Chinese company, preceding the implementation of the strategy. The lack of ODI experience was at least partly accountable for the company's problems.

Marcona is the only iron ore mine in use in Peru. It also benefits from having a Pacific port, San Nicolas de Marcona, which is able to receive cargo ships of up to 200,000 tonnes. This port is operated by SHP, as part of the package acquired from Hierro Peru in 1992 (Willer 2000). As with the operation rights of the port, many of the specifics of the acquisition have remained vague. Although this is not the only unclear deal made by the Peruvian government at the time to privatize some of its state-owned companies, it is noted that SHP failed to pay the agreed investment in time (US$150 million in three years) and there were irregularities around the buying price (US$120 million when its listed price was US$22 million) and later problems with its unionized workers (CIDEF 2002a; Manco and Maldonado 2003).

The privatization of some state-owned companies took place in the context of political turmoil in Peru. In 2002 the Peruvian Congress established a commission to investigate these companies on economic and finance offences from 1990 to 2001 (CIDEF 2002a). In the case of SHP, CIDEF concluded that the government should further investigate the matter, to resolve whether Shougang had access to insider information at the time of the acquisition and to address workers' complaints and the environmental consequences of the company's polluting practices (CIDEF 2002b).

There was some suspicion among Peruvian Congress members, when reviewing the privatization of the mine, that Shougang had privileged information at the time of buying which could explain the wide difference between the listed and the buying price. These suspicions emerged through the decrees that were issued by the government right after the buying of the company in November 1992, which greatly benefited Shougang; together they are called the 'Shougang Laws' and they transferred the company's debt to the Ministry of Economics and Finance in some cases and converted the debt to capital investment for the new company in another (CIDEF 2002a). To date, it remains unclear as to why Shougang bought the Marcona mine for US$120 million when its listed price was US$22 million, and why it committed to invest another US$150 million in the mine in the three years following the acquisition.[8]

However, of particular concern to this case study is the troubled relationship of SHP with its unionized workers. The fact that the miners are highly unionized has been a big challenge to the company, not least because it has had little experience of dealing with independent trade unions in China. Since 2002 SHP has faced a strike each year. Workers' grievances include lower than average wages, poor working conditions, safety issues, failure to meet social responsibilities, and environmental pollution, among others. The workers have complained that Shougang lacks a sense of social responsibility. There has not as yet been much progress on the issues raised by the workers with the exception of increasing wages and the workers' yearly bonus (Garcia 2009; ElComercio.pe 2010).[9]

By taking a relatively uncompromising line, the company has arguably failed in key elements of its engagement with local unions. The failure to invest the US $150 million in the first three years after the acquisition, and arguably some underinvestment (US$137 million over seven years), has led to inefficiency (for example, an increasing rate of accidents among the workers operating the mine's old machinery) and high costs of production. Union officials claim there were 450 accidents at the mine in 2004, including 22 that disabled workers; five workers having been killed in accidents since 2002 from electrocution and lack of safety harnesses (Emmott 2005).

Since at least 2002, the workers, in particular through the National Federation of Miners, Metalworkers and Steelworkers of Peru (FNTMMSP), have requested the company to reconsider and negotiate on: salary increases to comparable levels of income of other miners in Peru; distribution of utilities without discounts of any sort; better safety regulations and provisions, and better community services (Emmott 2005).[10] Nevertheless, SHP's practices are only a part of the problem. A more in-depth look at the yearly strikes reveals that one of the main challenges is embedded within the Peruvian legal system.

The Peruvian Constitution (1993) limits the role of the government to that of a promoter of collective bargaining and peaceful settlements, agreeing upon the solutions reached by the parties themselves. 'The Peruvian legal system ... establishes the right of parties to freely regulate their labour relations, defining the issues and subjects to be covered during the bargaining process' (International Labour Organization 2010). However, the procedure, after direct negotiation, provides for conciliation, mediation or voluntary arbitration to reach a solution. From 2002, the workers' union and SHP have turned to voluntary arbitration but both safety and community services issues remain problematic.

After 2007, the workers' union took a further step against SHP by filing a formal complaint against the government of Peru at the International Labour Organization (ILO). This complaint followed the company illegally bringing in temporary miners to work while the unionized workers were on strike. The strikes in Marcona had government approval and were thus legal. The workers also complained that they feared they would be laid off; this fear was silencing workers from speaking up about perceived injustices. Even in the face of such strident opposition, the company has continued to break the strikes illegally and has sued the workers claiming that they have committed violent acts during the strikes, a claim that was subsequently proved to be unfounded (ICEM 2009; MTPE 2011).

The company has resorted to the Peruvian Constitution and Laws and has conceded little to the unions. The union thus argues that where SHP has failed, the former American owner of the mine, Marcona Mining Company (MMC), had actually succeeded in that MMC had established union support and more easily engaged with the local community. Local perceptions are paramount to any company's successful engagement with the community, and in this case they lay at the heart of the problem. The Marcona community now regards MMC as socially responsible in that it had provided the means and services for the community to live decently. Conversely, the perception is that Shougang has poor social responsibility. From the union's point of view, the situation at Marcona is described by Peruvian Mining Workers Federation leader Luis Castillo in comments on reasons for the strike in June 2010: 'the company is not used to negotiating with the workers and this is the eighth year the miners [have had to] strike to get the Ministry of Work to resolve the grievances' (LaRepublica.pe 2010). The company, on the other hand, does not wish to kow-tow to local union demands that it sees as excessive.

Conclusion

This chapter has considered case studies in three contrasting locations: Australia, Papua New Guinea and Latin America. Insights are gained from these as they examine SOE experiences in an advanced industrialized host nation, a poor developing nation and a politically volatile scenario. The cases reveal characteristics of China's SOEs 'going out'. Each study shows that the SOEs' involved had lacked adequate prior knowledge of the beliefs and institutionalized practices of the host country's domestic environment. This lack was coupled with an apparent initial reluctance and even refusal to recognize and engage with, or adapt to, local norms, beliefs and practices. In Meitan's case these issues were compounded by low English proficiency among staff recruited on the basis of their Chinese experience and connections rather than host-nation expertise.

Despite the state providing substantial support for its 'go-global' strategy, state authorities and SOE investors have not always conducted appropriate due diligence to comply with host-country commercial practices. Sufficient training has not always been provided to staff; nor have appropriate personnel with the prerequisite ODI experience and business acumen always been selected. Thus, SOE managers charged with implementing the 'go-global' strategy are often inadequately equipped to do the job expected of them. As such, one option is for them to fall back on their China experience and adopt a 'learn-as-you-go' or 'cross the river by groping for pebbles' strategy. Such uncertain trial and error processes were, however, shown to be costly, causing operational delays and in some cases leading to legal disputes, attracting local resentment and unnecessary misunderstandings.

A centrepiece in SOEs China experience is the centrality of the state (and state support) to successful business. They have been able to rely on state agencies and officials in financial and business operations. For example, Meitan's parent board of directors had initially based their Australian business decisions on their experience in China. From this experience they had expected the Australian government to expedite their position in its legal disputes and provide them with policy and legal knowledge and consequent reductions in legal costs. This demonstrates the board's lack of knowledge about the 'separation of powers' in the Australian political and common law legal system, and inadequate feedback loops between Meitan's Australian-based staff and headquarters in China. Similarly, CMC worked with the PNG government on the Ramu project, viewing the project as a 'state-to-state' matter and thus by-passing the local actors who may have had genuine grievances about aspects of the project. Attempting to bypass local actors was more complex than anticipated. A key difference in this case was that the PNG government also wanted to bypass local actors, seeing them as potentially expensive and counterproductive to 'national' interests. In Shougang's case in Latin America, it too negotiated deals directly with the Peruvian government, but the content of these deals remain commercial and in-confidence, with unions claiming they lack transparency and may even be tinged by corruption. In short, the Peruvian deals are the subject of much speculation.

With the Chinese SOEs having little experience to fall back on in dealing with trade unions and local communities, Shougang in particular has responded to strident opposition in the same way that most SOEs inside China would have responded in the past. It has even gone so far as to illegally break strikes. One of the reasons for the company's hard-line approach to the unions and illegal behaviour appears to be some connivance on the part of the Peruvian government which, for its own purposes, does not wish to jeopardize Shougang's business interests and yet cannot distance itself too far from the workers' causes. This case study reveals the government's pragmatism and the volatile nature of Peruvian rule of law, and the SOE involved has responded to that 'pragmatism'. The rule of law in the PNG is similarly volatile. In this developing nation scenario, the government has been shown to sometimes rewrite laws in the face of the lobbying of powerful international mining companies. In more developed nations with established rule of law systems, SOEs cannot apply the same type of 'pragmatic' pressure.

That does not mean, of course, that Chinese SOEs invariably get their own way in countries like Peru and PNG. What the studies show is that there are varying pressures emanating from host environments and these make considerable differences to SOE behaviour. It has been argued that Chinese corporations are themselves being 'socialized' as a result of exposure to international norms and through the process of trial and error in interacting with host states (Haglund 2009 and Lee 2009). The studies presented in this chapter tend to confirm this. Furthermore, the pressures on Chinese SOEs to reform their practices have been accentuated in particular by court proceedings. Each of the Chinese enterprises under discussion had experienced some difficulties in adapting to local legal and political systems. This illustrates the challenges that China's enterprises face in 'going out'. The 'going out' strategy has occurred in a relatively brief period of time. The challenge now is to absorb those lessons so that China can fulfil its role as a responsible big state rather than using its economic and political might to pressure sovereign host nations in ways that may be unsustainable and perhaps counterproductive.

Notes

1. An economy can be considered a global economic superpower if it is large enough to significantly affect the world economy, sufficiently dynamic to contribute importantly to global growth, and sufficiently open to trade and capital flows to have a major impact on other countries. The three criteria were first proposed by Bergsten *et al.* (2009). Only China, the US and EU meet these criteria (Cheng 2011: 139).
2. Privately owned enterprises have been allowed to undertake outbound investment projects since 2003, but their investment is insignificant by comparison with that of the SOEs.
3. From discussions with a contracted geologist at the company.
4. From discussions with unnamed (for confidentiality reasons) executives at the company.
5. For further details on the technical and financial aspects of the project, see: www.highlandspacific.com/pdf/Ramu_Nickel_Cobalt_Project.pdf (accessed 17 July 2011).
6. In that case, Slater and Gordon, the legal firm representing landowners in their case against BHP for environmental damage to the Fly River system, identified that the word-processing codes on the PNG government's 'Eight Supplement Agreement' were precisely the same as BHP's own Port Moresby law firm (Gordon 1997).
7. In addition to PNG, MCC's overseas mining portfolio involves projects in Afghanistan, Pakistan and Argentina.
8. The company paid a penalty of US$12 million for not fulfilling its investment commitments (CIDEF 2002a: 26).
9. In the resolution of the July 2010 strike, the wage was increased by PEN$3.10 (US$1.13) and the bonus by PEN$.1000 per day (US$.036) (ElComercio.pe 2010).
10. SHP is responsible for providing electricity and water to Marcona (CIDEF 2002a).

9 China's taxation law reforms in the context of 'market socialism'

John Garrick

Introduction

Tax is complicated and China's system is no exception. China is using its tax system as a maze of fiscal valves to rapidly steer its giant economy. We have seen from the earlier chapters that a new form of socialism has entered into China's official ideology quite recently, allowing the private economy to co-exist with the socialist public economy. In addition to China's well-documented economic growth rates, today it is also outbound foreign direct investment (OFDI) that attracts particular attention due to its short but spectacular history.[1] By allowing mixed economic forms, the CPC has been given the latitude to reform China's economic and social systems without undermining its leadership or socialist discourse. The rhetoric of 'socialism with Chinese characteristics', on one hand, claims the CPC's adherence to its orthodox ideology of socialism. On the other hand, it legitimizes the party's arguably non-socialist policies and practices as so-called 'Chinese characteristics'. The capitalist productive forces that have been promoted can be viewed through one lens of the party as a means to an end, perhaps even a 'preliminary' form of socialism.[2] Alternatively, it may be argued that the introduction of 'socialism with Chinese characteristics' was actually the beginning of the end of socialism.[3]

Taxation policy and reform provides an example of the ambivalence and seemingly contradictory nature of the CPC's private/market-based reforms and its stated commitment to furthering socialist principles. Marx (1973: 532) actually anticipated that government infrastructure and services, non-market in character and funded out of taxation, would eventually become 'marketized', and central to China's 'marketization' is reform of the taxation system. Under the Constitution, power to make tax law is vested in the National People's Congress (NPC) (or its standing committee) which has delegated this authority to the State Council. In turn the State Council has designated key responsibilities for the development of taxation policy and strategy to the Minister of Finance and the key role of drafting tax laws to the State Administration of Taxation (SAT). Provinces, autonomous regions, municipalities and standing committees of local people's congresses can also make local taxes and do not contravene the Constitution as administrative regulations give them this right – to account for conditions within their local jurisdiction.

China's tax collection and management authorities thus include state tax bureaux, local tax bureaux and also customs. This arrangement has, in the past, favoured the more affluent development centres of the east and is in part why the central government now offers significant tax concessions for Chinese businesses and foreign investors to move west and to 'go green'. Indeed, this complex structure partly accounts for China having so many interim tax regulations instead of tax laws, but it is SAT which is the primary operational unit for administration and implementation of tax law in China.[4]

Tax law reform under these authorities faces intriguing dilemmas inherent in the hybrid public/private economic reforms in that some private entrepreneurs have become conspicuously very wealthy, very quickly, and many consider aspects of this outcome unfair. In some cases the transfer of wealth from public to private is seen as a betrayal of Marxist–Leninist principles. This chapter first outlines the new principles of key Chinese tax law reforms and then explores examples of critical reform dilemmas Chinese authorities have faced including burden shifting, unifying a divided taxation system and implementing the value added tax (VAT), *Enterprise Income Tax Law* (EITL) and *Individual Income Tax Law*. The contentious issue of 'wealth hatred' and its connections to tax avoidance is also examined before conclusions are made about the explicit transitions in China's taxation laws.

The principles of Chinese taxation law reform

The guiding principles for the ongoing reform of China's industrial and commercial tax system are to unify the tax law, equalize the tax burden, simplify the tax system, rationalize the division of power between different levels of government, straighten out the distribution system, guarantee financial revenue and establish a tax system which conforms with the requirements of the 'socialist market economy' (Stoianoff 2008: 313–19). Government policies have also sought to stem the growth in inequality, which has been fairly steep since the 1980s.[5] Such policies further seek to 'improve conditions in rural areas nationwide by way of substantial reductions in the burden of regressive taxes and fees' (Herd 2010: 9).

Using the EITL[6] as an illustration, China's State Council rules may be summarized into five basic reform principles as follows:

1 *Rationalizing the distribution relationship between the central and local governments:* including strengthening the macro-control capability of the former, readjusting the structure of the tax system, rationalizing tax categories and re-setting tax rates to establish a foundation for a system of sharing tax revenues between central and local authorities.
2 *Realizing fair tax burdens:* involving creating conditions for fair competition among enterprises in the market.
3 *Regulating personal income and economic development between regions:* including developing the role of taxation to promote coordinated economic and social development.

4 *Promoting the readjustment of the economic structure*: for tax reform to embody the industrial policies of the state.
5 *Simplifying and standardizing the tax system*: to safeguard the 'unity and solemnity' of the tax law.[7]

These principles frame the discourse legitimizing current tax law reforms. At their heart is the expansion of a market base to the economy and consolidation of the central government's taxation and redistributive powers. Indeed, Marx (1978: 220) identified the expansionary dynamic of market capitalism and the tendency towards universalization of market forms 'so that all production becomes commodity production'. His theory helped inform CPC policy for many decades following the successful 1949 revolution and commodification under market forms definitely fuels some critical dilemmas for socialist governance.

Critical dilemmas in the reform process

The first dilemma concerns *the theory* that guides reform. Interpreting the principles of tax law reform relates to the question of the extent to which Chinese 'market-socialism' shapes tax law reform strategy (or not). For instance, to what extent is the social distribution of wealth guided by socialism, and to what extent is the strategy influenced by the need to promote a thriving market economy with a healthy private sector? With private entrepreneurs and privatized companies constantly lobbying for tax concessions to ensure capital growth and access to funding, a pertinent question is whether the socialist discourse is now more symbolic, perhaps even irrelevant, in shaping reform theory. Regulation (and deregulation) is being engineered for economic reform with non-state and hybrid actors now overtly (and covertly) seeking to influence state-controlled regulatory space. At the same time, Ho in Chapter 12 of this volume shows how the power of government was recently mobilized in Chongqing to adopt revolutionary and cultural resources from Mao's era to deal with organized crime. This suggests that far more than socialist symbolism remains.

The second dilemma relates to *the practice*: some tax reforms are now directly influenced by lobbying efforts of private (and foreign) investors who ostensibly are not meant to be motivating such reforms. As illustrations, Minglu Chen (2011: 229) showed how Zhang Yin, one of China's richest women, instigated a 'pro-rich' proposal in the 2008 Chinese People's Political Consultative Conference to amend new laws; foreign investors also reacted strongly to the draft of the *EITL* under which the Chinese government intended to immediately eliminate tax benefits previously offered to foreign investors. A number of large foreign companies in China petitioned the relevant authorities protesting against the legislative proposal.[8] The Chinese government compromised and tax benefits for foreign investment were phased out over five years (Article 57). The dilemma relates to the CPC facing new and further forms of lobbying from powerful, private local and foreign-equity interest groups *and* cadres melding seamlessly with crony capitalism. Foreign investment is sought, but policy-making is now more contested with more say from outside actors.

There are of course many other intriguing *implementation* dilemmas facing Chinese tax reformers including the central/local division of taxation. There are dilemmas of 'burden shifting': that is, how to balance fairly wealth differences between eastern and western China, rural and urban, rich and poor, and of unifying a divided tax system. There are significant obstacles to achieving balanced wealth distribution and questions of how to encourage industrial growth yet discourage pollution and environmental degradation. Local governments have strict limitations in borrowing from banks or issuing bonds. To get around these restrictions, they create state-owned commercial entities or 'investment platforms' which plough capital into the local property market. Hu points out in Chapter 5 of this volume that this occurs through the process of acquiring land, re-classifying it as 'commercial', building on it and then selling the buildings. About 50 per cent of local government revenues come from property. This essentially means tax revenue for local governments is significantly based on the perpetuation of property price increases.

The country is also faced with great pressure from huge social security spending. The reform of the pension system needs to be further promoted with ways of changing the social security *fee* to social security *tax* being examined to help build a unified national social security system.[9] At the same time, Credit Suisse (Wang 2010) estimates there are almost RMB10 trillion in hidden income, or 30 per cent of GDP. This estimate is, not surprisingly, disputed by the Chinese government but it is based on a survey correlating income and spending patterns over 4,000 samples and across 19 provinces in China. The survey author, Professor Wang Xiaolu, estimates that the per-capita disposable income of urban Chinese households in 2008 was in fact closer to RMB32,154 (90 per cent above official data). Total hidden income could thus amount to RMB9.3 trillion or 30 per cent of GDP, with about 63 per cent of hidden income in the hands of the top 10 per cent of urban households.[10]

Burden shifting

Burden shifting has been one of the CPC's significant taxation dilemmas. In the 1980s and through the 1990s, peasants in particular suffered disproportionately, and their resentment against their rising tax burden 'fuelled waves of riots and other violent clashes between peasants and officials in the countryside' (Pan 2008: 183). Pan makes strong assertions on this topic, and with justification, as taxes grew faster than incomes across the countryside during the early 1990s; by 2000 a peasant paid an average four times more in taxes than an urban resident despite earning six or seven times less (2008: 181). Most city residents only began paying taxes in 1994, and only if their monthly income exceeded ?800 (about US$100), but peasants paid taxes no matter how little they made as long as they produced 'agricultural products'.[11]

Alarmed by growing unrest, the party leadership tried in 1993 to set a limit on peasant taxes of 5 per cent of average local incomes. But local officials ignored regulations or found ways around them, sometimes 'coming up with ingenious new tax schemes' (Pan 2008: 184). To combat such 'ingenuity' and to promote taxation law reform generally, China's Ministry of Finance began more radical reforms of its individual, commercial and industrial tax systems effective 1 January 1994. Six key tax regulations including the VAT (or turnover tax), consumption tax, business tax, enterprise income tax, resource tax and land VAT were implemented simultaneously with a revised *Individual Income Tax Law*. These will be discussed in more detail below as they are interrelated and central to the overall reform programme affirmed in the call for *Advice for the 12th Five-Year Plan* from the CPC Central Committee (27 October 2010; Xinhua 2010f).

Unifying a divided tax system

China's divided enterprise income tax system was unified with the EITL promulgated 1 January 2008. Article 5 of this law defines 'taxable income' as: 'the gross income in a tax year less the non-taxable income, tax exempt income, deductions and allowable prior-year losses'.[12] Article 19 determines the taxable income for non-resident enterprises with no establishment in China and for non-resident enterprises that have an establishment in China. Where there is a conflict with regard to the provisions of a tax treaty between China and a foreign government, Article 58 states that the provisions of the treaty or agreement will prevail over the *Enterprise Income Tax Law*.

The EITL confirms the principle of preferential policy treatment for certain industries such as strategic SOEs, environmental protection, high-tech development, agricultural improvement, infrastructure construction and safe production equipment. The previous preferential policy favoured certain developed areas and foreign investment and eastern development centres benefited from this. Various new methods of granting preferential tax treatment now take into account the economic gap between western and eastern China (with some preferential tax benefits now benefiting the west). Essentially, the provisions of the EITL deal with the operation and application of the law, but beyond these substantive law reforms are intriguing questions as to how the reforms should be interpreted against the backdrop of a transforming PRC and 'command capitalism'.

Tax reform and the rise of 'command capitalism'

The publication and implementation of a range of new taxation laws and regulations indicate that recent reforms to the tax system are not simply a patchwork effort or a reform of individual tax categories. Rather, they are a comprehensive structural reform of the country's tax system. Official state rhetoric suggests that the goal of the new laws is to establish an overall tax system that conforms to national conditions and generally accepted international practices. Many of the reforms of the 1990s were made, argues Stoianoff (2008: 311), to satisfy the requirements of 'transparency, equity and fair treatment, essential elements for [China's] entry to the World Trade Organisation (WTO)'. At same time, there is another argument that the new laws reflect China's revenue distribution requirements in a market economy facilitated by macro-control over economic development – the so-called 'command-economy' of the one-party state (see State Council Information Office 2008).

Recent analyses by China tax law specialists Asia Trade Hub.com suggest that reforms of the tax system, conducted in line with the principle of a combination of 'planned economy' and 'market forms', have been characterized by 'a tendency towards excessive use of the tax system to interfere with market mechanisms' (Asia Trade Hub 2009). Their argument is that the multiple tax system – characterized by multiple tax categories (with multiple levels within each category) – no longer suits the further development needs of a market economy. This claim is made on the basis that it has been difficult for the state system to play its 'proper' regulatory role due to inconsistencies and conflicts between central and local governments. When one considers the period and scope of tax reform beginning in 1980s, Asia Hub's critique may be a little harsh as the system has undergone radical change and does require time to be constantly improved. Not every change can lead immediately to satisfying results especially in tax areas that have to consider equity. Perhaps the key point that Asia Hub glosses over is the potential for conflict between the regulatory authorities and the central government as they are in fact separate arms of the same body-politic.

On this analysis, the ideological influence of socialism with Chinese characteristics as a guide to tax reform is downplayed in that the requirements of the market and need for market *efficiencies* have become influential. But Marxism is clearly not eliminated even though the tax reforms of China Inc. indicate market pragmatism currently rules over socialist ideological justifications. Despite this pragmatism, Asia Trade Hub (2009) argues that major inefficiencies remain in the current tax system, manifesting themselves in three key ways, that: (1) an unfair tax burden is carried by the less well-off; (2) the (discretionary) power of management over the division of tax income is too great; and (3) the distributive relationship between the state and private enterprises can be disproportionate. The following section examines the veracity of such claims by considering various illustrations of China's complex taxation system.

The benzhi 本质 *('nitty-gritty') of taxation law reform*

It is, of course, impossible to summarize in one chapter the sweeping reforms of China's taxation system.[13] Critical issues flagged earlier in this book such as changes to the company law regime, bankruptcy, environment, climate change and implementation of the sweeping new labour laws all carry very significant taxation implications for the future. For instance, tax incentives and imposts are very likely to be more extensively used to regulate industries with respect to air pollution, water usage (and water pollution), toxic waste management and disposal, sustainable consumption (including motor vehicle usage) and carbon emissions (Ye and Wang 2010; Wang and Voituriez 2010). China is taking steps towards imposing new resource taxes as a means of conserving resources, slowing environmental destruction and rebalancing an economy that delivers bloated corporate profits at the expense of households.[14] Each of these major issues requires specific attention in its own right but space permits just some brief discussion of examples of strategic (elements of) changes to the taxation system – to enable theoretical analysis of the overall reform package. These elements include a new 'turnover' or VAT tax system, new consumption taxes, new business taxes levied on labour transactions and tertiary industry, a unified individual income tax system and other initiated tax items including interim regulations on *land, private property and inheritance*.

The VAT system

Premier Wen Jiabao through the State Council Information Office (2008) stated that:

> In order to ... reduce the tax burden of equipment investments for enterprises, accelerate technology development with industrial structure adjustment and transfer economic growth type, it is decided by the State Council that starting from January 1st 2009 the transformation and reform of VAT will be established in all of areas and industries throughout the whole nation.

At that time, Wen's narrative indicated that a key element of the overall tax reform strategy was to be the turnover tax based on the VAT. The Standing Committee of State Council decided the transformation of China's VAT system will be established for the whole nation.[15] In China's multiple tax system, the turnover tax is a major source of tax revenue and a significant fiscal lever. When China's State Council announced that it would spread the reform of its value-added tax regime to all industries nationwide (Xinhua 2008a), the plan was to cut the tax burden on enterprises by ¥120 billion (about US$17.6 billion). The idea behind this reform was to *encourage technological upgrading* at Chinese enterprises. At the same time, and in response to effects of the GFC, the State Council also put forward a stimulus package of ¥4 trillion to expand domestic demand.[16]

One year later the government called for 'Advice' (Xinhua 2010f) for China's 12th Five-Year Plan. Part 10, Paragraph 42 of the Plan addresses the 'Reform Progress of the Fiscal and Taxation System' and this reconfirms the intentions to:

> develop a better set of taxations policies in order to facilitate the reconstruction of industries and development of service industry, the main prospects of reform would be made to increase the collection scope of VAT tax ... reduce the scope business taxation and correspondingly adjust the scope and *tax rate structure* of consumption tax.
>
> (Xinhua 2010f)

The current Plan (2011–15) aims to improve the individual taxation system, additional tax categories shall be provided together with a comprehensive calculation system ... with the following reforms carrying over in the future, to: (a) progress the shift from fees to tax; (b) start comprehensive reform of resource tax; (c) promulgate the environmental protection tax; and (d) continue with the research on real estate tax.

Essentially, the aims of VAT reform in this broad context are to shift from the production-based value-added tax regime to a *consumption-based* one. The shift enables

Chinese companies to get tax deductions for spending on fixed assets and focuses on the implementation of a standardized VAT, establishing consumption and business taxes centred on the new pattern of a dual-level turnover tax. VAT becomes a 'wide-ranging' regulation, and the consumption tax a 'special' regulation. The new tax maintains the characteristics of the turnover tax in terms of its wide-ranging scope, and stable tax revenues are said to 'demonstrate the principle of unity between the tax system and market mechanisms'.[17]

The VAT is held out to be a type of 'neutral tax' with a relatively high degree of transparency. Based on the simple principle of economic returns, the theory is that this tax will 'encourage' enterprises to select the best form of production, management and organization, and facilitate the implementation of tax reimbursement for export products more in line with common international practices. Arguably, the bottom line appears to be that it aims to strengthen the competitiveness of China's products on international markets rather than redistribute wealth according to Marxist principles; proponents may argue that ultimately this can amount to the same thing.

In terms of present taxation reform, VAT becomes *the* major tax item and central component of the whole. The goal, in line with generally accepted international practices and conforming to existing conditions in China, is to establish a relatively comprehensive VAT mechanism that fits into the entire taxation system and meets the requirements of the market economy.[18] An effect is that this mechanism expands the scope of taxation. Industrial products previously exempt from VAT and product tax such as wholesale retail commodities, public utilities of water, electricity, heat and gas (which previously paid business taxes) and salt (which was subject to salt tax), all now fall within the scope of the new VAT. All industrial and commercial enterprises engaged in selling products (and dutiable labour) and individuals must pay VAT, although the provisional regulation on VAT s.2(3) allows a *zero tax rate* for approved export commodities: that is, all tax payments may be refunded following the declaration of exports (except if stipulated otherwise by the State Council).[19]

Following the VAT reforms, taxpayers who calculate their tax amounts in accordance with the standardized method are subject to a special tax registration and have to use special VAT invoices. Here the state's goals are to establish an auditing system to cross-check both purchasing and selling taxpayers, and to strengthen the internal mechanisms of VAT self-control. In turn these measures aim to prevent tax evasion and ensure the application of appropriate tax reductions and exemptions. Such goals are laudable of course, but given the extent and scale of informal financing in China and its significant economic effects, management and enforcement across the entire system are likely to be very difficult.[20] Further and ongoing improvements to the value-added tax and sales tax systems and expanding the scope of the value-added tax are clearly central to China's tax reform agenda.[21]

Consumption tax and business taxes levied on labour transactions (which are not subject to VAT)

The consumption tax is a relatively new tax category of the turnover tax system reform. On the basis of a general VAT levy on commodities, a consumption tax is further levied on selected consumer goods mainly for the purpose of adjusting consumption patterns, providing guidance to consumers and guaranteeing the country's financial revenue. At least that is the official government line. It is a line with many historical antecedents. Chinese governments have in the past sought to satisfy special needs by levying heavy taxes on certain consumer goods. For example, to curb burgeoning real estate market bubbles, one fiercely debated option has been the idea of levying a high rate of tax on certain luxury housing. Indeed, it is common international practice for relatively high taxes to be levied on targeted consumer products such as beer, wine, cigarettes, certain categories of cars and fuel, and to have capital gains taxes on investment property.

Business taxes are another tax category coming under this 'turnover tax' umbrella, taxes levied on the basis of business volume (such as sales). Reform to the collection of business taxes has been applied to two types of business activity: *providing labour services* and *selling immovable assets*.[22] When these reforms are read in conjunction with the implementation of the new Company Laws (Zhang Xianchu in Chapter 2 of this volume), Anti-Monopoly Laws (Zhang 2011: 142) and the 1 March 2007 amendment to the EITL (unifying the taxation systems of enterprises with different forms of ownership), there are clearly efforts being made to improve level playing conditions in the market and to more equitably distribute wealth via taxation. At the same time preferential conditions remain for SOEs as there are clear tax advantages for Tier-1 SOEs, just as there are for other comparably large, major market players. The main advantages accruing to Tier-1 SOEs are not necessarily preferential tax treatments although these are built in, but rather their capacity to tap into sovereign funds for structured financing.[23] Indeed, bank lending, which funds the bulk of domestic fixed-asset investment, amounted to $US220 billion in January 2011 alone. Three-quarters of the capital goes to SOEs (Lee 2011).

Unified individual income tax

In the mainland's personal tax system, the individual income tax rate varies from 5 per cent to 45 per cent depending on how much income has been generated. The Finance Ministry reported (19 June 2009) that of the ¥372.2 billion in personal income tax collected in 2008, 35 per cent (¥129.4 billion) was paid by the top 3 per cent of income earners (2.4 million people). Personal income tax collected in 2010 grew to ¥483.7 billion – 22.5 per cent more than 2009. In first quarter of 2011 alone tax collection was ¥203.8 billion – 37 per cent more than the first quarter of 2010. Based on Ministry of Finance figures (2011) this increased tax revenue is mainly from capital gains tax (which jumped 121 per cent compared to the corresponding period of the previous year) and includes a CGT tax increase of 57.2 per cent from real estate.[24]

Individual income tax reform is thus an important means of offsetting some social disparities even though it is now commonly argued that solutions (to the extent of wealth inequality) may revolve around a more fully marketized economy and democratized political system. This is generally acknowledged in China but remains a fierce subject of debate (Zhao 2006; Garnaut 2010g).[25] Notwithstanding this political debate, the importance of two tax types in China for social equity – individual income tax and inheritance tax – cannot be understated, as private wealth is now an accepted part of the system. The general legislative principle for individual income tax adopted in various countries around the world is to regulate gaps in personal income and ease contradictions resulting from major disparities in social distribution. The social distribution of wealth via the tax system was precisely one of the purposes of the revised *Individual Income Tax Law of the PRC* adopted by the National People's Congress in October 1993 to ensure income taxes were levied on high-income earners, with a lesser tax (or no income tax) levied on medium- and low-income earners respectively.

The goals of China's revised income tax laws were thus two-fold: to prevent excessive increases in the tax burden carried by lower-income earners on the one hand, and to ensure a reduction in the overall tax burden to stimulate entrepreneurial activity on the other hand. To achieve these dual goals, the overall taxation system was standardized by incorporating *the original* taxes of individual income tax, the individual income regularity tax and the income tax on urban and rural individual industrial and commercial households, into *the new* (unified) *individual income tax*. The revised individual income tax law applies to both Chinese citizens and foreign personnel earning income in China.[26]

China's methods of levying individual income tax differ from those used in most Western countries where income tax tends to be calculated annually on a lump-sum basis. China has adopted the method of itemized deductions and fixed rate items, and levies taxes on a monthly, annual or specified time basis. The levy method was selected to address specific Chinese conditions, with the aim to block loopholes in tax collection and management. There are still many problems with China's existing personal income tax system, with the tax for many simply deducted from a worker's salary by his or her company. But the number of breadwinners in a family is not taken into consideration, creating the potential for some workers to pay overly high personal income tax.[27]

The unified individual tax reforms have been made, however, to radically accommodate the government's promotion of private enterprise and market base with additional tax levied on exceptionally high income (earned as remuneration for non-recurring short-term labour services) strengthening the regulatory dynamics by restricting excessively high income levels.[28] See Figure 9.1.

'Wealth hatred' and the critical importance of readjusted, abolished, merged and initiated tax items

The topics of taxation and 'wealth hatred' are commonly perceived to be interconnected in China. New tax categories are thus politically very sensitive. In the overall tax reform programme several new initiates have included: VAT on *land* to regulate excessive profits involving land transactions; a stock exchange tax to assist in regulating the stock market; inheritance tax to regulate property inheritance; and a social insurance tax to provide fund guarantees for the comprehensive

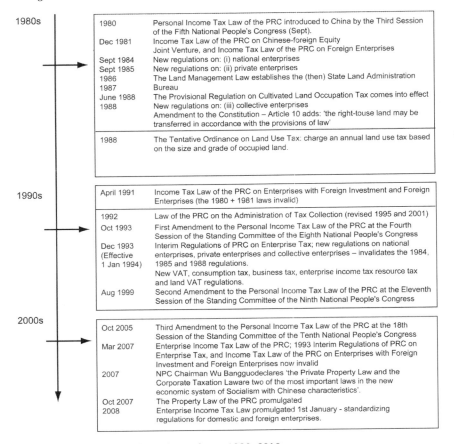

Figure 9.1 China's landmark tax law reforms 1980–2010

reform of the state social security system. All of these tax initiatives are worthy of disaggregated examination. However, the land VAT is examined in more detail here as an example; its material effects are pronounced and it directly and indirectly affects the other reforms.

Land VAT is levied on the value of transferred real estate – that is, the balance of earnings gained from the transfer of state land, including use rights, surface structures and other attachments (which are referred to as transferred real estate after deducting related costs, expenses and tax paid). The sums of money involved in this terrain are vast and stir emotions on a grand scale. The regulations stipulate that all units and individuals are subject to VAT, irrespective of their economic nature, whether domestic- or foreign-funded enterprises, whether Chinese or foreign (and whether operating real estate and earning exclusively or concurrently, so long as they operate real estate and earn income from within the territory of the PRC).[29]

Taxation on transferred real estate is a very sensitive area of law reform in China for several reasons as it is related to 'wealth hatred'. In the years since 1978 vast wealth has been transferred from the state to the expanded private sector. Between 1993 and 2001 approximately 25 per cent of global growth went to China, with the private sector responsible for about three-quarters of economic output and employment in China (Zang Xiaowei 2008: 54). The new rich (and their family members) probably do not exceed 4 per cent of the total PRC population (approximately less than 45 million) or less than 0.74 per cent of the world population. In 2007, 20 of the world's 946 billionaires came from the PRC. By 2010 this number had grown to 64 out of 1,011 billionaires globally (27 being from the mainland). By 9 March 2011 the total known billionaires had reached 1,210 world-wide, with 115 being from mainland China (second to the US), indicating the trajectory in private wealth holdings among the privileged elite in the PRC was not unduly affected by the 2009 GFC (Sina.com 2011).

With respect to OFDI, efforts to bring 'hot money' out of the country may partly explain the sharp increase in outward bound investment since 2004. But it is really only a small proportion of private entrepreneurs who have accumulated a large amount of wealth and who have come to play a high-profile role in the Chinese economy. At the same time they have often been intriguingly linked to powerful government officials and cadres of the CPC (Zang Xiaowei 2008: 54). Since 2000 there have been heated discussions on 'wealth hatred' in China's mass media and on the internet. On this point Zang Xiaowei (2008: 56) mentions that 'wealth hatred' (*choufu xinli*) is a popular term used by ordinary citizens to reject the legitimacy of the claim to wealth by private entrepreneurs. Zang further points out that:

> Seething popular discontent resulting from the 'unjustifiable' inequalities and suspect sources of wealth in part explains why private entrepreneurs seem to have developed a profound sense of distrust in ordinary citizens and a general opposition to democracy if it means majority rule.
>
> (2008: 56)

An underlying reason for the so-called 'wealth hatred' lies in this inherent dilemma of China's socialist ideology which aims at capitalist-style reforms. To an extent this reform process was anticipated to lead to some social injustice and disparity of wealth distribution. Many became rich virtually overnight during China's development boom in the transition towards a market economy. It could be argued that they were able to become rich simply because the economy had not yet 'marketized' enough: that is, competition had not yet evolved and, with the government owning the land, developers with 'close connections' to government officials gained a competitive advantage. Zang Xiaowei (2008) refers to the collaboration between the wealthy and government officials with the immediate interests of some residents on the land having been, to an extent, sacrificed. A significant example was seen in preparations for the 2008 Olympic Games with the disappearance of many *hutongs* as developers 'bought' entire neighbourhoods, and everyone, even those holding full title and not just possessory rights, had to go. Almost everybody facing eviction was offered compensation, and when asked about this process one developer, Chen Lihua (reportedly China's richest woman at the time of writing), stated unequivocally that 'in the real estate business, you can't succeed without a political patron behind you' (Bernstein 2009: 7).

Land-use monies

As mentioned earlier, local governments do not raise money for development through bank loans, direct taxes or bond issues, but from the sale of land-use rights (see Chapter 5). This system is a key factor related to both wealth generation and distribution, and a key point in relation to land-use rights is that since the 1994 changes were made to the previously more divided tax system (i.e. between the central and local governments), the central government became more powerful in collecting tax. Local governments experienced, to varying degrees, some financial burden as a consequence. One important source of revenue for local governments has thus been to sell land to private developers, justifying their deals under the rhetoric of 'developing the local economy'.

Important measures have subsequently been introduced to break the interest-alliance between local governments and developers. Since 2002, all land-use rights must be transferred through *public bidding*. Before that, most land-use rights were transferred through bilateral contracts, which engendered non-transparent cooperation between, in the public's view, corrupt government officials and greedy developers. Praise initially heaped on private developers and entrepreneurs for helping China's economic miracle has in some instances turned to blame for many social problems including recent massive lay-offs of workers affected by the economic downturn of 2009, the increase in unaffordable housing, and a widening gap between rich and poor. The magnitude and intensity of 'wealth hatred' has apparently alarmed some PRC leaders with legal and administrative measures introduced to protect private property.

The Fifth Session of the Tenth National People's Congress (March 2007) enacted new laws on property rights to protect legally acquired private properties (see Hu 2011: 199). One effect has been that some private property developers and entrepreneurs have been viewed as gaining personal profit at the expense of both state assets and workers. Indeed, it can be argued that capital gains tax on investment property profits is not always effective, giving some support to this view.[30] The profound sense of injustice magnifies the importance of taxation law reform as a way of equitably redistributing wealth and of *being seen* to be fair. In rural China, for instance, for the purpose of social redistribution, peasants are subsided for farming, and social security and health systems are being spread in rural areas as important measures to build a 'new socialist rural China' under the official 'social harmony' programme.

In city and urban developments in particular, however, it appears that much depends on a corrupt complicity between capitalists and officials with 'minimal' transparency about this powerful combination. Reforms that include the urban land-use tax to ensure it is applicable to both urban and rural areas do not mask this underlying 'power' nexus. Increasing the tax value and revising the urban maintenance and construction tax to create an independent tax category simply enables a further means of raising funds for local construction – with the well-connected rich getting richer.

Resources tax

An expansion in the scope of tax collection for resources including all mineral resources is foreseeable. Taxable items now include crude oil, natural gas, coal, non-metal raw ores, ferrous metal raw ores, nonferrous metal raw ores and salt.[31] At the same time a number of former tax categories have been cancelled, including the fair trade tax, domestic animal trades tax, special consumption tax, special tax on enterprises that use petroleum as a principal fuel, the salt tax, bonus tax and wage regularity tax. The special consumption tax and special tax on enterprises that use petroleum as a principal fuel are now incorporated into the consumption tax, with the salt tax becoming a part of the resource tax.[32]

Tax avoidance

That the government is seriously concerned about the magnitude of tax avoidance is reflected in Wen Jiabao's declaration that to combat this endemic issue 'the government will firmly crack down on and ban illegal income; regulate off-the-books income; gradually form a transparent, fair and rational pattern of income distribution; and resolutely reverse the widening income gap' (Wen Jiabao 2010: 24).

There is little doubt that China's mass media is convinced that tax avoidance (and corruption more broadly) occurs on a significant scale. Media reports over the past two decades have often featured both corporate tax avoidance (including the use of phoenix companies) and personal income tax avoidance as a common way for many Chinese business people to become rich. This avoidance has, to an extent, been tolerated by the public and legitimized in government discourse as a required 'stepping stone' in market reformation. As argued earlier, tax avoidance has been possible on a wide scale owing to elements of corruption between some business people and some government officials, and the technical incapacity to link tax, banking and credit. In this way some tax can be avoided in certain types of informal financial transfers. Similarly, a factor potentially contributing to the dramatic increase in OFDI is what Rosen and Henemann (2009: 3) refer to as 'round-tripping': reporting OFDI (mostly to Hong Kong or tax havens[33]) only to bring it back into China in order to enjoy preferential FDI treatment and other advantages (although as mentioned earlier these are now being phased out).

To combat tax avoidance, the PSB has the power to target a business person it has suspicions about by investigating tax 'irregularities'. The precondition for commencing the investigation is that the PSB and the government officials behind the scenes are convinced that the business person(s) should be punished, often for reasons other than tax avoidance. In the media-shaped public opinion, if a business person is investigated and imprisoned for tax avoidance, a constructed common perception is that he or she must have done something wrong with the government, not necessarily for having avoided tax. Being unable to maintain good relations with the government can be a significant problem, with tax avoidance and corruption being interwoven. A good example of this conflation of tax avoidance and corruption is the imprisonment for tax avoidance in 2003 of Liu Xiaoqing. At that time one of China's most famous movie stars, Liu's case was portrayed in the media as an illustration of the government's determination to address tax avoidance by businesses and individuals by using a celebrity's name.

One of China's richest men, Huang Guangyu,[34] disappeared from his home in November 2008 with Chinese and Hong Kong media reporting that he was being questioned by the PSB. It has been subsequently confirmed that Huang Guangyu was held by the PSB for many reasons, tax avoidance one of them (although not necessarily the primary reason). The media's enthusiasm for Huang's case illuminates how many Chinese journalists (and readers/viewers) have come to expect successful business people and officials to 'cut corners' to succeed.[35] Pew's 2008 survey of global attitudes found that corruption was China's third greatest public grievance behind inflation and the rich–poor gap (Garnaut 2008: 16).

Against this emotive backdrop of 'wealth hatred' in the broader Chinese community and the associated government crackdown on corruption, it would seem breathtakingly unwise to improperly or illegally avoid taxation. At the same time it is clear that in China key issues extend not only to tax policy, but to tax implementation. In the context of an evolving system that is not universal (in that it does not, at this stage, integrate banking, tax and credit records), tax evasion may not be too difficult for the resourceful, with costs relatively low compared to potential gains. Perhaps this is connected to one of the reasons President Hu Jintao highlighted in his 2008 five-yearly work report the importance of fighting corruption: 'addressing both the symptoms and root causes ... and in particular ... to tackle the problems of excessive concentration of power and lack of checks on power' (ibid.).

Conclusion

Several conclusions may be drawn from this study. First, extensive reforms have been made to China's tax system to accompany and facilitate its economic reform policy with the effect of significantly centralizing China's extensive system of taxation. The central government now has relatively firm control of the country's fiscal levers, and with it the resources and capacity to steer overall social and economic development and tighten political control. Second, this central control of taxation has had significant effects on local authorities' abilities to raise revenue and some 'creative measures' have been adopted by local officials to replace lost sources of local tax revenue. A prime example surrounds transferring land-use rights to various SOE investment platforms and private developers and stimulating property development to grow local government revenues. A net effect of the new tax laws along with the inflationary pressures of a rapidly growing economy is excessive, speculatory property price increases in some Chinese cities – especially the leading cities – where property prices have evolved from being economic concerns to social and political issues for China's central government. The introduction of new targeted property taxes and policies to cool off property markets and to control bank lending for property investment are indicative in this scenario, including the prospects of increasing the holding costs of property investments for the rich with a more effective capital gains tax.[36] Yet at the same time the government aims to 'keep property tax as a stable main component of the tax revenue of local governments'.[37] Third, since implementing the tax reforms described herein, the number of tax categories belonging to China's original consolidated industrial and commercial taxes, excluding customs duty and the agricultural tax, has decreased, inferring a more efficient, simplified tax system is evolving. However, the objectives of the tax system are fulfilled mostly by extensive regulations rather than formal tax laws and getting consistent interpretations remains a challenge.[38] Fourth, the *Enterprise Income Tax Law* (2008) standardizes regulations for domestic and foreign enterprises simplifying the previous dual system and balancing benefits. Some foreign investors have had an adjustment period of five years (which commenced 1 January 2008), but the 25 per cent tax rate is relatively low compared to most developed nations. These reforms will tighten a key loop-hole for OFDI being syphoned from the mainland to offshore tax havens via Hong Kong, then reinvested back in China at beneficial rates. The reforms will not, of course, eliminate tax avoidance without further supportive regulatory control and strong enforcement measures.

Broader conclusions can also be drawn. As taxation law reforms are a tool for social and economic change during a transitional stage of the PRC, they are not merely 'neutral'. If taxation is insufficient, gaps can be left in the pension system, health care and social security insurance, worker and consumer protection, public education, environmental protection, addressing corruption and so on. In turn, such 'gaps' ultimately influence public and consumer confidence. Ultimately, the success of China's 'going out' policy is co-dependent on these internal elements being in place. China is thus clearly faced with new dilemmas as it develops and refines its taxation laws and regulations. At the heart of the dilemmas is balancing the mixed public/private economic reforms. In this balancing act, local officials can exercise formidable influence over local bank branches and they rely on a seemingly endless flow of capital to local SOEs. The favouring of SOEs (and corresponding suppression of the domestic private sector through capital deprivation) is a key pillar of how the CPC maintains economic dominance and influence at grassroots levels, allowing it to dispense the most valued business and career opportunities (see Lee 2011). Some privileged private entrepreneurs have become conspicuously wealthy in socialism's devolution from Mao's era (of strident collectivism) to socialism with Chinese characteristics (pragmatic collectivism) to a new, hybrid-form collectivism.[39] The conspicuous new wealth of a few is considered by some critics as unfair, perhaps even a betrayal of China's brand of socialism. 'Trickle-down' benefits to ordinary citizens are not always clear and the existence of hidden income has contributed to an expanded income gap.

During the transition to a market economy and 'open-door' phase the emphasis has been on implementing a new taxation regime for both domestic and foreign enterprises that complies with WTO requirements. The reforms are in fact a corporate tax strategy that is 'catching up with the individual taxation reforms made in the 1990s' (Stoianoff 2008: 319). The new tax regime better suits the strategic requirements of China Inc. The relevant tax law principles were not, however, embedded in the PRC Constitution. Conditions thus exist whereby the people who make the laws also enforce them, which can result in power imbalances and potential injustice: one arm of government being *market player*, another arm being *the regulator*. However, according to official ideology, socialism with Chinese characteristics views the law reforms as an extension of the economic system and the system of ownership which determines modes of production. It follows that when taxation law reform is viewed as an integral part of the *political structure*, reforms are merely the instrument of the political will of the ruling power.

From this perspective key questions about the future tax law reforms of 'market socialism' arise. Can the tensions and contradictions inherent in China's economic and ideological systems be glossed over without inadvertently creating structural imbalances? To what extent do the tax reforms serve the socialist goal of fair wealth redistribution and, in the delicate balancing act of taxation policy, to what extent do reforms serve the self-interest of China's new rich who possess economic power and the requisite political connections?

Notes

1 Virtually nonexistent when economic reform began in 1978 and remaining insignificant to 2004, by 2007 the annual volume of OFDI had grown to around US$25 billion, doubling to more than US$50 billion in 2008. The stock of Chinese cross-border investments reached approximately US$170 billion at the end of 2008 (see Rosen and Hanemann 2009: 3 and for updates, *The China Investment Monitor* at: www.rhgroup.net/china-investment-monitor).
2 'Preliminary' in the sense that socialist China emerged in 1949 from a semi-colonial, semi-feudal period, without passing through a stage of highly developed capitalism – its productive forces thus lagged behind those of developed capitalist countries – thus having to undergo a long period of preliminary socialism with the private economy allowed to co-exist with the socialist public economy (see Peter de Cruz 1999: 132).
3 Lee Feigon (Lee 2002: 179) argues that 'postsocialism' is the ideological counterpart of postmodernism, a cultural crisis unique to societies that have undergone decades of 'Leninist–Stalinist' development.
4 Mandate of the Ministry of Finance at: www.mof.gov.cn, March 2008.
5 OECD 'Economic Survey of China 2010' at: www.oecd.org/document/43/0,3343, en_2649_34571_44477419_1_1_1_37443,00.html.
6 *Zhonghua Renmin Gongheguo Qiye Suodeshui Fa* [Enterprises Income Tax Law of the People's Republic of China] (promulgated by the National People's Congress 16 March 2007 and effective from 1 January 2008).
7 Source: www.asiatradehub.com/china/tax.asp.
8 Source: http://theory.people.com.cn/GB/40551/3145450.html.
9 *People's Daily* (2010b). The original article foregrounding this shift by Minister Xie Xuren (1 April 2010) ?[Intensify the fiscal levy with constancy], *Qiu Shi Magazine* [Seeking

China's taxation law reforms   161

10 Truth], explains that 'research on social security tax is underway to find alternatives in funding social security', at: www.qstheory.cn/zxdk/2010/201007/201003/t20100326_25267.htm.
10 Professor Wang's 2010 report, 'Chinese annual household income understated by almost 10 trillion RMB?' is at: www.sinocism.com/archives/953; also see the Credit Suisse website: www.credit-suisse.com.
11 Individual income tax law, first introduced into China in 1980, subjected only a small number of city residents to the tax owing to the relatively high starting income base. The Law, amended in 1993 with a lower levy floor, enlarged the tax base significantly and it was in this sense Pan argued many city residents did not have to pay tax until 1994.
12 With regard to foreign-owned enterprises it is important to distinguish 'Chinese sourced' and 'non-Chinese sourced' income (see Article 6 which lists the types of monetary and non-monetary income that comprises 'gross income'): www.asiatradehub.com/china/tax.asp.
13 For a full list of current effective laws of the PRC published by the State Council Information Office (2008) see China's Efforts and Achievements in Promoting the Rule of Law at: www.china.org.cn/government/news/2008-02/28/content_11025486_12.htm.
14 Professor Huang Yiping (China Centre for Economic Research, Peking University) asserts that a resources tax will be imposed in the next five years following China's 1 June 2010 unveiling of its first resources tax, at a rate of 5 per cent on fossil fuels in Xinjiang, as a way of retaining some of the region's mineral wealth in local hands. Since then, Li Keqiang (a vice-premier), has advocated in the Communist Party's leading theory magazine *Seeking Truth* a national resources tax at: www.smh.com.au/business/now-china-mulls-tax-on-resources-20100609-xwwn.html.
15 For the main contents of this reform, see: http://202.108.90.130/n6669073/n6669088/index.html.
16 Source: www.chinaview.cn (Xinhua 2008a).
17 www.asiatradehub.com/china/tax.asp.
18 *Value Added Tax Implementing Rules of the People's Republic of China* Articles 1 and 2.
19 The provisional regulations on VAT were implemented 1 January 2009 adopting a tax withholding system with taxable amounts calculated in accordance with the purchase tax withholding law.
20 In 2005 the People's Bank of China estimated the annual scale of informal lending to be 950 billion RMB (US$118 billion) (i.e. 6.96 per cent of the country's GDP) in *China Management News*, 6 August. Tsai (2006) argued the main engine of China's reform-era growth (the private sector) has relied on informal rather than formal sources of credit despite efforts of the People's Bank of China and the China Banking Regulatory Commission to limit informal finance by increasing private sector access to the banking system. These efforts are not likely to eliminate informal finance owing to various local political, economic and social advantages.
21 As stated by Xu Lin, director of the Department of Fiscal and Financial Affairs (under the National Development and Reform Commission): *People's Daily* (2010b).
22 The *Regulations on the Business Tax of the People's Republic of China* are provided at: www.fdi.gov.cn/pub/FDI_EN/Laws/law_en_info.jsp?docid=99461; and www.fdi.gov.cn/pub/FDI_EN/Laws/law_en_info.jsp?docid=100542.
23 See: http://seekingalpha.com/article/166968-2009-a-chinese-energy-acquisition-odyssey; and www.eeo.com.cn/ens/Politics/2009/11/10/155247.shtml.
24 Ministry of Finance, 1 February 2011 (for 2010 figures) and 21 April 2011 (for 2011 figures), in Chinese only at: http://szs.mof.gov.cn/zhengwuxinxi/gongzuodongtai/201104/t20110421_539744.html.
25 Garnaut (2010g) quotes General Liu Yazhou (political commissar of the National Defence University):

> If a system fails to let its citizens breathe freely and release their creativity to the maximum extent, and fails to place those who best represent the system and its people into leadership positions, it is certain to perish ... The secret of US success is neither Wall Street nor Silicon Valley, but its long-surviving rule of law and the system behind it.

This may indicate China's political and ideological struggles are livelier than commonly thought. A key is not what *is* said, but *who* says it (General Liu's father was a senior military officer and his father-in-law was Li Xiannian, one of Chinese communism's 'Eight Immortals' and a one-time president of China). Full text: www.smh.com.au/world/china-must-reform-or-die-20100811-11zxd.html.

26 Any individual income from contracted operations of enterprises, institutions, leasing arrangements, royalties, occasional income and property transfers is caught although some exemptions apply. See recent SAT announcements at Xinhua (2011c).

27 See note 23 (Xu Lin 2010).

28 This approach contrasts with failed attempts in the US and other Western nations to curb excessive private sector greed at executive levels, particularly bonuses paid in the insurance, banking and finance sectors following the collapse of Wall Street giant Lehman Brothers and US government bail-outs of failed private corporate enterprises such as General Motors.

29 See: State Administration of Taxation 'Tax Law', at: http://202.108.90.130/n6669073/n6669088/index.html.

30 At the time of writing calculating capital gains tax from the sale of real estate in China was based on the purchase cost being deducted from the sale price at the 20 per cent rate (i.e. an individual's capital gains and investment income are taxed at 20 per cent). Capital gains tax for a Chinese company is added to the regular tax: www.worldwide-tax.com/china/china_tax.asp. See also: www.fdi.gov.cn/pub/FDI_EN/Laws/law_en_info.jsp?docid=51616.

31 China's method of calculating taxes is from the 'quantity quota' (in accordance with the category of product) and sets the tax value with upper and lower limits, tax rates varying with the different resource conditions even for the same product.

32 Cancelling the 'urban real estate' tax, taxes on vehicles and boats (and the operating licence tax on vehicles and boats) and introducing a unified housing property tax, a tax on vehicles and/or boats, reforming the banquet tax (and tax on slaughter-houses) to lower levels, and allowing various localities to decide whether or not to levy such taxes in light of local conditions are all part of the reform process.

33 China's OFDI data are unclear; however, Chinese companies are required to submit OFDI destination 'region and country' in the registration and approval process. According to Rosen and Hanemann (2009: 4) firms tend to 'report the first, not the final, destination of their investment, weighting the numbers towards stop-over locations such as Hong Kong'. The implication is that 'final' destinations such as tax havens in the Cayman Islands, the Bahamas and the British Virgin Islands are not caught. In MOFCOM data around 80 per cent of Chinese OFDI stock lies in Hong Kong or tax havens (ibid.).

34 Said to have a fortune of up to $US6 billion, Huang Guangyu, Chairman of Gome Electronics, was listed by *Forbes* magazine in 2008 as China's second richest person.

35 Huang Guangyu was sentenced to 14 years' jail in May 2010. See Garnaut (2010e).

36 Between 2008 and 2010 individuals in the two lowest tax brackets paid zero long-term capital gains tax, while everyone else paid 15 per cent. From 2011 individuals in the lowest tax bracket will pay 10 per cent while the rest will pay 20 per cent. The majority of foreign stock investors are in the higher brackets and face a 5 per cent increase: http://au.ibtimes.com/articles/29669/20100622/the-2011-capital-gains-tax-rate-hike-and-its-impact.htm.

37 See note 23 (Xu Lin 2010).

38 Professor Liu Jianwen (Peking University tax law) in a 2002 internet interview, and other China tax law experts on how in 2010 the reforms are reflected in practice, at: www.fdi.gov.cn/pub/FDI_EN/Laws/law_en_info.jsp?docid=76240.
39 The term 'hybrid collectivism' is used here in relation to outcomes of the surge of hybrid laws and the amalgam of policies emerging from the pragmatic stage of collectivist justifications for market reform on one hand, and the state's use of seductive elements of the high capitalist road (such as privileging certain individual private entrepreneurs and hybrid state/non-state actors) on the other hand.

Part III
Courts, alternative dispute resolution and anti-corruption measures in China

10 Economic and social rights

The role of courts in China

*Randall Peerenboom**

Compared to the average lower-middle income country, China has done relatively well on most social and economic indicators.[1] Chinese courts however have generally played a limited, and rather ineffectual, role in implementing economic and social rights (ESR).[2]

Not surprisingly, one of the concerns flagged by the Committee for Economic, Social and Cultural Rights (CESRC) was the extent to which ESR could be invoked before the courts.[3] In its Concluding Remarks, the committee specifically urged China 'to ensure that legal and judicial training takes full account of the justiciability of the rights contained in the Covenant and promotes the use of the Covenant as a source of law in domestic courts.[4]

This chapter considers what the role of the courts could and should be in implementing ESR in China. Part I surveys recent global developments giving greater bite to economic and social rights, as well as some of the main controversies, debates, and approaches to promoting, protecting and fulfilling ESR, with particular attention to the role of the courts. Part II provides a general introduction to the social, legal, political and economic context in China. The overall environment in China is, if not hostile, at least not promising for a robust role for the courts in protecting ESR. Nevertheless, there is still some room for the courts to play a positive role in implementing ESR. Part III provides some suggestions regarding the way forward, suggesting that what is needed is an approach that considers all factors: absolute minimums and core rights; the level of development nationally, regionally and locally; community consensus and popular opinions; institutional constraints; and the role of courts within the Chinese constitutional structure and polity. Part IV concludes.

Global trends: The increased salience of ESR

Although civil and political rights still receive more attention, the global salience of ESR has been increasing. The International Covenant on Economic, Social and Cultural Rights (ICESCR), passed in 1966, has now been signed by 69 states and ratified by 160. The Optional Protocol to the ICESCR, adopted on 8 December 2010, has given a further boost to ESR. The Protocol provides a mechanism for the CESRC to hear complaints from individuals, groups or other states.

There has also been a change in attitudes. Whether ESR are indeed 'rights' is still debated, but less so. It is also now generally accepted that it is not possible to draw a sharp line between civil and political rights (CPR) and ESR: both sets of rights have negative aspects (in the sense of limiting government action) and positive aspects (in the sense of requiring state action and support); the realization of CPR also requires government expenditures (for example, to hold elections, fund the judiciary and legal aid centers, etc.); and the two sets of rights are interdependent in the sense that neither can be fully realized without the other.

The constitutional basis of ESR is also increasingly secure. Many new constitutions in 'third wave' democracies have incorporated individual or comprehensive ESR, although the piecemeal approach remains more common. Most importantly for present purposes, regional tribunals and domestic courts have assumed a more prominent role in enforcing ESR. Social rights are now litigated directly and indirectly before the African Commission on Human Rights, Inter-American Commission of Human Rights, Inter-American Court of Human Rights, European Committee of Social Rights, and European Court of Human Rights.[5] Among the jurisdictions in which social and economic rights have been deemed justiciable and judicially enforceable are Bangladesh, Colombia, Finland, Kenya, Hungary, Latvia, the Philippines, Switzerland, Venezuela, South Africa, Ireland, India, Argentina and even the US.[6] These states represent a wide diversity in terms of regions, philosophical and cultural traditions, political systems, constitutional structures and levels of wealth, suggesting that some role for the courts in realizing ESR is possible in all states.

Nevertheless, ESR remain controversial. Among the many contested issues and debates, three issues stand out.

The first is the nature of the state's obligation with respect to ESR, and the tension between the need to take immediate steps to realize some or all of them at least in part and their ultimate full realization on a progressive basis over time. In contrast to the International Covenant on Civil and Political Rights (ICCPR), which imposes an immediate obligation on state parties to respect and ensure all such rights, the ICESCR infamously provides that each state party 'undertakes to take steps ... to the maximum of its available resources, with a view to achieving progressively the full realization of the rights recognized in the present Covenant by all appropriate means, including particularly the adoption of legislative measures'.[7] The CESCR has interpreted this article to mean that although the state need not achieve the full realization of ESR immediately, it does have an immediate duty to construct a program or action plan,[8] as China has done.[9] States must also 'within a reasonably short time' after becoming a party, take 'deliberate, concrete and targeted' steps to meet their obligations.[10] Moreover, the CESCR will carefully scrutinize any 'deliberately retrogressive measures', and insist that they be 'fully justified by reference to the totality of the rights provided for in the Covenant and in the context of the full use of the maximum available resources'.[11]

Nevertheless, this leaves states with considerable discretion in determining the means to realize ESR, the amount of resources to allocate to their realization, and ultimately the pace and extent of their realization.

A second and related issue is whether there are core rights or minimal standards that must be realized immediately, and whether a minimum core approach is the best way to go. The CESCR has stated:

> [A] minimum core obligation to ensure the satisfaction of, at the very least, minimum essential levels of each of the rights is incumbent upon every State party. Thus, for example, a State party in which any significant number of individuals is deprived of essential foodstuffs, of essential primary health care, of basic shelter and housing, or of the most basic forms of education is, *prima facie*, failing to discharge its obligations under the Covenant ... In order for a State party to be able to attribute its failure to meet at least its minimum core obligations to a lack of available resources it must demonstrate that every effort has been made to use all resources that are at its disposition in an effort to satisfy, as a matter of priority, those minimum obligations.

Even when resources are inadequate, states are obligated to ensure the widest possible realization of ESR given the circumstances, and to adopt 'relatively low-cost' targeted programs during periods of economic recession or adjustment to protect the most vulnerable members of society.

The notion of a minimum core has been subject to many criticisms, including that it is conceptually problematic; it is not workable in practice (what exactly does 'every effort' to use 'all resources' to meet the minimum core entail?); it is still too indeterminate and requires context-specific balancing and decision making based on local circumstances; it targets only developing countries or, if applied to developed countries as well, undermines the alleged universality of ESR since the minimal core in India will be considerably lower than in the US; and it undermines efforts to achieve a more robust form of ESR.[12] Accordingly, some ESR-friendly courts, such as in South Africa, have rejected the minimum core approach in favor of a reasonableness test that gives the government discretion even when it comes to the realization of the minimum core.

The third issue, or set of issues, and perhaps the most controversial, is the justiciability of ESR, the role of the courts in implementing ESR, and the proper standards to be applied in doing so. The CESCR has noted, 'The [ICESCR] contains no direct counterpart to ... the [ICCPR], which obligates States parties to, inter alia, "develop the possibilities of judicial remedy".'[13] Nevertheless, the CESCR has strongly urged states to provide judicial remedies:

> a State party seeking to justify its failure to provide any domestic legal remedies for violations of economic, social and cultural rights would need to show either that such remedies are not 'appropriate means' ... or that, in view of the other means used, they are unnecessary. It will be difficult to show this and the Committee considers that, in many cases, the other means used could be rendered ineffective if they are not reinforced or complemented by judicial remedies.[14]

More specifically, the CESCR has 'made clear that it considers many of the provisions in the Covenant to be capable of immediate implementation', including Article 3, equal right of men and women to the enjoyment of all economic, social and cultural rights; Article 7(a)(i), fair wages and equal pay for equal work; Article 8, the right to form and join trade unions; Article 10(3), child labor; Article 13, free primary education and other educational rights; and Article 15(3), the freedom indispensable for scientific research and creative activity.[15] Indeed, the Committee has asserted that 'there is no Covenant right which could not, in the great majority of systems, be considered to possess at least some significant justiciable dimensions'.[16]

As noted, there is a growing global trend for ESR to be directly or indirectly justiciable. However, resistance remains strong, as the CESCR recognizes:

> State practice is mixed. The Committee notes that some courts have applied the provisions of the Covenant either directly or as interpretive standards. Other courts are willing to acknowledge, in principle, the relevance of the Covenant for interpreting domestic law, but in practice, the impact of the Covenant on the reasoning or outcome of cases is very limited. Still other courts have refused to give any degree of legal effect to the Covenant in cases in which individuals have sought to rely on it. There remains extensive scope for the courts in most countries to place greater reliance upon the Covenant.[17]

Concerns about the justiciability of the courts fall into two categories: general concerns about the legitimacy and competence of the court to handle ESR cases, and the limits of litigation as a means to bring about the type of systemic changes needed to fully realize ESR; and more specific concerns such as the proper standards for handling ESR cases (e.g. minimum core versus reasonableness standard) or whether ESR should be enforced directly or indirectly through civil and political rights.[18] Although it is not possible to address the many specific issues here, a brief discussion of the general issues may be useful.

Legitimacy concerns

Legitimacy concerns come in two forms. The first reflects concerns about separation of powers and the relation between domestic courts and the legislature. The CESCR has rejected the common objection that implementation of ESR involve decisions about the allocation of resources which should be left to political authorities.

Nevertheless, ESR cases may raise serious resource-allocation issues that could have a significant impact on economic growth and social stability. Moreover, in most cases, courts do suffer from a democracy deficit relative to the legislature. However, the seriousness of this issue will depend on various local factors, including the constitutional structure, whether ESC are incorporated into the constitution, the power of the courts to engage in constitutional and judicial review, and the remedies available to the courts, which will depend to some extent on the level of development.

Thus, while separation-of-powers issues suggest a more cautious approach in some circumstances, they do not preclude a role for the courts. A more case- and context-specific analysis is required.

A second legitimacy issue involves sovereignty concerns, and the relation between domestic legal-political systems and international and regional rights committees, tribunals and related bodies. There is always the worry that international law will usurp domestic policymaking space, and that decisions by far away international bodies, whose members are not elected by or directly accountable to domestic constituents, will encroach on state sovereignty. Indeed, several states, including the US and Canada, opposed the Optional Protocol for the ICESCR, arguing inter alia that it is inappropriate for international bodies to interfere with governments' decisions about socio-economic policy.[19]

Although the CESCR has been firm on several issues, including the need for judicial remedies, in its non-binding general comments and concluding comments, it has been careful to avoid imposing too detailed a plan for realizing ESR on state parties. For instance, in urging state parties to set specific goals for the reduction of infant mortality, child vaccination rates, the intake of calories per person and so on, it acknowledged that 'global benchmarks are of limited use, whereas national or other more specific benchmarks can provide an extremely valuable indication of progress'.[20] Given the potential legitimacy deficit, some scholars have sensibly cautioned that supranational litigation of ESR must be practiced in a manner respectful of non-legal contextual factors to be effective. It should be one element in an integrated strategy toward achieving meaningful social change, tied to broader advocacy strategies, and closely coordinated with social movements, media engagement and other forms of pressure.[21]

In short, while such concerns should not be dismissed lightly, given the relatively weak enforcement powers of the CESCR and most regional bodies, as well as a general trend to accept the encroachment of international law and human rights on state sovereignty, most states need not be overly concerned that their policymaking space will be excessively restricted by overreaching international bodies coercively enforcing robust versions of ESR.[22] States certainly cede a great deal more autonomy over economic and development policymaking when they join the WTO. In any event, such concerns do not preclude some role for domestic courts in ESR cases.[23]

Competence concerns

Even assuming domestic courts are legitimate venues for implementing ESR, whether the courts have the competence to do so remains contested. Nolan *et al.* provide a useful breakdown, and point by point refutation, of competency concerns:

> (i) the courts lack the information required to deal with social and economic rights; (ii) the judiciary lacks the necessary expertise, qualification or experience to deal with social and economic rights issues; (iii) the courts are incapable of dealing successfully with 'polycentric' tasks, such as those entailed by

adjudication involving social and economic rights; and (iv) the courts lack the necessary tools and remedies to deal effectively with social and economic rights.[24]

As with legitimacy concerns, the competency concerns should not be dismissed lightly. But closer analysis and the ever-accumulating body of experience with domestic courts implementing ESR demonstrate that such concerns need not preclude some constructive role for domestic courts in implementing ESR.

Rather, the competency concerns, like the legitimacy concerns, suggest that the court should adopt a cautious approach. It should take steps to mitigate these concerns, and take local circumstances into consideration when deciding cases and formulating remedies.

Take the information problem, for example. Some courts have responded to the information problem by inviting amicus curiae filings. In South Africa, the court 'routinely issues orders to the parties prior to the hearing, during the hearing, or even during post-hearing deliberations that invite one or both of the parties to make submissions of reports, studies, or other factual documentation for the justices to review'.[25] In some cases, courts may seek testimony from experts or even hold public hearings.

Such measures clearly help, but they do not completely alleviate information concerns. Accordingly, courts may still in some cases have to deny relief to plaintiffs if they lack adequate information on a particular issue, as the South African Constitutional Court did in overturning the lower court's order for the state to provide infant formula to poor mothers.[26]

Similarly, courts can mitigate the legitimate fear that the court decisions will have a negative impact on economic growth or in the extreme bankrupt the state by acknowledging the risk, tailoring their remedies and more generally adopting a cautious approach. Again, the experience of the South African Constitutional Court is instructive. The Court has expressly acknowledged the problem: '[Courts] are ill-suited to adjudicate upon issues where the Court orders could have multiple social and economic consequences for the community. The Constitution contemplates rather a restrained and focused role for the Courts.'[27] More importantly, it has responded

> by deferring to the legislature where no clear violation of a right has occurred, by assuming as little traditionally legislative authority as possible regarding remedial program specifics, and by rejecting any form of unqualified rights that might otherwise call for non-discretionary remedies.[28]

Courts have a variety of remedies at their disposal, including the award of monetary damages or reparation in-kind to individual parties. They may also 'read in' additional protections in a legislative scheme to protect socially vulnerable groups. They may issue declaratory orders noting a rights violation but leaving it to the state to devise a remedy, mandatory orders requiring specific actions to be taken or supervisory orders providing for ongoing supervision of government action by the court and/or requiring the relevant agency to report back within a set time-frame.[29]

There is a risk of judicial overarching and excessive judicial activism, with negative consequences for individual plaintiffs and the judiciary alike. Remedies that lack popular support or are too costly are likely to go unenforced.[30] Overly ambitious judicial decisions may invite a backlash against the court, and undermine support for other ESR. Nevertheless, courts have the ability to mitigate the risk by adopting a restrained approach and carefully selecting their remedies.

The limits of litigation

One final general concern is that the focus on litigation is misguided in that litigation cannot address the main causes of poverty, inequality and ESR violations, which are systemic and tied in most countries to a neoliberal free-market ideology and the dismantling of the welfare state.[31] At minimum, the focus should be on good policy design and effective policies that promote sustainable and equitable growth. More ambitiously, greater 'thought work' is required to replace the dominant ideology with a more progressive one.

This is a necessary caution given the recent trend toward judicialization, the court-centric approach of the rule of law promotion industry, and the CESCR emphasis on judicial remedies. In many developing countries, the judiciary may be weak and overburdened. Nevertheless, in most countries, including China, ESR have been promoted primarily through government policies and implemented through political and administrative channels.[32] Even advocates of a robust role for the courts allow that litigation alone will not suffice to ensure the realization of ESR, and that litigation must be part of a broader strategy carried out on many fronts and in many venues. That does not mean, however, that the potentially positive role of the courts should be discounted or ignored.

Background conditions

Dispute resolution of socio-economic cases has been characterized by: (i) notably less effective resolution than the vast majority of commercial cases; (ii) a trend toward dejudicialization, in contrast to the judicialization of most commercial disputes: that is, the government has steered socio-economic disputes away from the courts toward other mechanisms such as administrative reconsideration, mediation, arbitration, public hearings and the political process more generally, when it became apparent that the courts lacked the resources, competence and stature to provide effective relief in such cases;[33] (iii) a sharp rise in mass-plaintiff suits, and subsequent attempts to limit such suits by both government and Party entities and the judiciary itself; (iv) an attempt to dismantle litigation support networks, including not only lawyers engaged in political cause lawyering (roughly, the pursuit of civil and political rights),[34] but 'social cause lawyers' focusing on issues that lie closer to the core concerns reflected in ESR;[35] (v) a dramatic rise in letters, petitions, and social protests in response to the inability of the courts and other mechanisms to address adequately citizen demands and expectations; (vi) a reallocation of resources toward the least well-off members of society as part of a government effort to contain social instability and create a harmonious society, combined with a simultaneous increase in targeted repression of potential sources of instability, including political dissidents, certain NGOs and the more aggressive muckraking segment of the media.

The ability of Chinese courts to implement ESR is constrained by law, institutional design, political realities, ideological conflicts and resource constraints. Although the PRC constitution does list a number of ESR, *no* rights in the constitution are directly justiciable absent implementing legislation, not even CPR. Moreover, there is no constitutional court in China.

China remains an effectively single-party socialist state with limited protection of CPR when the exercise of such rights is deemed to threaten socio-political stability. While the PRC constitution provides for judicial independence in deciding cases, and courts are able to handle many cases independently, the CPC continues to make major policy decisions, and to exert an influence on the judiciary both indirectly and directly.[36] Moreover, the Chinese system is more akin to a parliamentary system, with the highest organ of state power being the National People's Congress. Given the legal system's civil law heritage, courts have relatively circumscribed powers. They cannot overturn acts of parliament, or even strike down administrative rules and regulations.[37] Lower-level courts have until recently been funded by the local government,[38] with judges appointed by local people's congresses. This has led to local protectionism in some cases, where the courts favor economically important local actors, with negative consequences for individuals in labor and environmental disputes.

Further, there is no clear popular mandate for the courts to play a leading role in transforming society. There are fundamental disagreements about social policy and the future of China among the New Left and the New Right, socialists and neoliberals. Moreover, as noted, China has been relatively successful among developing states in reducing poverty and improving living standards. It has done so mainly through government policies and programs, with a greater role for political and administrative mechanisms to redress problems than for the courts.

The vast differences in local circumstances suggest that courts in different countries will and should play different roles in implementing ESR. While it would be unrealistic to expect courts in China to play as forceful a role in implementing ESR, Chinese courts may still play a positive role.

Toward a constructive role for Chinese courts in implementing ESR

The fundamental guiding principle for the courts is to adopt an approach based on 'the three Cs': consultation, collaboration, and caution.

Most judges in China, like most judges everywhere, are realistic. They want to do their jobs as best they can, to follow the law, and at the same time provide an adequate remedy where possible. Given the weak powers of the courts, shortcomings in the legal framework particularly with respect to individual remedies, and the lack of resources to address systemic socio-economic claims, cooperation with government agencies to resolve the immediate case is often the best, if not the only, option.

Chinese courts have a number of institutional mechanisms to facilitate consultation and cooperation. Most importantly, the party political-legal committee serves as an intermediary between government branches, and has the authority to resolve institutional conflicts. While many commentators fear an expanded role for political-legal committees would undermine judicial independence, there is little point denying their existence. On balance, it would be better to accept them as part of China's living constitution and maximize their positive role while minimizing their negative impact in terms of judicial independence. Similarly, every court has an adjudicative committee of senior judges, headed by the court president. The court president often has a political background, and is well suited for negotiating responsive solutions with other government agencies.

Chinese courts have already recognized the importance of working with, rather than against, the government to resolve ESR cases.[39] For instance, when the 2009 global recession led many businesses to close shop, disgruntled workers took to the streets in protest. In response, government officials and judges, acting under the authority of the recently established Social Stability Maintenance Office (an office under the political-legal committee) met the protesters in the street in an effort to mediate a settlement, thus transforming the streets into a courtroom. This 'street as courtroom' approach is a result of the weak capacity of the legal system, including a restrictive and cumbersome regulatory framework that encourages mediation and requires arbitration before parties can access the court and the court's inability to provide an adequate remedy given limited resources, together with a government-wide campaign to build a harmonious society based on sustainable and equitable development and social justice.[40] It also reflects the populist turn of the judiciary under the new president of the Supreme People's Court, Wang Shengjun. Wang has called for a more 'democratic' judiciary that is responsive to citizen needs, and promoted mediation and settlement of disputes as part of the effort to realize a harmonious society.

The judiciary's response to these labor disputes is part of a longer-standing approach to the dramatic rise in the number of mass plaintiff cases, many of which involve social and economic claims. Given the large number of parties, and often media attention, such cases threaten social stability. In response, the courts have developed a number of techniques to reduce public pressure, including breaking the plaintiffs up into smaller groups, emphasizing conciliation, and providing a spokesperson to meet with, and explain the legal aspects of the case to, the plaintiffs and the media in the hopes of encouraging settlement or even withdrawal of the suit. Some courts also try to pacify the protesters by providing accelerated procedures to access government-sponsored funds. To deal effectively with these cases, basic-level courts have found it helpful to work closely with higher-level courts and other government entities.

In a further effort to transform these emotionally charged and highly adversarial lawsuits into a less confrontational process more likely to provide some level of satisfaction to the parties, the All-China Lawyers Association issued guidelines that seek to reach a balance between social order and the protection of citizens and their lawyers in exercising their rights.[41] The guidelines remind lawyers to act in accordance with their professional responsibilities. Lawyers should not encourage parties to interfere with the work of government organ agencies; they should accurately represent the facts in discussions with the media and refrain from paying journalists to cover their side of the story; and they should report to and accept the supervision of the bar association. On the other hand, bar associations shall promptly report instances of interference with lawyers lawfully carrying out their duties to the authorities, and press the authorities to take appropriate measures to uphold the rights of lawyers. Where necessary, local bar associations may enlist support from the national bar association.

Given the circumstances, an aggressive role for the courts in developing ESR jurisprudence is simply not possible. Chinese courts have exercised, and will have to continue to exercise, caution in handling ESR cases. Like courts everywhere, Chinese courts have at their disposal a number of procedural techniques to avoid being overwhelmed by ESR cases. They can, and have, limited standing, for instance interpreting standing requirements narrowly to prevent 'private attorney general' lawsuits, or denied jurisdiction.[42] They have emphasized mediation. They have found employers in violation in employment discrimination cases but not provided the requested remedy of a job. They have decided for parties in labor dispute cases but limited the remedy to monetary damages, often in an amount less than requested. Citing legal barriers and enforcement difficulties, they have pushed disputes back to political and administrative channels, requiring parties first exhaust their administrative remedies, while at the same time claiming the right to review the government's decisions in administrative litigation.[43]

Yet a cautious approach alone is clearly inadequate as evidenced by the ever-increasing number of mass protests, many of them in response to the failure of the courts to adequately address ESR claims. Thus, in addition to working with government agencies, the judiciary should consider a somewhat more proactive, multi-pronged approach.

First, drawing on the experiences of courts elsewhere, the Chinese judiciary should focus more on the duties to respect and protect ESR than the more costly and ambitious duty to fulfill. When the state has a clear obligation to individuals, particularly with respect to the core minimum, the judiciary should be more assertive in providing a remedy. For instance, cases suitable for individualized judicial remedy include forced evictions to ensure proper procedures have been followed and adequate compensation has been paid; violations of the prohibition against child labor; some labor cases where the issue is failure to pay wages, wrongful termination of individual employees, or unsafe working conditions, particularly where life-threatening;[44] and the failure to provide emergency medical treatment to protect life rather than turning people away because they have no insurance and cannot pay out of their pocket. This will go a long way toward meeting the requirement of protecting the most vulnerable members of society.

Second, the court should be more assertive in enforcing the duty to protect against third parties. For instance, the government has repeatedly issued regulations and notices prohibiting schools from charging fees, thus depriving children of the right to free primary education. In enforcing the government's regulation, particularly against private and for-profit schools, the courts would be enforcing government policies and meeting the legitimate, minimal and essential rights of children to the education needed to compete equally and become a productive member of society. Similarly, many environmental and labor cases involve violations by third parties, often for-profit businesses.

Third, although the indirect strategy of framing ESR claims in terms of traditional CPR is generally not promising in China given the limits on political lawyering and CPR more broadly, the courts may still be more assertive in developing a jurisprudence of equality and non-discrimination. The courts have been relatively successful in handling ESR cases based on anti-discrimination principles, although they have been reluctant to order employers to hire the person even when they find a violation. One reason is that the EPL is unclear about remedies. Another is that many of the cases have involved persons applying for civil servant positions, and the court may be reluctant to order local government agencies to take on someone against their wishes. Nevertheless, these cases have had a positive impact in that they attracted media attention and led to legislation to address the problem. The courts could continue to find violations, but leave it to the legislature to address. Alternatively, they might experiment with more robust remedies, including money damages or specific performance in the form of requiring the government agency to offer the next available job to the plaintiff.

Fourth, the court should be more assertive in promoting the procedural dimension of ESR protection. They can use the opportunity provided by such cases to hold government bodies to their commitment to make information publicly available under the national and local freedom of information acts. They can also decide against the government on procedural grounds – for not holding a hearing, denying the parties the opportunity to be heard, failing to obtain or make available to the public a environmental impact study, and so on.[45] In this way, the courts could avoid a direct confrontation with the government agency on the substantive issue, while allowing the government agency the opportunity to correct the procedural shortcomings.

Fifth, with respect to the duty to fulfill, courts should avoid broad remedies, adopt the reasonableness approach, and show deference to other state organs. In terms of remedies, the courts should mainly emphasize declaratory relief. Given their limited powers within the constitutional framework, they simply are not in a position to issue mandatory orders telling the government what to do, in most cases with far-reaching economic and social implications. For instance, state-owned enterprise reform and the transition to a market economy have led to many disputes over pension payments and other welfare benefits, including unemployment insurance, job relocation and training expenses, workers' compensation benefits and medical care. In handling such cases, the court could and should find a violation, but then leave it up to the discretion of the government how best to address the problem where a general policy issue is involved.

In addition, the court could find that the government has failed to develop the program to address ESR as required by law, and if so, request that the government remedy the situation by developing the required program. For instance, the *Employment Promotion Law* (article 25) provides 'governments at every level shall create a fair employment environment, eliminate discrimination in employment, formulate policies and take measures to support and assist the hard-to-employ'.

Supervisory orders may also be possible in some circumstances, where for instance the government has established a program. However, it is highly unlikely that the courts will be able to require other government actors to report back on a regular basis. Under the constitution, the people's congress and procuracy are charged with supervising the courts, not the other way around. In recent years, there has been a great deal of tension between people's congress and courts over whether this right of supervision permits individual case supervision. Although the procuracy's right to protest individual cases is clear, the scope of right and the manner in which it is to be exercised are still subject to vigorous debate. Moreover, the general transition to rule of law has increased the authority of courts relative to other state organs, particularly the procuracy and the police. This has led to a certain amount of resentment on the part of the procuracy and police. Accordingly, now would not be a good time to be challenging their authority by issuing supervisory orders that require the procuracy, police or people's congress to report back to the court on how they are implementing particular policies.

Fortunately, a more positive alternative approach is available. In recent years, there have been local experiments in environmental cases with more relaxed standing rules that allow the procuracy and certain NGOs to bring public interest suits.[46] Expanding these experiments to allow the procuracy a broader role in representing the public in ESR suits may help defuse the tension between the courts and procuracy, and provide adequate assurance to the government and judiciary alike that the courts will not be inundated by ESR suits.

Similarly, the courts could follow the example of the Indian Supreme Court in asking the procuracy or government agencies to investigate the facts and supervise implementation of court-ordered remedies or government programs.[47] In India, this has helped transform the adversarial litigation process into a more cooperative process, with the government officials who appear in public interest litigation cases seeking to find constructive solutions to pressing problems rather than viewing their role as to defend government policy at all cost. The Indian Supreme Court has emphasized that public interest litigation is:

> not a litigation of an adversary character for the purpose of holding the State... responsible for making reparation, but it is a public interest litigation which involved a collaborative and cooperative effort... for the purpose of making human rights meaningful for the weaker sections of the community.[48]

Sixth, in applying the reasonableness standard, the courts should pay particular attention to the minimum core and the most vulnerable members of society. This is not only consistent with the advice of the CESCR, but also reflects the large number of people who are still living in poverty, the high level of inequality, and the negative consequences of economic reforms and rapid social transformation over the last 30 years. Thus, if plaintiffs claim a violation of a minimum core right, the court could shift the burden to the government to prove that it has taken reasonable legislative and other measures, within its available resources, to achieve the progressive realization of the right, and to show that any limitation 'is reasonable and justifiable'.

Although the reasonableness standard means that the court will not inquire whether there are other more desirable measures that could have been adopted, there may still be a high level of scrutiny of the state's actions and justifications for its actions. In particular, the court should scrutinize with great care government claims of inadequate resources. They may ask, for example, with respect to the rights of migrant workers to education and health, whether enough is being done. They may request that the government provide information about the costs of enforcing the right, promote cost–benefit analysis, review budgets, and encourage people's congresses and government agencies to articulate minimal national and local standards so that the courts can effectively evaluate the government's response to plaintiff claims.[49] They may also assess the performance of the government against the performance of similarly situated regions by drawing on empirical data and objective indicators.[50] Of course, cost–benefit analysis, transparent budgetary reviews, objective indexes, impact assessments and the like are also important tools for improving policymaking by the legislature and government agencies, and thus should be seen as part of a broad, less threatening, cooperative effort to govern more rationally, efficiently and equitably.

Conclusion

The PRC government is by no means hostile to ESR per se. Even a cursory glance at China's initial report on the implementation of the ICESCR demonstrates the government's commitment to alleviating poverty, improving living standards and promoting more sustainable and equitable development. Nor is the government opposed to constructive advice from the international community. As noted, the government has developed a national human rights action plan, and formulated many other plans to promote ESR. It has also taken many 'deliberate, concrete and targeted' steps to ensure the realization of ESR.

Nevertheless, the judiciary has played a limited role in enforcing ESR, and is likely to continue to do so. In comparison to the courts in many countries, Chinese courts are inhibited in implementing ESR by a variety of factors, among them shortcomings in the regulatory framework including the lack of specific and robust individual remedies in many laws, institutional design that limits the power of the judiciary within the Chinese constitutional structure, political limitations inherent in an effectively single-party social state, ideological conflicts between New Left advocates of socialist justice and New Right proponents of neoliberalism, and resource constraints typical of lower-middle-income countries. Even in South Africa, the courts, mindful of the cost implication of their decisions, have exercised caution, often finding a violation but allowing the government to figure out what to do about it or providing relief to individual parties but denying relief when a wider class would be affected.

There is of course no reason to expect that courts will play the same role in all countries; nor is a court-centric approach necessarily the most appropriate or effective way to implement ESR. In China, political and administrative mechanisms have played and will continue to play a more prominent role. The role of civil society, NGOs, and self-governing private and public–private hybrid regulatory systems are also important complements to the courts.[51] No doubt changes to the incentive structure for evaluating and promoting government officials, now biased toward economic growth and social stability, would have a more immediate and dramatic impact on the full realization of ESR than all of these other remedial mechanisms combined.

The long-term solution to socio-economic cases is growth, although growth alone is not sufficient. As the government has realized, development raises many social justice issues, including how the wealth generated by development is to be distributed. A comprehensive policy approach that goes well beyond judicial remedies is required.[52]

Nevertheless, international experience demonstrates the limitations of implementing ESR without some role for the courts. The key, however, is to develop a feasible strategy that allows the judiciary to play a constructive role and yet is consistent with the operating environment. While a robust role for an activist judiciary in China may have normative appeal to many, it is not realistic in the current circumstances. Pie-in-the-sky proposals serve a positive function in pressing for a more ambitious agenda, but a piece or two of pie in the belly may be more important to the most vulnerable members of society. A more moderate, gradual, pragmatic approach along the lines suggested herein may lead to better protection of ESR. Over time, the judiciary will accumulate experience and China will continue to develop, thus growing out of many of the problems and providing the courts greater leeway to order costly remedies. The judiciary's role in implementing ESR will therefore need to be continually assessed, updated and adjusted, with the overall trend being towards a more expansive and assertive role for the courts.

Notes

* The author thanks Otto Malmgren and the participants at the 2010 Beijing International Conference on Human Rights for their insightful comments.
1 See the government's data-filled initial report to the Committee on Economic, Social and Cultural Rights, http://daccess-dds-ny.un.org/doc/UNDOC/GEN/G04/406/56/PDF/G0440656.pdf?OpenElement. For a comparative perspective, see Peerenboom (2007), showing that China outperforms the average country in its lower–middle income class on most human rights measures and indicators of human well-being, with the notable exception of civil and political rights. Despite relative overall progress, there are wide regional differences and many specific areas in need of substantial improvement.
2 On the role of the courts in enforcing economic and social rights generally, see Fu and Peerenboom (2010: 112–16); Peerenboom and He (2009); on the role of the courts in protecting (or not) the right to education, see Peerenboom (2007: 136–7); Xia (2006);

on the somewhat more positive but still limited role of the courts in combating various forms of discrimination, Timothy Webster (2007); Orianne Yin Dutka (2007); on the role of the courts in labour disputes, see Ronald Brown (2008) (labour disputes increased from under 20,000 in 1994 to over 300,000 in 2006; most are resolved through arbitration, although there were over 120,000 litigation cases in 2005, of which one-third were settled through judicial mediation); see also Su and He (2009) (discussing the extra-legal role of the courts in responding to worker claims in the wake of insolvencies resulting from the global recession); on environmental litigation, see Bie (2007); Gao (2010) (discussing creation of special environmental courts and more permissive standing rules in some jurisdictions that allow NGOs to bring suit, and noting that environmental civil cases increased from 96 to 1,509 from 1998 to 2008, while criminal suits rose from 1,912 to 10,075 during the same period); Rachel Stern (2010: 79–103; and 2012) (noting that the 'vast majority of environmental disputes are handled through government-brokered deals, private concessions or simply when plaintiffs give up and go away').

3 See List of Issues to be taken up in connection with the consideration of the initial report of the PRC, E/1990/5/Add.59, http://daccess-dds-ny.un.org/doc/UNDOC/GEN/G04/420/41/PDF/G0442041.pdf?OpenElement. Although China's response did not provide complete statistics, the government did respond to the general question about the justiciability of the treaty by stating:

> All the human rights and associated institutions specified in the [ICESCR] are provided for in the basic laws and regulations of the People's Republic of China. They are enforceable and can by and large meet the needs of Chinese court proceedings. The principles and spirit of the Covenant, for all practical purposes, are reflected in China's judicial system, namely, fulfilling the requirements of the Covenant by invoking domestic laws to protect citizens' economic, social and cultural rights.

See *China, Replies to the List of Issues* HR/CESCR/NONE/2004/10, 34th session, 2004.
4 *Concluding observations of the Committee on Economic, Social and Cultural Rights PRC (including Hong Kong and Macao)*, E/C.12/1/Add.107 13 May 2005, para. 42, www.unhchr.ch/tbs/doc.nsf/898586b1dc7b4043c1256a450044f331/a206bffcd68c76b1c125700500478168/$FILE/G0542245.pdf.
5 See Aoife Nolan *et al.* (2009) at: http://ssrn.com/abstract=1434944.
6 See Nolan *et al.* (2009); Ghai and Cottrell (2004).
7 ICESCR, art. 2(1).
8 CESCR General comment 1, para. 4, www.unhchr.ch/tbs/doc.nsf/(Symbol)/38e23a6ddd6c0f4dc12563ed0051cde7?Opendocument.
9 See National Human Rights Action Plan (2009–10).
10 General comment 3, para. 2.
11 General comment 3, para. 9.
12 See Katharine Young (2008).
13 General comment no. 9, para 3.
14 General comment 9, para 3.
15 General comment 3, para 5; General comment 9, para 10.
16 General comment 9, para 10.
17 General comment 9, para 13.
18 Compare Cavallaro and Schaffer (2005) and Takele Soboka Bulto (2009) (favouring indirect approach), with Tara Melish (2006) (arguing in favour of the direct approach). The indirect approach usually seeks to pursue ESR via reference to the principles of equality, non-discrimination or human dignity, or to the general principles of due process and fairness, or to the right to life, although there have also been cases based on freedom of expression and association, the right to privacy and personal integrity rights. See, generally, Nolan *et al.* (2009); Rory O'Connell (2009); see also Sandra Fredman

(2006: 498–520) (arguing that the guiding principle for adjudication of the positive duties of the states should be reinforcement of democracy).
19 See Nolan *et al.* (2009: 4). The draft text provided various options

> to address the different and sometimes complex proposals to limit the scope of a communications procedure to: (a) 'core rights' or 'minimum contents' of rights; (b) non discrimination; (c) serious violations of Covenant rights; and (d) 'respect' and 'protect' aspects of the rights, with an opt-out procedure allowing States to exclude 'fulfil' aspects.
> (*Draft Optional Protocol To The International Covenant On Economic, Social And Cultural Rights*, Human Rights Council, Sixth session, Open-ended Working Group on an Optional Protocol to the International Covenant on Economic, Social and Cultural Rights, Fourth session Geneva, 16–27 July 2007 A/HRC/6/WG.4/2 (23 April 2007))

On the duties to respect, protect and fulfil, see Henry Shue (1996).
20 General comment 1, para 6.
21 Cavallaro and Schaffer (2005).
22 The degree of threat will vary by region, depending on many factors, including the powers of the regional body, the extent to which the decisions of the regional body are binding domestically, and the regional body's ESR jurisprudence. Thus, there may be more grounds to worry in Latin America than in Asia. In Latin America, the American Convention on Human Rights is considered national law in most countries and the Inter-American Court on Human Rights has more aggressively sought to bring about social transformation through an ambitious jurisprudence of ESR that interprets the right to life to encompass the right to a 'dignified existence' and a 'decent life'. In contrast, there is no regional human rights convention in Asia, and the human rights arm of ASEAN remains weak and apparently committed to the sovereignty-respecting 'diplomacy of accommodation'. Moreover, the indirect approach may be more effective in Europe and the US where there is a general antipathy to ESR and strong philosophical and jurisprudential support for CPR than in China and other Asian countries. See Monica Feria Tinta (2008).
23 Nor would it preclude other positive roles for international law. See Rimmer and Gail (2010). (International human rights law can influence domestic courts in other ways than by giving rise directly to litigation, for example as a tool for statutory interpretation; to influence the development of the common law; as a basis of judicial review in administrative law; in the exercise of judicial discretion; and as an indicia of contemporary standards and values and therefore relevant to the context in which the state's constitution should be interpreted and applied. Moreover, international treaties can form the basis of a wide suite of policy and budgetary tools.)
24 Nolan *et al.* (2009: 19–20).
25 Eric Christiansen (2007: 12).
26 *Minister of Health v. Treatment Action Campaign (No. 2)* 2002 (5) SA 721 (CC) (S. Afr.) [hereafter TAC].
27 TAC, para 38.
28 Christiansen (2007: 25).
29 Nolan *et al.* (2009: 19–20).
30 Indian courts have been among the most active in promoting ESR – even though ESR are considered 'directive principles' rather than justiciable fundamental rights in the constitution – by interpreting the right to life to include the right to a clean environment, food, suitable working conditions, emergency medical treatment and even free legal aid. In so doing, they have issued a series of far-reaching decisions with significant cost implications. The right to food, for instance, was interpreted to entail the

distribution of food grain and other basic commodities at subsidized prices, assistance to destitute households, and the provision of cooked midday meals to children in all government schools. While the provision of midday meals has been relatively effective, the other remedies have encountered resistance in implementation. See Jayna Kothari (2008).
31 See Otto and Wiseman (2001: 5–46).
32 For example, 'The State Council's progress on human rights situation in China in 2009' (Xinhua 2010e) includes a section on the judicial protection of rights. However, rather than a discussion of specific cases, that section emphasizes law and order concerns and criminal law issues (including the number of people arrested and convicted); new regulations to ensure that the police, procuracy and other legal complex actors are held accountable and cannot abuse their power; efforts to increase government transparency and legal aid; new rules to protect lawyers in carrying out their duties; and mediation. The section on economic, social and cultural rights emphasizes government policies to mitigate the negative effects of the global economic recession, including efforts to create jobs, strengthen the social security system, and ensure (free) compulsory education through the ninth grade (which reportedly reached 99.7 per cent).
33 Peerenboom (2008).
34 Scheingold and Sarat (2004).
35 Peerenboom (2010c).
36 Judicial independence is a complicated topic. Simplistic assertions about the 'lack of judicial independence' in China fail to capture a much more complex reality. The extent of independence depends on many factors, including the type of case, level of court and region. See, generally, Peerenboom (2010a). While judges enjoy the most independence in commercial cases, they also may have adequate autonomy to decide many ESR cases independently, including labour and environmental cases. See, e.g., Stern (2010: 84–5). The problem in many ESR cases is not the lack of judicial independence, but that the courts are unable to resolve the dispute and provide an adequate remedy without reaching out to the government for assistance.
37 The courts have the power to review specific administrative acts but not abstract acts.
38 There has been a recent attempt to centralize funding. However, to what extent this new policy is being carried out remains unclear.
39 On the need for a cooperative approach to employment discrimination cases, see Webster (2007). For environmental disputes, see van Rooij and Wing-Hung Lo (2009: 114–37).
40 Su and He (2009).
41 Guidance Notice of the All-China Lawyers Association regarding Lawyers' Handling of Multi-party Cases, 20 March 2006.
42 One media report widely discussed on the Internet claims that Guangxi courts would not accept 13 types of cases including securities litigation, land-taking claims and compensation for resettlement, disputes arising out of illegal *ponzi* schemes and other chain sale scams, cases involving laid-off workers and retraining as a result of economic transition or as a result of bankruptcy, large-scale government cancellation of rural responsibility system contracts, and remaining problems regarding how to divide collectively owned assets. Many of the cases fall into the ESR category. Many also involve large multi-party suits. In most if not all cases, the parties would have available a variety of political, administrative and private channels to pursue their claims, each of which has advantages and disadvantages, none of which ensures success. See '*Guangxi fayuan bu shouli 13 lei anjian; shenggaoyuan cheng you guoqing jueding*' [Guangxi courts refuse to accept 13 types of cases; High Court claims decision in accordance with national conditions], *Zhongguo nianqing bao, Zhongqing zai xian*, 24 August 2004. See also Stern (2011) (noting judges routinely refuse filing of environmental cases; they often refuse to provide a written reason despite being required by law to do so, thus preventing parties from challenging the decision; in many cases, they refuse to accept the case because an administrative solution is underway or litigation is not an effective way to resolve the issue).

43 See He Xin (2010) (discussing the handling of cases involving 'married out women', i.e. women who leave their home village once they are married and then are denied economic benefits from their home village).
44 There are a number of steps that the courts and lawmakers could take to facilitate these sorts of labour claims, such as reducing the barriers to litigation by permitting parties to bypass arbitration, lowering or waiving court fees, improving legal aid, and more aggressively exploiting fee-shifting rules to impose costs, including attorney fees, on the employer if a violation is found. See Brown (2008) (recommending changing the current de novo review of arbitrated labour disputes to a deferral policy that accepts the finality of arbitration, absent a showing of illegality or procedural irregularity, as well as clarification of the definition of 'labour dispute' to allow more cases to proceed to direct court review).
45 Confer *Guerra* v. *Italy* (1998) 26 E.H.R.R. 357, where failure to provide information about pollution from a chemical factory was a violation of ECHR, article 8.
46 See Gao (2010) (noting that in Yunnan, only the procuracy and public interest organizations registered in China have standing).
47 Kothari (2008).
48 *Dr Upendra Baxi v. State of UP* (1986) 4 SCC 106 (Indian Supreme Court).
49 See Harvey and Rooney (2011) (discussing how courts might use economic techniques to appraise public expenditure in line with international obligations under ICESCR).
50 Terra Lawson-Remer *et al.* (2009: 195–221); Sital Kalantry *et al.* (2010).
51 See, e.g., Jin *et al.* (2010) (noting that environmental performance rating and disclosure has emerged as an alternative or complementary approach to conventional pollution regulation, especially in developing countries, the authors provide an empirical study of the impact of one such performance rating and disclosure program in China).
52 See Randall Peerenboom (2007), advocating inter alia (i) preventing disputes from arising in the first place by improving the welfare system, and increasing resources to address some of the major social cleavages; (ii) developing and strengthening procedural mechanisms to handle the increasingly diverse views in society, and in particular increasing political participation in the decision-making processes, whether through public hearings, consultative committees or participation in the nomination or election of officials; (iii) enhancing non-judicial mechanisms for addressing citizen concerns in ESR cases, including administrative reconsideration, the letter and petition system, mediation, arbitration and supervision by the administration, people's congress and Party; (iv) improving procedural justice in all mechanisms for resolving disputes, whether through mediation, the letter and visits system, court cases or other means: participants must perceive the mechanisms to be fair, regardless of the outcome in the particular instance; and (v) explaining the proper role *and the limits* of the legal system and rule of law in resolving these controversial issues. In addition to these general recommendations, specific types of cases give rise to specific issues, and require specific policy responses and reforms. See Fu and Peerenboom (2010) for further area-specific proposals.

11 Alternative dispute resolution in China

Fan Yu

Introduction

Traditionally, alternative dispute resolution (ADR) in China has been characterized by 'mediation'.[1] Scholars such as Lubman (1967), Fu Hualing (2001), Clarke (2007), Palmer (2007, 2008) and Cohen (2010) have variously termed pre-1980s mediation as 'the mediation of Mao Zedong's era' – embodying the political function of dispute resolution, permeating the 'pro-struggle' philosophy and playing an essential role in socialist adjustment. This era coincided with an almost non-existent formal legal system or rule of law. In this sense, the development and success of mediation in Chinese society before the 1980s was an outcome and indication of an inadequate legal system as well as the prevailing political ideology.

It follows that post-1980s mediation may be referred to as 'the mediation of Deng Xiaoping's era'. Mediation in Deng's opening up and reform period is perhaps best characterized by the co-existence and mutual development of the legal system *and* mediation. Fu Hualing (2001: 310–11) pointed out that ironically this occurred when Western societies were seeking alternative dispute resolution methods while 'China was following the age-old Western route to law and order via a popular judicial system and public participation'. Indeed, many predicted that with the development of China's modern legal system (and the arrival of a new wave of litigation), mediation would inevitably decline. Considering the relatively limited first-hand data available on China's emerging ADR systems, even in Chinese, this chapter's main purpose is analytical and descriptive. It argues that the predictions about the demise of ADR in China were largely wrong. In the 'era of Hu Jintao', the role of mediation has been strengthened, becoming a vital element of China's movement towards a market economy. The following sections outline arguments as to why earlier predictions about ADR were wrong, commencing with a brief historical overview of ADR since reform and opening up. The basic forms and main systems of ADR are then examined with an emphasis on how specialized mediation and arbitration have evolved in contemporary China, including programs for foreign and domestic investors. The chapter then considers emerging directions of ADR in China with grassroots mediation being restored by the *People's Mediation Law*. Justice does not rest solely on judicial authority. Much rests upon China's traditional culture of negotiation, mediation and arbitration.

The development of ADR in China since reform and opening up

The 1990s saw China's 'people's mediation', 'administrative mediation' and 'court mediation' decline and there were several reasons for this. China was in a period of social transition and rapid economic development in which social disputes were frequent, sometimes complicated, and statutory provisions and procedures either inadequate or uncertain (or both). Under these circumstances, court procedures were the most important route for dispute resolution and as a rule-making mechanism. The state needed social governance through a uniform legal approach to ensure social stability (see Fan Yu 2007a). In addition, social awareness of the benefits of modern law was expanding. With China undergoing rapid social change it was helpful to establish the authority of the courts in general and the judiciary in particular. Court procedure was viewed as a favourable way to popularize the concept of a *rule of law* for China. As an illustration, Ronald Brown (2008) found that labour disputes alone increased from under 20,000 in 1994 to over 300,000 in 2006. Most were resolved through arbitration, although there were over 120,000 litigation cases in 2005 with one-third of these settled through *judicial* mediation.

The rapid increase in lawsuits and in social adjustment have brought a renewed focus on dispute resolution mechanisms. This chapter identifies five key contextual influences that frame the government's renewed focus on ADR as follows:

1 *The need for law reform and court development*
   In the development of China's modern legal system, the court has actively recruited more staff, improved working conditions and court facilities. At the same time courts have, in striving to do a good job in case trials and extending their jurisdiction, increased their authority and social status. Nevertheless, the state's investment in the judiciary is limited when one considers the expanding source of cases and rising trial numbers (especially cases involving considerably large claims). Against this background, and in the light of expensive new litigation fees, it could be argued a turn to ADR was inevitable.[2] In the turn to ADR courts have displayed various attitudes (from supportive of ADR to dismissive): supportive as the Supreme People's Court decreed it to be so, dismissive as non-litigation mechanisms had fallen out of legal fashion. But as I shall argue in a moment, fashions are notoriously fickle!

2 *The 'passive' attitude of administrative authorities and local governments*
   Many administrative authorities and local governments were known to be passive about resolving civil disputes, in that they readily transfer disputes to courts to avoid responsibility. Such passiveness can also be partly explained by a conflict between judicial and administrative procedures. Court and administrative handling mechanisms were not effectively harmonized, lacking mutual communication and holding different philosophical understandings. This was reflected in dramatically different underlying rules and procedures including ways of handling disputes. Nor did courts always respect administrative ways of handling disputes and administrative authorities did

not always understand judicial trial and review methodology. Simultaneously, the just management of disputes was being increasingly demanded by powerful interested parties. In this scenario it can be readily inferred that the function of the administrative dispute resolution mechanism was gradually weakened – corresponding with a rise in court influence.

3 *Procedural design and quality problems*
By the late 1980s, traditional mediation with patriarchal authority no longer existed in most villages. The influence of the local hero-type and governmental leaders was dropping in most regions and the demand for mediation according to law was making it increasingly difficult for 'old-style' mediation to operate. These factors together contributed to a reduction in access to and success of mediation. Furthermore, mediation agreements were without binding force. Where a party went back on their word and brought an action to court, courts in the past usually did not take the mediation agreement into consideration; hence it did not even have the force of a simple contract.

A consequence of the state (and society at large) not having attached adequate importance to, nor made enough investment in, ADR, is that there are some residual problems in procedural design, quality of organization, and availability of suitably trained personnel. These are all needed now but there has not been a developed, integrated mediation mechanism and, as such, procedures tend to be poorly coordinated, with ineffective set-ups, and simplistic in operation. The combination of a lack of quality of mediation organizations with trained personnel and ineffective administrative authorities generated a low percentage of successful mediation case outcomes.

4 *The 'court' of public opinion*
Public opinion remains influential in shaping some government policies and the media (and legal community) are constantly trying to make the public aware of the power of litigation. These interest groups are seeking to overturn a traditional Chinese dislike of litigation on the grounds that having greater awareness about rights will deliver citizens increased power in that they are encouraged to go to court to claim their right to resolve disputes through that forum. As a result, litigation has become more fashionable, especially among the new rich. In this way the rich are able to use public opinion to further secure their wealth and power through their ability to use the formal legal system. Nonetheless, the fashion has been created and now it has to be managed.

5 *Tensions in social relations add difficulty to reconciliation through consultation*
China's social transition has, of course, produced many benefits for citizens. At the same time there have been gradual losses related to the binding force of many generally accepted social norms. Moral standards, customs, conventions and administrative regulations have rapidly changed with visible effects on social members. Public opinion and social evaluation are less

influential than they once were. In some senses this has positive features, but in other ways it can be argued there has been a loss of cohesion resulting in no self-discipline awareness among social members. Individualism combined with money worship has entered the collective ethos and in this context it has been extremely easy for all manner of disputes to arise and to be intensified (Zang Xiaowei 2008: 53).

Disputes between family members or between neighbours that were previously seldom brought to court are now attracting court adjudication. An apparent collapse of integrity and other moral standards have made it difficult for interested parties to carry on 'good faith' consultations or dialogue once a dispute arises. Against this backdrop of moral turpitude there remains considerable uncertainty about applicable law and yet there are high public expectations of court procedure. This is one reason why some citizens continue to use the *xinfang* (petitioning) system to help deal with their grievances.

Xinfang

Xinfang or *shangfang* is an administrative system for receiving complaints and grievances from individuals in the PRC via petitions. Under the system of *xinfang*, the State Bureau for Letters and Calls (*guojia xinfang ju*) and local bureaus receive complaints or grievances and then channel these to the relevant departments, monitoring the progress of settlement. This system has been in operation since the establishment of the People's Republic in 1949 and remains a 'last resort' for resolving grievances – often adopted by citizens out of ignorance (and/or frustration) – and a largely ineffectual method for resolving disputes. As a social barometer, however, it is noteworthy that the number of petitioners in Beijing alone has allegedly reached more than 100,000 people (not counting those grievances that remain at provincial capital bureaus).[3]

When the sheer number of complainants is viewed alongside the five points raised above, it becomes more evident why ADR has faced operating difficulties during the early years of reform and opening. The situation for ADR began to change significantly after 2000 partly through the government's recognition that more had to be done to address the consequences of dramatic social change. Alternatives to clogged (and expensive) court procedures had to be found. Since 1990 *xinfang* complaints have included some serious group events such as the relocation of residents affected by development through urbanization, dissatisfied victims of sub-standard buildings affected by earthquakes, and so on, and these have increasingly affected social stability. Such a grim situation forced policy-makers to adjust the governance model. The traditional comprehensive model of social organization has had to be re-established, with the idea of building a socialist 'harmonious society' promulgated. This idea stresses a 'people-orientation' with the livelihood of ordinary citizens brought to the fore and a diversity of dispute resolution mechanisms promoted. The central government has gone as far as to identify 'dispute handling' as an important component of accountability, requiring local government to 'resolve disputes seriously' (see Xinhua 2009a).

Court credibility and the court-mediation interface

A range of legal reform issues has had a direct impact on the evolution of China's ADR and none more so than the rise of litigation. Litigation, to an extent, removes power and control from disputants in that it entails a transfer of control to the court which 'decides' (but does not necessarily 'resolve') the dispute and does not allow for the complex and creative solutions which may be more satisfactory for the parties than an imposed decision. The law itself has had gaps and areas of confusion; the legal environment is poor with the existence of some judicial corruption well documented, resulting in doubts about court credibility (Li Ling 2010: 196). Furthermore, there have been implementation difficulties partly due to the sheer weight of growing litigation cases brought to court, intensifying pressures on court capabilities.

At the same time, state financial investment in the judiciary has been strengthened and it is against this backdrop that the Court's judicial policy of 'fundamental change' helps bring the development of ADR back to the fore. In September 2002, the Supreme Court issued 'Several Provisions on the Trial of Civil Cases Involving the People's Mediation Agreement'.[4] This states that a People's Mediation Agreement has the effect of a contract. From that Supreme Court ruling on judicial practice, courts have strengthened mediation proceedings (i.e. mediation before a lawsuit), constituting 'Court Annexed ADR', and entrusting administrative organs and grassroots participants to actively engage in diverse local dispute resolution mechanisms. The Supreme People's Court further held in August 2009 that the justice model now placed 'mediation first' – that is, 'mediation combined with adjudication' – and that litigation should be based on the establishment of sound convergence of non-litigation dispute resolution mechanisms to first attempt to resolve contradictory opinions. It has thus been the Supreme People's Court that has directly promoted the development of a variety of ADR processes to interface with the judicial process.

ADR with Chinese characteristics

In promoting a variety of ADR mechanisms, the theory and practice of ADR in Western countries has had a significant impact on China. Some foreign experiences have provided a basis for the legitimacy of ADR – in promoting legal circles and public opinion of the value of ADR and reducing misunderstandings and resistance to it. One of the architects of the modern ADR movement in the West, Harvard Professor Frank Sander, put it this way: 'picking the right dispute for ADR is always important … it is a question of fitting the forum to the fuss' (Sander and Goldberg 1994). A courtroom is not always the best forum to resolve a dispute.

The role of the judiciary in promoting a more vibrant ADR sector in China cannot, however, be understated. It has had the power to explore and communicate with other countries to benefit from foreign ADR legislation, system construction, education and training. China's current and emerging ADR can thus be viewed as an important development opportunity. This is consistent with a world-wide trend, with ADR becoming a more prominent part of many legal systems. There are, however, important differences between China's ADR concepts, systems, procedures and technical capacities and those in Western countries. Important Chinese features of ADR are underpinned by the following specific laws:

- *The Arbitration Law* (1994)
- *Labour Dispute Mediation and Arbitration Law* (2008)
- *Rural Land Contract Disputes Mediation and Arbitration Law* (2010)
- *The People's Mediation Law* (2010).[5]

Although these valuable ADR laws have been promulgated, their role in promoting and protecting ADR remains insufficient. In addition to the legal framework being established, other characteristics are also essential in shaping China's ADR.

Political ideology

Local governments often use political ideology in various ways to promote ADR. This is a relatively easy way to avoid lawyers and, at the same time judges, regulators and even mediators still often lack enough enthusiasm for and knowledge of ADR to put up spirited resistance to unfair or dominating practices of local department officials. These influences enable the continued use of political ideology at local levels in ways that can have a negative impact on both the quality and credibility of ADR.

Traditional culture (or its weakening?)

The role of traditional culture and community morality as underpinning dispute resolution has certainly been weakened since opening and reform. With ADR's social credibility at a low ebb, the risk of using it may be commonly perceived as too big – as the culture and atmosphere conducive to negotiation and honesty is not sufficiently established. When social autonomy and self-discipline is limited, the parties' ability to negotiate (or mediate) is weakened and, by definition, ADR's operations and capacity to resolve disputes are correspondingly weak (see Fan Yu 2003, 2004, 2005).

Dispute resolution mechanisms and procedures

Dispute resolution mechanisms are by no means perfect. There is one key target value to be sought: the people's mediation aims at institutionalization and standardization with the entire dispute resolution mechanism devoted to 'mediation according to law'. This strong legal focus is helpful, but at the same time it fails to adequately legitimize ADR as an autonomous, consultative, market-based approach to dispute resolution. It backgrounds ADR as an adjunct to the formal legal system rather than a worthwhile enterprise in its own right. The procedural interests and value of ADR *per se* are not fully recognized. This includes confidentiality, full and voluntary participation of the parties – without lawyers – and respect for the integrity and flexibility of procedures and the substantive regulations governing ADR.[6]

Contemporary Chinese ADR: basic form and main systems

The current Chinese approach to ADR may be divided into several categories as follows:

- **Non-governmental ADR**
  This includes, inter alia, the following:

  (i) People's mediation based on the 'grassroots autonomy system' (the villagers' autonomy and the urban dwellers' autonomy). This is the basic form of autonomous civil mediation. Besides people's mediation organizations, community autonomy organizations exist in other forms such as house-owners' committees and property management boards (although these may not be in all regions and cities). These can resolve disputes too and more recently there has been an upswing in legal volunteers and civil mediators in dispute resolution.

  (ii) With increased socialization, some judicial or administrative dispute resolution organizations are becoming non-governmental including, for instance, arbitration and notary offices, law firms and grassroots community legal services.

  (iii) Some social bodies or departments attached to administrative authorities exist between autonomous and administrative organizations. These are civil bodies in function and legal status despite depending on government financial support and employees being public servants. Examples are Consumer Associations and labour–management arbitration organizations. Looking ahead it is possible that these types of bodies may become more detached from the government system, with increased roles for hybrid and non-government organizations or neutral dispute resolution organizations that have less dependence on government funding and may be more responsive to China's open market conditions.

- **Specialized ADR**
  Specialized alternative procedures are based on the types and nature of disputes and the applicable legislation. These specializations relate mainly to mediation, administrative treatment and arbitration of labour disputes, consumer disputes, traffic accidents, the attribution of right of land use and woods, medical disputes and disputes over intellectual property, e.g. disputes of trademark, copyright and patent rights. These mechanisms are quite diverse with some administrative and others non-administrative, comprehensive or occupational. Indeed, some procedures such as labour arbitration function separately from (although in collaboration with) court procedures.

- **Industry-based ADR**
  Autonomous sectoral or industry-based organizations which are at an early stage of their evolution and not yet completely detached from government administration, are now being quickly promoted in China. For instance, autonomous industrial organizations have been established, or are being established for industry professionals in accountancy, public health, finance, real estate, home appliances, building, chemical engineering and the tourism industry. Respective standards have been or are being formulated and relevant dispute resolution procedures established. For example, on 18 January 2000, the Ministry of Information Industry promulgated the Telecommunication Services Standards – the first set of compulsory standards issued by a competent department of the Chinese government. Standards have been put in place for handling both user and administrative complaints in the telecommunication services. Since that precedent was set, the Ministry of Information Industry has promulgated the 'Interim Measures for Handling Telecommunication Users' Complaints', outlining special procedures for dispute resolution in that sector. It is anticipated other industries will follow suit.

- **Administrative ADR**
  This category may itself be divided into administrative 'mediation' and 'adjudication' sub-categories:
    (i) Administrative mediation handles damages claims for both *personal* and *property* injury caused by public security events, some consumer disputes, damages for injury suffered because of traffic or medical accidents handled by competent administrative authorities. The resolution of a dispute is in the form of a 'mediation agreement', and the administrative authority acts as both mediator/witness *and* supervising/enforcement authority. Where mediation fails, the administrative authority closes the mediation procedure and at that point an interested party may bring proceedings to the People's Court.
    (ii) Administrative adjudication is an 'administrative judgement', quasi-judicial in nature. In the past, some administrative adjudication involved a final procedure with courts having no jurisdiction over those cases. But recent years of reform have involved promotion of a variety of civil rights, and administrative adjudication has become subject to judicial review or normal court procedures. This has meant that disputes over such matters as the attribution of the right to use woods and land, pulling down or removal of houses in urban developments, copyright or trade mark violations and so on may commence as administrative proceedings but end with parties seeking judicial remedies. In this way the government can avoid the accusation of biased or corrupt outcomes determined by local departmental officials.

- **Administrative reconsideration system**
  This system is essentially one of administrative appeals. It treats administrative disputes as the object of its operation with dispute resolution its essential function. Action in this forum is 'quasi-judicial', but compared with court procedures,

'administrative reconsideration' is procedurally simple, free of charge, expedient and easily accessible. Once made, an administrative decision has the authority and effect of being enforceable. However, such decisions are not necessarily final in that an interested party retains the right to bring proceedings to court. The administrative reconsideration procedure thus offers parties an alternative route to resolving administrative disputes to the formality of court. Opinions are divided as to whether the administrative reconsideration procedure involves modern ADR although on balance most consider it to be ADR in a 'broad sense'.

- **Criminal reconciliation: A case for reform**
  ADR has been widely used in civil and commercial disputes, labour and other specialized disputes, administrative disputes and some criminal areas of reconciliation. The *Administrative Procedure Law*, however, prohibits mediation in administrative litigation. Technically, this means that mediation is termed 'administrative co-ordination' or 'administrative conciliation'. At the time of writing, the Legislature is planning to amend this law to remove some restrictions on mediation.[7] For instance, in public order and criminal cases involving public security authorities, prosecutors and courts are actively seeking 'criminal reconciliation' as a judicial reform. Such reforms are being legitimized by their potential positive effects on public safety where significant violations have occurred such as in the Sanlu contaminated milk-powder case.[8] Reforms to the Criminal Code are ongoing and some ADR procedures may be considered for certain categories of crime.[9]

In addition to the categories of ADR in China outlined above, there are several systems and procedures specifically designed to address disputes concerning foreign investors.

Commercial arbitration and mediation for foreign investors

China's arbitration is characterized by an emphasis on mediation: The pattern and culture of arbitration is combined with mediation in the *Arbitration Law* (Article 51(1)), indicating that mediation is based on the parties 'volunteering to the arbitration processes'. Its characteristics are: the arbitrator is also a mediator; when mediation is unsuccessful the arbitrator should, in a timely way, give the arbitration award. After a mediation agreement is reached the arbitral tribunal prepares the conciliation statement or agreement and this has legal effect like an award. China's commercial arbitration and mediation is also divided according to foreign and domestic trading.

International arbitration

Foreign trade arbitration was established during the 1950s. In May 1954 the Central People's Government established the China International Trade Promotion

Committee in the Foreign Trade Arbitration Commission. In November 1958 the State Council then promulgated the Promotion of International Trade and China Maritime Arbitration Committee – established within the Commission. These accepted foreign arbitration cases and are now known as the China International Economic and Trade Arbitration Commission (China International Chamber of Commerce Court of Arbitration) and the China Maritime Arbitration Commission.[10]

For foreign investors in China, the process of solving disputes requires close attention to several issues. Despite many similarities, China's ADR in functions, values and mode of action is very different to Western countries. For example, negotiation and mediation has no clear demarcation between adjudication and sentencing; the role of mediator is 'active' and there is an emphasis on the function of law (and legal effects) combined with social effects. In this sense mediation has a political function in China. By contrast, mediators in common law Western countries are required to 'be careful to avoid making suggestions and appearing to exert pressure on a party to proffer or accept a particular settlement' (Limbury 2010: 65). It is substantively up to the parties to work out solutions, with the mediator predominantly a 'facilitator'. Conceptually, dispute settlement mechanisms in China are sensitive to the varying economic, social and cultural differences across its different regions. Notwithstanding the 'one-China' policy, cultural differences across this vast nation are quite large. Departments have formed practices that accommodate differences at local levels, and the attitude and approach of courts (and local lawyers) to ADR vary accordingly. It follows that foreign investors need to be 'tuned-in' to local operating contexts of ADR mechanisms. The value of knowing local conditions cannot be overstated.

Where disputes between local operators and foreign investors occur, the fullest possible use of ADR by negotiation and mediation should be made to resolve them – especially given the large numbers of labour and consumer disputes nowadays. If one of the parties belongs to a disadvantaged group, media attention may become a factor in the dispute, especially if it involves a complex event, legal issues or the public interest. In such situations, non-litigious dispute resolution can greatly reduce costs and risks. Foreign investors should also pay careful attention to managing the relationship with the government. In the case of ordinary disputes, a foreign investor can request the local government (or relevant administrative authority) to help or resolve a dispute. In this situation there is a focus on the *coordinating role* of government. If the dispute is with the local government or administrative authority – over, say, land acquisition and resettlement, government procurement contracts, investment, law enforcement (for example, labour, industry and commerce, taxation, quality control or health circumstances) – then help of a superior government authority may be sought. This can be by way of administrative reconsideration or, if not settled, then civil or administrative proceedings may be brought.

Where parties have not been able to reach a settlement or have rejected mediation they can sue directly, but in recent years the court has emphasized mediation first (see Fan Yu 2007b). To set this up, several protocols are to be followed:

(1) Mediation before litigation; (2) Settlement (if the parties negotiate a settlement the lawsuit is withdrawn); (3) Mediation before trial (mediation here is by a judge's assistant or the presiding judge in a pre-trial process); and (4) Mediation in civil proceedings (trial judge conducts mediation).[11] The court has the power, of course, to entrust other social organizations – such as a chamber of commerce, people's mediation and so on – to assist. Mediation is voluntary, but restricted by prescribed completion times so as not to delay the lawsuit (and clog the courts with unresolved mediations). Litigation mediation has the same effect as a judgement and can therefore restrict appeal rights and be enforced.[12]

Domestic

Domestic arbitration was built in the early 1960s with the Economic Commission responsible for arbitration at all levels of organization. Belonging to the category of 'administrative arbitration', it essentially dealt with economic contract disputes in the planned economy. In 1994, however, the promulgation of the *Arbitration Law* marked the formal establishment of a modern arbitration system required for transition to a market economy. The *Arbitration Law* has a revised schedule characterized by three main issues, as follows:

- First, the arbitration committee became a *non-governmental organization*.[13] With 'market mechanisms' becoming more mainstream, it is anticipated that arbitration will in the future draw increasingly on grassroots participation as high costs currently mean it is, according to Chen Fuyong (2010), largely used for 'high-end' commercial dispute resolution.[14]
- Second, the *Arbitration Law* has provided a framework for the standardization of arbitration facilities in each region. Although laudable, this has the effect of marginalizing the temporary arbitration services and potentially creates regional arbitration monopolistic practices. Lack of competition may constitute a trade obstacle to the development of arbitration.
- Third, the law has sought to improve the 'judicial tendency' of arbitration. Trade arbitration has tended to imitate the courts' 'judicial patterns'. As the arbitration system's history evolved from a planned economy it has lacked a commercial tradition, arbitrators are often recruited from legal backgrounds and the arbitration culture still lacks experience of a market economy. It mainly exists as a high-end commercial dispute resolution mechanism, but for general civil dispute solution and sharing litigation cases has relatively limited significance.

Directions in China's ADR

It is impossible to summarize in one chapter the range of domestic and international ADR systems and approaches in the PRC. Indeed, this is not necessary. There are, however, several key institutions and mechanisms outlined below which illustrate the philosophical orientations of ADR in China. With market reforms,

ADR mechanisms now include a range of government and non-government (fee-for-service) mechanisms. This section thus highlights concepts underlying these mechanisms including the development since 1987 of the Mediation Centres, approaches to solving labour and consumer disputes, and the new *People's Mediation Law*.

Mediation Centres

The first Mediation Centre was set up in 1987 by the China Council for the Promotion of International Trade (CCPIT) in conjunction with the China Chamber of International Commerce (CCOIC) and by 2006 the association had 42 Mediation Centres across China. Individual commercial Mediation Centres are not completely independent as they come under a model of central governance whereby the organization of arbitration requires mediation rules to be applied in a unified, nationwide network. Mediation Centre employment advertises the mediator role as requiring arbitrator qualifications *and* mediation skills training (according to the international general standard). The Centre serves a wide range of industries involved in trade and commerce including the financial services sector, negotiable securities, investment management and so on, and addresses intellectual property rights, technology transfer, real estate, project contracts, transportation and insurance disputes (among others).

At this stage, mediation has involved domestic and international disputes with big high-end traders taking up the service in order to avoid protracted court litigation. Mediation Centres are more economical, have 'nimble procedures' and the high standards of mediation have attracted high praise from both domestic and foreign litigants. More sceptical readers may, however, view such appraisals as predictable outcomes of the types of evaluations used by fee-for-service providers. Nonetheless, the Supreme People's Court has approved that mediation organizations set up by the arbitration committee to carry on fair and neutral mediation have the right to reach mediation agreements. When signed (or stamped) by both parties these have the force of a civil contract which the court can confirm. The Centres comply with this. Philosophically, then, Mediation Centres are 'market-oriented', relying on fees to maintain their operations rather than being dependent on government funding to support them, and are thus a hybrid form directly reflecting a reform era that encourages some market development and diversity in the mediation space.

Labour dispute resolution

In the planned economy period, China had no special labour dispute resolution mechanism per se. After the reform and opening-up policy and with the growth of non-public ownership, however, all manner of labour disputes have arisen. These have become a significant source of social problems. After the 1980s, China gradually set up the labour dispute arbitration committee with a system of compulsory arbitration based on a two-level judicial trial. In June 2007 the NPC Standing Committee formulated *The People's Republic of China Labour Contract Law* (promulgated 1 January 2008), and on 29 December 2007 *The Labour Dispute Mediation and Arbitration Law* (promulgated 1 May 2008). These laws provide the legislative basis of the present labour dispute processing mechanism, constituting the two-level 'mediation-arbitration' judicial trial.[15] A labour dispute arbitration committee is composed of representatives of labour departments, trade unions and the enterprise. But in fact it is mainly managed by the labour administrative department. In practice, therefore, it is an 'administrative arbitration' yet it tends to imitate court proceedings and the adversarial process.

Labour arbitration does not charge fees and after an application for labour arbitration is made the parties are still free to negotiate settlement. Alternatively, if a settlement agreement is reached, the parties can withdraw their application. Furthermore, before making an award, the tribunal is first required to attempt to conciliate.[16] Some wage claims, work injury medical expenses, economic compensation or damages, social security and other issues are finalized by an arbitration award which becomes legally effective from that date. On the other hand, if the parties refuse to accept the arbitration award they can bring a lawsuit – within 15 days after receipt of the award.

Since the implementation of the *Labour Contract Law* and *Labour Dispute Mediation and Arbitration Law* and in the wake of the global financial crisis, labour disputes have hit new peaks. In 2008 at all national levels of labour arbitration, facilities processed more than 964,000 cases and the courts settled a further 286,221 labour disputes – a 93.93 per cent rise compared to the previous year.[17] This massive increase in numbers has placed extreme pressure on the present arbitration system in terms of a design based on processing according to legal procedure and the cumbersome nature of the two-level judicial trial system. Philosophically, the consideration of labour disputes has several characteristics. It must address both political imperatives to protect workers' interests – through the functions of the tripartite consultative mechanism. This goal operates at a practical level with low efficiency – which is, not surprisingly, counterproductive to worker interests. It is precisely the movement *from* a planned *to* a market economy that is reflected in this conundrum.

Consumer Association mediation

Since 1994 the *Consumer Protection Law* has operated to protect consumers (and business operators) by making provisions for dispute resolution. Set up and funded by the government, it provides several options, as follows: (1) *negotiate* a settlement with the operator; (2) *mediate* through a Consumer Association; (3) *refer* the dispute to the relevant administrative department; (4) *arbitrate* – to reach an arbitral award; and (5) *lawsuit*. The first four of these options are ADR, and of particular interest to this analysis is the role played by the Consumer Associations. Concerned with the legal rights and interests of consumers, they provide civil ADR but have no judicial function. In mediation proceedings, Consumer Associations act as a 'neutral third party'. As such, they do not represent a particular party (consumers) and must obey the principle of mediation being voluntary. Philosophically, then,

China's Consumer Associations are closer to the Western theory of 'non-interventionist' mediation and they cannot prevent the parties from exercising their rights to commence legal proceedings. As dispute resolution is a statutory duty of Consumer Associations they are not meant to refuse requests for mediation and in recent years have played an invaluable role in resolving consumer disputes, including some affecting foreign investors.

Reasonably equal dialog needs to be a foundation for successful mediation to avoid power imbalances or overly confrontational meetings. As China's market mechanisms are not yet mature, however, sometimes this 'equality' is missing. For instance, some industry organizations are now developing and it is not always easy for them to establish an equal dialog with the government-backed Consumer Associations. On the other hand, however, there are some powerful industry groups that can exercise significant power over Consumer Associations and there remains some dependence on administrative authorities and judicial procedure to resolve consumer disputes to balance competing interests. This is especially so where one party has greater access to wealth and power. Furthermore, in a recent study of the China Consumer Association (CCA), the CCA's silence in the Sanlu contaminated milk case may be linked to the institutionalizing of a close relationship between the CCA and the government, likely to result in 'the alignment of interests of the CCA with the concerns of the government' (Bath and Ip 2011: 241).

The People's Mediation Law

The people's mediation system was born in the Communist revolutionary base-period after 1949. It is legally recognized as an important grassroots organization of social governance. By December 1982 the government had established the Constitution. Article 111 indicates that urban and rural residential areas (can have) residents' and villagers' committees set up by the grassroots mass self-organization. The residents' and villagers' committee chairman, vice chairmen and members are elected by residents and there is a direct relationship between the committees and grassroots political power established by law.

Neighbourhood or village committees have a range of responsibilities including setting up people's mediation, public security and public health, the residential area, public affairs and public welfare, mediating civil disputes and helping to maintain public order. The committees are intended to reflect the opinions of the masses to demands of the people's government and may make recommendations. Village committees have had delegated authority to make certain local regulations and, in June 1989, the State Council promulgated the 'People Redressing Committee Organic rules'. In 1990 the *Civil Procedure Law* further strengthened management and guidance to people's mediation by transferring its organization to an informal justice system. By 2002 the Ministry of Justice formulated the 'People to Mediate Works Certain Stipulations', expanding the organization and functions of people's mediation.

More recently, people's mediation has been further elevated by the National People's Congress and the State Council with a work plan, drafted by the

Ministry of Justice, in August 2010: the *People's Mediation Law*. This was adopted by the 28th NPC Standing Committee as the *People's Mediation Act*. Essentially, this reflects the Constitution in that it enables towns, streets and certain areas (such as bazaars, tourist areas, development zones), grassroots trade unions, women's federations, federations more generally, Consumer Associations and other mass organizations such as trade organizations to build 'people's mediation organizations'.[18]

The *Mediation Law* creates the opportunity to resist the tendency of ADR becoming legalistic and overly standardized and preserves informal, flexible and convenient features. Philosophically, the mediator can take the initiative to intervene in disputes and conduct on-site, 'real-time' mediation. This community orientation differs from the conventional Western notion of the 'neutral', non-interventionist mediator. Although confidentiality is not explicitly recognized in the Law, the principle is retained and the parties have the right to mediation that is not open to the public. The Law also confirms the legal effect of the People's Mediation Agreement. In this Law there is a convergence of people's mediation, administrative and judicial proceedings.[19]

A most important reform for ADR was clearly the judicial confirmation of the People's Mediation Agreement. If parties consider it necessary, within 30 days from the date of the agreement, they can apply to the People's Court for judicial confirmation and once confirmed the mediation agreement can be enforced by the court. This system deepens the legal status of people's mediation, improving its security. On the other hand, however, it simply reflects the desires of parties, the public and practical departments to improve the effectiveness of mediation.

There is a risk for ADR in the new Law in that the emphasis on legal enforcement may tend to gloss over the importance of good faith and the spirit of voluntary compliance in parties reaching an agreement. Time will tell. ADR rapidly evolves, and in recent years people's mediation has not been limited to resolving community disputes. It has begun to develop in many professional fields such as traffic accident compensation, medical disputes and labour dispute processing – to name a few. After implementing the *People's Mediation Law*, this expansion will be faster and may combine with the insurance system to play an even greater role in society.

Conclusion

As is the case elsewhere in the world, ADR in contemporary China is in a period of transition both practically and philosophically. The transition coincides with the rapid development of Chinese society and the introduction of market reforms to its economy. ADR, and indeed the entire dispute resolution network, has been given a special place in the reconstruction process. It is impossible, however, to be precise about ADR's future. Its patterns are evolving. Nevertheless, from the ongoing changes outlined in this chapter, it appears inevitable that diversified dispute resolution programs will be gradually instituted in China's drive to modernize its legal system. The diverse demands of society for just, quick and efficient dispute resolution mechanisms require no less. The Supreme People's Court has already confirmed that a People's Mediation Agreement is binding. The *People's Mediation Law* highlights that it is not limited to resolving neighbourhood or community disputes but helps in many professional fields. This is likely to expand in the future. Furthermore, some tradition-based, grassroots alternative procedures may be re-invigorated and become integral to ADR specifically and the legal system more generally.

At the same time, China has opened up to foreign investors. Along with the 'going out' policy which has seen significant investment flowing from the mainland to secure China's national interests overseas, China's ADR system has had to grow to meet the special demands of resolving international disputes. While a variety of political, legal and policy factors have clearly had an impact on China's modern approach to ADR, there are signs the people are becoming more aware of the value of drawing on traditional culture to help resolve disputes. This growing awareness is likely to influence decisively the directions of China's law reforms generally and ADR more specifically.

Notes

1 In previous treatises on mediation in China, scholars did not particularly distinguish 'people's mediation' from 'court mediation'. For this article I refer to mediation as 'extra-court mediation' (i.e. an alternative to court dispute resolution) and, in particular, 'people's mediation' and the rich variety of social and administrative mediations now available.
2 Although 'revenue' and 'expenses' are separately calculated, the court may financially benefit from litigation fees on the basis of the amounts involved in the cases. These benefits may be used for the provision of court facilities and improvements to the livelihood of staff. As a result of this practice, the income gap between urban centre courts and remote rural areas has widened. See Wang Yaxing (2001) for more detailed analysis of this matter.
3 Chinese official website: http://www.gjxfj.gov.cn/.
4 The Supreme People's Court of China issued the legal authorization in its 'judicial interpretations', indicating the mediation agreement, while binding, should not conflict with laws and administrative regulations.
5 *The People's Mediation Law* was passed on 28 August 2010 effective from 1 January 2011. Source: www.npc.gov.cn (available in Chinese and English).
6 The court is presently trying to simplify court procedures for citizens to bring litigious actions. This may have the side-effect of devaluing ADR as an option in its own right. Ironically, courts' efforts to make court procedures more convenient may make it more difficult for interested parties to be attracted to using ADR and instead rely on the courts.
7 See: www.gjxfj.gov.cn/.
8 [Editor's note] In the Sanlu case, reports suggest that

> neither the China Consumer Association nor its local counterpart assisted consumers in any way and that in September 2008, lawyers representing victims appealed to the Ministry of Health and the China Consumer Association to participate in discussions about formulating a compensation plan with the responsible milk producers ... Consumer associations in China were set up under the auspices of the government and since 2007 have been totally funded by the government. The silence of the Chinese consumer associations in such a significant case strongly suggests

that they are more aware of their obligations to government than their duty to consumers.

(Bath and Ip 2011: 247)

On criminal reconciliation, also see: www.hi138.com/e/?i162554.
9   Also see Fan Yu (2009) with respect to multiple ways to resolve group Tort law incidents.
10 Internationally accepted arbitration practices in China can be traced to the China International Trade Promotion Committee with the China International Chamber of Commerce revising the 'China Maritime Arbitration Commission Arbitration Rules'; the 'China International Economic and Trade Arbitration Commission Arbitration Rules' and 'China International Economic and Trade Arbitration Commission, Financial Disputes Arbitration Rules'.
11 See Vai Lo Lo (2001) at: http://works.bpress.com/vai_lo/8 for a useful history of judicial mediation.
12 Despite the judges in mediation working under the critical incentive of 'mediation rates', the mediation *must* be based on the parties' voluntary participation. If mediation does not meet the parties' own interests and expectations they can initiate further action.
13 Currently, arbitration agencies operate on two different models: nongovernmental and administrative. Some arbitration committees in central cities are better equipped to implement self-financing and have high independence (e.g. the Beijing Arbitration Commission); but most arbitration agencies still depend on government support (mainly the Office of Legislative Affairs). The Arbitration Commissions receiving very few cases and relying on government funding and operations for survival, not surprisingly, have questionable independence.
14 See also Albert H.Y. Chen (2003: 257–87) regarding mediation and folklore. Also please note that Chen Fuyong's work makes other points about arbitration problems, not just costs (Chen Fuyong 2010).
15 Mediation is not strictly a legal procedure, but can be hosted by the enterprise of a labour dispute mediation committee or local people's mediation organization (or mediation organization established in towns or streets by local governments).
16 Mediation agreements should state the arbitration request and the result of agreement. Conciliation statements should be signed by the arbitrators, with the seal of the labour arbitration commission, and served on both parties. But if the parties cannot reach agreement, the arbitral tribunal shall make a timely decision.
17 The data has been extracted from the original labour, social security and Supreme People's Court announcements.
18 The *Mediation Law* stipulates state policies and responsibilities for supporting the people's mediation; provides for the judicial administrative organs' management system of the people's mediation work; and guides the grassroots work of the People's Mediation Committee with respect to links to court.
19 Explicitly stipulated by the People's Conciliation Committee, a mediation agreement is legally binding on the parties. The Law provides grassroots People's Courts and public security organs with guidance about case applications (and suitability) for people's mediation.

12 Organized crime in China

The Chongqing crackdown (重庆打黑行动)

Norman P. Ho

The 'crackdown' on organized crime in Chongqing (2009–10) and the general nature of Chongqing's organized crime elements and activities are explored in this chapter. By situating the Chongqing crackdown in a broader history of organized crime in China and government responses to it, this chapter argues that Chongqing's crime-world is best viewed as representative of trends in Chinese organized crime over the past few decades. This includes an increasingly strong nexus between high-ranking, corrupt government officials and criminal gang members, more sophisticated organized crime groups that penetrate legitimate business and economic sectors, and the increasingly brazen use of violence. Violent crime related to syndicate activity is now often perpetrated in audacious disregard of Chinese law and is characterized frequently by a total lack of concern for the welfare of fellow urban residents. In many ways, Chongqing's twenty-first-century organized crime is reminiscent of the strong gangs that controlled Shanghai in the early twentieth century.

In terms of government responses in Chongqing, it will be shown that a mixture of old and new techniques to combat organized crime has been utilized. While relying on anti-crime and 'strike-hard' style campaigns as used in the 1950s, the Chinese government has also utilized the power of the media, including the internet, to mobilize the populace against organized crime. Indeed, the media has been used to put a 'personal face', namely Bo Xilai, to its anti-crime effort.

In this chapter, a brief historical overview of Chinese organized crime since the late imperial era is provided, as well as a short history of the central government's responses towards organized crime. Then, the Chongqing crackdown is examined and situated in its historical context, analysing the nature of Chongqing's organized crime problem and the government's responses. Finally, the implications of the government's strategy in Chongqing will be discussed. Ultimately, the message of this analysis is optimistic, as despite the severity of organized crime in Chongqing, the government has been able to use a variety of methods to control it while gaining popular support. At the same time, some serious concerns (which should not be ignored) regarding the sacrifice of legal rights of individual defendants in the government's quest for swift verdicts are highlighted.

Contexts: history and trends in Chinese organized crime and government responses

China has dealt with the presence of organized crime for centuries. In late imperial China, organized crime elements rose to become powerful enough to directly challenge the government.[1] Triads had in fact sought to overthrow the imperial Qing dynasty and played a major role in both the Boxer Rebellion (1899–1901) and the 1911 Revolution (Schloenhardt 2010: 161). Dr Sun Yat-sen was himself a triad member (ibid.). From 1911 to 1949, underground criminal groups actively nurtured and developed relationships with the KMT party (He 2003: 281). Their criminal activities included selling drugs, gambling and prostitution, and they also penetrated many legitimate business industries such as entertainment, real estate and banking (ibid.). The Shanghai Green Gang, for example, actively participated in municipal politics, assisting Chiang Kai-shek's anti-Communist activities in the 1920s (Martin 1996: 6). Du Yuesheng, the leader of Shanghai's criminal underground, also led a legitimate life as a shareholder, manager and chairman of many top businesses (He 2003: 281–2). The period of 1911 to 1949 can be characterized as one where organized crime flourished in China, strengthened by its guanxi and mutual cooperation with the ruling government.[2]

Shortly after the establishment of the People's Republic of China in 1949, organized crime almost completely disappeared as activities such as gambling, opium drug trading and prostitution were strictly prohibited and attacked by the central government (Lo 2009: 14). The CPC employed aggressive measures to stamp out organized crime, including the issue of strict regulations buttressed by swift enforcement and popular support for such measures. In February 1950, the CPC promulgated an order banning opium and drugs, a major source of organized crime income (He 2003: 288).[3] Thousands were arrested, and within two years, 1,223.5 tons of illegal drugs had been confiscated. In Shanxi province alone, the number of drug addicts dropped from 620,000 to 220,000 in just one year (ibid.). In 1952, Beijing promulgated 'Instructions for Eliminating Drug Influence' which encouraged the civilian population to take an active role in cleaning up drugs; over 51,000 drug offenders were arrested and punished (ibid.). Pornography, gambling and loan-sharking were virtually eliminated (ibid.).

Other political campaigns were also launched, vilifying the image of criminal gangs and their corrupt government official co-conspirators, painting them all as enemies of the revolution. These campaigns included 'The Suppression of Counterrevolutionaries Campaign' and 'The Rooting Out of the Secret Societies Campaign' (Keith and Lin 2006: 92). In 1951, the CPC launched the 'Three-Antis' campaigns to 'flush out corruption, waste and harmful bureaucracy' (Tsai 2007: 46–7). These campaigns were later merged with the 'Five-Antis' campaigns which targeted Chinese citizens who were committing various economic crimes such as bribery (ibid.). Those who were detained and arrested were tried in mass trials for maximum public humiliation and also as a deterrent to would-be criminals (ibid.). All of these strong, centrally directed regulations and campaigns largely eradicated organized crime in China from 1950 to around 1980.

Organized crime, however, was revitalized partly as a consequence of Deng's liberal economic reforms. With the accompanying decrease in central control, prosperity and wealth has grown in China with a simultaneous increase in the general crime rate. According to Lo (2009: 15) the overall crime rate in China since 1970 has tripled. From 1979 to the 1990s, the net number of criminal organizations also increased (Liang 2008: 89–90). Scholars estimate that from 1988 to the twenty-first century, underground criminal groups may have comprised 20–30 per cent of all criminal groups in China (He 2003: 282). Over the past 20 years, mafia-style gang crime is also estimated to have increased by roughly 700 per cent (Trevaskes 2007: 25). Other Chinese sources indicate that between 2000 and 2004 China had over one million members in secret societies. Of these, 4,200 groups were mafia-style syndicates (Schloenhardt 2010: 164). The BBC (2008) reported that in 2007 alone there was an estimated 160 per cent increase in gang-related crime across China. The rise of organized crime in China over the past three decades is not, however, unique. Many other developing and post-Soviet nations engaged in economic liberalization and development have also had to deal with organized crime as it provides members with 'a shortcut to wealth' (Bakken 2005: 99).

Besides the increase in sheer numbers, there have been other disturbing trends in the composition and the substantive activities of organized crime after Deng's reforms. Some represent new forms and some can be seen as virtually a continuous line since the KMT ruled on the mainland.

Organized crime groups have become more specialized, participating in the drug trade and the abduction of women for the sex business (He 2003: 282). Similar to the Shanghai Green Gang in the 1920s, post-1980s organized crime groups have infiltrated legitimate enterprise sectors to launder money, bribe government officials and law enforcement personnel and actively recruit accomplices to serve in the Party, government and judicial departments (He 2003: 284). As with the KMT in 1920s Shanghai, government officials have cultivated their relationships with organized crime elements for personal wealth, influence and power. Public security and customs officials are often targeted with bribes by 'snakeheads' and Chinese gangs in order to allow 'private trespassing', or to 'assist' with passport applications and the provision of 'official' documents for gang smugglers (Zhang 2008: 121). In November 2006, five judges from the Shenzhen Intermediate Court were arrested for taking bribes from criminals; notably, one court official had 'kept 30 million RMB in his personal home and enjoyed five mistresses, fruits from his dealings with criminal organizations' (Lo 2009: 96). Local officials in Wenzhou in the early 1980s frequently ignored illegal financial activities in order to 'locate promising rent sources for themselves' (Tsai 2002: 128). In Macao, casino operators and businessmen paid corrupt officials for protection (Lo 2009: 16). Organized crime activity in China over the past few decades has been largely made possible by the symbiotic relationship or nexus that has been formed between criminal organizations and corrupt government officials, especially at local levels.[4]

Underground groups have also become increasingly organized with defined hierarchies, some even forming corporations of sorts that control every step of the purchase and sale of illicit substances (He 2003: 283). There has also been a trend towards the use of more violence, as underground groups and gangs are 'increasingly arming themselves with guns, radio transmitters, submachine guns and other technologically advanced devices' (ibid.).

To deal with the resurgence of crime in general and organized crime in particular, the CPC has utilized various strategies. These have ranged from the passage of legislation to informal measures such as organizing academic conferences on combating organized crime. In 1997, the *Criminal Law of the PRC* 1997 (Article 26) was revised to include the following definition of a criminal organization as being: 'formed by three or more persons for the purpose of committing crimes jointly'. In 2000 the Chinese government further recognized their new dangerous status by giving them a special title: 'criminal gangs of underworld organizations'. According to Beijing, these criminal gangs shared the following characteristics:

> they were highly organized with an internal hierarchy and leadership structure; they had strong economic power and utilized illegal means to make profits; they had substantial and deep connections with government officials and enjoyed their protection (in Chinese, this is referred to as *baohusan*, or 'protective umbrella'); and they controlled specific, demarcated 'fixed turfs' where they committed their crimes.
>
> (Liang 2008: 89–90)[5]

This linguistic recognition of criminal gangs, through the provision of a standard definition of their characteristics, was a clear indication of Beijing's growing concern with organized crime and its potential to destabilize society and challenge central governmental power. In some coastal cities and provinces, local rules were also drawn up to combat organized crime. In 1989, for example, Shenzhen issued the 'Notice on Banning Underground Societies and Underground-type Gang Organizations' which listed specific, dangerous activities undertaken by such organizations, such as 'extortion, forcing people to lend money and creating trouble' (He 2003: 288–9). In 1993, the eighth conference of the Guangdong Standing Committee of the NPC passed the 'Issue for Punishing the Activities of Underground Criminal Organizations in Guangdong Province' (He 2003: 289).

From the 1980s to the present day, Beijing has also launched several 'severe strike-hard' (known in Chinese as *yanda*) campaigns, characterized by their emphasis on severity of punishment and swiftness in the criminal legal process in conviction and sentencing against criminals and criminal organizations. The first of these campaigns, in August 1983, targeted gangs, rape crimes and general hooliganism; harsher punishments were levied and arrest as well as execution quotas were reportedly implemented (Liang 2008: 91). In April 1996, Beijing organized another wave of campaigns, this time aimed at 'armed and violent crimes and prostitution' (ibid.). In April 2001, a campaign was launched specifically against the notorious 'criminal gangs of underworld organizations' with over 12,000 gang members arrested across China (Liang 2008: 91–2). In February 2006, the Chinese Communist Central Political and Legal Committee (CCPCLC) called for more serious crackdowns against underworld organizations operating in rural areas (Liang 2008: 96). In these crime campaigns, trials and punishments were carried out swiftly so as not to disrupt the momentum of the crackdowns, and mass trials were also employed (ibid.).

Local governments have also relied on similar strike-hard campaign directives and initiatives to fight organized crime, often with limited success. The Zhuhai authorities have employed 'cultural teams' to canvass the city to fight prostitution and combat crimes instigated from internet cafes, setting up a public phone 'hotline' for ordinary citizens to quickly report crimes (Lo 2009: 72). Problems with implementation, however, rendered this well-intentioned campaign ineffective (ibid.). Sometimes, local governments have been so powerless to stop organized crime that urban residents have had to take matters into their own hands. In Guangdong, for example, vigilante civilian groups formed to 'combat out-of-control crime, capturing pickpockets and conducting neighborhood watches' (Lo 2009: 73). At other times, local governments have pleaded for help from Beijing. In October 2003, Shenzhen requested help from Beijing to fight urban crime, and Beijing responded by sending 5,000 paramilitary People's Armed Police to patrol the city. While the immediate effect was to reduce the crime-rate, this solution did not solve any root-causes of the problem including 'inefficacy at the local level' (Lo 2009: 74).

In addition to the enactment of domestic legislation, regulations and 'strike-hard' campaigns, there has also been an emphasis (and resources spent) on developing improved 'police investigative practices and surveillance skills' (He 2003: 289). Furthermore, the Chinese government has entered into several anti-organized crime international treaties, including the *International Drug Treaty*. Beijing has joined Interpol and signed numerous judicial-assistance treaties, notably an anti-drug collaboration programme including China, Burma and the United Nations, as well as a joint anti-drug programme with Vietnam and Laos (He 2003: 284). It can thus be argued that the Chinese government has attempted to deal with organized crime in a variety of ways encompassing, inter alia, legislative change, 'tough' local measures and internationally-linked strategies.

The Chongqing case study

Having provided an historical context for examining the nature, development and scope of organized crime including government responses to it, the 2009–10 crackdown against organized crime in Chongqing is now examined in more detail. For readers who may not be familiar with Chongqing, the Chongqing Municipal Government describes it as a major city in southwestern mainland China 'with a population of 31.4 million', making it the largest municipality by population in the world.[6] This vast, rapidly modernizing and newly urbanized city is organized into 19 districts apparently awash with development cash and with real estate a 'dragon-head' that drives industry. Benefiting as it does from the central government's 'Go West' campaign, its mayor, Huang Qifan, describes Chongqing as having a booming economy with 'huge tracts of land reserved for development'.[7]

The criminal activities of underground groups in Chongqing that sparked the 2009–10 crackdown were similar to those perpetrated by underground groups in the past few decades. Intriguingly, they are comparable in power and influence to Du Yuesheng's notorious 'Green Gang' in Shanghai. Indeed, one of the disturbing points about Chongqing's organized crime groups and the corrupt officials who protected them is that many gang elements had become fully integrated into Chongqing's mainstream economy and the municipality's five primary industries: transportation, real estate, loans, the meat industry and the entertainment sector (Ji 2009: 28). This was akin to Du's involvement in legitimate businesses in Shanghai, as well as the operations of certain groups from the 1980s onwards, many of which were highly organized, actively recruiting government officials to protect their interests. Likewise, Chongqing's gangs were not merely engaging in peripheral activities or their own private, individual criminal operations (such as brothels or human smuggling), they were immersing themselves into critically important and, prima facie, legitimate business sectors. Symbiotic relationships between government officials and gang criminals – a behavioural trend in post-1986 groups – were perpetuated in Chongqing and appear to have intensified in both scale and scope. Indeed, as many corrupt officials had done in the past three decades, Chongqing officials (or former officials) did not just become 'passively' involved in organized crime groups simply for personal monetary gain. Rather, they had fully integrated into these criminal organizations by actively engaging in criminal enterprises for power and influence as well as money. These corrupt officials were not only turning a blind eye to economic crimes committed by criminal gangs, they were ignoring, indeed openly tolerating, increased levels of violent crime – fitting the broader post-Deng reforms trend towards increased violent and aggressive behaviour in organized crime.

Chongqing's cast of criminal characters has therefore been representative of continuing, identified trends in organized crime in China. For instance, Wen Qiang, the former head of the Chongqing Municipal Judicial Bureau – a critically important, high-ranking post in Chongqing's legal and police apparatus – was found to be implicated in the Chongqing crackdown as one of the central figures in the municipality's violent organized crime scene. Arrested in August 2009, he was accused of running gambling dens, illegally jailing people and also bribing police officials (BBC 2009b). He was also found guilty of raping a university student back in August 2007, and eventually executed on 7 July 2010, becoming the highest-ranking official at that stage to fall in the crackdown (Xinhua 2010d). Another key target of the crackdown was Wen Qiang's sister-in-law, Xie Caiping, who was labelled as the 'crime godmother' of Chongqing. She was accused of sheltering drug users, running gambling dens, bribing police, and also other violent crimes. Media reports also stated that she had 16 young lovers at her disposal (BBC 2009b). Xie's actions were also representative of trends related to the increased use of violence. She had been accused of hiring gang members to beat an undercover police officer who was later put into a bag and dumped in the countryside (Sanderson 2009). She is now behind bars, having been sentenced to a prison term of 18 years (Macartney 2009). Several top

Chongqing judges (Canaves 2010a) and six district police chiefs were also arrested in the crackdown, another sign of the widespread corruption in Chongqing and the severity of the organized crime problem (BBC 2009b).

Li Qiang, a rich businessman and former Chongqing Municipal People's Congress deputy, also epitomizes post-1980s trends towards heightened symbiotic relationships between government officials and gang criminals. Accused of being a gang leader, Li faced charges of disrupting public transportation, disturbing public order and bribery (*Global Times*, 2009). Like many of the other officials or former officials detained in the Chongqing crackdown, Li did not just take a back-seat role in criminal affairs, but instead was actively running full-scale criminal enterprises himself. His four seemingly legitimate companies were related to sectors critical to the smooth running of Chongqing, such as public transportation (one of his companies was responsible for more than 100 municipal bus routes) and real estate. The *Global Times* (2009) argues that this reflects broader trends of increasing sophistication in the organization of criminal gangs in China and their infiltration into mainstream, legal business sectors. Furthermore, he had used his power and influence to hire gang members to penetrate taxi companies, organizing a disruptive strike of 8,000 taxi drivers (Sanderson 2009). Li's accomplices too were not minor crooks. They were also relatively important Chongqing officials such as district transport administration directors (*Global Times* 2009). Li is now serving a 20-year prison sentence (Xinhua 2010a).

In addition to similarities with broader organized crime trends from the 1980s onward, the Chongqing 2009–10 crackdown also reveals a possibly new and disturbing demographic component of organized crime in China, namely, its 'youthification'. For instance, twin brothers Zhang Bo and Zhang Tao, who were both sentenced to 17 years in jail in November 2009, had been convicted of running criminal gangs in Chongqing since 2007. Born in 1987, the twins were, at the age of 20, leaders of a large gang running illegal casinos. Their gang also consisted of young men, mostly under the age of 30 and armed with knives (Xinhua 2009b). Although it is just one example, the Zhang brothers represent a new generation of youthful gang leaders who, apparently, have the necessary acumen to run a crime organization mainly comprised of older, violent members.

In many ways, Chongqing's cast of shadowy underworld characters has similarities to the powerful nexus of gang members and politicians in 1920s and 1930s Shanghai. As discussed above, in early twentieth-century China, Chinese gangs and secret societies were not just tangential actors engaged in limited criminal realms, but were strong forces in urban life and in politics. The Shanghai Green Gang and other contemporary criminal organizations were, for example, remarkably resilient and flexible, integrating into Shanghai's economic life and cosmopolitan social environment, 'participating in middle-class, legitimate political organizations and economic sectors' (Martin 1996: 2–6). As with the Shanghai gang, the various Chongqing gangs have also proved to be hardy and many have been run by officials (or former officials) operating in some of the most important sectors of Chongqing's economic and civic sectors. In other words, Chinese organized crime, as seen through the situation in Chongqing, is returning to its pre-1949 status, affirming the existence of disturbing trends in organized crime from the 1980s, including the increased use of violence.

Government responses to organized crime in Chongqing

The response of the Chinese authorities in dealing with organized crime in the municipality combined old and new methods. The government continued to rely on anti-corruption and anti-crime campaigns similar to those dating back to the 1950s and the post-1980s. Specifically, the Chongqing crackdown reflects continued government reliance on mass anti-crime and *yanda* campaigns and speedy, lightning-fast trials and imprisonment as a method of fighting organized crime.

The government reaction in Chongqing was arguably similar to anti-crime campaigns Beijing had formulated in previous decades. Perhaps most notably, the Chongqing crackdown was very much a 'mass campaign' with a relatively clear commencement date (mid-2009). Rather than gradual crackdowns against gang enterprises in the municipality, the selected Chongqing government officials launched a large crackdown at one time, arresting hundreds of people in a short time frame. As with the historical anti-crime *yanda* campaigns, swiftness of trial and punishment was a prominent feature of the Chongqing crackdown. By late October 2009, six ringleaders had already been sentenced to death and prison sentences were often handed down just weeks after the initial arrests (Elegant 2009). By 5 May 2011, *The Standard* estimated that the Chongqing crackdown had led to more than 3,300 detentions and the prosecutions of hundreds of individuals, including nearly 100 senior officials.

A central limitation to such *yanda* campaigns is that while they may cause immediate reductions in organized crime, such effects are not necessarily long-lasting. Peerenboom (2006: 71) argued that moral campaigns, for instance, are not effective at rooting out corruption and related crimes – what needs to be done is critical reform that changes the incentive structure for officials prone to corruption (such as increasing government officials' salaries to keep pace with market reforms, thus reducing incentives to favour the 'dark side').

The Chinese government also utilized new strategies to fight and prevent future organized crime in Chongqing. One newer strategy to deal with the rising criminal–corrupt official nexus was harnessing the media. The media was used to produce sensational and shocking stories about the detained criminals. Proceedings at Chongqing's No. 5 Intermediate People's Court, for example, attracted hundreds of onlookers who sat and listened to the trials, many of them victims themselves (Sanderson 2009). The crackdown and trials were turned into a spectacle, with wide (and seemingly unrestricted) media and internet blog coverage across China.[8]

Another strategy used by the CPC has been the active promotion and publicity (through the media and the internet) of a charismatic, reliable, almost heroic government official, creating a directly opposing image to that of the corrupt officials who had been arrested. In Chongqing's case, Bo Xilai, the municipality's head and CPC Committee Secretary, has arguably been groomed as this figure (and force) to combat organized crime. By creating an heroic figure, the CPC was able not only to fight crime, but to provide China's citizenry with hope via a human face to the anti-crime campaign. This was a crucial step as it was brought about under the gaze of intense media coverage of both the general crackdown and the specific lives and activities of individuals in Chongqing's criminal cast. More importantly for the CPC, this human face, exemplified through Bo, was no ordinary human face but a 'hero figure' representing the central government. In other words, the reliance on and praise of Bo was another effective way for the CPC to strengthen and consolidate its own power, attempting to prove to the public that not all its officials were corrupt like Wen Qiang. Russell Moses (in Elegant 2009, web version) put it this way: 'there is clearly a concerted effort by sections of the party [CPC] to give credit [for the crackdown] to Bo and make him more of a political rock star'.

Bo appeared to have the right credentials to be 'the face' of anti-organized crime in China. Prior to taking the helm at Chongqing, his reputation was solidified during his tenure as mayor of Dalian in the 1990s, where he was widely credited with revitalizing the city's economy, having previously served as China's Commerce Minister (Beck 2008). Selected as Chongqing's head in 2008 (to popular support) Bo enjoyed a formidable Communist pedigree, with his father one of the 'eight immortals' of the CPC (Elegant 2009).

After the crackdown, Bo was lauded by numerous 'netizens' – another testament to the government's influence on and engagement with the media and, more specifically, the internet. Some wrote: 'Bo Xilai is the hero in the hearts of the people' (in Wang 2009: 27). Other online comments included: 'Bo Xilai, please come over here to Hunan province – we need a leader like you!' (ibid.). Bo Xilai was also compared to a 'red sun rising in China's West', and some hoped he would become 'the Chairman of the CPC ... because he is the hope of the country, the hope of the people' (ibid.). A cult of personality may have even been formed; for example, a former motorcycle worker named Li Lei composed and performed a song praising Bo for his efforts in cracking down on organized crime. The lyrics, written by Meng Fanxiao, included lines such as: 'Your [Bo Xilai's] eyes are like a pair of swords flickering cold light' and 'Bo Xilai, Bo Xilai, China needs tens of hundreds of heroes like you!' (Canaves 2010b). From such comments, it certainly appears Bo was being set up as a national hero for his fight against organized crime and corruption.

The Chongqing crackdown can also be analysed in the context of Bo's other municipality-wide initiatives to fight organized crime and in light of the unique geographic and economic significance of Chongqing itself. In examining the crackdown in such a way, other newer strategies deployed by the Chinese government to combat organized crime at its source can be seen. For instance, in early 2008, Bo launched forth with an initiative in Chongqing focused on 'singing the red song, reading the classics, sharing stories, conveying maxims, and building a seven-story high statue of Mao Zedong at Chongqing University' (Wang 2009: 27). These reforms show Bo pushing what he sees as 'a purer, positive form of Marxist values [advocating] the promotion of a "*hongse* GDP" ("red GDP"), an economy where everyone can partake of and enjoy China's economic development' (Ji 2009: 24). Specific policies presented as pursuing a 'red GDP' included government intervention to stabilize housing prices and the provision of three different kinds of housing (a price-tiered system) suitable for different income levels. Under Bo's leadership, there are now efforts in Chongqing to expand cultural and educational programmes 'so agricultural workers can also enjoy municipal services' (Ji 2009: 25–6). Given Chongqing's estimated 30:70 ratio of urban to rural workers (Beck 2008) this focus on promoting the interests of rural workers is hardly surprising.

Clearly, Bo did not deal solely with existing criminal elements and, with the central government, an attempt was being made to build a new Chongqing, taking advantage of its geographic and economic significance and as an 'experiment zone' for new policies. Through this analytical lens, the leadership style of Bo is noteworthy. In handling the taxi drivers' strike, for instance, Bo 'eschewed heavy-handed political tactics and organized a public dialogue with forty taxi drivers in order to reach a solution' (Ji 2009: 28). Other 'heroes' have also emerged, such as Wang Lijun, a top policeman who had previously earned a strong anti-gang reputation while serving in Liaoning, and who had been brought into Chongqing to oversee police efforts (BBC 2009a). Chongqing's importance to the CPC was also made very clear when Vice President Xi Jinping (and successor to President Hu Jintao) travelled to Chongqing in January 2011 for a study tour, lauding the 'efforts of the city's law enforcement personnel in combating organized crime' (Ji 2011: 16–17).

In summary, the government has relied not only on old, mass anti-crime 'strike-hard' campaign tactics to fight organized crime, it has also utilized a newer strategy, that of tapping into and promoting specific individuals to serve as the public faces of honest officialdom to counter the proliferation of organized crime in Chongqing. This required harnessing the media's power. At the same time a range of socio-economic reforms were pushed through to fight root causes of corruption and crime.

The heroic treatment of Bo simultaneously reveals problems in the Chongqing crackdown. First, some observers have pointed out numerous legal problems with the Chongqing crackdown with respect to the treatment of those arrested and detained. There have been reports that lawyers were prevented from meeting their clients, accessing trial records or adequately defending clients owing to the breakneck speed of trials (Wang 2009). There were also concerns about the harassment of lawyers. A notable case emerged on 14 December 2009 when police detained Li Zhuang, a criminal defence lawyer representing some of the alleged gangsters in the Chongqing crackdown. Since then, Li's case has been marked by a series of bizarre developments. According to the relevant government authorities, Li had asked one of his clients, Gong Gangmo, to lie and say that the police had tortured him while in custody. Li was eventually found guilty of violating Article 306 of the PRC Criminal Law, which makes it illegal for lawyers to 'destroy or forge evidence, help any parties destroy or forge evidence, or coerce and entice witnesses into changing their testimony in defiance of the facts or giving false testimony' (Canaves 2009). He was initially sentenced in early January

2010 to two years and six months in prison (Blanchard 2010). However, in early February 2010, Li's sentence was reduced to 18 months on appeal.[9] During the appeal period, Li maintained that his earlier confession was false and made under his mistaken belief that there was in place a plea agreement with the government to avoid jail time. Many observers had already questioned the legitimacy of his earlier confession owing to its suspiciously clichéd, scripted nature and hesitant delivery marked by language mistakes (Clarke 2010; He Xin 2010, 9 February).

There have thus been severe doubts as to whether Li received a fair trial. Immediately after his arrest, Li was attacked in a '4,000-word character assassination' published in the *China Youth Daily*. Some even believe that Bo himself may have, for political gain, engineered Li's arrest (Garnaut 2010c). The case has generated considerable controversy in the media and the internet (ibid.), two of the vehicles the CPC itself harnessed to fight organized crime in Chongqing. Some Chinese newspapers have pejoratively labelled the case 'Lawyer fake-gate'. While Li was serving his 18-month sentence, prosecutors brought new charges of falsification of evidence against him, based on allegations made by his former clients and leads in Chongqing, Shanghai, Liaoning and Sichuan; these charges were however later dropped on grounds of insufficient evidence in late April 2011, another bizarre development in the saga of the Li case (He Xin 2011). It is bizarre in that, despite government rhetoric to the contrary, more broadly Li's case can be viewed as an illustration of continued government suppression of attorneys working on sensitive cases or representing unpopular clients (Cohen and Pils 2010).[10] Furthermore, in September 2010 the SPC upheld the execution of Chongqing gang member Fan Qihang despite allegations by Fan that to coerce his confession he was tortured by police while being held in detention. Despite the new exclusionary rule which would have prohibited the use of Fan's confession because of evidence of his torture, the SPC affirmed the death sentence (Lynch 2010; Ng 2010).[11]

Second, the adulation bestowed on Bo gives rise to further questions about the still weak nature of the Chinese legal apparatus to deal effectively with Chongqing-style organized crime as problems arise. If the police force and the court system were fully functional, would there be a need to publicize crime-busting heroes like Bo? Indeed, why would such an anti-crime/anti-corruption face be necessary? Might the use of carefully planned (and timed) mass campaigns and the recent personalization of anti-crime crackdowns in Chongqing testify to possible weaknesses in Chinese legal institutions to deal with certain types of criminals – even after they are apprehended? Some might say that the 'paternalistic' nature of the CPC is evident in the Chongqing crackdown. The Party still appears not to trust the judiciary in dealing with organized crime, and believes central directives and campaigns continue to be necessary (Peerenboom 2006: 61).

Conclusion

The nature of Chongqing's organized crime, when analysed in an historical context, should not be viewed as a completely new form. It is not. Rather, it reflects broader trends and developments in organized crime in China from the 1980s onwards and shares characteristics with the power Shanghai gangs wielded in the 1920s. Officials and former officials involved in organized crime continue to be motivated by the desire for a fast track to personal profit and the seduction of gaining power in urban society. Chongqing is replete with examples of officials who became active gangsters themselves establishing criminal enterprises. The sophistication of Chinese mafia organizations is continuing to rise. Many members, even leaders, are very youthful, and form the new generation of organized crime heads. Chongqing revealed that organized criminal elements are capable of fully infiltrating (and even monopolizing) critical economic and social sectors of large urban areas – even though these may be directly controlled by the central government. They are increasingly violent, apparently unafraid of directly attacking investigative and judicial institutions.

Given the historical continuity in the nature of organized crime faced in Chongqing, it should be no surprise that the government has utilized some old techniques to combat it, relying on traditional anti-crime mass campaigns. But the government has also been thorough in harnessing the power of media (and the general population) and in putting a human face on the anti-crime effort. This was well illustrated by Bo Xilai's savvy use of the media and his Chongqing urban policies. Indeed, new policies were promulgated to deal with socio-economic imbalances that may contribute to the causes of organized crime.

It is too early, however, to speculate on how successful the crackdowns may have been. Nor should we unquestioningly construct the notion that organized crime, as represented by the Chongqing case, is overrunning China. It is not. As Bakken (2005: 89) points out, we should be cautious of assuming high levels of organized crime in China or that there has been a huge increase in the amount of organized crime. Nonetheless, it is present and we can say about Chongqing that it has affirmed some disturbing trends in post-1980s organized crime. It has shown that a monopolization of power over an entire municipality by organized crime can still occur in the twenty-first century, just as the so-called 'Green Gang' had largely controlled Shanghai in the 1920s. Continued concerns over organized crime remain strong; Chen Xiaocun, of the Criminal Investigative Division of the PRC Ministry of Public Security, said it best when laying out some of his principal worries regarding the growth of organized crime in China:

> Our main concerns are that (1) organizations with an underworld nature will penetrate into the legitimate business sector; (2) gangsters will get involved in politics and run for public office, and (3) they will eventually hook up with foreign-based organized crime groups.[12]

Yet ultimately, there are grounds to be optimistic. The government has shown itself to be remarkably adaptive in dealing with organized crime, employing traditional *yanda* campaigns while engaging the public via a range of media to stand up against crime. This fight is far from over. The ways in which the government deploys the courts and the judiciary in this fight will be a primary indicator of progress in China's promotion of rule of law.

Notes

1 The Qing government took secret societies, especially those grounded in religious teachings, very seriously. For a discussion of the Qing's treatment of religious secret societies and a translation and compilation of records from actual cases involving secret societies in late imperial China, see Hegel (2009: 183–200, 201, 247–51).
2 For an investigation and analysis of how guanxi and corruption work in China see Li Ling (2011).
3 For the Chinese text of this opium and drug ban, entitled *Guanyu yanjin yapian yandu de tongling*, see Xinhua (2004).
4 For an extended analysis of this nexus see various chapters in Garrick (2011)
5 It is not possible to provide here a detailed overview or history of the development of Chinese legislation dealing with organized crime; however, for an excellent discussion see Schloenhardt (2010: 164–77).
6 For more demographic and geographic details see: http://english.cq.gov.cn/Chongqin gGuide/MountainCity/1918.htm.
7 Cited in Garnaut (2011a).
8 For an evaluation of the media's role in the Chongqing crackdown see Gao (2010).
9 Li was released from prison in June 2011. For the BBC News report (in Chinese), see: www.bbc.co.uk/zhongwen/simp/chinese_news/2011/06/110611_china_lawyer_releas ed.shtml.
10 Numerous Chinese lawyers and prominent law professors in Chinese universities have called for the repeal of Article 306 *of* China's *Criminal Law* (CL) which provides criminal liability and a prison term of up to seven years to lawyers who entice their clients to change their testimony in opposition to the facts, or to give false testimony. This is to ensure that lawyers do not encourage their clients to lie; however, Article 306 has been used by police and prosecutors to intimidate defence counsel from questioning the validity of any confession, even when torture may be obvious. Success with the repeal call may be difficult with Yu Ning, head of the All China Lawyers Association (ACLA) (a government-controlled body), indicating that it is neither practical nor realistic to do away with Article 306 (see Xu *et al.* 2010).
11 For further discussion of the background of the Fan Qihang case, see Cohen and Pils (2010).
12 As quoted by the US Department of Justice (Office of Justice Programs 2007: 6).

13 Conclusion

Law and policy for 'opening up' [*kaifang*] and 'going out' [*zou chu qu*]

John Garrick

Introduction

The context of law and policy making for China's socialist market economy includes economic reform and 'opening up' [开放] and, after achieving WTO membership, for Chinese enterprises to 'go out' [走出去]. China has emerged as a superpower that seeks to secure its interests and resource needs internally and externally, guided by the CPC.

On the key issues raised in the book, conclusions share similarities or differences depending on the perspectives and methodological approaches of the authors. The main themes raised by the contributors are discussed here. At the heart of the matter are arguments that China's laws and regulations are radically improved and more integrated with international best practice. At the same time the nature of government intervention sometimes remains an issue, as do judicial reforms and the protection of certain economic and social rights. Rules are often ambiguous and place huge administrative discretion in the hands of officials, especially the powerful Party-Secretaries. In fact China's 1982 Constitution (as amended in 1988, 1993, 1999 and 2004) remains non-justiciable and 'insists on CPC leadership' (Lin 2011: 254) as well as adherence to, variously, Socialism, Marxism, Leninism and Mao Zedong Thought. Guanxi is still often required to support complex transactions. Indeed, media coverage has at times portrayed law, politics and corruption as so entwined in China that it is impossible to invest faith in any given legal outcome. But this 'broad-brush' portrayal may be unfair as China is the world's second largest economy, with economic growth largely driven by export-oriented development through frequent commercial transactions with the world. The vast majority of this trade is being carried out through legal structures acceptable to the parties involved.

The more optimistic interpretations are that extraordinary advances in rule of law promotion have been made. Yet there are so many laws and regulations in this vast country it is almost impossible for officials not to, at times, 'bend' some of them. Further, this 'discretion' may be viewed as reasonable in the context of China's rapid economic growth, modernization and urbanization. This perspective is tied to Deng's legitimizing aphorism: 'crossing the stream feeling for the rocks with your feet' ('*mozhe shitou guohe*'). On another interpretation, however, there remain questions as to whether China's commercial law reforms have advanced while the protection of economic and social rights may have actually receded in recent times and that some laws and regulations have been 'bent' by officials not because there are so many, but because of the lack of sufficient legal transparency and regulatory development to guide them. This argument holds that compared with European democracies, for example, China's problem may be not so much the large number of laws, but insufficient and transparent enforcement of such laws.

In addition to extensive official discretion, courts also face transitional challenges. For instance, Howson (2010) found in a study of over 1,000 corporate law cases that, following the 2006 amendments to the *Company Law*,[1] Shanghai courts are now more competent and independent, having made rulings against government entities, SOEs and other powerful, well-connected commercial actors and investors. He also found that courts continue to defer to national economic and social policies in contravention of the Company Law, and are reluctant to hear cases involving companies limited by shares. Peerenboom (2011: 275) points out several reasons for these limitations, including 'the limited experience of the courts with new types of claims; plaintiff and judicial deference to the China Securities Regulatory Commission and public prosecutor; and concerns for market and social stability'. To explore the varying views of the book this chapter is divided into three broad subsections reflecting its parts.

China's evolving legal and policy context

In the broad context of China's 'market socialism', policy and regulation of ODI have been gradually transformed from a practice of strictly controlled 'trial and error' to a more simplified, liberalized regime. As Jianfu Chen argues in Chapter 1, however, various financial supports and foreign exchange controls remain firmly in central government hands. Although much is now left to enterprises and to the market, the government retains the capacity to strategically guide ODI. As Chen points out, China must also find ways of utilizing its US$3 trillion in reserve, 'if only to reduce losses due to any appreciation of the yuan' (see Xinhua 2011d). At the same time any significant depreciation of the US dollar can also hurt.

Although it is difficult to measure, Chen refers also to government involvement in large state-owned firms' decision-making, arguing that 'intervention is selective, operating more through providing financial and other supports rather than by vetoing [ODI] investment'. At the heart of his argument is data indicating that given the significant growth in ODI and liberalization of the ODI examination and approval regime, 'the government's capacity to control and direct ODI is now more limited ... [and] bound to be shaped more by commercial than political considerations'. Looking ahead, China is going global for a range of national strategic and business enterprise reasons, and the outcomes of this policy will have deep local and global ramifications.

Xianchu Zhang notes in Chapter 2 the rapid development of the company law regime that has accompanied China's economic reforms and increasing integration into international markets. Increasing sophistication is having profound political implications for rule of law promotion, with China's new company laws closing gaps between China and international best practice. This is reflected in corporate governance, corporate social responsibility and business-enabling approaches in legislation. To achieve this quantum leap forward, China has transplanted a range of legal doctrines from developed countries and, in particular, from common law jurisdictions. Zhang points out, however, that the reforms remain incomplete with elements missing, adding ambiguity to company, business and political relationships in China. It remains the case that directors and other senior officers may have to seek 'political protection' in dealing with risks. Legal modernization has faced the interrelated challenges of political ideology, infrastructure and cultural constraints. Zhang's argument holds that for the foreseeable future, Chinese company law developments are likely to allow for compliance with international norms, yet 'contextualized' to conditions in China.

Roman Tomasic and Zinian Zhang extend this theme in Chapter 3, focusing on reform directions since the *EBL* 2006 and in particular 'corporate reorganization' where there are indicators of insolvency. They point out that government concerns about social unrest shape outcomes in ways that do not always match the principles that underpinned the EBL reforms and that there is already a need for further reform and development of the administrator system. The rationale behind the old EBL 1986 was not to try to close many SOEs but to make SOEs aware of the possibilities and implications of themselves becoming bankrupt. This changed, at least in theory, the common belief that an SOE could not be declared bankrupt regardless of how badly it operated. This in itself was an achievement. But with bankruptcy administrators, who were professional intermediary firms and often merely functioning as expert consultants, there has been a scarcity of alternative expertise to run the company being reorganized. Furthermore, local courts face pressures from the local governments and early resolution is sometimes hindered by the current administrator system.

Detailing China's extraordinary progress in transitioning from a command economy towards a market economy, in Chapter 4 Yan Chang Bennett points out that such progress has been aided since 1978 by China first codifying its contract law and then creating a uniform contract law. The law reformers had correctly foreseen that foreign companies doing business in China might seek to litigate their concerns in Chinese courts and arbitration tribunals and a uniform contract law (UCL) would be required. Bennett shows how the CISG has impacted on China's UCL which helps bring China's contract law into conformity with international standards. She points out that Chinese courts and arbitration tribunals have also shown growing sophistication in applying the CISG and CIETAC arbitration decisions, especially in applying law to specific facts and in determining damages.

At the same time, the application of CISG is still uneven across Chinese courts and arbitration tribunals, along with litigants' fear of taking on a Chinese enterprise. This fear includes loss of future business opportunities even if their case is successful. Bennett's review of decisions suggests this 'unevenness' is levelling out, and that Chinese jurisprudence on the CISG is likely to influence decisions in other countries, creating new international standards of interpretation and application. Involvement with the CISG may be an indicator of China's apparent willingness to engage with and influence international legal architecture and indeed, the fostering of an international common culture in cross-border dispute resolution will almost certainly see China with more sway over developments.

Critical challenges for China's law reform and policy agendas

Property

With regard to property law reform there is a range of challenges facing the Chinese government. Privatizing property creates policy paradoxes for a socialist country. Richard Hu in Chapter 5 refers to the changing, hybrid nature of CPC ideology and the fact that some well-connected individuals have become enormously wealthy from property development in China. Wealth inequality and related questions about how best to promote good governance and a transparent rule of law for land privatization and ownership transferability in the land market are sensitive issues in China. Local governments throughout China have created 'investment vehicles' to enable them to borrow funds and develop property for speculative profit. Wong (2011) asserts this borrowing has created substantial, often non-transparent, debt that will face 'a day of reckoning' in the not too distant future.

Hu argues that land privatization would 'signify the collapse of one of the CPC's ideological platforms upon which the current central government is based'. His argument is that land privatization may be possible in the longer term as the CPC has clearly shown flexibility in adjusting its ideological doctrines; however, privatization will not be an easy task. Land privatization is more than an ideological issue as it affects the livelihood of China's rural residents, the overwhelming majority of the population, and therefore the sociopolitical stability in the country. It's not surprising then that much of the imperial and Maoist statecraft says the peasants should not be removed from (or allowed to leave) the land. In this light, it's hard to imagine the CPC contemplating large-scale land privatization in the near to medium future. Much of the land that has gone into private hands has been privatized through 'back door methods' rather than as a result of ideological or policy changes.

'Back door methods' primarily refer to China's local government investment model mentioned above, which involves appropriating land from peasants and urban households and transferring it into government investment vehicles. The land is then used as collateral for debt, or portions of the land are sold to fund ongoing construction costs. This model depends on ever-rising land prices, on the one hand, and 'ever-greater coercive force to hold down compensation payments for the dispossessed on the other ... the battle for land is where China's economic and political crises intersect' (Garnaut 2011d). Property law reform challenges are made more difficult with central control of taxation affecting local authorities' abilities to raise revenue. 'Creative measures' have therefore been adopted by local officials to replace lost sources of local tax revenue. The transfer of some land-use rights to private developers to stimulate property development and grow local government revenues is a prime method.

One consequence of this method is that some well-connected individuals have become spectacularly wealthy in a relatively short time-frame. Another net effect of China's evolving tax regime, along with the inflationary pressures of a rapidly growing economy, has included the speculatory property price increases in some Chinese cities. Property prices have in fact grown from being economic problems to becoming social and political concerns for China's central government. At the same time the government aims to keep property tax as a stable main component of the tax revenue of local governments (see *People's Daily Online* 2010). There are clearly some winners and some losers in this game.

In addition to developments in real property law, China's intellectual property strategy has radically evolved since the Maoist era. Then, under Marxist–Leninist ideology and Mao Zedong Thought, the state retained ownership of inventions, preventing investors from benefiting from their efforts to the exclusion of others (Article 23, *Regulation on Awards for Inventions* 1963). In fact, copyright during Mao's period was 'stamped out' (Stoianoff 2011: 185). Since the 'open-door' policy, however, China has begun to embrace an intellectual property rights system, in part to attract foreign investment and technology but also to encourage local innovation. China has caught up with the rest of the industrialized world and is now in the next phase of its development, notwithstanding some ongoing piracy and enforcement issues (see Stoianoff 2011).

The environment

Transitioning to cleaner, more highly skilled industries is in part contingent upon China's environmental law reforms. In Chapter 6, Lin, Chan and Cheung point out that China has progressively enacted, since 1989, a suite of environmental laws governing pollution prevention and control. They claim there is a national framework in place that promotes local incentives and disincentives to help control sources of pollution. China has also entered various international agreements and has set challenging and quantifiable goals to 2020. At the same time, these authors point out that the autonomous domestic mitigation actions are essentially voluntary in nature and that *enforcement* becomes *the* key issue. Stern (2011: 294; and 2012) extends this point in her examination of civil environmental lawsuits in China whereby 'plaintiffs and lawyers agree that environmental cases are hard and wringing concessions out of polluters requires remarkable persistence; how Chinese courts work depends on "local circumstances" with disaggregating expansive concepts like rule of law a helpful way of exploring complexity'. Lin, Chan and Cheung also identify two central discourses serving the purposes of the current government. These discourses seek to legitimize actions taken in the name of 'environmental protection', but in fact there are some virtually irreconcilable differences between the requirements of continual economic growth and environmental protection. This chapter argues that the balance currently favours economic growth.

Attempts by the Chinese government to increase consumerism to reduce dependency on its export-led economic model can also create unprecedented burdens on the environment. Another associated burden is what to do with toxic waste disposal and hazardous exposure. These researchers highlight a range of initiatives that provide some hope, with new policies promoting technologies that will decrease dependence on fossil fuels. They look back over the past 60 years to assert that 'China today is taking environmental protection more seriously than ever before'. Looking ahead, their stance is cautiously optimistic about how balancing economic growth with environmental protection is effected so as to achieve sustainable development.

Labour

The firm-level case studies of the implementation of China's new labour laws reveal how high-skilled workforce firms appear to embrace key provisions, while low-skilled workforce firms have resisted. Hurst, Kinkel and Sowash, in Chapter 7, found that 'the skill level of a firm's workforce plays a significant, perhaps decisive, role in shaping its reaction to new legal protections for its workers'. This knowledge is essential to understanding both Chinese labour politics and the effectiveness of the law reforms. It is argued that the government may run the risk of driving down the profitability of some of its 'ubiquitous exporters' as it engineers the industrial shift towards higher-skilled (and cleaner-technology) workplaces. In addition, younger workers are increasingly less willing to 'eat bitterness' by accepting sweat-shop conditions that characterized earlier generations. Getting the correct balance in the industrial transition by implementing regulations in the segmented fashion outlined in this chapter will be a particularly delicate act and these researchers predict some 'wrenching times' ahead for some lower skill-based industries.

China's SOEs 'going out'

Guo *et al.* examine in Chapter 8 three case studies of SOE experiences in contrasting locations: Australia, Papua New Guinea and Latin America. They found that despite the state providing substantial support for its 'go-global' strategy, state authorities and SOE investors have not always conducted appropriate due diligence to comply with host country commercial practices. Sufficient training has not always been provided to staff; nor have appropriate personnel with the prerequisite ODI experience and business acumen always been selected. SOE managers implementing the 'go-global' strategy thus sometimes fall back on their China experience, adopting a 'learn-as-you-go' strategy. At times this approach caused operational delays, unnecessary misunderstandings and local resentment. In some instances, expensive legal disputes occurred. Chinese managers in these studies had in the past been able to rely on state agencies and officials to support them. From that prior experience they had expected host nation governments and local officials to provide them with policy advice and legal information and to expedite their position in legal disputes – as may have happened in China. These assumptions were not always accurate and attempts to by-pass local actors were far more complex than anticipated. Some anti-Chinese sentiment in host nations has subsequently forced internal debate between the Chinese Ministry of Foreign Affairs and those who are primarily concerned with maximizing overseas profit. These case studies argue that Chinese corporations are themselves being 'socialized' as a result of exposure to international norms and business practices. Indeed, the 'going out' strategy has occurred in a relatively brief period of time, and as a result of this experience foreign policy tools used to support Chinese ODI have become more sophisticated, including conditional overseas development assistance, loans from policy banks coupled with service contracts or equity stakes for Chinese firms and missions and delegations sent out to identify 'win–win' investment opportunities and regional or bilateral agreements (Rosen and Hanemann 2009: 12). Despite this increased international engagement and sophistication at senior government levels, from a firm-level perspective the case studies make it clear the liberalization process is far from complete, and while lending money to foreign governments is easy, running real businesses is hard – particularly for SOEs that dominate the flow of investment.

Tax

In balancing economic growth with environmental protection, taxation law reforms figure prominently. This study shows that China's tax law reforms have been incremental with extensive reforms having been made to facilitate the transition from a centrally planned to a socialist market economy. The central government now has control of the country's fiscal levers, but centralization of taxation has had significant effects on local authorities' abilities to raise revenue. Creating investment vehicles (and other creative measures) to compensate, this local government strategy has in turn significantly affected urban development and property prices. At the same time, central regulation of domestic and foreign enterprises has also been simplified with the unification of the previous 'dual' system. Yet the tax reforms do not guarantee revenue is distributed evenly from the centre to provincial and through to local and township levels; nor do they eliminate some tax avoidance schemes. For example, it is possible for OFDI to be siphoned from the mainland to offshore tax havens via Hong Kong, then reinvested back in China at beneficial rates. Chen in Chapter 1, however, suggests this practice may eventually disappear under the new laws.

If one views the success of China's 'going out' policy as being co-dependent on having internal law reforms firmly in place, there are clearly some emerging dilemmas. Balancing the mixed public/private economic reforms is a key to the CPC's maintenance of economic dominance and influence at grassroots levels, and the new tax regime better suits the strategic requirements of *Team China*. But a particularly challenging condition exists whereby the people who make the laws also enforce them, with one arm of government being *market player* and another arm being *regulator*. This highlights a conundrum as to the extent the apparently contradictory philosophies of socialist central planning and market economics can operate harmoniously. There are no clear precedents to inform us what the offspring of this mixed economic marriage is likely to look like in future.

Enforcing economic and social rights, the courts, ADR and anti-corruption strategy in China

Randall Peerenboom argues in Chapter 10 that China's initial report on the implementation of the ICESCR demonstrates the government's 'commitment to alleviating poverty, improving living standards and promoting more sustainable and equitable development ... the government has developed a national human rights action plan, and formulated many other plans to promote ESR'. But the judiciary has played a limited role in enforcing ESR, with Chinese courts inhibited in implementing ESR by a variety of factors. Peerenboom notes some of these as being:

> Shortcomings in the regulatory framework including the lack of specific and robust individual remedies in many laws, institutional design that limits the power of the judiciary within the Chinese constitutional structure, political limitations inherent in an effectively single-party social state, ideological conflicts between New Left advocates of socialist justice and New Right proponents of neoliberalism, and resource constraints typical of lower-middle-income countries.

In China, political and administrative mechanisms have played and will continue to play a more prominent role. The role of civil society, NGOs and self-governing private and public–private hybrid regulatory systems are also important complements to the courts, but their important roles are not fully developed in China at this stage. Peerenboom's analysis indicates that changes to the incentive structure for evaluating and promoting government officials, now biased towards economic growth and social stability, 'would have a more immediate and dramatic impact on the full realization of ESR than all of these other remedial mechanisms combined'. His call is for a comprehensive policy approach that goes well beyond judicial remedies, although limitations to implementing ESR are likely unless there is a clear role for the courts.

Peerenboom argues that a more moderate, gradual, pragmatic approach offers the more likely pathway to protect ESR in China, with the judiciary's role needing continual assessment, updating and adjustment, with an overall trend 'towards a more expansive and assertive role for the courts'.

In addition to the role of courts, alternative dispute resolution (ADR) in China is also in a period of transition. Fan Yu in Chapter 11 shows how this transition parallels the promotion of the socialist market economy. As with Peerenboom's analysis with respect to the gradual and pragmatic upgrading of court roles, Fan asserts that it appears inevitable that diversified dispute resolution programmes will also be gradually instituted in China's legal modernization. The demands for just, quick and efficient dispute resolution mechanisms are backed up by the Supreme People's Court confirmation that a People's Mediation Agreement is binding. The *People's Mediation Law* indicates mediation is not limited to resolving neighbourhood disputes but extends to many professional contexts and is likely to expand in future. Fan also points out that with China opening up to foreign investors and, with the promulgation of its 'going out' policy, China's ADR system has had to grow to meet the special demands of resolving international disputes. With this growth has come an increased awareness of modern ADR and this is likely to have some sway over directions in Chinese law reform.

Norman Ho in Chapter 12 examines the nature of Chongqing's organized crime in an historical context, concluding that it should not be viewed as something new but reflects trends and developments in organized crime in China from the 1980s onwards, and in fact shares characteristics with the notorious Shanghai gangs of the 1920s. The Chongqing case study reveals examples of government officials who themselves became active gangsters with sophisticated criminal enterprises. Organized criminal elements are shown as capable of infiltrating the mainstream economic and social sectors of large urban centres, including areas directly controlled by the central government. Ho's analysis indicates the government has used some old techniques to crackdown on organized crime and corruption, including traditional anti-crime mass campaigns. The government has also strategically utilized newer techniques, such as the power of modern media (harnessed by Bo Xilai) to mobilize the general population in its anti-crime efforts. Bo has also subsequently thrown thousands of lesser 'Black Society' gangsters and their Communist Party protectors into jail, with several executions. As well as 'striking black' he has also been 'singing red' by leading Chongqing in rousing Cultural Revolution songs and using Chairman Mao quotations. Smashing the Chinese mafia is deeply popular, but it is too early to say how successful the crackdowns may have been. The old 'movement' style of crackdowns on organized crime and turning to 'singing red' revolutionary songs has been controversial, especially for intellectuals, and reminiscent for some of the Cultural Revolution (Andrew Chan 2011: 89). Continued concerns over organized crime remain strong and, as Ho points out, this fight is far from over. The ways in which the government deploys the courts and the judiciary in this fight will be indicators of China's progress in its often stated promotion of rule of law.[2]

Conclusion

So, what do all of these legal and policy developments reflect about China's past and future? For three decades the Chinese Communist Party has forged ideological unity around Deng's 'two-hands' formula of a market-based economy and uncompromising political control. The law and policy reforms described in the different sections of this book reflect this conflation of socialism and market economics. Progress in legal sophistication mirrors the great strides taken in economic growth and urban development, especially in the various commercial areas of company and business law and international sale of goods dispute resolution.

That China's law reforms are directly affected by the CPC's organizational structures and policy directions is also clear. What is less clear is what the new directions will hold, with the Party entering a period of leadership transition and realignment.

On the one hand extraordinary economic growth has been accompanied by equally extraordinary, but far less trumpeted, law reforms. The numbers of people living in poverty have been radically reduced since Deng's reforms commenced. China is now engaging in a range of international forums commensurate with its major-power status. On the other hand there has also been an upsurge of wealth inequality, corruption and organized crime, as the need for a crackdown in Chongqing has shown. The CPC has 'strengthened its organizational structures to keep itself unified and embedded in every facet of organizational life' (Garnaut 2011b: 6). This increase in state power, especially since the GFC, has been attacked by some Chinese lawyers, journalists, civil society writers of the liberal right and academics who refer to many instances of nepotism, crony capitalism and corruption. Garnaut (ibid.) claims that 'whether you are in private equity, a state-owned enterprise or a village enterprise the end game is the same: connect the right Party official (or relative) with the market and turn public money into private gold'. He adds that 'left and right agree that Deng's consensus is crumbling under the weight of inequality and corruption but they cannot agree on whether to dismantle the "open market" or "political control" side of his legacy' (ibid.).

In 'Law, wealth and power in China', Peerenboom (2011: 291) captured this ideological conundrum, observing that the jury is still very much out on where China is headed and whether it will continue the impressive march towards superpower status:

> As China's stature rises in the new world order, it is both natural and inevitable that China will exert greater influence over international systems. Many pundits already accuse China of adopting more aggressive policies, and seeking to undermine the current international infrastructure ... Yet China remains fragile. It is still a lower-middle income country, facing many of the challenges that have prevented other middle-income countries from graduating to the ranks of high income countries that enjoy rule of law, democracy and reasonably robust protection of human rights.

The chapters in this book do not contradict these points. A key descriptor is 'fragile'. Although it might appear incongruous that a superpower could be fragile, the word is apposite. There are several possible interpretations of fragility in this context: economic, social, legal, political and ideological, historical and so on. For each argument there are counter arguments. As Stern (2011) suggests, disaggregating expansive concepts can be helpful to exploring such complexity. At the same time, China's one-party state does promote its own grand narrative for one 'harmonious society' and this warrants some deconstruction. When the suite of reforms over the past 30 or so years is considered, there have clearly been periods of rapid acceleration followed by more restrained or conservative development.

The various contributors have examined the effects of specific legal and policy reforms as a market economy expands, private entrepreneurship is encouraged, SOEs adapt to the new market conditions and China begins to 'go global'. China's government keeps claiming to be a 'responsible big state', a Chinese euphemism for 'superpower', in global affairs. China is, rhetorically and in some cases practically, committed to establishing a new kind of domestic as well as international order to match her new international settings.

Her rise sees 'rule of law' promotion as central to the government's legitimizing discourses. China strives to develop laws, regulations, legal institutions, courts, judicial and dispute resolution competence; yet a rule of law state does remain a challenge for the future. Nonetheless, we can say at least some things with certainty. Over the past few decades there has been a rise in private equity investment, foreign and domestic capital *is* competing for transactions and there has been significant reform and poverty reduction. There is, and has been, intense ideological debate around reform direction. What the nature of China's 'marketization' will be, going forward, remains to be seen. There is a growing recognition that the mercantilist export-led growth model is no longer viable, and that there must be a transition to a more 'consumption based model' (Peerenboom 2011: 281). Tensions between a more 'consumption based economy' and 'sustainable consumption' (including environmental consequences) are likely to generate intense debate in the foreseeable future.

This debate spills immediately beyond the local to global economics and politics. At stake are major environmental and legal issues, including regulation of water and air pollution, climate change and the effects and enforceability of international conventions. China's future affects us all. The basic principles that have guided economic and legal reform thus far appear likely to continue, with the process gradual, pragmatic and results-driven rather than based on hard-line ideology. Making law and policy for China's socialist market economy is probably best viewed in this light, but it is certainly not the only light, as the preceding chapters have revealed.

Since the Communist Party's 17th Congress in late 2007, a legitimizing narrative of the CPC has been to promote the goals of socialism through a 'harmonious society'. A new Party leadership of the courts has emphasized this harmonious approach by encouraging the settling of disputes through informal mediation in preference to formal trials, to be more 'democratic and congenial to ordinary people and China's traditions than adjudication' (Cohen 2009: A11). However, fostering social stability and promoting such reforms do not necessarily sit comfortably with the logic and application of Marxist–Leninist theory. The law and policy reforms will, in the first instance, tend to favour those who are already wealthy, as *capitalist production mostly takes place on the basis of unequal ownership of capital* (Marx 1976: 169). In this view, the extension of capital markets in a socialist system will help those with prior economic advantage to consolidate their position. It cannot be overlooked that the justificatory framework for the CPC has historically rested heavily on this Marxist ideology. Some revolutionary slogans survive to this day, and Mao's portrait is still hung above Tiananmen Square in Beijing, as it is in many average rural households (Gao 2008: 198). Bo Xilai's much publicized efforts in Chongqing (see Chapter 12) illustrate that some Maoist tenets are not merely symbolic. If the goals of the CPC are to further socialism and 'social harmony' through a preliminary stage that includes economic, tax and legal reforms that promote capital markets, private property, foreign investment and so on, then this strategy carries substantial risk.

It is risky because the gulf between the elitist, privileged class of 'haves' and 'have nots' has, unfortunately, widened despite grand fiscal reform and official rhetoric to the contrary. Liberalization over the past decade has shown the costs of reform are outweighed by the benefits. But dissent has been dealt with severely. There are strong public emotions around issues such as 'wealth hatred' and corrupt connections between elements of the new rich and some government officials. Current Chinese law and policy is in a state of transition and a prudent strategy for law reform may be to assume that the dilemmas outlined above are to an extent inescapable whether socialist, capitalist or 'hybrid'. It is extreme views that become unhelpful.

While acknowledging progress in China's overall legal reforms, the contributors note that China can build further upon its steps towards rule of law. The stage of legal development still sees law as very much *an instrument*, with implementation and enforcement facing many problems. There is much at stake. The highest aspirations for a harmonious society, backed up by a fair social distribution of wealth via the reforms outlined herein such as new commercial, property, labour, environment and taxation laws, may at least partly help to improve circumstances. At a time of leadership transition and some uncertainty, as Qianfan Zhang (2006: 163) aptly reminds us, 'the fruits of law rarely grow out of despotic soil'.

Notes

1 The amendments marked a shift away from a self-enforcement to a litigation-centred model for resolving corporate disputes (see Zhang in Chapter 2).
2 The task of cracking down on organized crime was welcomed by virtually all walks of society; however, the way the government implemented the task appeared problematic to some. For instance, the way the Chongqing government deployed the courts and the judiciary has been criticized as lacking transparency, restricting lawyers' involvement, embracing a 'movement-style' propaganda campaign reminiscent of Maoist times.

Bibliography

ACFTU (All China Federation of Trade Unions (2006) *Qi ye gong hui gong zuo tiao li (Shi xing)* (Provisions on the Work of Enterprise Trade Unions (For Trial Implementation)), 6 July, ACFTU regulations.
All-China Lawyers Association (2006) Guidance Notice regarding Lawyers' Handling of Multi-party Cases, 20 March.
Anderson, C. (2001) 'The Australian corporate rescue regime: bold experiment or sensible policy?' *International Insolvency Review*, 10: 81–113.
Anderson, J. (2008) 'How to think about China (Part I)', *UBS Investment Research*, 10 January.
Anderson, J. (2011) 'China's economic system and reflections on market reform', in J. Garrick (ed.) *Law, Wealth and Power in China: Commercial Law Reforms in Context*, London: Routledge.
Anonymous (1998) 'Class action litigation in China', *Harvard Law Review*, 111(6): 1523–41.
Ansfield, J. and Bradsher, K. (2010) 'China report shows more pollution in waterways', *The New York Times*, 9 February. Online. Available: www.nytimes.com/2010/02/10/world/asia/10pollute.html (accessed 12 December 2010).
Antkiewicz, A. and Whalley, J. (2006) 'Recent Chinese buyout activities and the implications for global architecture', *National Bureau of Economic Research Working Paper 12072*, Cambridge, MA.
Antkiewicz, A. and Whalley, J. (2007) 'Recent Chinese buyout activity and the implications for wider global investment rules', *Canadian Public Policy*, 33(2): 207.
Anwar, S.T. (2010) 'CFIUS, Chinese MNGs' outward FDI, and globalization of business', *Journal of World Trade*, 44(2): 419.
Asia Times (2006) 'New bankruptcy law puts creditors first', *Asia Times Online*, 31 August. Online. Available: www.atimes.com/atimes/China_Business/HH31Cb02.html (accessed 16 July 2011).
Asia Trade Hub (2009) 'China tax system'. Online. Available: www.asiatradehub.com/china/tax.asp.
Ayer, J.D. (1989) 'Rethinking absolute priority after Ahlers', *Michigan Law Review*, 87: 963–1025.
Baidu Bulletin Board (2007) '*Woerma li de heian de gonghui*' (The horrible union in Walmart store #3424) *Baidu Bulletin Board* 202.105.101, 22 October. Online. Available: http://tieba.baidu.com/f?kz=277996673 (accessed 10 September 2010).
Baird, D.G. (1998) 'Bankruptcy's uncontested axioms', *The Yale Law Journal*, 108: 573–99.
Baird, D. and Rasmussen, R.K. (2002) 'The end of bankruptcy', *Stanford Law Review*, 55: 751–90.
Bakken, B. (2005) 'Comparative perspectives on crime in China', in B. Bakken (ed.) *Crime, Punishment and Policing in China*, Lanham, MD: Rowman & Littlefield.

Ballard, C. and Banks, G. (2003) 'Resource wars: the anthropology of mining', *Annual Review of Anthropology*, 32: 287–313.
Balme, S. (2010) 'Local courts in western China', in R. Peerenboom (ed.) *Judicial Independence in China*, Cambridge: Cambridge University Press.
Barboza, D. (2010) 'In China, unlikely labor leader just wanted a middle-class life', *The New York Times*, 13 June.
Bath, V. (2009) 'The company law and foreign investment enterprises in the People's Republic of China: parallel systems of Chinese–foreign regulation', *Legal Studies Research Paper of Sydney Law School*, No. 09/42. Online. Available: http://ssrn.com/abstract=1410383 (accessed 3 March 2011).
Bath, V. and Ip, M. (2011) 'Wealth and loss in changing economic times: reforms in bankruptcy and consumer protection laws', in J. Garrick (ed.) *Law, Wealth and Power in China: Commercial Law Reforms in Context*, London: Routledge.
BBC (2008) 'China plans new anti-gang effort', 22 December. Online. Available: http://news.bbc.co.uk/2/hi/asia-pacific/7795415.stm.
BBC (2009a) 'Police held in China gang probe', 21 August. Online. Available: http://news.bbc.co.uk/2/hi/asia-pacific/8213357.stm.
BBC (2009b) 'Chinese crime "godmother" jailed', 3 November. Online. Available: http://news.bbc.co.uk/2/hi/asia-pacific/8339773.stm.
BBC (2011) *BBC News report*, June (in Chinese). Online. Available: www.bbc.co.uk/zhongwen/simp/chinese_news/2011/06/110611_china_lawyer_released.shtml.
Beck, L. (2008) 'New party boss brings hope to Chongqing', *New York Times*, 20 February. Online. Available: www.nytimes.com/2008/02/20/business/worldbusiness/20iht-chong.1.10221880.html?_r=1.
Beijing Metals & Minerals v. American Business Center Inc. (1993) 993 F 2d 1178.
Bergsten, C.F., Freeman, C., Lardy, N. and Mitch, D. (2009) *China's Rise: Challenges and Opportunities*, Washington, DC: Peterson Institute for International Economics.
Bernstein, R. (2009) 'The death and life of Beijing', *The Australian Financial Review*, 12 June, p. 7.
Bie, Tao (ed.) (2007) *Public Interest Environmental Litigation (Huanjing Gongyi Susong)*, Beijing: Law Press.
Blanchard, B. (2010) 'Jailing of China gang lawyer alarms legal world', *Reuters*, 8 January. Online. Available: http://in.reuters.com/article/idINIndia-45241920100108.
Blazey, P. and Govind, P. (2008) 'Environmental law in China', in P. Blazey and Kay-Wah Chan (eds) *The Chinese Commercial Legal System*, Sydney: Thomson Lawbook.
Booth, C.D. (2008) 'The 2006 PRC Enterprise Bankruptcy Law: the wait is finally over', *Singapore Academy of Law Journal*, 20: 275–315.
Booth, C.D. and Zhang Xianchu (2001) 'Chinese Bankruptcy Law in an emerging market economy: the Shenzhen experience', *Columbia Journal of Asian Law*, 15: 1–32.
Brandt, L. and Rawski, T.G. (2008) *China's Great Economic Transformation*, Cambridge: Cambridge University Press.
Brown, R.C. (2008) 'China labour dispute resolution'. Online. Available: www.fljs.org/uploads/documents/Brown%231%23.pdf.
Brown, R.C. (2010) *Understanding Labor and Employment Law in China*, Cambridge: Cambridge University Press.
Buckley, P.J., Clegg, L.J., Cross, A.R., Xin, L., Voss, H. and Zheng, P. (2007) 'The determinants of Chinese Outward Foreign Direct Investment', *Journal of International Business Studies*, 38: 499.
Buckley, P.J., Cross, A.R., Tan, H., Xin, L. and Voss, H. (2008) 'Historic and emergent trends in Chinese Outward Direct Investment', *Management International Review*, 48(6): 715.

Buckley, P.J., Clegg, L.J., Cross, A.R., Xin, L., Voss, H. and Zheng, P. (2010) 'The determinants of Chinese Outward Foreign Direct Investment', in P. Buckley (ed.) *Foreign Direct Investment, China and the World Economy*, Basingstoke, UK: Palgrave Macmillan.

Bulto, Takele Soboka (2009) 'The indirect approach to promote justiciability of socio-economic rights of the African Charter on Human and Peoples' Rights', *University of Tasmania Law Review*, 29(1). Online. Available: http://ssrn.com/abstract=1408826.

Business Week (2004) 'Big Blue's bold step into China', 20 December, pp. 33–4.

Cai, K.G. (1999) 'Outward Foreign Direct Investment: a novel dimension of China's integration into regional and global economy', *The China Quarterly*, 160: 856.

Cai, Y. (2002) 'The resistance of Chinese laid-off workers in the reform period', *The China Quarterly*, 170: 327–34.

Campanella, T. (2008) *The Concrete Dragon: China's Urban Revolution and What it Means for the World*, New York: Princeton Architectural Press.

Canaves, S. (2009) 'Lawyer detained in Chongqing crackdown', *Wall Street Journal China Realtime Report*, 14 December. Online. Available: http://blogs.wsj.com/chinarealtime/2009/12/14/lawyer-detained-in-chongqing-crackdown/ (accessed 7 January 2010).

Canaves, S. (2010a) 'As Chinese judge takes stand, court corruption goes on trial', *Wall Street Journal*, 4 February. Online. Available: http://online.wsj.com/article/SB10001424052748703357104575044890834624852.html (accessed 7 January 2010).

Canaves, S. (2010b) 'Gangbuster Bo Xilai gets a musical homage', *Wall Street Journal China Realtime Report*, 24 February. Online. Available: http://blogs.wsj.com/chinarealtime/2010/02/24/gangbuster-bo-xilai-gets-a-musical-homage/ (accessed 7 January 2010).

Cannings, J. (2011) 'Louis Mediang vs MCC and the State', in *WS No. 1192 of 2010*, Papua New Guinea National Court of Justice, 67, Madang, 2011. Online. Available: ramumine.files.wordpress.com/2011/07/medaing-v-mcc-the-state-iamo.pdf (accessed1 August 2011).

Carl Hill v. Cixi City Old Furniture Trading Co. (2001) Cijingchuzi No. 560. Online. Available: http://cisgw3.law.pace.edu/cases/010718c1.html (accessed February 2011).

Cavallaro, J.L. and Schaffer, E.J. (2005) 'Less as more: rethinking supranational litigation of economic and social rights in the Americas', *Hastings Law Journal*, 56: 217.

CCPIT (China Council for the Promotion of International Trade) (2010a) 'Survey on current conditions and intention of outbound investment by Chinese enterprise', April. Online. Available: http://trade.ec.europa.eu/doclib/docs/2010/may/tradoc_146193.pdf (accessed 11 May 2011).

CCPIT (2010b) 'China goes global: survey of Outward Direct Investment intentions of Chinese companies', December. Online. Available: www.asiapacific.ca/sites/default/files/filefield/china_goes_global_2011_web_v2.pdf (accessed 25 May 2011).

CCPIT (2011a) 'China goes global: survey of Outward Direct Investment intentions of Chinese companies', April. Online. Available: www.asiapacific.ca/sites/default/files/filefield/china_goes_global_2011.pdf (accessed 7 September 2011).

CCPIT (2011b) 'Survey on current conditions and intention of outbound investment by Chinese enterprise 2008–10', April. Online. Available: www.ccpit.org/yewu/docs/Survey_on_Current_Conditions_and_Intention_of_Outbound_Investment_by_Chinese_Enterprises_2011.en.pdf (accessed 11 May 2011).

Centre of Corporate Governance Study of World Economy and Politics Institute, China Social Science Academy and others (2010) 'Assessment of corporate governance of top 100 listed companies in China'. Online. Available: www.protiviti.com.sg/zh-CN/Headlines/Documents/2009%20guide.pdf (accessed 10 May 2011).

Chan, A. (2008) 'The emergence of real trade unionism in Wal-Mart stores', *China Labor News Translations*, 4 May. Online. Available: http://clntranslations.org.

230 Bibliography

Chan, A. (2011) 'Power narratives and lessons from the Chinese Cultural Revolution', in J. Garrick (ed.) *Law, Wealth and Power in China: Commercial Law Reforms in Context*, London: Routledge.
Chan, H.L. (1995) 'Chinese investment in Hong Kong: issues and problems', *Asian Survey*, 35(10): 941.
Chan, K.W. (2011) 'China's labour laws in transition', in J. Garrick (ed.) *Law, Wealth and Power in China: Commercial Law Reforms in Context*, London: Routledge.
Chang, L.T., Fan, C.C., Huang, Y., Zhang, L. and Gallagher, M. (2010) 'What do China's workers want?' *New York Times*, editorial, 13 June.
Chao, X. (2005) 'Transforming Chinese enterprises: Ideology, efficiency and instrumentalism in the process of reform', in J. Gillespie and P. Nicholson (eds) *Asian Socialism and Legal Change: The Dynamics of Vietnamese and Chinese Reform*, Canberra: Asia Pacific Press, Australian National University.
Chen, A.H.Y. (2003) 'Mediation, litigation and justice: Confucian reflections in a modern liberal society', in D.A. Bell and H. Chaibong (eds) *Confucianism for the Modern World*, Cambridge: Cambridge University Press.
Chen, B. (2008) 'Overseas M& a by Chinese Enterprises: current conditions, difficulties and a responses analysis', *Journal of Shenyang Agricultural University (Social Science Edition) (Shenyang Nongye Daxue Xuebao – Shehui Kexue Ban)*, 10(4): 395.
Chen, F. (1999) 'Chinese bankruptcy law: milestones and challenges', *St Mary's Law Journal*, 31: 49–61.
Chen Fuyong (2010) *Unfinished Transformation: An Empirical Study of the Current Status and Future Trends of China's Arbitration Institution*, Beijing: Law Press.
Chen, J. (2008) *Chinese Law: Context and Transformation*, Leiden/Boston: Martinus Nijhoff.
Chen, J. (2011) 'China's civil and commercial law reforms: context and transformation', in J. Garrick (ed.) *Law, Wealth and Power in China: Commercial Law Reforms in Context*, London: Routledge.
Chen, M. (2011) 'Women, enterprises and the state', in J. Garrick (ed.) *Law, Wealth and Power in China: Commercial Law Reforms in Context*, London: Routledge.
Chen, Y.F. and Funke, M. (2009) 'China's new labor law: no harm to employment?' *China Economic Review*, 20: 558–72.
Cheng, H. (2004) *ODI Development Strategies for Chinese Private Enterprises (Zhongguo Minying Qiye Duiwa Zhijie Touzi Fazhan Zhanlue)*, Beijing: China Social Sciences Press.
Cheng, Y.-S. (2011) 'China's foreign trade: from self-reliance to outward-orientation', in Chan Lai-ha, G. Chan and K. Fung (eds) *China at 60: Global–Local Interactions*, Singapore: World Scientific.
Cheung, Y.-W. and Qian, X. (2009) 'Empirics of China's Outward Direct Investment', *Pacific Economic Review*, 14(3): 312.
Child, J. and Rodrigues, S.B. (2005) 'The internationalisation of Chinese firms: a case for theoretical extension?', *Management and Organisation Review*, 1(3): 381–410.
China Daily (2003) 'Bankruptcy laws need review', 17 March. Online. Available: http://app1.chinadaily.com.cn/highlights/nbc/news/317law.htm (accessed 16 July 2011).
China Daily (2008) 'NDRC chief: macroeconomic control effective', 6 March. Online. Available: www.chinadaily.com.cn/china/2008npc/2008-03/06/content_6513843.htm (accessed 16 July 2011).
China National Metal Products Import Export Company v. Apex Digital, Inc. (2001) 141 F.Supp.2d 1013.
Chinability (2011) 'GDP growth in China 1952–2009', 26 April. Online. Available: www.chinability.com/GDP.htm (accessed 26 April 2011).

Chinese Communist Party (1999) 'The decisions of the SOEs' reform and development', 22 September. Online. Available: www.molss.gov.cn:8080/trsweb_gov/detail?record=52 0& channelid = 40543 (accessed 16 July 2011) (in Chinese).

Chongqing Municipal Government (2011) 'Demographic'. Online. Available: http://english.cq.gov.cn/ChongqingGuide/MountainCity/1918.htm (accessed 26 August 2011).

Christiansen, E. (2007) 'Adjudicating non-justiciable rights: socio-economic rights and the South African Constitutional Court', *Columbia Human Rights Law Review*, 38(2): 12.

CIDEF (Comisión Investigadora de los Delitos Económicos y Financieros entre) (2002a) *Primer Informe de Investigación, Caso: El Proceso de Pruvatización de Hierro Perú*, in C.d.l.R.d. Perú (ed.) Lima. Online. Available: www.congreso.gob.pe/comisiones/2002/CIDEF/oscuga/informeHierro.pdf (accessed 10 May 2011).

CIDEF (Comisión Investigadora de los Delitos Económicos y Financieros entre) (2002b) *La Privatización de la Empresa Shougang Hierro Perú S.S.A. (Resumen de Caso)*, in C.d.l.R.d. Perú (ed.) Lima. Online. Available: www.congreso.gob.pe/comisiones/2002/CIDEF/resumenes/privatiza/hierro.pdf (accessed 10 May 2011).

CIETAC Arbitration Proceeding (1991) 'Metal Silicon Case' 19 April. Online. Available: http://cisgw3.law.pace.edu/cases/910419c1.html (accessed 25 February 2011).

CIETAC Arbitration Proceeding (1995) 'Jasmine Aldehyde Case' 23 February. Online. Available: http://cisgw3.law.pace.edu/cases/950223c1.html (accessed 25 February 2011).

CIETAC Arbitration Proceeding (1997a) 'Fishmeal Case' 1 April. Online. Available: http://cisgw3.law.pace.edu/cases/970401c1.html (accessed 25 February 2011).

CIETAC Arbitration Proceeding (1997b) 'Black Melon Seeds Case' 4 April. Online. Available: http://cisgw3.law.pace.edu/cases/030418c1.html (accessed 2 May 2011).

CIETAC Arbitration Proceeding (1997c) 'Germanium Case' 15 April. Online. Available: http://cisgw3.law.pace.edu/cases/970415c1.html (accessed 25 February 2011).

CIETAC Arbitration Proceeding (1998) 'Waste Paper Case' 26 November. Online. Available: http://cisgw3.law.pace.edu/cases/981126c2.html (accessed 25 February 2011).

CIETAC Arbitration Proceeding (1999) 'PVC Suspension Resin Case' 7 April. Online. Available: http://cisgw3.law.pace.edu/cases/990407c1.html (accessed 25 February 2011).

CIETAC Arbitration Proceeding (2003) 'Desulfurization Reagent Case' 18 April. Online. Available: http://cisgw3.law.pace.edu/cases/030418c1.html (accessed 25 February 2011).

CIETAC Arbitration Proceeding (2006) 'Water Heater Production Line Case' 1 April. Online. Available: http://cisgw3.law.pace.edu/cases/060400c1.html (accessed 25 February 2011).

Clarke, D.C. (2006) 'The independent director in Chinese corporate governance', *Delaware Journal of Corporate Law*, 31: 125–228.

Clarke, D.C. (2007) 'Introduction: The Chinese legal system since 1995: steady development and striking continuities', *China Quarterly*, 191: 560.

Clarke, D.C. (2010) 'Li Zhuang gets 18 months on appeal; disavows earlier confession', *Chinese Law Prof Blog*, 9 February. Online. Available: http://lawprofessors.typepad.com/china_law_prof_blog/2010/02/li-zhuang-gets-18-months-on-appeal-disavows-earlier-confession.html (accessed 6 August 2011).

CNA International Inc. v. Guangdong Kelon Electronical Holdings et al. (2008) U.S. Dist. LEXIS 113433.

Cohen, J.A. (2009) 'People's justice', *South China Post*, 25 June.

Cohen, J.A. (2010) 'Cohen holds court: reflecting on the last five decades of Chinese legal development', *National Committee on United States–China Relations*. Online. Available: www.ncuscr.org/?q=programs/jerome-cohen-holds-court (accessed 1 February 2011).

Cohen, J.A. (2011) 'China's shame over Ai Weiwei', *The Wall Street Journal*, 24–26 June.

Bibliography

Cohen, J.A. and Pils, E. (2010) 'Rule and reality', *South China Morning Post*, 2 September. Online. Available: www.usasialaw.org/wp-content/uploads/2010/08/20100902-Rule-and-Reality.pdf.

Colebatch, T. (2011) 'China to lead world economy', *The Age*, 25 April. Online. Available: www.theage.com.au/national/china-to-lead-world-economy-20110424-1dt1j.html (accessed 25 April 2011).

Committee on Economics, Social and Cultural Rights (2005) *Concluding Observations of the Committee on Economic, Social and Cultural Rights People's Republic of China (including Hong Kong and Macao)*, E/C.12/1/Add.107 para. 42, 13 May. Online. Available: www.unhchr.ch/tbs/doc.nsf/898586b1dc7b4043c1256a450044f331/a206bffcd68c76b1c125700500478168/$FILE/G0542245.pdf (accessed 6 September 2011).

Communist Party of China (2000) *Proposals of the Communist Party of China on the Making of the 10th Five-Year National Economic and Social Development Plan*, October, Beijing: People's Publishing House.

Congress Research Service (2008) 'China's Sovereign Wealth Fund', a *Congress Research Service* Report, 22 January. Online. Available: www.fas.org/sgp/crs/row/RL34337.pdf (accessed 16 July 2011).

Contract Law of the People's Republic of China (1999) 15 March. Online. Available: www.novexcn.com/contract_law_99.html (accessed 1 July 2011).

Cooney, S. (2007) 'China's labor law, compliance and flaws in implementing institutions', *The Journal of Industrial Relations*, 49(5): 673–86.

Criminal Law of the People's Republic of China (1997). Online. Available: www.china.org.cn/english/government/207319.htm.

Das, S. (2009) 'Beijing stuck with a fistful of dollars', *SMH Business Day*, 29 December.

Das, S. (2010) 'Foreign treasure not all it's cracked up to be', *SMH Weekend Business*, 2–3 January, pp. 1–3.

Davies, K. (2010) 'Outward FDI from China and its policy context', Vale Columbia Center on Sustainable International Investment, 18 October. Online. Available: www.vcc.columbia.edu/files/vale/documents/China_IFDI_final-18_Oct_0.pdf (accessed 18 April 2011).

de Cruz, P. (1999) *Comparative Law in a Changing World*, London: Cavendish Publishing.

Dempsey, J. (2011) 'Chinese Prime Minister's visit to Europe shows concern over Euro', *New York Times*, Global Business, 24 June.

Deng, P. (2004) 'Outward investment by Chinese MNCs: motivations and implications', *Business Horizons*, 47(3): 8.

Deng, P. (2007) 'Investing for strategic resources and its rationale: the case of outward FDI from Chinese companies', *Business Horizons*, 50: 71.

Ding, Q. and Bao, C. (2011) 'China's ODI "set to grow" despite setbacks', *China Daily*, 6 May. Online. Available: http://europe.chinadaily.com.cn/business/2011-03/23/content_12212765.htm.

Ding, X.L. (2000) 'Informal privatization through internationalization: the rise of nomenklatura capitalism in China's offshore business', *British Journal of Political Science*, 30(1): 121.

Dittrick, P. (2010) 'Chinese oil companies invest heavily abroad', *Oil and Gas Journal*, 108(5): 20.

Dr Upendra Baxi v. State of UP (1986) 4 SCC 106 Indian Supreme Court.

Dryzek, J. (2007) 'Paradigms and discourses', in D. Bodansky, J. Brunnee and E. Hey (eds) *The Oxford Handbook of International Environmental Law*, Oxford: Oxford University Press.

Dutka, O.Y. (2007) 'Turning a weapon into a shield: using the law to protect people living with HIV/AIDS in China from discrimination', *Columbia Human Rights Law Review*, 38(2): 421–57.

Eisenberg, T. and Tagashira, S. (1994) 'Should we abolish Chapter 11? The evidence from Japan', *The Journal of Legal Studies*, 23: 111–57.
Electrocraft Arkansas, Inc. v. Super Electric Motors, Ltd (2009) 70 UCC Rep.Serv.2d 716 (E.D. ARK. 2009) (not reported).
ElComercio.pe (2010) '*Suspenden Huelga en Shougang tras Publicacion de Resolucion del Ministerio de Trabajo*' 9 July. Online. Available: http://elcomercio.pe/peru/508201/noticia-suspenden-huelga-shougang-publicacion-resolucion-ministerio-trabajo (accessed 2 August 2011).
Elegant, S. (2009) 'China's underworld on trial in Chongqing', *Time World*, 21 October. Online. Available: www.time.com/time/world/article/0,8599,1931342,00.html (accessed 7 January 2010).
Emmott, R. (2005) 'Perú miners feel oppressed by China's Shougang', *Mines and Communities*, 21 July. Online. Available: www.minesandcommunities.org/article.php?a=7748 (accessed 24 May 2011).
Evans, P.C. and Downs, E.S. (2006) 'Untangling China's quest for oil through state-backed financial deals', *Brookings Institute Policy Brief No. 154*, May.
Fan, J.P.H., Jun, Huang and Zhu, Ning (2011) 'Institutions, ownership structures, and firm distress resolution' (unpublished). Online. Available: www.hkimr.org/cms/upload/seminar_app/sem_paper_0_401_Paper_2011-04-08.pdf (accessed 12 April 2011).
Fan Yu (2003) 'Development of ADR in contemporary China', *Zeitschrift für Zivilprozess* (ZZP Int.) 7 Band, Cologne: Carl Heymann's Verlag, pp. 533–55.
Fan Yu (2004) 'The People's mediation system in social transformation in Shanghai–Changning district people's mediation reform', *Justice of China*, No. 10.
Fan Yu (2005) 'On the Mediation Law', *Justice of China*, No. 10–11.
Fan Yu (2007a) *Theory and Practice of Dispute Resolution*, Beijing: Tsinghua University Press.
Fan Yu (2007b) 'Pre-litigation mediation and the court's social responsibility', *Law Application*, No. 6.
Fan Yu (2009) 'Multi-ways to resolve group tort incidents', *Lawyers*, No. 2.
Fang, Liufang (1995) 'China's corporatization experiment', *Duke Journal of Comparative and International Law*, 5: 149–269.
Farnsworth, E.A. (1988) 'Review of standard forms or terms under the Vienna Convention', *Cornell International Law Journal*, 21: 439.
Fazhi Ribao (Legal Daily) (2008) 7 December. Online. Available: http://news.cnfol.com/081207/101,1591,5167034,00.shtml.
Feenstra, R.C. and Hanson, G.H. (2003) 'Ownership and control in outsourcing to China: estimating the property-rights theory of the firm', *National Bureau of Economic Research*, Working Paper No. 10198, December.
Feinerman, J.V. (2007) 'New hope for corporate governance in China?' *The China Quarterly*, 191: 609–11.
Feng, Fei (2010) 'Guangdong Henfu takes over Zhonggu and the new sugar king is born', *Zhanjiang Evening News*, Guangdong (in Chinese), 16 September.
Feng, Fei and Li, Ruozhu (2010) 'Zhonggu reorganization is terminated as Henfu stepped in', *Zhanjiang Daily* Guangdong (in Chinese), 15 September. Online. Available: www.gdzjdaily.com.cn/zjnews/fortune/2010-09/15/content_1258804.htm (accessed 1 July 2010).
Ferguson, B. (2010) 'Plenty of reasons to be concerned about China', *The Age*, 3 December. Online. Available: www.theage.com.au/business/plenty-of-reasons-to-be-concerned-about-china-20101202-18i5j.html (accessed 3 December 2010).
Feria Tinta, M. (2008) 'The Inter-American Court and the role of National Courts in protecting socio-economic rights', Foundation for Law, Justice and Society Conference (paper on file with R. Peerenboom).

Flechtner, H.M. (2008) 'Funky mussels, a stolen car, and decrepit used shoes: non-conforming goods and notice thereof under the United Nations Sales Convention ("CISG")', 26 *B.U. Intl L.J.*, 1.

Fredman, S. (2006) 'Human rights transformed: positive duties and positive rights', *Oxford Legal Studies Research Paper No.38/2006, Public Law*, pp. 498–520.

Frisby, S. (2004) 'In search of a rescue regime: the Enterprise Act 2002', *The Modern Law Review*, 67: 247–72.

Frost, S. (2005) 'Chinese outward direct investment in Southeast Asia: how big are the flows and what does it mean for the region?', *The Pacific Review*, 17(3): 323.

Fu Hualing (2001) 'The people's mediation system in the post-Mao Zedong China', in Qian Shigong (ed.) *Mediation, Legal System and Modernity: On Mediation System in China*, Beijing: China Legal System Publishing House, pp. 310–11.

Fu, Y. and Peerenboom, R. (2010) 'A new analytical framework for understanding and promoting judicial independence in China', in R. Peerenboom (ed.) *Judicial Independence in China*, Cambridge: Cambridge University Press.

Fung, H.G., Liu, Q.W. and Kao, E.H.C. (2007) 'China's outward direct and portfolio investments', *China and World Economy*, 15(6): 53.

Gallagher, M. E. (2005) *Contagious Capitalism: Globalization and the Politics of Labor in China*, Princeton: Princeton University Press.

Gallagher, M.E. (2009) 'China's old workers: between law and policy, between laid-off and unemployed', in T.B. Gold, W.J. Hurst, J. Won and L. Qiang (eds) *Laid-Off Workers in a Workers' State: Unemployment with Chinese Characteristics*, New York: Palgrave Macmillan.

Gao, J. (2010) 'Environmental public interest litigation and the vitality of Environmental Courts: the development and future of environmental courts in China' Online. Available: www.greenlaw.org.cn/files/reports/GaoJieEPCourts_En.pdf (accessed 10 February 2010).

Gao, L. (2010) 'The monopoly and SOEs' reform', *Politics and Economy Review* (in Chinese), 3: 64–71.

Gao, M. (2008) *The Battle for China's Past: Mao and the Cultural Revolution*, London: Pluto Press.

Gao, Y. (2010) '*Ping Chongqing dahei xingdong zhong de meiti yu sifa*', *Faxue zazhi*, 4: 11–14.

Garcia, F. (2009) '*Trabajadores Piden a Shougang Mejorar Condiciones Laborales*', *LaRepublica.pe*, 8 February. Online. Available: www.larepublica.pe/08-02-2009/trabajadores-piden-shougang-mejorar-condiciones-laborales (accessed 2 August 2011).

Garnaut, J. (2008) 'Tycoon vanishes on graft rumours', *SMH*, 25 November, p. 16.

Garnaut, J. (2010a) 'Assertive China goes a great leap too far', *SMH Business Day*, 18 January, p. 5.

Garnaut, J. (2010b) 'China's runaway growth train on a dangerous course', *SMH Business Day*, 25 January, p. 2.

Garnaut, J. (2010c) 'Children of the revolution', *SMH*, 13 February. Online. Available: www.smh.com.au/world/children-of-the-revolution-20100212-nxjh.html.

Garnaut, J. (2010d) 'China's land disputes at crisis point as revolutionary turmoil beckons, says professor of disenfranchised', SMH Business, 1 March. Online. Available: www.smh.com.au/business/chinas-land-disputes-at-crisis-point-as-revolutionary-turmoil-beckons-says-professor-of-disenfranchised-20100228-pb4n.html.

Garnaut, J. (2010e) 'It is not what you know, it's Hu you pay', 25 May. Online. Available: www.smh.com.au/business/it-is-not-what-you-know-its-hu-you-pay-20100524-w83h.html#ixzz1XR9h7zxZ.

Garnaut, J. (2010f) 'China race to invest in Australian resources', *SMH*, 6 April, p. 1. Online. Available: www.smh.com.au/business/china-race-to-invest-in-australian-resources-20100405-rn22.html.

Garnaut, J. (2010g) 'China must reform or die', *SMH*, 12 August, p. 1. Online. Available: www.smh.com.au/world/china-must-reform-or-die-20100811-11zxd.html.
Garnaut, J. (2010h) 'In China, it's always (Communist) Party time', *SMH Business Day*, 14 September. Online: Available: www.smh.com.au/business/in-china-its-always-communist-party-time-20100913-159ff.html.
Garnaut, J. (2010i) 'The princelings', *SMH Business Day*, 2 October. Online: Available: www.smh.com.au/business/the-princelings-20101001-613l.html.
Garnaut, J. (2011a) 'Crouching tiger, soaring cranes, rumbling doubts', *SMH Business Weekend*, 29 January, p. 9.
Garnaut, J. (2011b) 'China won't take the Cairo route', *SMH Business Day*, 15 February.
Garnaut, J. (2011c) 'Companies feel pinch as credit crunch hits', 4 May. Online. Available: www.smh.com.au/business/companies-feel-pinch-as-credit-crunch-hits-20110503-1e6q6.html.
Garnaut, J. (2011d) 'Hard landing for a financial circus', 14 June. Online. Available: www.smh.com.au/business/hard-landing-for-a-financial-circus-20110613-1g0fo.html#ixzz1PaKCMVeM.
Garnaut, R. and Song, L. (2004) *China's Third Economic Transformation: The Rise of the Private Economy*, London, RoutledgeCurzon.
Garnaut, R., Song, L., Tenev, S. and Yao, Y. (2005) *China's Ownership Transformation: Process, Outcomes, Prospects*, Beijing: International Finance Corporation of Australian National University and China Centre for Economic Research, Peking University.
Garrick, J. (ed.) (2011) *Law, Wealth and Power in China: Commercial Law Reforms in Context*, London: Routledge.
Ge, G.L. and Ding, D.Z. (2008) 'A strategic analysis of surging Chinese manufacturers: the case of Galanz', *Asia Pacific Journal of Management*, 25: 667.
Geng, W. (2007) 'Institutional deficiencies and perfection of foreign exchange regulation' (*Jingwai Touzi Waihui Guanli de Zhidu Quexian ji Wanshan*), *Foreign Exchange (Zhongguo Waihui)*, 12: 72.
Ghai, Y. and Cottrell, J. (eds) (2004) *Economic, Social and Cultural Rights in Practice*, London: Interights.
Giles, J., Park, A. and Zhang, J. (2005) 'What is China's true unemployment rate?' *China Economic Review*, 16: 149–70.
Gillespie, J. (2009) 'The role of state, non-state and hybrid actors in localizing global scripts in East Asia', in J. Gillespie and R. Peerenboom (eds) *Regulation in Asia: Pushing Back on Globalization*, London: Routledge.
Gillespie, J. and Chen, A.H.Y. (eds) (2010) *Legal Reforms in China and Vietnam: A Comparison of Asian Communist Regimes*, London: Routledge.
Global Nutri Co. v. Sichuan Xinguang Industrial Import & Export Co. Ltd (2005). Online. Available: http://cisgw3.law.pace.edu/cases/051209c1.html (accessed 25 February 2011).
Global Times (2009) 'Billionaire Li Qiang on gang crime trial in Chongqing', 26 October. Online. Available: http://china.globaltimes.cn/society/2009-10/479691.html (accessed 20 December 2010).
Gordon, J. (1997) 'The Ok Tedi lawsuit in retrospect', in G. Banks and C. Ballard (eds) *The Ok Tedi Settlement: Issues, Outcomes, Implications*, Canberra: AP Press.
Guang Dong Light Headgear Factory Co. Ltd. v. ACI International Inc. (2007) 521 F.Supp.2d 1153 (not reported).
Guang Dong Light Headgear Factory Co. Ltd. v. ACI Intern. Inc. (2008) WL 1924948 (D. Kan.) (not reported).
Guanyu yanjin yapian yandu de tongling (1950). Online. Available: http://news.xinhuanet.com/ziliao/2004-12/14/content_2332921.htm (accessed 1 May 2011).

Guerra v. *Italy* (1998) 26 E.H.R.R. 357, article 8.
Gunter, F.R. (1996) 'Capital flight from the People's Republic of China 1984–94', *China Economic Review*, 7(1): 77.
Guo, Y. (2011) 'In search of wealth and power: the character of the Chinese state and limits to change', in J. Garrick (ed.) *Law, Wealth and Power in China: Commercial Law Reforms in Context*, London: Routledge.
Haglund, D. (2009) 'In it for the long term? Governance and learning among Chinese investors in Zambia's copper sector', *The China Quarterly*, 199: 627–46.
Halliday, T.C. (2007) 'The making of China's Corporate Bankruptcy Law'. Online. Available: www.fljs.org/uploads/documents/Halliday.pdf (accessed on 12 April 2011).
Halliday, T.C. and Carruthers, B.G. (2009) *Bankruptcy: Global Lawmaking and Systematic Financial Crisis*, Stanford: Stanford University Press.
Hang, J., Silverberg, D. and Levine, M. (2008) 'Update on China labor contract law: China promulgates implementing regulations to labor contract law', *EpsteinBakerGreen – Client Alert*, 1–3 December. Online. Available: www.ebglaw.com/files/24877_ChinaContractLawAlert.pdf (accessed 27 September 2010).
Harmer, R.W. (1988) 'Report No. 45: General insolvency inquiry', *Australian Law Reform Commission*, Commonwealth of Australia, Volume 1, Sydney.
Harvey, C. and Rooney, E. (2011) 'Integrating human rights? Socio-economic rights and budget analysis', *European Human Rights Law Review*, 3: 266–79. Online. Available: http://ssrn.com/abstract=1590214 (accessed 18 December 2010).
He, B. (2003) 'Organized crime: a perspective from China', in J. Albanese, D. Das and A. Verma (eds) *Organized Crime: World Perspectives*, Upper Saddle: Pearson, pp. 279–99.
He, W. and Lyles, M. A. (2008) 'China's outward foreign direct investment', *Business Horizons*, 51: 485.
He Xin (2010) '*Er shen huo pan xing yinianban, Li Zhuang zaici "fangong"*', *Caixin*, 9 February. Online. Available: http://policy.caing.com/2010-02-09/100116950.html (accessed 13 June 2011)
He Xin (2010) 'The judiciary pushes back: law, power and politics in Chinese courts', in R. Peerenboom (ed.) *Judicial Independence in China: Lessons for Global Rule of Law Promotion*, New York: Cambridge University Press.
He Xin (2011) 'Prosecutors withdraw charges against Li Zhuang', *Caixin*, 22 April. Online. Available: http://english.caing.com/2011-04-22/100251500.html (accessed 16 July 2010).
He, Xuqiang (2011) 'Bankruptcy of listed companies, choices of reorganization solution, its efficiency and legal underpinning'. Online. Available: http://www.cqvip.com/qk/95499X/200607/22423831.html (accessed 9 April 2011).
Hegel, R.E. (2009) *True Crimes in Eighteenth-Century China: Twenty Case Histories*, Seattle: University of Washington Press.
Herd, R. (2010) 'A pause in the growth of inequality in China?' *Organisation for Economic Development and Co-operation (OECD)* Economics Working Paper 748 (4), 1 February.
Hilton, I. (2011) 'Beijing's growing might threatens state sovereignty', 25 May, originally published in the *Guardian*, republished in *The Age*, 'Business Day', p. 17.
Hirschman, A.O. (1970) *Exit, Voice, and Loyalty: Responses to Decline in Firms, Organizations, and States*, Cambridge, MA: Harvard University Press.
Ho, S. and Lin, G. (2003) 'Emerging land markets in rural and urban China: policies and practices', *The China Quarterly*, 681–707.
Hong, E. and Sun, L. (2006) 'Dynamics of internationalization and outward investment: Chinese corporations' strategies', *The China Quarterly*, 610.

Howlett, A. and Hong, L. (2007) 'The new property law in the People's Republic of China', *The Real Estate Finance Journal*, 1–3.

Howson, N.C. (1997) 'China's company law: one step forward, two steps back? A modest complaint', *Columbia Journal of Asian Law*, 11: 127–73.

Howson, N.C. (2010) 'Judicial independence and the company law in Shanghai Courts', in R. Peerenboom (ed.) *Judicial Independence in China: Lessons for Global Rule of Law Promotion*, Cambridge: Cambridge University Press.

Hsing, Y. (2006) 'Land and territorial politics in urban China', *The China Quarterly*, 575–91.

Hu, J. (2007) 'Hold high the great banner of socialism with Chinese characteristics and strive for new victories in building a a moderately prosperous society in all respects', *Beijing Review*, 8 November: 45. Online. Available: www.bjreview.com.cn/document/txt/2007-11/20/content_86325.htm (accessed 10 December 2010).

Hu, R. (2008) 'China's urban age', in C. Johnson, R. Hu and S. Abedin (eds) *Connecting Cities: China*, Sydney: Metropolis Congress.

Hu, R. (2011) 'Property, wealth and law reforms in China's urban revolution', in J. Garrick (ed.) *Law, Wealth and Power in China: Commercial Law Reforms in Context*, London: Routledge.

Huang, H. (2009) 'The regulation of foreign investment in post-WTO China: a political economy analysis', *Columbia Journal of Asian Law*, 23(1): 189–218.

Huawei (2010) *Corporate Governance*. Online. Available: www.huawei.com/en/about-huawei/corporate-info/coporate-governance/index.htm.

Human Rights Council (2007) *Draft Optional Protocol to the International Covenant on Economic, Social and Cultural Rights*, Sixth session, Open-ended Working Group on an Optional Protocol to the International Covenant on Economic, Social and Cultural Rights, Fourth session Geneva, 16–27 July, A/HRC/6/WG.4/2.

Hung, V.M.-Y. (2005) 'Judicial reform in Chinas: lessons from Shanghai', *Carnegie Papers*, No. 58. Online. Available: www.carnegieendowment.org/files/CP58.Hung.FINAL.pdf.

Hurst, W.J. (2009a) *The Chinese Worker after Socialism*, Cambridge: Cambridge University Press.

Hurst, W.J. (2009b) 'A China model or just a broken mould?' in R. Springborg (ed.) *Development Models in Muslim Contexts: Chinese, 'Islamic' and Neo-Liberal Alternatives*, Edinburgh: Edinburgh University Press, pp. 13–25.

Hurst, W.J. (2011) 'Politics, society and the legal system in contemporary China', in J. Garrick (ed.) *Law, Wealth and Power in China: Commercial Law Reforms in Context*, London: Routledge.

Hurst, W.J., Gold, T.B. and Won, J. (2009) 'Introduction', in T.B. Gold, W. Hurst, J. Won and L. Qiang (eds) *Laid-off Workers in a Workers' State: Unemployment with Chinese Characteristics*, New York: Palgrave Macmillan, pp. 1–12.

ICEM (International Federation of Chemical, Energy, Mine and General Workers' Unions (2009) 'Chinese mine firm Shougang Hierro Perú again reneges on salary hike', *ICEM*.) Online. Available: www.icem.org/en/78-ICEM-InBrief/3508-Chinese-Mine-Firm-Shougang-Hierro-Per%C3%BA-Again-Reneges-on-Salary-Hike (accessed 24 May 2011).

Ifeng TV News (2009) 'Premier Wen, the government should seriously deal with the unemployment of migrant workers'. Online. Available: http://finance.ifeng.com/news/hgjj/20090202/343638.shtml (accessed 14 July 2011) (in Chinese).

Innotex Precision Ltd v. Horei Image Products Inc. (2009) 679 F.Supp.2d 1356, 1358–59.

Institute of International Commercial Law (2010a) *CISG Database*. Online. Available: www.cisg.law.pace.edu/ (accessed 24 May 2010).

Institute of International Commercial Law (2010b) 'Contracting states: China'. Online. Available: www.cisg.law.pace.edu/cisg/countries/cntries-China.html (accessed 24 May 2010).

International Labour Organization (2010) 'Complaint against the government of Perú presented by the General Confederation of Workers of Perú (CGTP)', National Federation of Miners, Metalworkers and Steelworkers of Perú (FNTMMSP) and the Trade Union of Miners of Shougang Hierro Perú SAA (SHMSHP). Online. Available: www.ilo.org/ilolex/cgilex/pdconv.pl?host=status01&textbase=iloeng&document=5028&chapter=3&query=(Peru)+%40ref&highlight=&querytype=bool&context=0 (accessed 24 May 2011).

ITS Global (2009) 'Foreign investment in Australia – China and common sense', report, Melbourne, Australia.

Jefferson, G.H. and Singh, I. (eds.) (1999) *Enterprise Reform in China: Ownership, Transition, and Performance*, Oxford: Oxford University Press.

Ji, S. (2009) '*Zhuixun hongse GDP, Chongqing changhong dahei xian xuanfeng*', *Youzhou Zhoukan*, 13 November, pp. 24–8.

Ji, S. (2011) '*Xi Jinping diaoyan Chongqing jiejin minzhong*', *Yazhou Zhoukan*, 2 January, pp. 16–17.

Jia, Li (2010) 'The uncertainty of Xiaxing's reorganization and its alleged inflated recapitalization', *Stock Daily*, 16 August, Beijing (in Chinese).

Jiang, Qiang and Li, Yuan (2007) '*Huawei Buchong 10 yi Guli Yuangong Cizhi Yi Guibi Laodong Hetong Fa*' (Huawei offers workers 1 billion RMB to resign in order to avoid the Labour Contract Law), *Xinhua Newswire*, 2 November. Online. Available: http://news.xinhuanet.com/legal/2007-11/02/content_6995564.htm (accessed 27 September 2010).

Jiang, Qunying (2003) *Research on the Current Situation and Countermeasures of Foreign Direct Investment Chinese Enterprises (Zhongguo qiye duiwai zhiji touzi de xianzhuang he duice yanjiu)*, Shanghai: Fudan University Press.

Jiang, Zemin (1992) 'CPC report', 12 October, delivered at the 14th Party Congress.

Jin, Yanhong, Hua, W. and Wheeler, D. (2010) 'Environmental performance rating and disclosure: an empirical investigation of China's Green Watch Program', *World Bank Policy Research Working Paper* No. 5240. Online. Available: http://ssrn.com/abstract=1678349 (accessed 4 August 2011).

Jingji, Guancha Bao (2008), *Economic Observer*, 17 July. Online. Available: www.lawtime.cn/info/gongsi/gsnews/2008070831717.html (accessed 17 July 2011).

Kaartemo, V. (2007) 'The motives of Chinese foreign investments in the Baltic Sea region', *Pan-European Institute Working Paper* No. 7/2007.

Kahl, M. (2002) 'Economic distress, financial distress and dynamic liquidation', *Journal of Finance*, 107: 135–68.

Kalantry, S., Getgen, J.E. and Koh, S.A. (2010) 'Enhancing enforcement of economic, social and cultural rights using indicators: a focus on the right to education in the ICESCR', *Cornell Legal Studies Research Paper* No. 09-031, *Human Rights Quarterly*, 32(2): 253–310. Online. Available: http://ssrn.com/abstract=1501293 (accessed 20 November 2010).

Kan, C. and Lam, J. (1999) 'Rules and regulations on insolvency and restructuring in China', *Journal of International Banking Law*, 14: 351–9.

Keidel, A. (2005) 'The economic basis for social unrest in China', Carnegie Endowment for International Peace for the Third European–American Dialogue on China, The George Washington University, 26–27 May. Online. Available: www.carnegieendowment.org/2005/05/26/economic-basis-for-social-unrest-in-china/56z (accessed 15 July 2011).

Keith, R.C. and Lin, Z. (2006) *New Crime in China: Public Order and Human Rights*, London: Routledge.

Kim, I. (2009) 'Inward and outward internationalization of Chinese firms', *SERI Quarterly*, July, p. 23.

Kim, J.C. (2006) 'The political economy of Chinese investment in North Korea: a preliminary assessment', *Asian Survey*, 46(6): 898.
Koehler, M.F. and Yujun, G. (2008) 'Acceptance of the Unified Sales Law (CISG) in different legal systems: an international comparison of three surveys on the exclusion of the CISG's application conducted in the United States, Germany, and China', *Pace International Law Review*, 20(45): 45–60.
Kothari, J. (2008) 'The role of the courts in enforcing socioeconomic rights: the Indian experience', Foundation for Law, Justice and Society Conference (paper on file with R. Peerenboom).
Kuhn, R.L. (2010) *How China's Leaders Think*, New York: John Wiley & Sons.
Labour Law of the People's Republic of China (2008).
Labour Contract Law of the People's Republic of China (2007).
Lan, C. (2000) 'Chinese privatization: between plan and market', *Law and Contemporary Problems*, 63(4): 13–62.
Lardy, N. (1998) *China's Unfinished Economic Revolution*, Washington, DC: Brookings Institution Press.
LaRepublica.pe (2010) '*Mineros de Shougang van a la Huelga*' 28 June. Online. Available: www.larepublica.pe/28-06-2010/mineros-de-shougang-van-la-huelga (accessed 2 August 2011).
Lau, K.L.A. (2007) 'Why are the initial paid-up capitals of private limited companies in China 2,000 times bigger than those in the United Kingdom?', *The Company Lawyer*, 28(8): 248–52.
Law of the People's Republic of China on Dispute Mediation and Arbitration (2008).
Lawson-Remer, T., Randolph, S. and Fukuda-Parr, S. (2009) 'An index of economic and social rights fulfillment: concept and methodology', *Journal of Human Rights*, 8(3): 195–221.
Lee, C.K. (2007) *Against the Law: Labor Protests in China's Rustbelt and Sunbelt*, Berkeley: University of California Press.
Lee, F. (2002) *Mao: A Re-interpretation*, Chicago: Ivan Lee.
Lee, J. (2000) 'From welfare housing to home ownership: the dilemma of China's housing reform', *Housing Studies*, 15: 61–76.
Lee, J. (2009) 'Structural flaws will limit China's rise', World Politics Review, November.
Lee, J. (2011) 'Party needs to loosen its grip', 9 March. Online. Available: www.afr.com (accessed 9 March 2011).
Leng, J. (2009) *Corporate Governance and Financial Reform in China's Transitional Economy*, Hong Kong: Hong Kong University Press.
Letter of Notification (1997) Letter of Notification of treaties applicable to Hong Kong, deposited by the People's Republic of China to the United Nations (27 June).
Letter of Notification (1999) Letter of Notification of treaties applicable to Macao, deposited by the People's Republic of China to the United Nations (13 December).
Leung, J.C.B. (2003) 'Social security reforms in China: issues and prospects', *International Journal of Social Welfare*, 12: 73–85.
Lewis, J.W. and Litai, Xue (2003) 'Social change and political reform in China: meeting the challenge of success', *The China Quarterly*, 176: 926–42.
Li, L.H. (1999) *Urban Land Reform in China*, London: Macmillan.
Li Ling (2010) 'Corruption in China's courts', in R. Peerenboom (ed.) *Judicial Independence in China: Lessons for Global Rule of Law Promotion*, Cambridge: Cambridge University Press.
Li Ling (2011) 'Performing bribery in China – guanxi-practice, corruption with a human face', *Journal of Contemporary China*, 20(68): 1–20.
Li, S. (2001) 'Bankruptcy law in China: lessons of the past twelve years', *Harvard Asia Quarterly*, 4: 1.

Li, S. (2009) 'China's administrator system: the legislation and enforcement', presented at the 6th Forum on Asian Insolvency Reform (FAIR), 17–18 July, Bangkok. Online. Available: www.oecd.org/dataoecd/61/8/44192202.pdf (accessed 12 June 2011).

Li, X. (2010) *China's Outward Foreign Investment: A Political Perspective*, Lanham, MD: University of America Press.

Li, Z. (2009) 'Regulatory framework of China's ODI: history, challenge and reform' (*Zhongguo Duiwai Touzi Guanli Tizhi: Lishi, Tiaozhan yu Gaige*), *International Trade and Investment Series*, Policy Brief No. 09021.

Li, Z. (2010) 'ODI by private enterprises: opportunities and bottleneck', *International Trade and Investment Series*, Policy Brief No. 1001, February.

Lian, C., Liu, D., Qiu, R. and Yuan, C. (2005) 'Thoughts on China's global mineral resources strategy' (*Guanyu Zhongguo quanqiu kuangchan ziyuan zhanlue de sikao*), *Geological Bulletin of China* (*Dizhi tongbao*), 24(9): 795–9.

Liang, B. (2008) *The Changing Chinese Legal System, 1978–Present*, New York: Routledge.

Limbury, A.L. (2010) 'Getting the best of both worlds with mediation–arbitration', *Law Society of New South Wales Journal*, 48(2): 62–5.

Lin, F. (2011) 'Where are China's economic and legal reforms taking the People's Republic: "democracy with Chinese characteristics"?' in J. Garrick (ed.) *Law, Wealth and Power in China: Commercial Law Reforms in Context*, London: Routledge.

Lin, F. and Buhi, J. (2009) 'Emissions trading across China: incorporating Hong Kong and Macau into an urgently needed air pollution control regime under "One Country, Two Systems"', *Journal of Transnational Law and Policy*, 19(1): 123.

Link, P. and Kurlantzick, J. (2009) 'China's modern authoritarianism', *The Wall Street Journal Asia*, 25 May.

Liou, Chih-shian (2009) 'Bureaucratic politics and overseas investment by Chinese state-owned oil companies', *Asian Survey*, 49(4): 670.

Liu, P.P. and Li. K. (2002) 'Strategic implications of emerging Chinese multinationals. Haier: the case study', *European Management Journal*, 20(6): 699–706.

Lloyd, J. (2010) 'Look east, young unionists, for inspiration', *Financial Times*, 8 August.

Lo, S. (2009) *The Politics of Cross-Border Crime in Greater China*, Armonk: M.E. Sharpe.

Lu, J. (2010) 'A report on the corporate reorganizations of Chaohua and Xingmei'. Online. Available: http://guba.eastmoney.com/look,000688,3009247126.html (accessed 20 August 2010) (in Chinese).

Lubman, S. (1967) 'Mao and mediation: politics and dispute resolution in Communist China', *California Law Review*, 55(1): 285–359.

Lubman, S. (2006) 'Looking for law in China', *Columbia Journal of Asian Law*, 20: 1–92.

Lubman, S. (2010) 'Are strikes the beginning of a new challenge?' *The Wall Street Journal*, editorial, 25 June.

Lynch, E.M. (2010) 'China's first test of the new exclusionary rules – a dog without a bite', *China Law and Policy*, 30 September. Online. Available: http://chinalawandpolicy.com/2010/09/30/china%E2%80%99s-first-test-of-the-new-exclusionary-rules-%E2%80%93-a-dog-without-a-bite/.

Ma, X. and Andrews-Speed, P. (2006) 'The overseas activities of China's national oil companies: rationale and outlook', *Minerals and Energy*, 21(1): 17–30.

Macartney, J. (2009) '"Godmother" of Chinese gangsters, Xie Caiping, jailed for 18 years', *The Times Online*, 4 November. Online. Available: www.timesonline.co.uk/tol/news/world/asia/article6900598.ece.

McDonald, H. (2011) 'Crisis of faith for nuclear brahmins', 19–20 March. Online. Available: http://smh.com.au.

Manco, J.E. and Maldonado, P.E. (2003) '*Hierro Perú: una Privatización Anormal del Estado Peruano al Estado Chino*', *Revista de la Facultad de Ciencias Economicas de la UNMSM*, 22: 103–35. Online. Available: http://sisbib.unmsm.edu.pe/bibvirtualdata/publicaciones/economia/22/a06.pdf (accessed 2 August 2011).

Mao, S. (2003) 'Eliminating the old, absorbing the new – the changes of the regulatory system of China's ODI', *China Foreign Exchange Administration (Zhongguo Waihui Guanli)*, 6: 34.

Martin, B.G. (1996) *The Shanghai Green Gang – Politics and Organized Crime, 1919–1937*, Berkeley: University of California Press.

Marx, K. (1973) *Grundrisse: Introduction to the Critique of Political Economy*, trans. M. Nicolaus, Harmondsworth: Penguin.

Marx, K. (1976) *Capital, Volume 1*, trans. B. Fowkes, Harmondsworth: Penguin.

Marx, K. (1978) *Capital, Volume 2*, trans. B. Fowkes, Harmondsworth: Penguin.

Melish, T. (2006) 'Rethinking the "less as more" thesis: supranational litigation of economic, social and cultural rights in the Americas', *New York University Journal of International Law and Politics*, 39: 171–343.

Milhaupt, C.J. (2008) 'Is the US ready for FDI from China? Lessons from Japan's experience in the 1980s', Vale Columbia Centre, November. Online. Available: www.vcc.columbia.edu/pubs/documents/MilhauptFinalEnglish.pdf (accessed 12 May 2011).

Minister of Health v Treatment Action Campaign (No. 2) (2002) (5) SA 721 (CC) (S. Afr).

Ministry of Commerce (PRC) (2011) *Report on Development of China's Outward Investment and Economic Cooperation (Zhongguo duiwai touzi hezuo fazhang baogao)*, Shanghai: Shanghai Jiao Tong University Press.

Morck, R., Yeung, B. and Zhao, M. (2008) 'Perspectives on China's outward foreign direct investment', *Journal of International Business Studies*, 39: 337.

MTPE (Ministerio del Trabajo y Promoción del Empleo) (2011) '*Shougang Hierro Perú y Sindicato de Obreros Sostuvieron Reunión Extraproceso*'. Online. Available: www.mintra.gob.pe/mostrarNoticias.php?codNoticia=3161.

National Bureau of Statistics of China (2011) 'Annual statistics report'. Online. Available: www.stats.gov.cn/tjgb/.

National Human Rights Action Plan 2009–10. Online. Available: www.gov.cn/jrzg/2009–04/13/content_1283983.htm (English version at: www.china.org.cn/archive/2009-04/13/content_17595407.htm).

Neumann, P.A. (2006) 'China's foreign-invested companies: a standardization of practice', *China Law and Practice*, July/August: 30–1.

Ng, T.W. (2010) 'Lawyer reveals grim details of client's torture', *South China Morning Post*, 29 July.

Nolan, A., Porter, Bruce and Langford, Malcolm (2009) 'The justiciability of social and economic rights: an updated appraisal', *CHRGJ Working Paper* No. 15. Online. Available: http://ssrn.com/abstract=1434944.

O'Connell, R. (2009) 'Social and economic rights in the Strasbourg Convention', in *Rule of Law and Fundamental Rights of Citizens: The American and European Convention on Human Rights*, London: Esperia Publications.

OECD (2005) 'Overview of governance of state-owned listed companies in China', DRC/ERI-OECD Document for Policy Dialogue on Corporate Governance in China, 19 May. Online. Available: www.OECD.org/dataoecd/14/6/34974067.pdf (accessed 12 June 2011).

OECD (2006) '5th Forum for Asian Insolvency Reform' (FAIR), Beijing, China, 27–28 April. Online. Available: www.oecd.org/document/63/0,3746,en_2649_34813_3814187_1_1_1_1,00.html.

OECD (2009) 'State owned enterprises in China: reviewing the evidence', Working Group on Privatisation and Corporate Governance of State Owned Assets, Occasional Paper, 26 January. Online. Available: www.oecd.org/dataoecd/14/30/42095493.pdf (accessed 12 June 2011).

OECD (2010) 'Economic survey of China', *OECD Economics and Growth*. Online. Available: www.oecd.org/document/43/0,3343,en_2649_34571_44477419_1_1_1_37443,00.html.

Office of Justice Programs (2007) 'Asian transnational organized crime and its impact on the United States', National Institute of Justice, Washington, DC: US Department of Justice.

Otto, D. and Wiseman, D. (2001) 'In search of effective remedies: applying the International Covenant on economic, social and cultural rights in Australia', *Australian Journal of Human Rights*, 7(1): 5–46.

Palmer, D.A and Rapisardi, J.J. (2009) *The PRC Enterprise Bankruptcy Law – The People's Work in Progress*, Washington, DC: Beard Books.

Palmer, M. (2008) *Dispute Processes: ADR and the Primary Forms of Decision Making*, second edn, Chinese translation, Beijing: Peking University Press.

Palmer, M. (2007) 'Mediation in China', in D.S. Clarke (ed.) *Encyclopedia of Law and Society: American and Global Experiences*, London: Sage Publications.

Pan, P.(2008) *Out of Mao's Shadow: The Struggle for the Soul of a New China*, London: Picador.

Pan, W. (2006) 'Toward a consultative rule of law regime in China', in S. Zhao (ed.) *Debating Political Reform in China: Rule of Law vs Democratization*, Armonck, NY: M.E. Sharpe.

Parry, R. (2010) 'Administrator: appointment and remuneration', in R. Parry, Y. Xu and H. Zhang (eds) *China's New Enterprise Bankruptcy Law – Context, Interpretation and Application*, Farnham, UK: Ashgate.

Pattison, P. and Herron, D. (2003) 'The mountains are high and the emperor is far away: sanctity of contract in China', *American Business Law Journal*, 20: 459–510.

Peerenboom, R. (2002) *China's Long March Toward Rule of Law*, Cambridge: Cambridge University Press.

Peerenboom, R. (2006) 'A government of laws: democracy, rule of law and administrative law reform in China', in S. Zhao (ed.) *Debating Political Reform in China: Rule of Law vs Democratization*, Armonk: M.E. Sharpe, Ch. 3.

Peerenboom, R. (2007) *China Modernizes: Threat to the West or Model for the Rest*, Oxford: Oxford University Press.

Peerenboom, R. (2008) 'More law, less courts: legalized governance judicialization and dejudicialization in China', *La Trobe Law School Legal Studies Research Paper* No. 2008/10. Online. Available: http://ssrn.com/abstract=1265147.

Peerenboom, R. (ed.) (2010a) *Judicial Independence in China: Lessons for Global Rule of Law Promotion*, Cambridge: Cambridge University Press.

Peerenboom, R. (2010b) 'The East Asian model and the sequencing debate: lessons from China and Vietnam', in J. Gillespie and A. Chen (eds) *Legal Reforms in China and Vietnam: A Comparison of Asian Communist Regimes*, London: Routledge.

Peerenboom, R. (2010c) 'The political economy of rule of law in middle-income countries: a comparison of Eastern Europe and China'. Online. Available: http://ssrn.com/abstract=1673581.

Peerenboom, R. (2011) 'Law, wealth and power in China', in J. Garrick (ed.) *Law, Wealth and Power in China: Commercial Law Reforms in Context*, London: Routledge.

Peerenboom, R. and He, X. (2009) 'Dispute resolution in China: patterns, causes and prognosis', *East Asian Law Review*, 4(1): 1–61.

Pen, J. (2010) 'The court is still delaying in accepting the reorganization petition of Hongshen', *The First Financial Daily* (Shanghai, in Chinese), 19 August. Online. Available: http://finance.jrj.com.cn/2010/08/1901357976672.shtml (accessed 27 May 2011).

People's Daily (2010a) 'Currency moves may imperil textile firms', 13 July. Online. Available: http://english.peopledaily.com.cn/90001/90778/90860/7063420.html (accessed 14 July 2010).

People's Daily (2010b) 'China to conduct large-scale taxation system reform', 25 August. Online. Available: http://english.peopledaily.com.cn/90001/90778/90860/7117359.html (accessed 26 August 2010).

People's Daily (2010c) 'The 10th anniversary of China's "go-global" strategy: there is enormous potential for Outward Direct Investment' (*'Zou chuqu' zhanlue shishi shi zhounian: duiwai touzi kongjian henda*), 14 December.

People's Daily Online (2010) 'China to conduct large-scale taxation reform', 25 August. Online. Available: http://english.peopledaily.com.cn/90001/90778/90860/7117359.html.

Philippopoulos, G. (2008) 'Awareness of the CISG among American attorneys,' *Uniform Commercial Code Law Journal*, 40(3): 357–71.

Ping, Jiang and Liu, Fang (eds) (2003) *Xinbian Gongsifa Jiaocheng* (new edn of company law textbook), China: Law Press.

PJC (2004) *Corporate Insolvency Laws: A Stocktake*, Canberra: Parliamentary Joint Committee on Corporations and Financial Services, Parliament House.

Potter, P.B. (2003) 'Globalization and economic regulation in China: selective adaptation of global norms and practices', *Washington University Global Studies Law Review*, 2: 119–50.

Qin, T. (2009) 'Chinese environmental law and its impact on foreign investment', *China Law Update*. Online. Available: http://article.chinalawinfo.com/Article_Detail.asp?ArticleID=22184.

Rapisardi, J.J. and Zhao, B. (2010) 'A legal analysis and practical application of the PRC Enterprise Bankruptcy Law', *Business Law International*, 11: 49–63.

Reisen, H., Grandes, M. and Pinaud, N. (2005) 'Macroeconomic policies: new issues of interdependence', *OECD Development Centre Working Paper* No. 241, January (DEV/DOC (2005)01).

Rimmer, H. and Gail, S. (2010) 'Assessing the relevance of the international legal framework in claiming economic and social rights', in A. Neville and S. Bessell (eds) Human Rights and Social Policy: A Comparative Analysis of Values and Citizenship in OECD Countries, Cheltenham: Edward Elgar.

Robinson, W.C. (1996) 'Statutory moratorium on proceedings against a company', *Australian Business Law Review*, 24: 33.

Rosen, D.H. and Hanemann, T. (2009) 'China's changing Outbound Foreign Direct Investment profile: drivers and policy implications', *Peterson Institute for International Economics Policy Brief* No. PB09-14 June.

Rosen, D.H. and Hanemann, T. (2011) 'An American open door? Maximizing the benefits of Chinese Foreign Direct Investment', Center on US–China Relations, Asia Society and Kissinger Institute on China and the United States, Woodrow Wilson International Centre for Scholars, May. Online. Available: http://asiasociety.org/policy-politics/center-us-china-relations/american-open-door (accessed 6 September 2011).

Rossi, V. and Burghart, N. (2009) 'Chinese investment in Europe: a shift to services', *China Business Review*, September/October: 26.

Rui, R. (2010) 'Tens of thousands in standoff with police in eastern China over land grabs by officials', 19 July. Online. Available: http://chinaview.wordpress.com/category/social/law/land-seizure/ (accessed 10 May 2011).

Rutwoski, R. (2010) 'China's battle for iron ore', *Asian Times Online*. Online. Available: www.atimes.com/atimes/China_Business/LE06Cb01.html.

Salidjanova, N. (2011) 'Going out: an overview of China's Outward Foreign Direct Investment', *US–China Economic and Security Review Commission Staff Research Report*, 30 March. Online. Available: www.uscc.gov/researchpapers/2011/GoingOut.pdf.

Sander, E.A. and Goldberg, S.B. (1994) 'Fitting the forum to the fuss: a user-friendly guide to selecting an ADR procedure', *Harvard Negotiation Journal*, 49(10): 49–67.

Sanderson, H. (2009) 'Gang crackdown, lurid mob trials transfix China', *Associated Press*, 21 October. Online. Available: http://abcnews.go.com/International/wireStory?id=8878331.

Sanyal, K. (2009) 'Australia's foreign investment relationship with partner countries', Background Note, Parliamentary Library, Parliament of Australia, 17 November.

Sauvant, K.P. (2005) 'New sources of FDI: the BRICs', *Journal of World Investment & Trade*, 6(5): 639–709.

Sauvant, K.P., Maschek, W.A. and McAllister, G. (2009) 'Foreign Direct Investment by emerging market multinational enterprises, the impact of the financial crisis and recession and challenges ahead', OECD Global Forum on International Investment, December.

Scheingold, S. and Sarat, A. (2004) 'Something to believe', in S. Scheingold and A. Sarat (eds) *Politics Professionalism and Cause Lawyering*, Stanford: Stanford University Press.

Schimmelfennig, F. (2000) 'International socialization in the new Europe: rational action in an institutional environment', *European Journal of International Relations*, 6(1): 111–12.

Schloenhardt, A. (2010) *Palermo in the Pacific: Organized Crime Offences in the Asia Pacific Region*, Leiden: Martinus Nijhoff.

Schüller, M. and Turner, A. (2005) 'Global ambitions: Chinese companies spread their wings', *IM Focus*, 10. Online. Availablet: www.giga-hamburg.de/ifa/kostenlos/ca/0504/Fokus-Schueller.pdf (accessed 25 May 2011).

Schwenzer, I., and Hachem, P. (2009) 'The CISG – successes and pitfalls', *American Journal of Comparative Law*, 57(2): 457.

Scissors, D. (2010) 'Chinese outward investment: better information required', testimony before the US–China Economic and Security Review Commission, 25 February–3 March 2009. Online. Available: www.heritage.org/Research/Testimony/Chinese-Outward-Investment-Better-Information-Required.

Scott, W.R. (2002) 'The changing world of Chinese enterprises: an institutional perspective', in A.S. Tsui and C.H. Lau (eds) *Management of Enterprises in the People's Republic of China*, Boston: Kluwer Academic Press.

Sekine, E. (2008) 'China's offshore investment boom – QDII for fund management companies', *Nomura Capital Market Review*, 11(1): 36.

Servant, J.-C. (2005) 'China's trade safari in Africa'. Online. Available: http://mondediplo.com/2005/05/11chinafrica (accessed 25 May 2011).

Shanghai Wangruixiang Fashion Co. Ltd v. US Trend Co. Ltd Shanghai Silk (Group) Co. Ltd (2003). Online. Available: http://cisgw3.law.pace.edu/cases/030623c1.html (accessed 25 February 2011).

Shanghai Weijie Electronic Devices Ltd v. Superpower Supply Inc. (2000) Hu Yi Zhong Jing Chu Zi Di No. 727t. Online. Available: http://cisgw3.law.pace.edu/cases/030000c1.html (accessed 25 February 2011).

Shanghai Yanko Engine Co. Ltd v. Shanghai Materials & Equipment Group Import & Export Co. Ltd (2004). Online. Available: http://cisgw3.law.pace.edu/cases/040224c1.html (accessed 25 February 2011).

Shen, S. and Zheng, H. (2009) 'Some considerations on establishing a legal supervision framework on ODI by our enterprises', *Western Law Review (Xibu Faxue Pinglung)*, 2: 41.

Shi, J. (2007) 'Twelve years to sharpen *one* sword: the 2006 Enterprise Bankruptcy Law and China's transition to a market economy', *Journal of Bankruptcy Law & Practice*, 16: 645–96.

Shu, M. (2008) 'Report on FDI in Chinese real estate' (W*ai zi tou zi zhong guo fang di chan bao gao*), 20 September. Online. Available: http://shumeilaw.com/news_view.asp?newsid=516 (accessed 20 September 2010).

Shue, H. (1996) *Basic Rights*, Princeton: Princeton University Press.

Sina.com (2004) '*Guangxi fayuan bu shouli 13 lei anjian; shenggaoyuan cheng you guoqing jueding*' (Guangxi courts refuse to accept 13 types of cases; High Court claims decision in accordance with national conditions). Online. Available: www.china.org.cn/government/news/2008-02/28/content_11025486_12.htm (accessed 27 November 2011).

Sina.com (2011) '2011 Billionaires List: record year in numbers, impact', 8 May. Online. Available: http://english.sina.com/business/p/2011/0310/363590.html (accessed 10 May 2011).

Sindicato de Obreros Mineros de Shougang Hierro Perú y Anexos (2010) *Oficio No. 477–2010/SOMSHP*, Lima, Perú. Online. Available: www.fntmmsp.org/noticiassindicales/files.php?file=sindicato_shougang.

Siyuan Think Tank (2010) 'Statistical chart of enterprise bankruptcy cases in China from 1989 to 2010'. Online. Available: www.caosy.com/view.asp?id=71 (accessed 1 July 2010).

Soble, J. (2010) 'Honda blames China managers for strikes', *Financial Times*, 20 July.

Solinger, D.J. (2010) *States' Gains, Labor's Losses*, Ithaca: Cornell University Press.

Song, X. (2006) 'The court's role in the proceedings of enterprise bankruptcy and restructuring and the problems that need to be solved', *Forum for Asian Insolvency Reform*, Beijing, China. Online. Available: www.oecd.org/dataoecd/17/30/38167340.pdf (accessed 28 April 2010).

State Administration of Foreign Exchange (2011) 'Scale of China's foreign exchange reserve, 1950–2010', 12 May. Online. Available: www.safe.gov.cn/model_safe/tjsj/tjsj_detail.jsp?ID=111100000000000000,3&id=5 (accessed 16 May 2011).

State Administration of Taxation (2011) '*Tax Law*'. Online. Available: http://202.108.90.130/n6669073/n6669088/index.html (accessed 10 September 2011).

State Council (2010) Progress on Human Rights Situation in China in 2009, issued 26 September. Online. Available: http://news.xinhuanet.com/politics/2010-09/26/c_12606421_3.htm (English version at: www.chinadaily.com.cn/china/2010-09/26/content_11348812.htm).

State Council Information Office (2008) 'China's efforts and achievements in promoting the rule of law', 24 August. Online. Available: www.china.org.cn/government/news/2008-02/28/content_11025486_12.htm (accessed 1 September 2011).

Steinfeld, E.S. (1998) *Forging Reform in China: The Fate of State-owned Industry*, Cambridge: Cambridge University Press.

Stender, N.A., Zeng, Yan, Cui, Lei and Sheet, N. (2006) 'PRC government restructuring continues', *China Law and Practice*, 20(6): 25.

Stephens, M. (2010) 'Locating Chinese urban housing policy in an international context', *Urban Studies*, 47(14): 2965–82.

Stern, R.E. (2010) 'On the frontlines: making decisions in Chinese civil environmental lawsuits', Law and Policy, 32(1): 79–103.

Stern, R.E. (2011) 'From dispute to decision: suing polluters in China', China Quarterly, 206 (June): 294–312.

Stern, R.E. (2012) In Safety's Shadow: Suing Polluters in China, Cambridge: Cambridge University Press.

Stoianoff, N. (2008) 'Chinese taxation law', in P. Blazey and K.-W. Chan (eds) *The Chinese Commercial Legal System*, Sydney: Thomson Lawbook.

Stoianoff, N. (2011) 'The development of intellectual property law in China', in C. Lai-Ha, G. Chan and K. Fung (eds) *China at 60: Global–Local Interactions*, Singapore: World Scientific Publishing.

Su, J. and Ye, M. (2010) 'History and prospect of Chinese ODI'. Online. Available: http://money.msn.com.cn/internal/20100907/16431132107.shtml.

Su, Y. and He, X. (2009) 'Street as courtroom: state accommodation of labor protest in South China'. Online. Available: http://ssrn.com/abstract=1447131.

Sung, Y.-W. (1996) 'Chinese Outward Investment in Hong Kong: trends, prospects and policy implications', *OECD Development Centre Working Paper* No. 113, July OECD/GD, (95)53.

Susskind, A. (2010) 'Copenhagen leaves room to move on climate change', *Law Society Journal* (Sydney, NSW), 48(3): 15–18.

Sydney Morning Herald (2010) 'China's land disputes at crisis point as revolutionary turmoil beckons says professor of disenfranchised', 1 March. Online. Available: www.smh.com.au/business/chinas-land-disputes-at-crisis-point-as-revolutionary-turmoil-beckons-says-professor-of-disenfranchised-20100228-pb4n.html.

Tan, R. (1999) 'Foreign Direct Investments flows to and from China', *PASCN Discussion Paper* No. 99–21. Online. Available: http://pascn.pids.gov.ph/DiscList/d99/s99–21.pdf (accessed 25 May 2011).

Tang, B., Wong, S. and Liu, S. (2010) 'Institutions, property taxation and local government finance in China', *Urban Studies*, 48(5): 847–75.

Taylor, L. (2011) 'China to tax the biggest polluters', 31 March. Online. Available: www.smh.com.au/national/china-to-tax-the-biggest-polluters-20110330-1cgb3.html (accessed 2 April 2011).

Taylor, R. (2002) 'Globalization strategies of Chinese companies: current developments and future prospects', *Asian Business and Management*, 1: 209.

The Standard: China's Business Newspaper (2011) 'Hilton shareholder given life amid Chongqing crackdown', 5 May. Online. Available: www.thestandard.com.hk/news_print.asp?art_id=110732& sid = 32251617 (accessed 6 May 2011).

Tolenntino, P. E. (2008) 'The determinants of the outward foreign direct investment of China and India: Whither the home country?' *United Nations University Working Paper Series* #2008-49.

Tomasic, R. (1998) 'Insolvency law principles and the draft bankruptcy law of the People's Republic of China', *Australian Journal of Corporate Law*, 9: 211–33.

Tomasic, R. (ed.) (2005) *Corporate Governance: Challenges for China*, Beijing: Law Press.

Tomasic, R. (2007) 'Insolvency law reform in Asia and emerging global insolvency norms', *Insolvency Law Journal*, 15: 229–42.

Tomasic, R. and Andrews, N. (2007) 'Minority shareholder protection in China's top 100 listed companies' *Australian Journal of Asian Law*, 9(1): 88–119.

Tomasic, R. and Little, P. (1997) *Insolvency Law and Practice in Asia*, Hong Kong: FT Law and Tax.

Tomasic, R. and Wang, M. (2006) 'The long march towards China's new bankruptcy law', in R. Tomasic (ed.), *Insolvency Law in East Asia*, Aldershot, UK: Ashgate.

Trade Union Law of the People's Republic of China (1992/2001) Formulated 3 April 1992, revised 27 October 2001).

Trevaskes, S. (2007) 'Severe and swift justice in China', *British Journal of Criminology*, 47(1): 23–41.

Tsai, K.S. (2002) *Back-alley Banking: Private Entrepreneurs in China*, Ithaca: Cornell University Press.

Tsai, K.S. (2006) 'Testimony before the US–China Economic and Security Review Commission on China's Financial System', 22 August, Washington, US–China Economic and Security Review Commission. Online. Available: www.uscc.gov/hearings/2006hearings/transcripts/aug_22/06_10_22_trans.pdf (accessed 6 September 2011).

Tsai, K.S. (2007) *Capitalism Without Democracy: The Private Sector in Contemporary China*, Ithaca: Cornell University Press.

Tudo, A. (2011) 'China to step up acquisitions in the energy sector', *The Wall Street Journal*, 4 January.

Tull, D.M. (2006) 'China's engagement in Africa: scope, significance and consequences', *Journal of Modern African Studies*, 44(3): 459.

UNCTAD (2007) *World Investment Report 2007*, New York and Geneva: United Nations.

UNCTAD (2010) *World Investment Report 2010*, New York and Geneva: United Nations.

United Nations (1980) 'United Nations Convention on Contracts for the International Sale of Goods'. Online. Available: www.cisg.law.pace.edu/cisg/text/treaty.html (accessed 20 May 2010).

US–China Business Council (2009) 'US–China trade statistics and China's world trade statistics'. Online. Available: www.uschina.org/statistics/tradetable.html (accessed 20 May 2010).

US Congress (2008) 'Report of the US–China Economic and Security Review Commission', November. Online. Available: www.uscc.gov/annual_report/2008/annual_report_full_08.pdf (accessed 30 April 2011).

Vai, Lo Lo (2001) 'Resolution of civil disputes in China', *UCLA Pacific Basin Law Journal*. Online. Available: http://works.bpress.com/vai_lo/8.

van, Rooij, B. and Wing-Hung Lo, C. (2009) 'Fragile convergence: understanding variation in the enforcement of China's Industrial Pollution Law', *Law and Policy*, 31(1): 114–37.

Vining, J. (2010) 'The effect of economic integration with China on the future of American corporate law', Working paper No. 10–012, Empirical Legal Studies Center of University of Michigan Law School. Online. Available: http://ssrn.com/abstract=1588968 (accessed 14 October 2011).

Wall, D. (1997) 'Outflows of capital from China', *OECD Development Centre Working Paper* No. 123, March, OCDE/GD (97) 37.

Walmart China (2010) 'Walmart China factsheet', *Walmart China: About Us*. Online. Available: www.wal-martchina.com/walmart/index.htm (accessed 9 September 2010).

Wang, J. (2007) 'The strange role of independent directors in a two-tier board structure of China's listed companies', *Compliance and Regulatory Journal*, 3: 47–55.

Wang, L. and Zhang, J. (2008) 'What is the effect of China's SOX-Act?'. Online. Available: http://ssrn.com/abstract=1542589 (accessed 12 April 2011).

Wang, M.Y. (2002) 'The motivations behind China's government-initiated industrial investments overseas', *Pacific Affairs*, 75(2): 204–5.

Wang, Q. and Liu, J. (2009) 'The judicial problems of listed companies' reorganization', in X. Wang and Z. Yi (eds) *The Summit of Bankruptcy Law*, Series 2, Beijing: Law Press (in Chinese).

Wang, Weiguo (1999) 'Adoption of corporate reorganization regime in China – a comparative study', in W. Wang and R. Tomasic (eds) *Reforms of PRC Securities and Insolvency Laws*, Beijing: Press of China University of Political and Legal Science (in Chinese).

Wang, Weiguo (2001) 'Strengthening judicial expertise in bankruptcy proceedings in China', Forum for Asian Insolvency Reform, Bali, Indonesia, 7–8 February. Online. Available: www.oecd.org/dataoecd/8/24/1874188.pdf (accessed 12 April 2011).

Wang, Xiaolu (2010) 'Chinese annual household income understated by almost 10 Trillion RMB?' Credit Suisse. Online. Available: www.sinocism.com/archives/953 (accessed 20 August 2011).

Wang, Xin and Voituriez, T. (2010) 'China's export tax and export VAT refund rebate on energy-intensive goods and their consequences for climate change', in C.D. Soares, J. Milne, H. Ashiabor, K. Deketelaere and L. Kreiser (eds) *Critical Issues in Environmental Taxation: International and Comparative Perspectives (Vol. III)*, Oxford: Oxford University Press, Ch. 23.

Wang Yaxin (2001) 'On acquisition and distribution of resources for court trial', in Wang Yaxin, *Civil Procedure in Social Change*, Beijing: China Legal System Publishing House.

Wang, Z. (2009) '*Chongqing changhong dahei zhengyi buduan*', *Yazhou Zhoukan*. Online. Available: www.yzzk.com/cfm/Content_Archive.cfm?Channel=ae&Path=2208184152/45ae1c.cfm (accessed 15 November 2010).

Warner, M., Hong, N.S. and Xu, X. (2004) 'Late development experience and the evolution of transnational firms in the People's Republic of China', *Asia Business Review*, 10(3/4): 324–45.

Warren, E. and Westbrook, J. (2009) *The Law of Debtors and Creditors*, sixth edn, Austin, TX: Wolters Kluwer Law & Business.

Webster, T. (2007) 'Ambivalence and activism: employment discrimination in China', *Vanderbilt Journal of Transnational Law*, 44: 643–711.

Wei, L.B. (2008) '*Yige Jiceng Gonghui Ruhe Yu Woerma Doufa*' (A grassroots trade union organization and Walmart in a battle of wits), *Nanfang Zhoumo* (Nanchang edition), 17 September. Online. Available: www.infzm.com/content/17314/0 (accessed 10 September 2010).

Wen Jiabao (2010) 'Continue to implement a proactive financial policy and appropriately more relax the currency policy' (*Jixu shishi jiji caizheng zhengce, shidu guansong huobi zhengce*), Report on the Work of the Government, presented at the 3rd session of the 11th NPC. Online. Available: http://news.sina.com.cn/c/2010-03-05/112019797023.shtml (accessed 10 May 2010).

White House (2011) 'The resurgence of the American automotive industry' (June, USA). Online. Available: www.whitehouse.gov/blog/2011/06/01/resurgence-american-automotive-industry (accessed 7 September 2011).

Willer, H. (2000) '*Del Sueño Americano que se Esfumó en un Barco Chino*', Instituto de Defensa Legal. Online. Available: www.idl.org.pe/idlrev/revistas/130/pag54.htm (accessed 24 May 2011).

Wong, C. (2011) 'Reforming public finance for the harmonious society in China: how far across the river?' public lecture, UTS China Research Centre, 3 August.

Wong, H. and Arkel, A. (2007) 'China's new property law: practical issues', *China Law & Practice*, 1 June.

Wong, J. and Chan, S. (2003) 'China's Outward Direct Investment: expanding worldwide', *China: An International Journal*, 1(2): 273–301.

World Bank (1993) *The East Asian Miracle: Economic Growth and Public Policy*, Oxford: Oxford University Press.

World Bank (2008) *Doing Business in China 2008*, China: Social Science Academy Press.

World Bank (2010) *Doing Business 2010 Report*. Online. Available: www.doingbusiness.org/documents/fullreport/2010/DB10-full-report.pdf (accessed 20 May 2011).

World Bank (2011) 'Data by country, China'. Online. Available: http://data.worldbank.org/country/china (accessed 7 July 2011).

WTO (2009) *International Trading Statistics 2009*, Geneva: WTO.

Wu, F., Xu, J. and Yeh, A. (2007) *Urban Development in Post-Reform China: State, Market and Space*, London: Routledge.

Wu, H.-L. and Chen, C.-H. (2001) 'An assessment of Outward Foreign Direct Investment from China's transitional economy', *Europe–Asia Studies*, 53(8): 1235.

Wu, W. (2004) 'Commencement of bankruptcy in China: key issues in the proposed new enterprise and reorganization law', *Victoria University of Wellington Law Review*, 35: 239–68.

Wu, X. and Wei, Z. (2009) 'The senior judge of China's Supreme Court is interviewed to clarify the EBL 2006's Interpretation 2009: the court should proactively hear bankruptcy petitions', *Legal Daily Weekend* (Beijing, in Chinese), 4 June. Online. Available: http://wenku.baidu.com/view/4de49c8a6529647d272852ea.html (accessed 30 June 2010).

Xia, C. (2006) 'Migrant children and the right to compulsory education in China', *Asia–Pacific Journal on Human Rights and Law*, 7(2): 29–74.

Xiao, Y.P. and Long, W.D. (2008) 'Selected topics on the application of the CISG in China', *Pace International Law Review*, 20: 61.

Xinhua (2003) 'The proposition of "rule of virtue"' (*yi de zhi guo li nian ti chu*), 20 January. Online. Available: http://news.xinhuanet.com/ziliao/2003–01/20/content_698038.htm (accessed 25 September 2010).

Xinhua (2004) '*Guanyu yanjin yapian yandu de tongling*',14 December. Online. Available: http://news.xinhuanet.com/ziliao/2004–12/14/content_2332921.htm.

Xinhua (2006) 'White Paper on Environmental Protection', 5 June. Online. Available: www.chinadaily.com.cn/china/2006–06/05/content_608520.htm (accessed 20 February 2011).

Xinhua (2008) 'China's VAT reform to shed corporate tax burden by 120 bln yuan', 9 November. Online. Available: http://news.xinhuanet.com/english/2008–11/09/content_10331645.htm.

Xinhua (2009a) 'The party and government leaders to implement the Provisional Regulations of Accountability', CPC Central Committee General Office, State Council declaration, 12 July. Online. Available: http://news.xinhuanet.co/legal/2009–07/12/content_11699908.htm (in Chinese only).

Xinhua (2009b) 'Twin brothers jailed for 17 years for organizing crime gang', 6 November. Online. Available: http://news.xinhuanet.com/english/2009–11/06/content_12400316.htm (accessed 7 January 2010).

Xinhua (2010a) 'Chongqing court upholds convictions of 54 gang members', 8 February. Online. Available: www.chinadaily.com.cn/china/2010–02/08/content_9446788.htm (accessed 24 May 2011).

Xinhua (2010b) 'China still faces serious employment pressure, says Premier Wen', 27 February. Online. Available: http://news.xinhuanet.com/english2010/china/2010–02/27/c_13190581.htm (accessed 8 July 2010).

Xinhua (2010c) 'Wang Qinfeng', 28 June. Online. Available: http://news.xinhuanet.com/video/2010–06/28/content_13762430.htm (accessed 30 June 2010).

Xinhua (2010d) 'Ex-justice Wen Qiang executed in Chongqing', 7 July. Online. Available: www.china.org.cn/china/2010–07/07/content_20441196.htm (accessed 24 May 2011).

Xinhua (2010e) 'State Council's progress on human rights situation in China in 2009', 26 September. Online. Available: http://news.xinhuanet.com/politics/2010–09/26/c_12606421_3.htm.

Xinhua (2010f) 'Advice for 12th Five-Year Plan from Chinese Communist Party Central Committee, Part 10, Para 42 Accelerate the Reform Progress of Fiscal and Taxation System', 27 October. Online. Available: http://news.xinhuanet.com/politics/2010–10/27/c_12708501_10.htm (Chinese version) (accessed 28 October 2010).

Xinhua (2011a) 'China's five-year blueprint significant to the whole world', 6 March. Online. Available: http://news.xinhuanet.com/english2010/indepth/2011–03/06/c_13764092.htm (accessed 10 September 2011).

Xinhua (2011b) 'Our foreign exchange reserve exceeded US$ 3 trillion for the first time', 14 April. Online. Available: http://news.xinhuanet.com/fortune/2011-04/14/c_12130 6024.htm (accessed 7 September 2011).

Xinhua (2011c) 'China's legislature ends bimonthly session, adopts revisions to road safety law', 23 April. Online. Available: http://news.xinhuanet.com/english2010/china/2011-04/23/c_13841986.htm.

Xinhua (2011d) 'Did China's reserve lose US$270 billion in the last years? SAFE said they were not actual loss', 8 May. Online. Available: http://news.xinhuanet.com/fortune/2011-05/08c_121391337.htm (accessed 9 May 2011).

XM International Inc. v. Jiangsu Metals & Minerals Import & Export (Group) Corp. (2000) Su Jing Zhong Zi Di No. 380. Online. Available: http://cisgw3.law.pace.edu/cases/001228c1.html (accessed 25 February 2011).

Xu, J., Li, D. and Wang, F. (2010) '*Lüxie dangjiaren shou tan Li Zhuang an: feichu lüshi weizheng zui bu xianshi*', 5 March. Online. Available: http://news.ifeng.com/mainland/special/2010lianghui/zuixin/detail_2010_03/05/673819_0.shtml (accessed 24 May 2011).

Yan, Jiangning (2010) '*Zhongye haiwai zhao kuang lu*' (MCC seeks mineral wealth abroad), *Xin Shijie (Century Weekly)*, 36. Online. Available: http://magazine.caing.com/news/chargeFullNews.jsp?id=100177070&time=2010-09-04&cl=115&page=1 (accessed 2 August 2011).

Ye, G. (1992) 'Chinese transnational corporations', *Transnational Corporations* 1(2): 125–33.

Ye, J., Wu, D. and Wu, J. (2006) 'A study on the Chinese housing policy during social transition: practice and development', *Housing Finance International* 20: 50–8.

Ye, R. and Wang, G. (2010) 'Roadmap for improving environmentally related taxation in China', in C.D. Soares, J. Milne, H. Ashiabor, K. Deketelaere and L. Kreiser (eds) *Critical Issues in Environmental Taxation: International and Comparative Perspectives (Vol. III)*, Oxford: Oxford University Press, Chapter 8.

Ye, Xie (2010) 'Higher yuan disastrous for China, says Wen', *SMH*, 24 September.

Yin, Xian-shu (2009) 'Current situation and future development trends of China's ODI', *Journal of China Central Financial and Economics University (Zhongyang Caijing Daxue Xuebao)*, 4: 63.

Yin, Xiaowei, Stender, N. and Song, J. (2003) 'PRC outward investment: liberalization momentum builds', *Chinese Law and Practice*, 17(10): 75.

Y.L.F. (USA) Inc. v. Jiangsu Overseas Group Haitong International Trade Co. Ltd (2006) Online. Available: http://cisgw3.law.pace.edu/cases/060126c1.html (accessed 25 February 2011).

Young, K. (2008) 'The minimum core of economic and social rights: a concept in search of content', *Yale Journal of International Law*, 33(1): 113–75.

Yu, A. and Huang, B. (2005) 'Chinese companies on the global M & A stage – domestic regulatory issues', *China Law and Practice*, 19: 25.

Yu, G. (ed.) (2010) *The Development of the Chinese Legal System: Change and Challenges*, London: Routledge.

Yu, M. and Zhao, X. (2007) 'The emergence of our "going out" strategy and an analysis on promotion policy framework', January. Online. Available: www.ccpit.org/Contents/Channel_1276/2007/0327/30814/content_30814.htm (accessed 3 May 2011).

Zafar, A. (2007) 'The growing relationship between China and sub-Saharan Africa: macroeconomics, trade, investment, and aid links', *The World Bank Research Observer*, 22(1): 106.

Zang Xiaoli (2008) '*Cong Huawei Shijian Kan Xianxing "Laodongfa" he Xin "Laodong Hetongfa"'de Lifa Loudong?*' (Based on the Huawei incident, are there legal loopholes in the Labour Law and the Labour Contract Law?) *Falu Shequ*, Zhaofa Wang, 11 January. Online. Available: http://china.findlaw.cn/law/179246/viewspace-4191 (accessed 27 September 2010).

Zang, Xiaowei (2008) 'Market transition, wealth and status claims', in D. Goodman (ed.) *The New Rich in China: Future Rulers, Present Lives*, London: Routledge.

Zhan, J.X. (1995) 'Transnationalisation and outward investment: the case of Chinese firms', *Transnational Corporations*, 4(3): 67–100. Online. Available: www.unctad.org/en/docs/iteiitv4n3a5_en.pdf (accessed 25 May 2011).

Zhang, A. (2009) 'The shares of Haiji Lvjian are sold at depressed price and the RMB 100 million investment of Mingtian Tech has evaporated' *Daily Economy News*, Beijing (in Chinese), 21 April. Online. Available: http://finance.sina.com.cn/stock/s/20090421/04076127208.shtml (accessed 7 September 2011).

Zhang, H. (2010) 'Corporate rescue', in R. Parry, Y. Xu and H. Zhang (eds) *China's New Enterprise Bankruptcy Law – Context, Interpretation and Application*, Farnham, UK: Ashgate.

Zhang, Haizheng and Tan, Xiaohe (2010) 'Bankruptcy petition and acceptance', in R. Parry, Y. Xu and H. Zhang (eds) *China's New Enterprise Bankruptcy Law – Context, Interpretation and Application*, Farnham, UK: Ashgate.

Zhang, K. (2005) 'Going global: the why, when, where and how of Chinese companies' outward investment intentions', *Asia Pacific Foundation of Canada*, November.

Zhang, Q. (2006) 'The People's Court in transition: the prospects for Chinese judicial reform', in S. Zhao (ed.) *Debating Political Reform in China: Rule of Law vs Democratization*, New York: M.E. Sharpe.

Zhang, S.X. (2008) *Chinese Human Smuggling Organizations: Families, Social Networks, and Cultural Imperatives*, Stanford: Stanford University Press.

Zhang, X.Q. (2000) 'Privatization and the Chinese housing model', *International Planning Studies*, 5: 191–204.

Zhang, Xianchu (1996) 'Piercing the corporate veil and regulation of companies in China', in W. Guiguo and W. Zhenying (eds) *Legal Developments in China: Market Economy and Law*, Hong Kong: Sweet & Maxwell, pp. 129–43.

Zhang, Xianchu (1998) 'Practical demands to update the company law', *Hong Kong Law Journal*, 28: 248–60.

Zhang, Xianchu (2003) 'Company Law', in Freshfields (eds) *Doing Business in China*, Huntington, NY: Juris Publishing (last updated 2010). Online. Available: www.jurispub.com/113/doing-business-in-china (accessed 7 September 2011).

Zhang, Xianchu (2010) 'Company law', *Doing Business in China*, Release 20 (Fall), Huntington, NY: Juris Publishing.

Zhang, Xianchu (2011) 'China's "dual-track" legislation on business organizations and the effects of Antimonopoly Law', in J. Garrick (ed.) *Law, Wealth and Power in China: Commercial Law Reforms in Context*, London: Routledge.

Zhang, Xianchu and Booth, C.D. (2001) 'Chinese bankruptcy law in an emerging market economy: the Shenzhen experience', *Columbia Journal of Asian Law*, 15: 1–34.

Zhang, Y. (2003) *China's Emerging Global Business: Political Economy and Institutional Investigations*, Basingstoke, UK: Palgrave Macmillan.

Zhang, Zhong (2007) 'Legal deterrence: the foundation of corporate governance – evidence from China', *Journal Compilation*, 15(5): 741–67.

Zhang, Zinian (2010) Unpublished material collected for PhD in Law, Durham Law School.

Zhao, J. and de Pablos, P.O. (2010) 'Chinese firms' Outward Direct Investment: technological innovation mechanisms, organizational modes, and improving strategies', *Human Factors and Ergonomics in Manufacturing and Service Industries*, 20(2): 149.

Zhao, S. (ed.) (2006) *Debating Political Reform in China: Rule of Law vs Democratization*, New York: M.E. Sharpe.

Zhejiang Shaoxing Yongli Printing and Dyeing Co. Ltd v. Microflock Textile Group (2008) F.Supp.2d, 2008 WL 2098062 (S.D.Fla.) (not reported).

Zhou, S. (2009) 'China's Outward Foreign Direct Investment: current situations, trends and policies' (*Zhongguo Duiwai Zhijie Touzi: Xianzhuang, Qushi yu Zhengce*) *East Asian Thesis (Dongya Lunwen)*, 75: 24. Online. Available: www.eai.nus.edu.sg/CWP75.pdf (accessed 30 April 2011).

Zhou, X. (2006) 'Policies, transitional characteristics, and suggestions for improvement of China's ODI' (*Zhongguo Duiwai Zhijie Touzi Zhengce, TIxizhuanxing Tedian ji Wanshan Jianyi*), 1. Online. Available: www.cbminfo.com/tabid/63/InfoID/216594/Default.aspx (accessed 25 May 2011).

Zhu, C. (2004) 'A critical analysis of the majority rule principle's and controlling shareholders' fiduciary duties: a Chinese perspective', *Australian Journal of Corporate Law*, 16: 248–67.

Zhu, E.M. and Hua, G.H. (2011) 'Thoughts on the reform of the management of SOEs' (*Guoyou qiye lingdao zhidu gaige de sikao*), *Jingji zhidu gaige*, 1: 86–9.

Zhu, S. (2010) 'The Party and the courts', in R. Peerenboom (ed.) *Judicial Independence in China*, Cambridge: Cambridge University Press.

Zhu, W. (2001) 'A study of China's direct investment: economic globalization and China's strategies' (*Zhongguo duiwai zhijie touzi yanjiu: jingji quanqiuhua fenxi he zhanlue*), unpublished doctoral dissertation of the Chinese Academy of Social Sciences.

Zimmer-Tamakoshi, L. (1997) 'When land has a price: ancestral gerrymandering and the resolution of land conflicts at Kurumbukare', *Anthropological Forum*, 7(4): 649–66.

Zweig, D. and Bi, J. (2005) 'China's global hunt for energy', *Foreign Affairs*, 84(5): 25.

Index

10th Five-Year Plan 28, 35, 132
11th Five-Year Plan 102
12th Five-Year Plan 12, 101, 102, 108, 109, 116, 148, 150

accountability 189, 216; CL 2006 43–44, 51; EBL 2006 65–66; land/real estate property 93, 98, 218; 'market socialism' 93; ODI 25, 28, 29, 31; SOEs directors/senior executives 44, 48, 63; SOEs 'going out' 138, 139–40, 142
ADR (alternative dispute resolution) 10, 11, 13, 73, 185–201, 222–23, 225; CISG, use of 73; demise of 13, 185; evolution 13, 186–88; local government 186, 189, 190, 201; media 187, 194; mediation 185 (administrative mediation 186, 192, 200; court mediation 175, 186, 200; non-interventionist mediation 198; people's/court mediation distinction 200; restrictions on mediation 193); renewed focus on ADR, context 186–88; Supreme People's Court 186, 189, 196, 199–200, 223; voluntary participation 191, 195, 197, 201, 219; Xinfang 188–89; *see also* ADR, categories/systems/procedures; ADR, Chinese characteristics; court
ADR, categories/systems/procedures 185, 191–95, 222; administrative ADR 192; administrative reconsideration system 192–93; commercial arbitration/mediation for foreign investors 185, 193; Consumer Association mediation 197–98; criminal reconciliation 193, 200–201; domestic arbitration 185, 195; industry-based ADR 192; international arbitration 193–95, 200, 201, 223; labour dispute resolution 196–97, 201; Mediation Centres 196; non-governmental ADR 191, 195, 196, 201; specialized ADR 191; *see also* ADR; ADR, Chinese characteristics
ADR, Chinese characteristics 189–91; legislation 190 (*Arbitration Law* 190, 193, 195; *Labour Dispute Mediation and Arbitration Law* 190, 197; People's Mediation Agreement 13, 189, 199, 200, 223; *People's Mediation Law* 13, 185, 190, 196, 198–99, 200, 201, 223); mechanisms and procedures 190–91; political ideology 13, 185, 190; traditional culture 185, 190, 200, 225; *see also* ADR; ADR, categories/systems/procedures
Africa 15; Chinese ODI 25, 33
Asia: Chinese ODI 25; ESR 182; Southeast Asia 15
Australia: Australian Law Reform Commission Report 57, 68; Corporations Act (2001) 57; EBL 57, 60, 66, 68–69; natural resources 37; ODI 33, 37; SOEs 'going out' 13, 15, 135–37, 141, 220

banking sector 3; bank lending 6, 9, 30, 38, 147, 152, 221; China Import—Export Bank 23, 28, 30; 'green credit policy', green securities, and licences 104, 107; privatization 8; reform 6; *see also* People's Bank of China
bankruptcy 10, 120, 127; *see also* EBL; EBL 2006
Bennett, Yan Chang: CISG 11–12, 70–84, 217–18

Chan, Andrew: environmental law reform 12, 101–17, 219–20
Chen, Jianfu 1; 'going out' policy 63–64; ODI 11, 21–38, 63–64, 131, 216; SOEs 63–64, 216; *see also* ODI

254 *Index*

Cheung, Wilson: environmental law reform 12, 101–17, 219–20
Chinese socialism 87, 144, 226; 1982 Constitution 15; end of socialism 144, 160; postsocialism 160; preliminary socialism 144, 160; 'socialism with Chinese characteristics' 4, 87, 144, 149, 159, 160; state/collective ownership system 7, 8, 12, 41, 87, 88, 97, 98–99; 'wealth hatred' 155, 159; *see also* 'market socialism'
CIC (China Investment Corporation) 31, 37
CISG (UN Convention on Contracts for the International Sale of Goods) 10, 11–12, 70–84, 217–18; adoption by China 72; alternative dispute resolution 73; Article 95 71, 72, 81, 84; CISG, impact on Chinese jurisprudence 11–12, 70, 83–84; CISG in practice 72–73; CISG interpretation/application 70, 79–83, 217–18 (Chinese arbitration tribunals 79, 80–82, 84, 217; Chinese case law 81–82; CIETAC 79, 80, 84, 217; US legal decisions 79, 82–83); definition 71; Hong Kong 72, 81, 83; Macao 72, 81; purpose 70, 71; UCL 12, 70, 73, 84, 217; US 73, 79, 84; *see also* CISG/UCL comparison
CISG/UCL comparison 70, 73–79, 84; breach of contract 76; contract formation 73–74; contract performance 75; contract validity 74–75; damages 78, 217; obligations of the buyer 77; obligations of the seller 76–77; other provisions of law affecting CISG application/contract interpretation 78–79; passing of risk/risk of loss 77; remedies 77–78; *see also* CISG
CL 2006 (Company Law 2006) 42–52, 216–17, 226; administrative regulations 46; appraisal 48–52, 216–17; capital contribution 42, 46, 47, 48, 50; corporate accountability 43–44, 51; corporate governance 43–44, 45, 52, 217; corporate liquidation 11, 47, 50; CPC 49; dual track incorporation system 50–51; judicial activism 46–48, 49, 216 (contribution of case law to corporation law development 48; judicial independence 49; Supreme People's Court 46–47, 48); legislation/practice gap 51–52; level playing field 51; political ideology 48–49, 52, 216; problems unsolved 44–46, 217;

regulation and market access 49–50; *see also* company law reform
company law reform 10, 11, 39–54, 152, 223; business autonomy 40, 41, 42, 50; CL 1993 40, 41–42, 45, 48–49, 53; directors 40, 41, 43, 44, 45–46, 48, 50, 51, 52, 53, 54, 217; evolution of company law 39–46, 52; 'going out' policy 39; integration with international best practice 217; JSC 41, 42, 43, 44, 45, 47, 50; LLC 40, 41, 42, 43, 47, 50; political ideology 39, 41, 48–49, 52, 216; *Securities Law* 42; SOEs 39–41; 'state advancing/private withdrawing' 11; *ultra vires* rule 41, 42, 46; WTO 42, 51; *see also* CL 2006; SOEs
competition 7, 8, 15, 155
Constitution: 1974 1, 15; 1978 114; 1982 15, 40, 103, 198, 215; 1988 88; CPC 215; environmental legislation 103–4, 114; ESR 174, 177, 178, 179, 222; land/property ownership 15, 88, 98; non-justiciable 215; SOEs 134; state control 215; tax law 144, 160
consumption: China, low consumption 2, 9; Consumer Association mediation 197–98; *Consumer Protection Law* 197; consumption tax 148, 150, 151–52, 157; increasing consumerism to reduce dependency on exports 102, 114, 150–51, 220, 225; internal consumption/currency valuation relationship 2; sustainable consumption 225; US 2
contract law *see* CISG
corporate governance 22, 217; CL 2006 43–44, 45, 52, 217; corporate accountability 43–44, 51; corporate social responsibility 42, 52, 104, 106, 115, 217; SOEs 37; *see also* EBL 2006
corruption 14, 158, 224; anti-corruption fight 11, 13–14, 158, 203, 207–9 (corporate accountability 43–44); bribery 204, 207, 208; CPC nepotism 94, 100, 224; CPC patronage 4, 52, 156–57, 159, 217, 224, 226; environmental law reform 110, 117; Hu Jintao 158; land/real estate property 89, 94, 98, 100, 155–57, 218; local government 110; 'market socialism' 94; media 14, 48, 94, 157; SOEs 9; tax avoidance 145, 157–58; tax reform 156–58; *see also* organized crime; organized crime, Chongqing; wealth

court 5, 174, 183, 216, 225; civil environmental lawsuit 117; company law reform 46–48, 49; CPC 11; court credibility/court-mediation interface 189; court development 186, 222; court mediation 186, 200 ('street as courtroom' 175); court procedure 188, 191, 192, 200 (and rule of law 186); funding 174, 183, 186, 200; sensitive case 11, 212; *see also* ADR; ESR and Chinese courts; Supreme People's Court

CPC (Communist Party of China) 1, 88, 223–24; Antimonopoly Law 51; civil and political rights 174; company law reform 49; Constitution 215; crackdown on corruption 13–14, 209–10, 212; democratization 4–5; 'Eight Immortals' 162, 210; ESR, party political-legal committee 174; judicial system 49, 174; 'hybridity' 98, 144; land 88, 99, 218; legal system 1, 4, 5–6, 11; legitimacy 12, 87, 93, 94, 99, 129, 225; liberalization 92; nepotism 94, 100, 224; one of the top six investors in the world 132; organized crime, involvement 13, 202, 203, 204, 207–9, 213, 223 (Party system 13–14, 209–10, 212); patronage 4, 52, 156–57, 159, 217, 224, 226; planned economy 39, 55, 73, 99, 195, 196; power–wealth coalition 94, 98, 100; princelings 94, 98, 99; private wealth 155; rule of party/ rule of law contradiction 92, 93; slogans 12, 14, 101–2, 225; state/collective ownership system 7, 12, 41, 87, 88, 97, 98–99; 'systematic problem' 92; trade union 124; 'wealth hatred' 155; working branches 49; *see also* political ideology; PRC; state control

Criminal Law of the PRC 205, 211; Criminal Procedure Law 5, 193; *see also* criminal law issues 183; criminal reconciliation 193; organized crime and criminal organizations 204–5; *see also* nexus with corrupt officials 14, 89, 110, 156, 202–10

Cultural Revolution 22, 223

currency valuation: foreign reserves 2, 16; internal consumption/currency valuation relationship 2; Renminbi (RMB) 3, 31, 32, 120; US dollar 2, 16, 216; yuan appreciation 2, 16, 34, 38, 120, 216; *see also* foreign exchange system

debt, government investment vehicles 3, 16, 90, 98, 99, 218

democracy 155, 162, 216, 225; CPC 4–5; democratic judiciary 175; ESR 168, 182; judicial independence 5–6; social equity 152

Deng Xiaoping 93, 94, 100, 215, 223; 1978 reform 1, 2, 3–4, 15, 22, 29, 39, 73, 83, 87, 134, 155, 160, 224; ADR 13, 185; mediation 13, 185; 'open door' policy 1, 3–4, 15, 27; organized crime 204, 224; pragmatic approach to law 1; slogan 102; Southern Tour Talk 27, 91, 99

deregulation 9–10, 39–40, 146

dissident 5, 93, 174, 226

EBL (Enterprise Bankruptcy Law): Australia 57, 60, 66, 68–69; EBL 1986 40, 55, 217 (1994 amendment 55); political ideology 55; UK 59, 60, 66, 68, 69; US 59, 60, 61, 66, 68, 69; *see also* EBL 2006

EBL 2006 11, 55–69, 217; accountability 65–66; corporate insolvency 10, 11, 55, 56, 63, 65, 67, 217; corporate liquidation 11, 56, 57, 58, 62; corporate reorganization 10, 56–67, 217; creditor recovery 56; drafting process 55–56, 57, 62, 63, 67, 68; legislation/practice gap 56, 64; local government 59, 64, 65, 66, 68; *pari passu* principle 64–65, 69; problems 56, 57, 217; social stability 56, 62–67 ('absolute priority' principle and shareholders 66–67; delayed process of EBL 1986's reform 62–64; employment relocation plan 64; small-creditor-first approach/creditor equality 64–66); social unrest 62–63, 64, 66, 67, 217; SOEs 59, 62–63, 64, 68, 69, 217; State Council 67; Supreme People's Court 57, 66, 67, 69; traditionalist perspective 60; *see also* EBL; EBL 2006, eligibility for reorganization

EBL 2006, eligibility for reorganization 56–62, 67, 68, 217; assessing a company's viability 57, 58–59; assessment, government's role 59, 68; financial/economic distress 58, 60–61; international comparison 59–60, 61; low threshold, desirable/necessary in China 58, 60–62; statutory threshold for corporate reorganization 57–58; *see also* EBL 2006

economic growth 2–3, 23, 33, 35, 215, 223, 224; Chinese economic 'miracle' 3, 156; 'East Asian Model, plus two' development policy 128–29; economic growth/environmental protection balance 12, 101–2, 113, 114, 219–20, 221; export-led economic model 2–3, 102, 114, 128–29, 215, 220, 225; export processing 119, 130; global economic superpower xvii, 131, 143, 215 (fragile superpower 224); policy framework 22; private sector 155, 156, 161; sustainability xvii, 2, 3, 128–29
economic reform 1; 1978 reform 1, 2, 3–4, 15, 22, 29, 39, 73, 83, 87, 134, 155, 160, 224; *Fifteen Measures on Economic Reform* 22; 'hybridity' 87; success 3; *see also* 'market socialism'
education 3; education industry 3, 16; free primary education 177, 183; free rural education programme 7
energy 2, 139; 'clean' energy 117; energy-efficiency projects 12, 103, 105, 106, 107, 108, 115, 116, 117; energy security 33; from fossil fuel to sustainable new technology 102–3, 110, 220; National Energy Commission 1; nuclear reactors, waste 112, 117; Wen Jiabao, energy consumption reduction 12, 108, 116; *see also* environmental law reform
enforcement 216, 226; environmental law reform 12, 102, 107, 110–13, 114, 117, 219; ESR 168, 171, 173, 174, 176, 179, 181; labour law reform 129; tax reform 151, 159, 221
environmental law reform 10, 12, 14, 15, 101–17, 183, 219–20, 225; 12th Five-Year Plan 12, 101, 102, 108, 109, 116; 'clean' technologies 12, 103, 110, 113, 114, 220; climate change 15, 102, 104; compliance/implementation 101, 102; corruption 110, 117; discourses of environmental law 12, 101–3, 114, 219–20; economic growth/environmental protection balance 12, 101–2, 113, 114, 219–20, 221; energy-efficiency projects 12, 103, 105, 106, 107, 108, 115, 116, 117; ESR, environmental cases 174, 177, 178, 181, 183, 184, 219; EU 106, 115–16; FDI 12, 103, 104; from fossil fuel to sustainable new technology 102–3, 110, 220; Hu Jintao, economic growth/ environmental protection balance 12, 102; industrial sector 102–3, 108, 116, 117; MoE/SEPA 107, 109, 111, 112–13; New Zealand, *Natural Resources Act* 103; political economy 12, 101, 225; political ideology 101, 225; SOEs 106, 112, 115; sustainable development 12, 101, 102, 106, 115; sustainable development/social stability 103, 106, 175; US 106; waste disposal 103, 105, 106, 110, 112, 113, 114, 138, 149, 220; Wen Jiabao, energy consumption reduction 12, 108, 116; *see also* environmental protection framework; pollution
environmental protection framework 103–10, 113–14, 219, 220; 2009 Copenhagen Accord 102, 103, 104, 105, 108, 114; CO_2 emissions and carbon taxes 104, 107–8, 116; enforcement 12, 102, 107, 110–13, 114, 117, 219 (case study 112–13); environmental legislation 103–4, 105, 112–13, 114–15, 117; environmental policies 104, 106, 108, 115; FDI options and preferences 109–10; 'green credit policy', green securities, and licences 104, 107; international agreements 104–5, 113, 219; Kyoto Protocol 104–5, 107, 115; pollution liability insurance 12, 109; tax reform 13, 104, 108, 147, 149, 221; trade practice and process management 104, 105, 106; *see also* environmental law reform
ESR (economic and social rights): CESCR 167, 168, 169, 170, 171, 173, 178; China 173, 179, 183; civil and political rights 168, 170, 174, 177, 181, 182; constitutional basis of ESR 168, 170, 172, 174, 182; debates on 168–73 (minimum core 169, 170, 176, 178–79; state's obligation 168); enforcement 168, 171, 173, 174, 176, 179, 181; ICESCR 167, 168, 169, 171, 179, 181, 222; increased salience of ESR 167–70; India 178, 182–83; justiciability 168, 169–73 (competence concerns 171–73; excessive judicial activism 173; legitimacy concerns 170–71, 172; limits of litigation 173); political ideology 173; social and economic indicators 167, 174, 180, 224; South Africa 172; *see also* ESR and Chinese courts

ESR and Chinese courts 5, 11, 13, 167–84, 215, 216, 222; China/South Africa comparison 173–74, 170–80; Chinese courts, implementing ESR 167, 174–79, 181, 222 (limited/ineffectual role 13, 167, 174, 179, 181, 183, 222; recommendations for constructive role 176–79, 180, 184, 222); civil and political rights 174, 177; Constitution 174, 177, 178, 179, 222; environmental cases 174, 177, 178, 181, 183, 184, 219; individual remedies, lack of 13, 175, 176, 177, 179, 222; judicial independence 174, 175, 183, 215; justiciability 167, 181; labour cases 174, 175, 176, 177, 181, 183, 184; media 174, 175, 176, 177, 183; mediation 175, 176; New Left socialists/New Right neoliberals conflict 13, 174, 179, 222; party political-legal committee 174; resource constraints 13, 174, 179, 222; social stability 175–76, 180, 222; 'the three Cs' 174; working with the government 175, 177; *see also* court

EU: civil and political rights 182; environmental law reform 106, 115–16; global economic superpower 131, 143

exports 2; export-led economic model 2–3, 102, 114, 128–29, 215, 220, 225; export processing 119, 120, 130; export tax rebates 28, 116, 133; increasing consumerism to reduce dependency on exports 102, 114, 150–51, 220; Japan 2–3; *see also* CISG

Fan Yu: alternative dispute resolution 13, 73, 185–201, 222–23
FDI in China 4, 7, 21, 98; commercial arbitration/mediation for foreign investors 185, 193; 'East Asian Model, plus two' development policy 128–29; environmental law reform 12, 103, 104, 109–10; foreign investors 91, 98, 118; international arbitration 193–95, 200, 201, 223; labour law reform 118, 128; land/real estate property 15, 90–91, 94–96, 98 (registration process 95–96; restrictions on FDI in real estate property 15, 94–96); regulation 26; state control 26; *see also* trade
financial crisis (2009) 3, 4, 5, 6, 7, 9, 39, 70, 150, 155, 156, 224; unemployment 62, 175

foreign exchange reserves 1, 2, 3, 15–16, 23, 24, 34, 35, 216; largest foreign exchange reserve 4, 35; yuan appreciation 16, 34, 38, 216
foreign exchange system 26; *Administrative Measures on Foreign Exchange Used by Domestic Enterprises for Outward Investment* 31, 36; foreign exchange control 21, 27, 30, 31, 34, 36, 216; liberalization 31, 120; *Measures on the Administration of Foreign Exchange for Overseas Investment* 26, 35; ODI 26, 27, 30, 31, 32, 34, 35, 36, 216; reform 26, 27; SAFE 23, 26, 27, 30, 35, 36; state control 23; *see also* currency valuation

Garrick, John 1–17; law and policy for 'opening up'/'going out' 215–26; taxation law reform 13, 133, 144–63
GDP (gross domestic product) 1, 2, 24; consumption 2; GDP index 16; increase 3–4, 16; 'red GDP' 210–11
globalization 25, 70
'going global' policy 28, 34, 216, 220, 225; 'going out' policy 23; Jiang Zemin 28, 132–33; 'open door' policy 23, 28; *see also* 'going out' policy; SOEs 'going out'
'going out' policy xvii, 2, 4, 5, 23, 35, 139, 142–43, 159, 200, 215; 10th Five-Year Plan 28, 35, 132; beginning 28, 35–36; company law reform 39; *Fifteen Measures on Economic Reform* 22; 'going global' strategy 23; SOEs 'going out' 132–33, 135, 141, 142; *see also* 'going global' policy; ODI; SOEs 'going out'
guanxi 203, 215
Guo, Yingjie: SOEs 'going out' 13, 131–43, 220–21

'Harmonious Society' policy 12, 15, 102, 103, 106, 156, 174, 175, 188, 224, 225, 226; *see also* Hu Jintao
health 110, 176; rural areas 7, 156
Ho, Norman P.: Chongqing's organized crime 13–14, 110, 146, 202–14, 223
Hong Kong 7; CISG 72, 81, 83; education industry 3; ODI 23, 25, 28, 31, 157, 159, 162; 'round-tripping' 23, 35, 157, 159, 221
Hou, Shumei: SOEs 'going out' 13, 131–43, 220–21
housing 92, 95, 156; Chongqing 211; *Further Deepening Urban Housing Reform and Accelerating Housing Construction* 90;

258 *Index*

privatization/marketization 89–90, 92, 99; *see also* land/real estate property
Hu Jintao 93, 100; ADR 13, 185; economic growth/environmental protection balance 12, 102; fighting corruption 158; 'going global' policy 133; mediation 13, 185; political reform 5; pragmatic approach to law 1; slogans 12, 102, 103 ('Harmonious Society' 12, 15, 102, 103, 106, 156, 174, 175, 188, 224, 225, 226; 'Putting People First' 12, 102; 'Scientific Perspective on Development' 12, 102); SOEs 40, 133
Hu, Richard: land/real estate property 12, 87–100, 147, 218
Hurst, William J. 9; labour law reform 12–13, 118–30, 220
'hybridity' 1, 226; CPC 98, 144; hybrid-form collectivism 159, 163; 'market socialism' 87, 144, 149, 159, 163, 221–22; rule of law xvii, 1, 9–10

income 2, 9; hidden income 147, 159; income gap 157, 159, 200; individual income tax 150, 152–53, 161, 162; *Individual Income Tax Law* 145, 148, 153; social and economic indicators 167, 174, 180, 224
industrial sector: energy consumption reduction 108, 116; environmental law reform 102–3; exploitation of workers 103; industry-based ADR 192; low-end manufacturing/high-end production shift 118–19, 120, 130; pollution 102–3, 117; taxation 117, 150; *see also* labour law reform
inequality 7, 145, 155, 156, 158, 179, 218, 224, 226; *see also* wealth
intellectual property rights 4, 14; labour law reform 16, 120, 122, 219; WTO 4, 16
international law 14, 71, 171, 182
internet 124, 155, 183; Chongqing, crackdown on corruption 202, 206, 209, 210, 212; *see also* media
intervention 26, 211, 215, 216; corporate reorganization 59, 61, 68; *see also* state control
IPO (initial public offering) 3, 16, 107

Japan 2–3, 7, 21, 25, 117
Jasmine Revolution 5
Jiang Zemin 93, 100; 'going global' policy 28, 132–33; pragmatic approach to law 1; slogan 102

judicial system: Chongqing's organized crime 13–14; CPC 49, 174; democracy 175; ESR, justiciability 168, 169–73, 181; judicial independence 5–6, 49, 174, 175, 183, 215; political negotiation 14; *see also* court; ESR and Chinese courts; Supreme People's Court

Kinkel, Jonathan: labour law reform 12–13, 118–30, 220

labour: cheap labour 14, 15, 118, 120; child labor 170, 176; *Employment Promotion Law* 178; ESR, labour cases 174, 175, 176, 177, 181, 183, 184; exploitation of workers 15, 103; *Labour Dispute Mediation and Arbitration Law* 190, 197; labour dispute resolution 186, 196–97, 201; tax advantages 14; *see also* labour law reform; unemployment
labour law reform 10–11, 12–13, 14, 15, 118–30, 220; enforcement 129; export processing 119, 120, 130; foreign direct investment 118, 128; incentives for companies to innovate 120, 219; intellectual property rights 16, 120, 122, 219; 'Iron Rice Bowl' 127; *Labour Contract Law* 118, 119, 120, 121, 122, 124–28, 197; *Labour Law* 118, 121; low-end manufacturing/high-end production shift 118–19, 120, 130, 220; media 125, 128; political economy 128–29; political ideology 118, 129, 220; social welfare 42, 45, 120, 121, 122, 123; trade union 120, 121, 122, 123, 124–26; *see also* labour law reform and types of firms; wages
labour law reform and types of firms 119, 220; firms' reactions 119, 120–21; foreign firms 119, 120, 121, 122, 125, 126, 128, 130; Honda 125–26, 129; Huawei 126–28, 129; implications for firms' interactions with the state/ China's development model 128–29; type of labour law reform implemented 119, 120, 121; types of firms 119, 120–28 (high-skill labour force firm 120, 121, 122–23, 126–28, 129, 220; low-skill labour force firm 120, 121, 122, 123–25, 128–29, 220; transitional firms 120–21, 123, 123, 125–26, 129); Walmart 123–25, 129; *see also* labour law reform

land/real estate property 12, 14–15, 87–100, 147, 150, 155–56, 218; accountability 93, 98, 218; corruption 89, 94, 98, 100, 155–57, 218; domestic private investment 91; FDI 15, 90–91, 94–96, 98; housing 89–90, 92, 95, 99; land market reforms 89–90; land/property price 159, 218, 219, 221; land use right market 87, 88–89, 97, 156 (allocation 89, 94, 97; conveyance 89); law reforms on land/real estate property 87–90, 94; local government 15, 91, 92, 147, 156–57, 158–59, 162, 218–19; market economy 12, 87, 99; 'marketization' 12, 87; media 93, 94; paradoxes 12, 15, 87, 96–98, 99; privatization of land/property 15, 87, 92, 98–99, 218; property law reform, drivers 90–92; property law reform, impediments 92–94 (lingering ambiguity 93; political factors 92–93, 94, 98–99, 100, 218; power–wealth coalition 94, 100, 218); real estate market 88, 89–90, 147; rural sector 88, 90; state/collective ownership system 12, 87, 88, 97, 98–99; urban sector, urbanization 12, 87, 88–89, 90, 91–92, 99; VAT on land 148, 153, 154–57

Latin America: American Convention on Human Rights 182; Chinese ODI 25; ESR 182; Peru 139–41, 142; SOEs 'going out' 13, 15, 139–41, 142, 143, 220

legal reform 4–6, 10, 224, 226; debates about 9; importance 14; objectives 4; political reform 5

legal system 174, 175; All-China Lawyers Association 176, 214; CPC 1, 4, 5–6, 11; evolution 1; increased sophistication 79, 84, 216–17, 223; integration with international best practice 215, 217; pragmatic approach to law 1; *see also* judicial system; rule of law

liberalization 221, 226; CPC 92; foreign exchange system 31, 120; land/real estate markets 99; ODI 26, 30, 31–32, 34, 36, 134, 216; and organized crime 204; political liberalization 5, 128; SOEs reform 6

Lin, Feng: environmental law reform 12, 101–17, 219–20

Liu Xiaobo 5, 17

local government: ADR 186, 189, 190, 201; corruption 110; debt 3, 16, 90, 98, 99; EBL 2006 59, 64, 65, 66, 68; environmental law reform 110, 112, 117; investment vehicles 3, 16, 90, 98, 99, 147, 158, 218, 221; land use rights/property tax 15, 91, 92, 147, 156–57, 158–59, 162, 218–19; organized crime 206; SOEs 135, 159

Macao: CISG 72, 81; ODI 25, 31; organized crime 204

Mao Zedong 7, 93, 100, 118, 215, 226; ADR 13, 185; intellectual property rights 219; mediation 13, 185; organized crime, crackdown on 14, 146, 203, 210, 223, 226; rule of law 185; 'rule of man' 93; slogan 14, 101–2

'market socialism' 4, 51, 55, 105, 134, 144, 160, 216, 225; 1978 reform 1, 2, 3–4, 15, 22, 29, 39, 73, 83, 87, 134, 155, 160, 224; accountability 93; ADR 222; ambivalence/contradiction 144; corruption 94; Deng Xiaoping 91; from communist planned to socialist market economy 6–7, 11, 16–17, 39, 83, 87, 91, 94, 149, 155, 160, 185, 187–88, 197, 217, 221; 'hybridity' 87, 144, 149, 159, 163, 221–22; land/real estate property 12, 87, 99; mediation 13; monitoring 134; 'red GDP' 210–11; regulation 225 (Amendments to the 1982 Constitution, Article 7 40; Decision on Certain Issues Concerning Establishment of the Socialist Market Economy 40); social change and tensions 187–88; state/collective ownership of land 12, 87; wealth distribution 13, 155, 159; 'with Chinese characteristics' 13, 40, 91, 99; *see also* Chinese socialism; Deng Xiaoping

marketization 49, 144, 155, 225

Martinez-Pacheco, Selene: SOEs 'going out' 13, 131–43, 220–21

Marx, Karl 144, 146, 225

media 131, 215; ADR 187, 194; corruption 14, 48, 94, 157; ESR 171, 174, 175, 176, 177, 183; Kyoto Protocol 105; labour law reform 125, 128; land/real estate property 93, 94; organized crime 202, 204, 209–10, 211, 212, 213, 223; propaganda 93; tax avoidance 157; 'wealth hatred' 155

mediation *see* ADR

mining 25, 110, 135–36, 137–38, 139–42, 143

Ministry of Finance 147, 152
MoE/SEPA (Ministry of Environment) 107, 109, 111, 112–13
MOFCOM (Ministry of Commerce) 51, 28–29, 31, 32, 51, 54, 95
MOFTEC (Ministry for Foreign Trade and Economic Cooperation) 26, 27

National People's Congress 63, 108, 133, 144, 153, 156, 174, 198
natural resources 3, 21–22; Australia 37; environmental law reform 110; ODI 33; resource tax 108, 148, 150, 157, 161, 162; *see also* raw material
neoliberalism 9, 13, 173
NGOs (non-governmental organizations) 174, 178, 180, 181, 222; non-governmental ADR 191, 195, 196, 201

ODI (outward direct investment) 4, 10, 11, 21–38, 131, 144, 155, 160, 200, 221; access to market 32, 33, 37; accountability 25, 28, 29, 31; China, the largest outward investor 21, 25; debates on 21; distribution around the world 25; introduction of 21; macro-economic context 22–25; macro-economic control/micro-economic management 32–34; ODI figures 23, 24, 25, 35; ODI growth 23, 25, 30, 32, 34, 37, 132, 216; ODI motivations 32–34, 37; private sector 28, 32, 36–37, 133, 143; 'round-tripping' 23, 35, 157, 159, 221; SOEs 9, 17, 25, 32, 34, 37, 132–35 (lack of ODI experience 139, 141, 220); studies on 21, 34, 37; *see also* Hong Kong; ODI, evolving policy/regulatory framework; SOEs 'going out'; trade
ODI, evolving policy/regulatory framework 11, 21, 25–32, 34, 36, 132, 216; 2004 reform 28–30; 2009 reform 31–32; *Administrative Measures on Outward Investment* 31, 36; China Import—Export Bank 23, 28, 30; decentralization 31; *Decision on the Reform of the Investment System* 29–30; *Fifteen Measures on Economic Reform* 22, 23; financial support 21, 28, 30, 32, 34, 36, 37, 216; foreign exchange 26, 27, 30, 31, 32, 34, 35, 36, 216; liberalization 26, 30, 31–32, 34, 36, 134, 216; MOFCOM 28–29, 31, 32; MOFTEC 26, 27; 'open door' policy 21, 22, 26, 29; *Opinion of the State Planning Commission on Strengthening the Administration of Overseas Investment Projects* 26–27, 35; *Opinions on Encouraging and Regulating Enterprises involved in Outward Investment and Economic Cooperation* 30, 36; relaxation 26, 36; SAFE 23, 26, 27, 30, 31, 35, 36; simplification 26, 31, 34; state control 21–23, 26–28, 30, 32–33, 34, 37, 133, 216; State Council 22, 23, 26, 27, 29–30, 35, 36; state engagement in ODI 132–35 (CPC, one of the top six investors in the world 132; 'a product of governmental policy' 132); transparency 25, 28, 29, 31; *(Trial) Provisions* 27; *see also* ODI
OECD 2, 55, 63
'open door' policy 1, 22, 34, 73, 91, 215; Deng Xiaoping 3, 27; *Fifteen Measures on Economic Reform* 22, 23; 'going global' strategy 23, 28; ODI 21, 22, 26, 29; SOEs 133; *see also* privatization
organized crime 202–14, 223; bribery 204, 207, 208; *Criminal Law of the PRC* 205, 211, 214; definition 205; drug trade 13, 203, 204–5; gambling 203, 204, 207; government officials involvement 13, 202, 203, 204, 213; government responses 202, 203, 205–6, 213 (*yanda* campaigns 202, 203, 205–6, 213); growth 204, 213; history of Chinese organized crime 202, 203–6, 223 (Deng's era 204, 224; Mao's era 14, 146, 203, 210, 223, 226); hooliganism 205, 208, 213; legitimate business infiltration 202, 203, 204, 213, 223; local government 206; Macao 204; money laundering 204; participation in politics 203, 204, 208; prostitution 13, 203, 204, 205, 206, 207; rural areas 206; Shanghai Green Gang 203, 204, 207, 208, 213, 223; syndicate activity 202 (mafia-style gang 204, 213; secret societies 203, 204, 208, 214; underground groups and gangs 203, 204–5, 207); trends 202, 204, 207, 212; use of violence 202, 205, 207, 208, 213; *see also* organized crime, Chongqing
organized crime, Chongqing 13–14, 110, 146, 206–14, 223, 224, 226; Bo Xilai 13, 14, 94, 202, 209–11, 212, 213, 223, 226; crackdown on corruption 13, 207–9; government officials involvement 13, 207–9, 223; government responses 202, 209–12, 213 (hero-figure

promotion 202, 209–11, 212, 213, 223; mass campaign 209–11, 213; 'singing red' 210–11, 223; *yanda* campaigns 209); internet 202, 206, 209, 210, 212; legitimate business infiltration 13, 207, 208; Li Qiang 208; media 202, 204, 209–10, 211, 212, 213, 223; Party system 13–14, 209–10, 212; problems in the Chongqing crackdown 211–12, 214, 223, 226; Wen Qiang 207, 210; *see also* organized crime

Papua New Guinea 13, 15, 137–38, 141, 220

Peerenboom, Randall 87, 209; China, fragile superpower 224; courts and ESR 5, 13, 167–84, 216, 222; rule of law 9, 119

People's Bank of China 3, 6, 16, 99, 107, 161; *Administrative Measures on the Trial Implementation of Renminbi Settlement for Overseas Direct Investment* 31–32; *see also* banking sector

political economy: environmental law reform 12, 101, 225; labour law reform 128–29; tax reform 148–49

political ideology 162, 225; ADR 13, 185, 190; company law reform 39, 41, 48–49, 52, 216–17; EBL 55; environmental law, discourses of 12, 101–3, 114, 219–20; environmental law reform 101, 225; ESR 173 (New Left socialists/New Right neoliberals conflict 13, 174, 179, 222); flexibility 99, 218; 'hybridity' 98, 218; labour law reform 118, 129, 220; land/real estate property 92–94, 98–99, 100, 218; tax reform 144, 146, 149, 160, 162; variations in CPC's ideology 93, 100; *see also* CPC

political reform 5; power–wealth coalition 94; Wen Jiabao 5

pollution 139, 140, 147, 184, 225; carbon dioxide emissions 102–3; control/prevention 101, 102, 103, 104, 105, 106, 107, 111, 112, 113, 114, 219; pollution liability insurance 12, 109; water pollution 103, 112, 149; *see also* environmental law reform

poverty 173, 179; poverty reduction 174, 179, 222, 224, 225; *see also* wealth

PRC (People's Republic of China): foundation 1, 55, 188, 203; legal system 1; *see also* Constitution; CPC; Chinese socialism

private land/property 4, 88, 150; confiscation 88, 90; protection 156; *see also* land/real estate property; privatization

private sector 4, 155, 162, 225; bank lending 6, 9, 38; Chinese economic growth 155, 156, 161; CPC working branches 49; informal lending 161; land/real estate property 91, 218; ODI 28, 32, 36–37, 133, 143; 'state advancing/private withdrawing' 6–9, 159; tax reform 146, 153; 'wealth hatred' 155

privatization 7–8; banking sector 8; housing 89–90, 92, 99; land/property 15, 87, 92, 98–99, 218; real estate property 87, 99; SOEs 7–8, 63

propaganda 10, 14, 93, 98, 100, 102, 226

property *see* land/real estate property; private land/property

Qing Dynasty 39, 203, 214

raw material 1–2, 27, 33, 37, 110, 139, 157; *see also* natural resources

rights: civil and political rights 168, 174, 177, 182; human rights 171, 178, 179, 180, 181, 182, 183, 222, 224; *see also* ESR

'round-tripping' 23, 35, 157, 159, 221; *see also* ODI

rule of law 1, 162, 178, 213, 215, 217, 223, 225, 226; accountability 93; ambiguity 93; court procedure and rule of law 186; critical issues 14–15; foundations 1; 'hybridity' xvii, 1, 9–10; Mao's era 185; Peerenboom, Randall 9, 119; rule of party/rule of law contradiction 92, 93; 'rule of virtue' 93; Wen Jiabao 14

rural sector 7, 225–26; exploitation of workers 103; health 7, 156; land privatization 218; organized crime 206; *PRC Land Reform Law* 88; private land ownership 15, 88, 90; reducing inequalities/promoting fairness 7, 156; *Rural Land Contract Disputes Mediation and Arbitration Law* 190; taxation 7, 145, 147–48, 156; unemployment 62; urban migration 92, 118, 211

saving 2, 33
security 131; energy security 33
services sector 3, 16, 196

Smith, Graeme: SOEs 'going out' 13, 131–43, 220–21
social stability 5, 186, 188, 216, 218, 225; EBL 2006 56, 62–67 (social unrest 62–63, 64, 66, 67, 217); ESR 175–76, 180, 222; social and economic indicators 167, 174, 180, 224; Social Stability Maintenance Office 175; social tensions 187–88; sustainable development/social stability 103, 106, 175
social welfare 140, 147, 159, 174, 177; labour law reform 42, 45, 120, 121, 122, 123, 127; social security system 33, 62, 147, 154, 156; social security tax 147
socialism *see* Chinese socialism
SOEs (state-owned enterprises) 4, 8, 63, 225; bank lending 6, 9, 38, 133; conflicts of interest 9; corporate social responsibility 106, 115, 140, 141; corruption 9; directors/senior executives 32, 37, 39, 53, 63, 134, 135; EBL 2006 59, 62–63, 64, 68, 69, 217; environmental law reform 106, 112, 115; financial support privileges 6, 9, 28, 32, 133–34, 141–42, 159; functions 134; Hu Jintao 40, 133; monitoring 134; 'open door' policy 133; power 4; privatization 7–8, 63; reform 6–8, 39–41, 62, 63, 133, 134, 142, 177 (deregulation 39–40; objectives 40; separating from state ownership/control 40, 134); regulation 40, 52; SASAC 40, 106, 115; 'state advancing/private withdrawing' 6–9, 11; state control 34, 37, 39, 40–41, 63, 93, 216; State Council 133–34; state ownership 7–9, 32, 132, 133, 134; as 'strategic' 8–9, 17, 132; tax reform, preferential policy treatment 148, 152; urban employment 62; Wen Jiabao 133; *see also* company law reform; EBL 2006; labour law reform; SOEs 'going out'
SOEs 'going out' 11, 13, 63–64, 131–43, 220–21; accountability 138, 139–40, 142; Africa 15; Australia 13, 15, 135–37, 141, 220; autonomy 134; CITIC 133; firm-level socialization 132, 142, 221; 'going global' policy 132–33, 135, 141, 142, 220; international socialization 131–32; lack of experience with trade unions 140, 142; lack of knowledge/engagement with local practices 136, 137, 141–42, 220–21;

Latin America 13, 15, 139–41, 142, 143, 220; mining 25, 135–36, 137–38, 139–42, 143; ODI 9, 17, 25, 32, 34, 37, 132–35 (lack of ODI experience 139, 141, 220); Papua New Guinea 13, 15, 137–38, 141, 220; Southeast Asia 15; state control on 132, 134; state engagement in ODI 132–35, 216; success 9, 134–35; trade union 139–41, 142; *see also* SOEs
South Africa 172, 173–74, 170–80
Sowash, Alexandra: labour law reform 12–13, 118–30, 220
state control 6–7, 92–93, 212, 215; Constitution 215; foreign exchange 23; ODI 21–23, 26–28, 30, 32–33, 34, 37, 133, 216; SOEs 34, 37, 39, 40–41, 63, 93, 132, 134, 216; *see also* intervention
State Council: EBL 2006 67; environmental policies 106; foreign M&As 51; ODI 22, 23, 26, 27, 29–30, 35, 36; SOEs 133–34; tax reform 144, 145, 150–51
Supreme People's Court 13, 212; ADR 186, 189, 196, 199–200, 223; CL 2006 46–47, 48; company law reform 46–47, 48; corporate insolvency 67; EBL 2006 57, 66, 67, 69; Wang Shengjun 175; *see also* court
sustainability: economic growth xvii, 2, 3, 128–29; from fossil fuel to sustainable new technology 102–3, 110, 220; sustainable consumption 225; sustainable development 12, 101, 102, 106, 115; sustainable development/ social stability 103, 106, 175

Taiwan 25, 31, 33, 36
tax reform 11, 13, 144–63, 218–19; 12th Five-Year Plan 148, 150; the *benzhi* of taxation law reform 149–50; corruption 156–58; dilemmas 146–48, 154, 159, 221 (burden shifting 147–48, 153; theory, practice, implementation 146–47; unifying a divided tax system 147, 148, 221); environmental issues 13, 104, 108, 147, 149, 221; export tax rebates 28, 116, 133; foreign investment 146, 148; hidden income 147, 159; industrial sector 117, 150; local government and land-use rights/ property tax 156–57, 158–59, 162, 218–19; political economy 148–49; political ideology 144, 146, 149, 160,

162; preferential policy treatment 148, 152; principles of 145–46; private sector 146, 153; rural sector 7, 145, 147–48, 156; social security system 147, 154; 'socialism with Chinese characteristics' 144, 149, 159, 160; State Administration of Taxation 144, 145; State Council 144, 145, 150–51; tax avoidance 145, 151, 157–58, 159, 221; urban sector 147, 161, 221; wealth distribution 13, 147, 152–53, 155, 156, 157, 160, 221; 'wealth hatred' 145, 153–56, 158, 159, 219, 226; WTO 148, 160; *see also* tax reform, regulations

tax reform, regulations: business tax 148, 150, 151, 152; consumption tax 148, 150, 151–52, 157; enforcement 151, 159, 221; enterprise income tax 148, 159; *Enterprise Income Tax Law* (EITL) 145, 146, 148, 152, 159; individual income tax 150, 152–53, 162; *Individual Income Tax Law* 145, 148, 153; inheritance tax 150, 153; resource tax 108, 148, 150, 157, 161, 162; VAT 109–10, 145, 148, 150–51, 161; VAT on land 148, 153, 154–57; *see also* tax reform

technology: 'clean' technologies 12, 103, 110, 113, 114, 220; from fossil fuel to sustainable new technology 102–3, 110, 220; intellectual property rights 219; 'know-how' 16, 22, 32, 33, 37; ODI, acquisition of technology 32, 33, 37; transfer of 4, 16

Tiananmen Square Incident 92, 99–100

Tomasic, Roman: Enterprise Bankruptcy Law 11, 55–69, 217

Tort Law 4, 16

trade 23, 215; China International Economic and Trade Arbitration Commission 79; China's top trading partners 84; commercial arbitration/mediation for foreign investors 185, 193; environmental law reform, trade practice and process management 104, 105, 106; global trade 1, 25; international arbitration 193–95, 200, 201, 223; trade law 4; trade protection 33; *see also* CISG; FDI in China; ODI

trade union: ACFTU 45, 124, 125, 126; CL 2006 45; Honda 125–26; labour law reform 120, 121, 122, 123, 124–26; Party branches 124; Provisions on Enterprise Trade Union Work 45; resistance against 124–25, 126; SOEs 'going out' 139–41, 142; unionization 120, 121, 122, 123, 124; Walmart 124–25; *see also* labour law reform

transparency *see* accountability

UCL (Uniform Contract Law) 12, 70, 73, 84, 217; *see also* CISG; CISG/UCL comparison

unemployment 61–62, 156; EBL 2006, employment relocation plan 64; employee redundancy 62, 63, 127

United Kingdom: EBL 59, 60, 66, 68, 69

United States 162; Chinese rivalry with 33; CISG 73, 79, 84 (US legal decisions 79, 82–83); civil and political rights 182; consumption 2; EBL 59, 60, 61, 66, 68, 69; environmental issues 106; global economic superpower 131, 143; ODI 25; private sector 162

urban sector, urbanization 12, 87, 91–92, 215; as driver of property law reform 90, 91–92; 'dual track' land use system 88–89, 99; nationalized urban land system, characteristics 88; *Regulation on Urban and Urban Fringe Land Reform* 88; tax reform 147, 161, 221; urbanization rate 91–92, 221

wages 64; fair wages 118, 120, 121, 122, 125; low wages 118, 127, 138, 140; unpaid wages 64, 176; *see also* labour law reform

wealth: inequality 7, 145, 155, 156, 158, 179, 218, 224, 226; money worship 188; the new rich 3, 98, 155, 160, 187, 226; organized crime, a shortcut to wealth 204, 213; power–wealth coalition 94, 98, 100, 218, 226; princelings 94, 98, 99; private wealth 153, 155; social equity 152–53; wealth distribution 13, 147, 152–53, 155, 156, 157, 159, 160, 180, 221, 225; 'wealth hatred' 7, 145, 153–56, 158, 159, 226; *see also* poverty; tax reform

Wen Jiabao 1, 14, 16, 95, 108, 150, 157; Chinese growth 2; energy consumption reduction 12, 108, 116; 'going global' policy 133; political reform 5; rule of law 14; SOEs 133; tax avoidance 157; VAT 150

World Bank 61–62, 128; *Doing Business Report* 49–50, 52
WTO (World Trade Organization) 33, 73, 134, 171, 215; company law reform 42, 51; intellectual property rights 4, 16; tax reform 148, 160

Zhang, Xianchu: company law reform 11, 39–54, 152, 216–17
Zhang, Zinian: Enterprise Bankruptcy Law 11, 55–69, 217
Zhu Rongji 36, 133